DARK CITY

TURNER CLASSIC MOVIES.

DARK CITY

THE LOST WORLD OF FILM NOIR

REVISED AND EXPANDED EDITION

EDDIE MULLER

RUNNING PRESS
PHILADELPHIA

Page ii: *Double Indemnity*
Page vi: *99 River Street*

Running Press
Hachette Book Group
1290 Avenue of the Americas, New York, NY 10104
www.runningpress.com
@Running_Press

Printed in China

First Edition: July 2021

Published by Running Press, an imprint of Perseus Books, LLC, a subsidiary of Hachette Book Group, Inc. The Running Press name and logo is a trademark of the Hachette Book Group.

The Hachette Speakers Bureau provides a wide range of authors for speaking events. To find out more, go to www.hachettespeakersbureau.com or call (866) 376-6591.

The publisher is not responsible for websites (or their content) that are not owned by the publisher.

Photography Credits: : All photos courtesy of the Film Noir Foundation unless noted below. All ephemera—posters, books, magazines, press materials, etc.—is from the author's personal collection unless noted below.

Academy of Motion Picture Arts & Sciences: pages 33, 34. Everett Collection: pages 9, 15, 23, 25, 35, 57, 60, 65, 66, 75, 98, 109, 112, 117, 118, 122, 124, 127, 132, 134, 135, 143, 152, 157, 159, 171, 180, 184, 186, 191, 202, 212, 215, 221, 226, 232, 238. Fossil Photos: pages i, xii. Warner Media: pages 10, 21, 25, 26, 35, 46, 49, 57, 65, 66, 106, 133 (2), 138, 143, 154, 178 (2), 180, 186, 195, 220.

Print book cover and interior design by Josh McDonnell.

Library of Congress Control Number: 2021903138

ISBNs: 978-0-7624-9897-0 (hardcover), 978-0-7624-9896-3 (ebook)

1010

10 9 8 7 6 5 4 3 2 1

For Kathleen

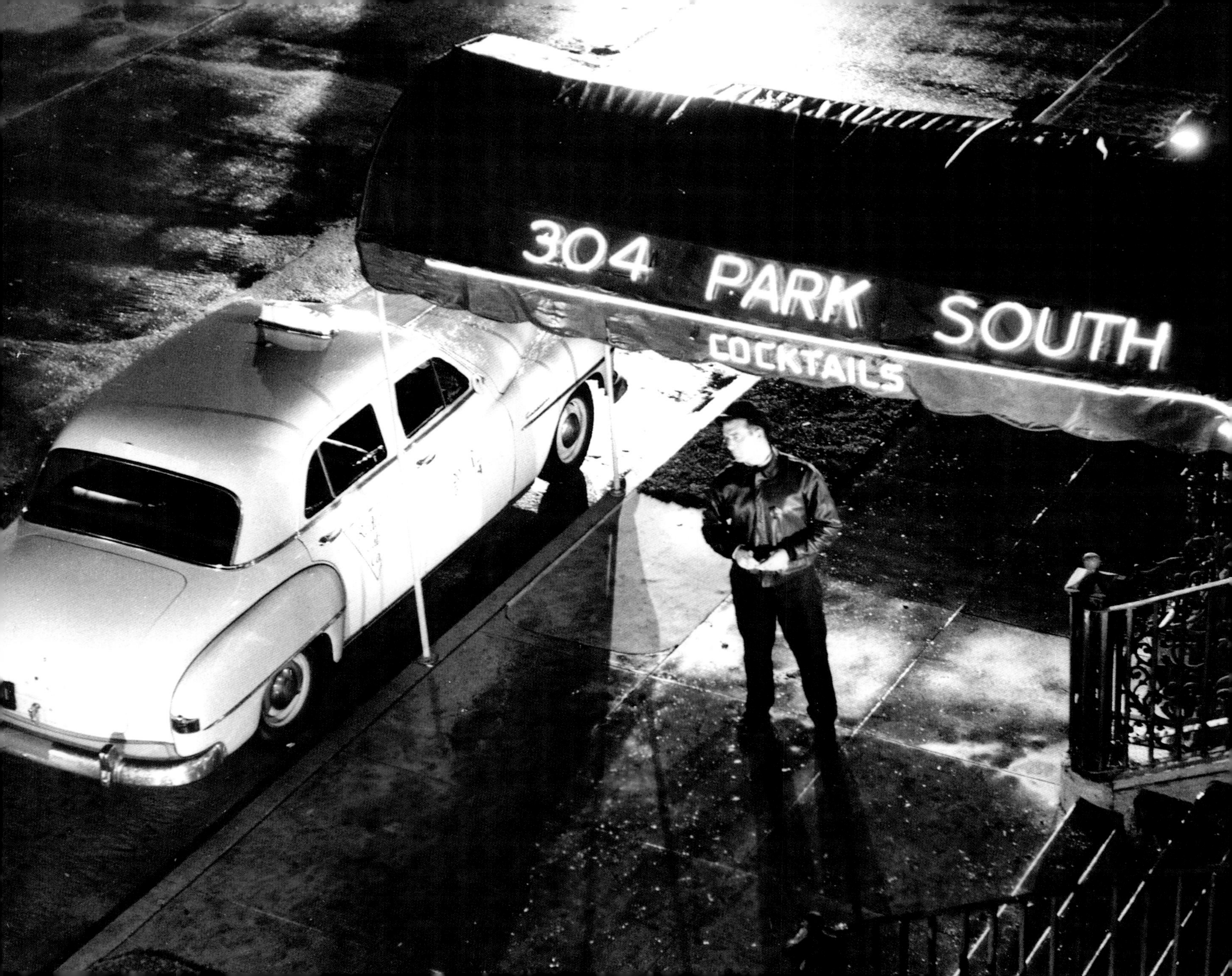

304 PARK SOUTH
COCKTAILS

CONTENTS

AUTHOR'S NOTE

When *Dark City* was first published in 1998, I subtitled it *The Lost World of Film Noir* for two reasons. First, *Lost* captured the sense of angst and alienation that permeates the films. But it also referred, in some cases, to the movies themselves. Research for the original edition took place during the decline of 35mm repertory cinemas and before the prevalence of digital media; it required tenacious detective work to find obscure movies like *The Sound of Fury, Jealousy, City That Never Sleeps*, and dozens more that had been "lost." I wrote the manuscript believing many of the movies referenced might never be seen again.

I like to think publication of *Dark City: The Lost World of Film Noir* spurred renewed interest in noir just as emerging technologies made access to obscure and vault-bound films more convenient and marketable than ever before. Producing a revised and expanded edition allows me to now include in this historical excursion movies once feared lost forever, gems such as *Woman on the Run, Too Late for Tears, The Guilty, Trapped*, and *The Man Who Cheated Himself.*

Further explanation awaits in the Afterword, at the conclusion of our journey.

INTRODUCTION

Film noirs were distress flares launched onto America's movie screens by artists working the night shift at the Dream Factory. Some shell-shocked craftsman discharged mortars, blasting their message with an urgency aimed at shaking up the status quo. Others were firecrackers—startling but playful diversions. Either way, the whiff of cordite carried the same warning: we're corrupt.

The nation's sigh of relief on V-J Day ought to have inspired a flood of "happily ever after" films. But some victors didn't feel good about their spoils. They'd seen too much. Too much warfare, too much poverty, too much greed, all in the service of rapacious progress. Unfinished business lingered from the Depression—nagging doubts about ingrained venality, ruthless human nature, unchecked urban growth throwing society dangerously out of whack. Artists responded by delivering bitter dramas that slapped romantic illusion in the face and put the boot to the throat of the smug bourgeoisie. Still, plenty of us took it—and liked it.

I took it later, because I grew up in the '60s. Before I could tell Richard Widmark from Richard Conte I knew the films I'd play hooky to watch on the family's Philco: *Thieves' Highway. Night and the City. Crime Wave. The Big Heat.* Any movie with *City, Night,* or *Street* in its title listed in that week's *TV Guide*— you could mark me absent from class. I went AWOL from catechism, as well. How could Sister Gretchen compete with Lizabeth Scott or Joan Bennett? The lessons Father McTaggart tried to impart weren't as crucial as the ones instilled by Robert Mitchum and Humphrey Bogart. If they wanted us to understand the Ten Commandments they should have screened *Out of the Past, Force of Evil, They Won't Believe Me, Side Street*—come to think of it, the Good Book would make one hell of a film noir.

In the '70s, an ever-expanding catalog of criticism emerged that tried to capture and deconstruct every frame of noir. Essayists argued over what it was and which films qualified. Was noir a genre? Was it a style? Academics tried to pin it down and dissect it. In the process they managed to drain the life's blood out of the films.

This book is an attempt to resurrect these movies for another generation, to make them as vivid as they were when I first saw them—or when our parents and grandparents did.

Of all the varieties of films Hollywood produced during the glory days of the studio system, noirs hold up best. They've got vivid characters and thematic weight and an inspired vision that preserves their vitality. When they fail to meet that tall order, they've got style and sass to die for. While some studio fare of the '40s and '50s has slid into campiness, or decayed into toothless nostalgia, film noir has kept its bite. Enjoy it for the surface allure, or venture further into the scorched existentialist terrain.

Conventional wisdom has branded these films bleak, depressing, and nihilistic—in fact, they're just the opposite. To me, film noirs were the only movies that offered bracing respite from sugarcoated dogma, Hollywood-style. They weren't trying to lull you or sell you or reassure you—they insisted you wake up to the reality of a corrupt world. Quit kidding yourself. Stand up, open your eyes, and be ready for anything. Prayers go unheard in these parts.

Film noir pointed toward the dark core of corruption in our "civilized" society and our primitive essence. The struggle of the individual to transcend or escape provided the emotional tension. That's the theme that makes noir so compelling for contemporary audiences. The films still connect, even without dissertations on the men and women who made them, or classes on the social pressures that informed their creation. Of all the postures proffered by Hollywood in the twentieth century, noir has proven to be the most prescient. Sadly, we're nowhere near as stylish anymore—but the corruption is thicker than ever.

So lock your door, would you? And hold on. We are taking a little ride. Seatbelts wouldn't do much good, even if we had them. Remember, once we cross the Dark City limits the meter's double and there's no going back.

This trip is going to take us through all the finer neighborhoods. We'll hit Sinister Heights, Shamus Flats, Blind Alley, Vixenville, and maybe Loser's Lane— if we make it that far. We'll be hustling in and out of cheap hotels, seedy nightspots, and lonesome roadside diners. You'll get reacquainted with some folks in these dank corners, ready to spill their bitter life story before retreating to the shadows. Be ready to crack wise even as a trickle of cold sweat runs down your spine.

While we're rolling, stay calm, act natural, keep the windows rolled up. Dark City was built on fateful coincidence, double-dealing, and last chances. Anything can happen, and it will.

Jean Hagen and Sterling Hayden in *The Asphalt Jungle*

SHUT UP AND GET IN THE CAR.

—Where are we going, Dix?

—To the pictures.

—What? Are you serious? They'll see us there for sure.

—Let 'em. I don't care anymore.

—Where's the Professor? I thought you were picking him up.

—He's not coming.

—Dix! How can we go through with this? The Professor had the plan, he knew every angle, he studi—

—Forget about him! We're improvising from here on. If you don't have the stomach for it—get out.

—What about Tony, the gunsel? Is he out, too?

—I'm picking him up in ten minutes. South Street and Third. He'll be there.

—Dix, what happened to the Professor? Is he all right? You two were so close, you'd been together for so many years—

—Leave it alone, Doll.

—He taught you so much, Dix. You always said you felt like a small-time chiseler until the Professor taught you about your—what did he call it? Your . . . manifest destiny! And what about all that French poetic realism, and Jacobean tragedy . . . and Expressionism! You used to love to listen to his theories. Why isn't he here, Dix? Wh—

—Because I killed him! I couldn't stand it anymore! I couldn't take another minute of his blather about Judeo-Christian patriarchal systems and structuro-semiological judgments. My head was going to explode!

—My God, Dix—what did you do?

—Let's just say I deconstructed him.

—You've finished us, Dix. I hope you know that. We're doomed.

—What else is new? Everybody dies. In the meantime, we'll be able to live again, like real people, not like little symbols on his big blackboard.

—And you think you can pull off this job without him?

—Did the Professor step up for me when Pete Hurley tried to kill me that night in Jefty's saloon? Was he in the car when I crashed that roadblock upstate? Did the Professor have to tell me where you like to be kissed?

—Give him his due, Dix. He was a great thinker.

—Thinking's overrated.

—Turn here.

—Shut up.

—Don't tell me to shut up. . . . I just might kill you.

—Let me see it coming, that's all I ask.

—There's Tony! See him? Sitting on the running board?

—This stinks. It's all wrong.

—Why doesn't he see us? Why doesn't he look over?

—Could be that bullet hole in his forehead, but it's just a hunch.

—What are you going to do now, Dix?

—We're gonna keep moving, Doll. Once a deal gets queered, that's when things get interesting.

—You're not going back to Dark City, are you? They'll kill you for sure.

—Well, I'm not running away. I'm through with that. What about you? You in or out?

—What else can I do? I've taken so many wrong turns I'm right back where I started. I may as well play it out.

—You could find yourself a rich guy. Break him. Drag him around until his knees are bloody.

—And leave you?

—I didn't say that.

—So it's back to the city, huh? No clear blue ocean, no boozy fruit drinks, no waiters in white?

—Later. I've got some housecleaning to do. Can I drop you someplace?

—Shut up, Dix. Just shut up and drive fast.

WELCOME TO DARK CITY

LIGHTS DOWN, CURTAIN UP, VOICE-OVER: OBSERVE THE MIGHTY BEAST, MANKIND'S RISKIEST EXPERIMENT. A SPRAWLING, SOARING MONSTER WITH A STEEL SKELETON AND CONCRETE OVERCOAT. SOME BRILLIANT ENGINEERS LEARNED HOW TO PUMP ELECTRICITY THROUGH ITS ARTERIES AND NOW IT LURCHES AND CRACKLES AND SPEWS NONSTOP. ON ITS DAYLIGHT STREETS YOU'LL WITNESS THE MOST COURAGEOUS OF HUMAN ENDEAVORS: THE WILL TO COEXIST. BUT WHEN NIGHT FALLS, HEAD FOR HOME. OR LEARN FIRSTHAND ABOUT OUR TRULY INGRAINED TRAIT: THE DESIRE TO DEVOUR.

A few years back, eminent philosopher Lewis Mumford came to Dark City. Bright guy, little full of himself—he was in town to lecture on his book *The Culture of Cities*. He climbed out of a cab in front of the downtown auditorium and gazed at the buildings looming around him. A knockout brunette who'd been hanging nearby rushed up.

"Spectacular, isn't it?" She gushed, ogling the skyscrapers with him. Even Mumford felt the blood rush a guy gets from a dishy dame.

"The city arose as a special kind of environment," he nattered, "favorable to cooperative association. It was a collective utility that ensured order and regularity in the comings and goings of men, that diminished the force of nature's random onslaughts, and reduced the menace of wild animals and the more predatory tribes of men. Permanent settlement meant not only continuity but security."

"Do tell," she said, nuzzling up to him.

"The big city becomes the prestige symbol for the whole civilization," he pronounced. "Life in all the subordinate regions is sacrificed to its temples of pleasure and towers of pecuniary aspiration."

The dame nodded. A guy leaped from behind a parked car, rapped Mumford's dome with a sap, and nailed his wallet before the philosopher hit the pavement.

A real trouper, Mumford still gave his lecture that night, but veered from his usual script:

"It is impossible here to go into all the perversions and miscarriages of civic functions because of the physical spread and the congestion and mis-planning of the mass city. . . . The physical drain, the emotional defeat of these cramped quarters, these dingy streets, the tear and noise of transit—these are but the most obvious results of megalopolitan growth. For what the metropolis gives with one hand, it takes back with the other: One climbs its golden tree with such difficulty that, even if one succeeds in plucking the fruit, one can no longer enjoy it."

Welcome to Dark City, professor. Mumford probably got the shakes when he watched film noir. One way or another, noir is all about people's struggle to survive in what he calls the "megalopolis." The square-off is usually short, nasty, and brutal. Urban omnipotence casts long shadows over the genre. Its power cowed some filmmakers, who slavishly began their stories by paying obeisance to the city: cameras swooping over rooftops, prowling labyrinthine streets, or simply displaying, with fearful reverence, the overwhelming skyline. It was a ritual, like making a hasty sign of the cross when confronted by the immensity of a cathedral.

In *City That Never Sleeps* (Republic, 1953), the metropolis, with the reverb

indicative of God's voice, narrates its own tale: "I am The City. Hub and heart of America. Melting pot of every race, creed, color, and religion in humanity. From my famous stockyards to my towering factories, from my tenement district to swank Lakeshore Drive, I am the voice, the heartbeat, of this giant, sprawling, sordid and beautiful, poor and magnificent citadel of civilization. And this is the story of just one night in this great city. Now meet my citizens . . ."

The City introduces us to some of its regulars: jaundiced cop, corrupt businessman, psychotic crook, scheming wife, lovelorn loser, sweet-natured stripper. The apostles.

As in every noir, these folks will carom through a story line with a structure reflecting the city itself. Unexpected intersections. Twisted corridors. Secrets hidden in locked rooms. Lives dangling from dangerous heights. Abrupt dead ends. The blueprints were drawn up by a demented urban planner. Down in the catacombs of the Dark City Department of Urban Development lived a wretched hermit trying like hell to conjure diagrams for a functional metropolis. Problem was, the designs had to account for human nature. He was up against an inevitable truth: There are too many rats in the cage and no bond issue or blue-ribbon civic panel will bail us out.

Screenwriters made this murky basement office a regular stop on nocturnal visits to Dark City. They fleshed out his tortured specs and the results were projected into the national psyche: *Whispering City, City of Fear, Naked City, Cry of the City, Captive City, Street of Chance, One Way Street, Terror Street, No Way Out.*

A FEVER DREAM OF MODERN LIFE erupted from these motion pictures. Something dreadful had crept into the social fabric, especially at the most bustling hubs of urban activity. A wounded cop-killer just escaped from the hospital and is leaving a trail of bodies behind him as he tries to reunite with his girlfriend in *Cry of the City* (Fox, 1948). Across town a tormented loner, guilty of murder, is holed up in a tenement, keeping at bay a squad of trigger-happy cops during *The Long Night* (RKO, 1947).

OPPOSITE: Charles Korvin flees the deadly touch of Evelyn Keyes in *Frightened City*, aka *The Killer That Stalked New York*.

Meanwhile, an unstable young man has escaped from a mental asylum and taken a saloon full of hostages in *Dial 1119* (MGM, 1950). Most of these poor saps had only come into the tavern because the evening commute was snarled at *Union Station* (Paramount, 1950), where a regular Joe went off his nut and kidnapped a blind girl. He's hiding in the subway tunnels, stalling service and ticking off hordes of angry commuters. As if that wasn't enough to keep the boys in blue hopping, a priest was just murdered at the local Catholic church. There's an APB out for the suspect—the son of a devout parishioner bludgeoned Father Kirkman when he wouldn't give his late mother a lavish burial (*Edge of Doom*, RKO, 1950).

Even the city's massive monument to mercy, the General Hospital, isn't immune from the societal cancers. The cops send in an undercover man, Fred Rowan (Richard Conte) to probe the violent demise of several doctors. *The Sleeping City* (Universal, 1950) won't rest any easier when it learns what happens on the night shift. Rowan discovers nurse Ann Sebastian (Coleen Gray), whom he's falling for, is the linchpin of a drug smuggling ring.

The Sleeping City was filmed at Manhattan's Bellevue Hospital in 1949, peak year in Hollywood's fascination with crime melodramas. Prior to its release, New York Mayor William O'Dwyer pressured Universal executives to attach a prologue advising viewers the story had nothing to do with the reality of big city hospitals, in New York or anywhere else.

This dichotomy—between overripe imaginings and disingenuous denial—was the cultural fissure upon which Dark City was built. Many of the stories you'll encounter here are a tantalizing blend of fact, fiction, and myth. Cinematic cocktails, if you will, in which a jigger of creative license and a dash of bitters put a dreamy edge on material rooted in ugly realities, both contemporary and timeless.

Sorting the facts and fictions of this place can be tricky. Consider *Frightened City* (Columbia, 1951; aka *The Killer That Stalked New York*), a more noir treatment of a modern urban plague than *Panic in the Streets* (Fox, 1950), the more heralded Elia Kazan–directed film released the previous year.

In *Panic*, the notion of a metropolis infected with "foreign bodies" was made explicit: The disease is carried into the city from a merchant ship filled with foreigners, one of whom is killed on leave by local crooks, who contract the virus and rapidly spread it throughout the city.

In *Frightened City*, writer Harry Essex threaded a crime narrative through the fact-based story of a smallpox outbreak that threatened New York in 1947. Sheila Bennett (Evelyn Keyes) and her husband Matt (Charles Korvin) run a diamond-smuggling operation. Sheila mails the gems home from Cuba, but unwittingly carries back the smallpox virus. While waiting for the diamonds to arrive, Sheila infects everyone she touches, including a young girl who later dies. Panic grips the city; the National Guard sets up an emergency inoculation program. A crusading health inspector spearheads a manhunt for the source carrier.

The story plays fast and loose with the actual epidemic that gripped New York, which was brief, well-controlled, and not very sensational. It's an example of how the truth was often stretched and artfully manipulated for the sake of a more exciting story. The old "Based on a true story" pitch has always lent authenticity.

But the blurring of reality and imagination sometimes got so extreme it created a strange half-world, a mythological movie metropolis, in which the truth swung

The Sleeping City: Undercover cop Fred Rowan (Richard Conte) learns from Pop Ware (Richard Taber) of a drug conspiracy in the city's General Hospital.

endlessly between what we think is real and what's merely a projection.

Fourteen Hours (Fox, 1951) was another urban drama based on a true story. On July 26, 1938, John Warde held downtown New York spellbound for a day as he perched on the seventeenth-floor ledge of the Gotham Hotel, threatening to jump. The first man at the scene, traffic cop Charles Glasco, valiantly bonded with Warde—consoling him for an anguished fourteen hours—but in the end he couldn't save the troubled man, who leapt to his death.

The film version exemplifies what you'll encounter on your journey through Dark City. It's a tense depiction of one man's despair amid the city's teeming indifference. As Robert Cosick (Richard Basehart) teeters on the verge of suicide, cabbies in the throng below wager on the hour he'll jump. A pair of young lovers meet in the glare of the searchlights. A wife filing for divorce in the attorney's office across the street is inspired to reconcile with her husband.

And in every shot of the distraught Cosick, the skyscrapers of Dark City loom above him and the endless avenues stretch to the horizon—the city's immensity mocking the insignificance of one man's travails. Despite the gallant effort of Officer Dunnigan (Paul Douglas) to talk him down, Cosick falls to his death. In the picture's final shot, a sanitation truck, moving like a lethargic antibody, washes away Cosick's splattered remains as the budding lovers walk past, arm in arm.

At least that's what audiences saw when the film premiered. That very day in New York, the daughter of 20th Century-Fox executive Spyros Skouras killed herself, leaping from the eighth floor of Bellevue Hospital. Devastated, Skouras pulled *Fourteen Hours* from theaters. Resourceful studio chief Darryl F. Zanuck rounded up some actors and a skeleton crew (Basehart not among them) and re-shot a new ending: Cosick at the last moment is whisked to safety.

This confounding waltz between fantasy and reality will be a leitmotif of our tour.

As we travel, be sure not to focus only on the major landmarks. Some of the most gripping stories emanate from the transient hotels in the town's Tenderloin, from within rooms clammy with the residue of spoiled hopes. Where wallpaper sweats from the radiator's steam and neon buzzes incessantly outside the window. Here, lifetimes are reduced to eighty minutes.

Somebody checked out earlier than expected; there's a vacancy on the third floor, ready for another story.

Richard Basehart resists rescue in *Fourteen Hours*.

Force of Evil

SINISTER HEIGHTS

U P THERE IN THE DIAMOND BRACELET OF PENTHOUSE LIGHTS, CHAMPAGNE CORKS POP, FECKLESS WOMEN SQUEAL, AND POWER COURSES MERCILESSLY AMONG THE INSULATED "BUSINESSMEN." DOWN HERE, FORTY FLOORS BELOW, THEIR CLERKS PROWL THE SELLING FLOOR, WHOLESALING FEAR AND MUSCLE WITHOUT CONSCIENCE. BUT THERE ARE CLIMBERS AMONG THE MINIONS. SOMEDAY THE BOSS WILL SLIP AND FALL IN THE TRAIL OF BLOOD MONEY, AND ONE OF HIS LOYAL BOYS WILL EASE THROUGH THE SIDE DOOR AND FINALLY BE UP THERE, ON THE INSIDE, LOOKING DOWN.

When crime flooded America's movie screens in the 1940s there was no such animal as film noir. Cineastes hadn't yet bestowed the academic nomenclature. At the picture factories in Los Angeles and in the boardrooms of Wall Street underwriters, they were called "crime pictures." Accurate, if not as highfalutin. For if there is a common denominator in film noir, it's crime. In Dark City, laws—and hearts—are trampled daily.

As popular as crime pictures were after World War II, they were also unnerving to great suburban swathes of the filmgoing public. In Monroe, Michigan, theater owner J. R. Denniston, a "small exhibitor in the sticks," declared in the March 10, 1951 issue of *Showmen's Trade Review*: "To get our theater programs in proper balance I would suggest production of all crime pictures be discontinued by all producers, and that those they now have on their shelves be withdrawn from the market."

Emboldened by the patriotic search-and-destroy mission of the House Un-American Activities Committee, Denniston requested Hollywood produce "Great romances about business, industry, farming, medicine, and education." In keeping with the Stalinist overtones of this wish list, he concluded, "To get these we will probably have to have a new set of writers, because the people who write the

stories must know and understand what they are writing about."

This diatribe, it should be noted, was motivated by dwindling audiences, not love of country. Better box office would have eased Denniston's mind. But his Babbittism shouldn't be dismissed merely as the whining of an exhibitor crying poor mouth. He knew his clientele, and, in the heartland, citizens were horrified by the barrage of movies depicting urban corruption as a spreading cancer.

During the Depression, the era in which noir germinated, Hollywood sold a glamorous vision of gangsters as renegade bandits. The Cagneys and Robinsons ran wild until the strong arm of our civilized society ran them to ground. Audiences loved flamboyant crooks, even if they did have to end up facedown in the gutter.

Post–World War II crooks were scarier. They weren't after the living wage the Depression robbed them of; they were after power. They didn't buck the system; they used it. Crime pictures of this era borrowed the trappings of traditional gangster pictures to present a vision of urban America in which the Have-Nots—angry and determined—battled the Haves for control of the gears and levers that operated the modern city.

In noir, crooks are shaved, shined, and high-toned. They've folded their rackets into the capitalist economy. Aspiring to the heights, they work their way in

Old-school racketeer Burt Lancaster learns that crime has moved uptown in *I Walk Alone*, with Wendell Corey and Kirk Douglas.

from the dark edges of society toward the light of legitimacy. They laughed at their scrappy forebears of twenty years earlier, knocking over banks with guns blazing. The noir crime boss has the bank president, and the police chief, in his pocket.

No film hit this nail on the head more squarely than *I Walk Alone* (Paramount, 1947). Producer Hal Wallis, who as studio production chief had helmed a number of Warner Bros.' gangster sagas in the 1930s, became an independent producer after the war and his adaptation of Theodore Reeves's Broadway play *Beggars Are Coming to Town* is a transitional landmark in cinematic crime.

The story revolves around a pair of former bootleggers, Frankie Madison (Burt Lancaster) and "Dink" Turner (Kirk Douglas), who ten years earlier would have been played at Warners by Jimmy Cagney and Humphrey Bogart. They once co-owned a speakeasy called the Four Kings and were low enough on the food chain to haul their own illegal hooch across the Canadian border. When a rum run in 1933 goes haywire (in flashback), the partners agree to split all spoils fifty-fifty whenever they reunite. But Frankie gets nabbed and serves a fourteen-year jolt. Upon release, he discovers that Dink, who never visited him in stir, is living the high life: As proprietor of the ritzy Regent Club, he's a rising player in the murkier margins of café society. Frankie's brother Dave (Wendell Corey) even handles Dink's ledgers.

Frankie demands his half of their handshake deal. Dink has no intention of cutting him in. "This isn't the Four Kings," he tells Frankie, "hiding out behind a steel door and a peephole. This is big business." Rather than take his old partner for a last ride, as in many a Prohibition-era potboiler, Dink has flunky Dave enlighten his brother as to the new rules of "legitimacy." Well-heeled crooks now have lawyers and accountants to bamboozle their rivals, their enemies, and the law. Douglas smirks as Dave drowns Frankie in a tidal wave of umbrella corporations, holding companies, and ever-dwindling subdivisions. In the final accounting, Frankie's fifty-fifty split nets him a measly $2,912.

The criminal element of capitalism was rendered more artfully the following year in *Force of Evil* (MGM, 1948). Adapted by Abraham Polonsky from Ira Wolfert's journalistic novel *Tucker's People*, the movie was originally going to be called *The Numbers Racket*. In Polonsky's hands it became more than an indictment of racketeering. It drew parallels between organized crime and big business, and offered a bleak picture of American industrial might, festering with institutionalized corruption. In Wolfert's words, crime was "the grease that makes things run."

"I wanted to be a success, to get ahead in the world, and I believed there were three ways to do it," explained protagonist Joe Morse in a voice-over Polonsky opted to cut from the film prior to release. "You could inherit a fortune, you could work hard all your life for it, or you could steal it. I was born poor and impatient."

Joe Morse (John Garfield) is a partner in a Wall Street law firm with clients on both sides of the law. He craves the fortune he will reap from transforming the policy racket into a legal lottery. He and his golden goose, gangster Ben Tucker (Roy Roberts), plan to break the small neighborhood policy banks by fixing the July 4th number, 776, to hit—paying off a multitude of superstitious bettors and leaving the penny-ante policy boys broke. Tucker will then bail them out—if they agree to be absorbed into an all-encompassing combination under his control.

The snag is Joe's guilty conscience. His brother Leo Morse (Thomas Gomez)

TOP: *Force of Evil*: Joe Morse (John Garfield) presides in his "office in the clouds," where he helps gangster Ben Tucker weave his rackets into mainstream society.
BOTTOM: Mama's boys: Sylvia Morse (Georgia Backus) watches son Joe try to convince brother Leo (Thomas Gomez) that there's nothing to lose by joining Tucker's combination.

runs a freelance numbers bank and has no desire to be consumed by the capitalist juggernaut. He likes his policy setup personal and communal; he won't follow Joe to "an office in the clouds." Leo's intransigence strains Joe's partnership with Tucker. Doris, Leo's secretary (Beatrice Pearson), further weakens Joe's resolve by spurning his advances. "You're a strange man—and a very evil one," she tells the cocky lawyer.

"I didn't have enough strength to resist corruption," Joe says, "but I had enough strength to fight for a piece of it." Joe spirals into ethical purgatory following Leo's murder. His resultant moral reawakening is unsatisfying, yet apt; Joe limps to the authorities with all the confidence of a lost man facing the force of evil.

In content and style, *Force of Evil* was pivotal. Its treatment of a formulaic story—ghetto kid takes a crooked road to the top, only to learn the error of his ways—undercut cliché at every turn. The character's moral agony was suffocating; Polonsky refused to opt for easy answers to complex questions. The film's dissection of the ground shared by free enterprise and criminal rackets invites viewers to connect the dots linking gangster Ben Tucker to corporate raiders and merger pirates of contemporary Wall Street . . . and all the way to the nation's capital.

"I do not write stories to sell a certain morality to the audience," Polonsky has said. "I accept the world and our place in it and I know we have to deal with it. I also know that if we have certain concerns about our nature in it, we're going to pay the price for that. The point of *Force of Evil* is that the price for stealing is Joe's destruction of himself, his brother, and everything else. If you're not willing to pay that price, then you can't live in that world. That's the soldier's attitude: That's how you survive a battle."

Polonsky, like John Garfield, was a Jewish street kid from New York, his head full to bursting with the fervor of Manhattan's 1930s art scene. Both survived the rugged road out of the Depression, lived through the war, and ascended to the rarefied air of Hollywood. "However appalled I was by the industry and its product,"

Abraham Polonsky

Polonsky said, "the medium overwhelmed me with a language I had been trying to speak all my life."

Stylistically, he was one of the first Hollywood filmmakers to attempt a form of cinematic poetry, using imagery, dialogue, and narration in three-part harmony. Revelatory speeches erupt almost unconsciously from the characters. Scenes are composed with the melancholy of Edward Hopper paintings. The editing is often daringly abrupt. Despite the bleakness at the film's core, the storytelling was fueled by creative adrenaline.

Neither Hollywood, nor the public, was receptive. At the same time Garfield and Polonsky were slipping their worldview into the stream of Hollywood pablum, studio heads were slavishly reading a booklet titled *Screen Guide for Americans*, concocted by the doyenne of social Darwinism, Ayn Rand. Published by the Motion Picture Alliance for the Preservation of American Ideals and distributed with the imprimatur of the House Un-American Activities Committee, the guide instructed: "Don't Smear Industrialists," "Don't Smear the Free Enterprise System," and "Don't Smear Success." Rand advocated the rejection of any script that implied villainy on the part of industrialists.

Imagine her reaction to Leo Morse's blustering anticapitalist tirade: "Living from mortgage to mortgage, stealing credit like a thief. And the garage! That was a business! Three cents overcharge on every gallon of gas. . . . Two cents for the chauffeur, and a penny for me. A penny for one thief, two cents for the other. Well, Joe is here now. I won't have to steal pennies anymore. I'll have big crooks to steal dollars for me."

PARALLELS EQUATING THE STUDIO SYSTEM and the rackets depicted in 1940s crime movies are too rich to ignore. Harry Cohn, boss of Columbia Pictures, even admitted: "This isn't a business; it's a racket." Its link to the mob was a wiseguy named Willie Bioff, a roly-poly racketeer from the same Windy City streets that produced Al Capone, Frank Nitti, Johnny Roselli, and Sam "Momo" Giancana. Bioff teamed up in the early '30s with George Browne, Chicago head of the International Alliance of Theatrical Stage Employees (IATSE) to help the workingman—and to make themselves rich in the process.

They started by hustling John and Barney Balaban. The brothers ran a Midwest theater chain and during the Depression they'd drastically cut the wages of IATSE projectionists. Bioff taught Browne mob tactics, demanding $50,000 from the Balabans. When they begged off, projection rooms had electrical fires, equipment broke, reels were shown out of order. The Balabans coughed up twenty Gs. Bioff and Browne were on their way.

They took their scheme of conquering the movie business to Frank Nitti, "The Enforcer," who'd taken control of the Chicago rackets after Capone was sent up. Nitti turned out the vote for Browne, getting him elected president of IATSE in 1934 (he'd eventually become a vice president of the American Federation of Labor). Bioff was named his "international representative." They roadshowed their extortion act coast to coast.

Nicholas Schenck, president of Loew's, exhibition overlord of Metro-Goldwyn-Mayer, met Bioff and Browne in a Waldorf Astoria hotel room with a fifty grand payoff stuffed in a paper sack. Schenck waited while Browne counted out the dough. Sidney Kent, president of 20th Century-Fox, walked in and dumped another fifty large on the bed.

Before long, the dynamic duo had a sweet deal in Lotus Land. They took control of the craft and stagehand unions, convincing members that a 10 percent wage hike would be extracted from the studios. But first the rank and file would need to donate 2 percent of their paychecks to a union war fund, in case of strikes. The slush was funneled straight to Nitti in Chicago.

While workers waited for a fair shake, Bioff and Browne were paid off by studio bosses, ensuring there'd be no walkouts. Bioff saw a future in which every Hollywood union was in the fold. "We had about 20 percent of Hollywood when we got in trouble," he testified, once the shakedown flamed out in 1941. "If we hadn't got loused up, we'd have had 50 percent. I had Hollywood dancing to my tune."

The Feds nailed him thanks to an investigation launched by Screen Actors Guild president Robert Montgomery. Faced with a stint at Alcatraz, Bioff ratted out the whole Nitti gang: Louie "Little New York" Campagna, Phil "The Squire" D'Andrea, Paul "The Waiter" Ricca, Charlie "Cherry Nose" Gioe, and Frank "The Immune" Maritone. Nitti promptly shot himself in the head in a Chicago railyard.

Joe Schenck (Nick's brother), chairman of 20th Century-Fox and the Motion Picture Producers Association, was convicted of paying the mobsters a $100,000 bribe and was sentenced to three years' hard time. Bioff and Browne pulled longer stretches. It was all symbolic. Trade papers played it as though Hollywood's respectable businessmen had been the prey of extortionists. But as journalist Otto Friedrich noted in his study of Hollywood in the '40s, *City of Nets*: "Bribery and extortion can turn out to be pretty much the same thing. Money is paid in exchange for a service; both sides agree on a price and a service; the only question is who is corrupting whom."

A ruling in Chicago tax court stated that studios "knowingly and willingly paid over the funds and in a sense lent encouragement and participated with full knowledge of the facts in the activities of Browne and Bioff." Payoffs, it was estimated in court papers, saved the studios as much as $15 million in wages.

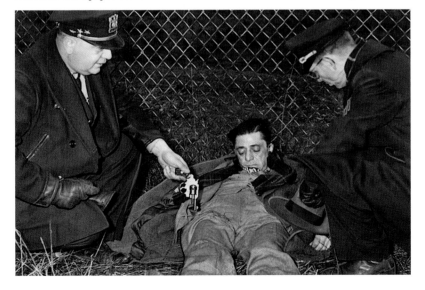

Gangster Frank Nitti killed himself in a Chicago railyard rather than face possible prison time after his role in studio extortion schemes was finally exposed.

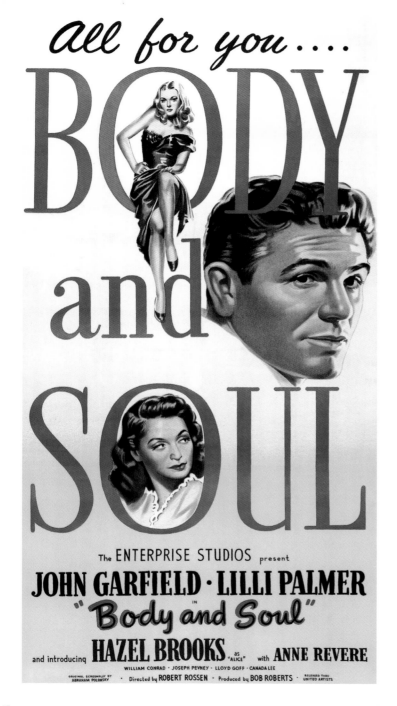

All for you....
BODY and SOUL

THE ENTERPRISE STUDIOS present
JOHN GARFIELD · LILLI PALMER
in "Body and Soul"
and introducing HAZEL BROOKS as "ALICE" with ANNE REVERE
WILLIAM CONRAD · JOSEPH PEVNEY · LLOYD GOFF · CANADA LEE
ORIGINAL SCREENPLAY BY ABRAHAM POLONSKY · Directed by ROBERT ROSSEN · Produced by BOB ROBERTS · RELEASED THRU UNITED ARTISTS

After leaving prison, Bioff changed his name to Bill Nelson and moved to Phoenix. But the garrulous gangster couldn't keep his profile low. He hooked up with the Riviera in Vegas—which was tied to the very mobsters he'd set up. He made showy contributions to Barry Goldwater's first Senate campaign. One day in 1955 Willie Bioff was blown apart by a bomb planted in his car, à la *The Big Heat*.

MOST MOVIE MOGULS, LIKE GANGSTERS, were poorly educated, ostentatious, vulgar, power hungry, insecure, and obsessed with being publicly respected. They ran Hollywood with a ruthlessness mob bosses envied. Their mission was to make money for investors; their job was to get power and keep it. Art was rarely invited to the party. It had to crash the gate.

In 1947 John Garfield, freed from contractual obligation to Warner Bros., used his newfound wealth to bankroll Enterprise Studios, an independent production house dedicated to challenging the status quo. To Hollywood's racket bosses, the actor was a brash upstart, cutting himself too big a piece of their pie.

To the artists Enterprise recruited, moviemaking presented a moral quandary akin to the one Joe Morse faced in *Force of Evil*: Was success worth anything if it came at the expense of integrity? Garfield set the tone, demanding his movies reflect the reality of a world beyond the soundstages. Hence his kinship with Abe Polonsky, whose passion for social justice was tempered by doubts about society's ability to ever achieve it. To them, you fought the good fight, damn the consequences.

Enterprise's first hit was *Body and Soul* (UA, 1947), about a Jewish kid from the Lower East Side, Charley Davis, fighting his way to the top but losing his soul by throwing in his lot with racketeers. Polonsky called his script "a fable from the Empire City," and it was given vivid life by the aggressive direction of Robert Rossen, the visual poetry of cameraman James Wong Howe, and a bristling performance by Garfield.

Beneath the story's emotionalism was a depiction of crime central to noir: No characters are crusading against the mob's infiltration of boxing. The corruption, as in the subsequent *Force of Evil*, is already too deeply entrenched. As Polonsky was writing *Body and Soul*, a Senate probe was seeking to expose the reach of racketeers into New York's boxing rings. Polonsky's script intimates that such efforts are futile. Government committees may squeeze token miscreants out of the system's bloodstream, but a true cleanup is impossible. In Polonsky's view, the notion of authority setting things straight, the reliable Hollywood square-up, was laughable at best—and at worst fascistic.

Body and Soul and *Force of Evil* chronicle a world in which it's too late to isolate corruption and root it out. The challenge for conscious people, which Charley Davis and Joe Morse eventually become, is to live with personal dignity in a society where the cancer is inoperable.

Other fight films followed in the wake of *Body and Soul*, solidifying the notion that the sweet science was corrupt, either by its nature or by criminal association. Some were created with strokes broad enough for audiences to see the prize ring as a metaphor for the win-at-all-costs struggle of modern life.

In *The Set-Up* (RKO, 1949), Robert Ryan portrays Stoker Thompson, a journeyman on the backside of his career, whose most cherished possession is the belief he can still win a title. His manager sells him out, assuring a local gangster that Stoker will tank that night's bout. When he tips to the setup, Stoker wages the fight of his life, battering his younger rival into submission. For his trouble, Stoker has his hands crushed, so he can no longer earn a living.

The picture, written by former sportswriter Art Cohn, was adapted from a poem by Joseph Moncure March, and directed by Robert Wise in real time—the seventy-two minutes before, during, and after the fight that are the solar plexus of Stoker Thompson's life. The film was a personal favorite of both Wise and Robert Ryan. *The Set-Up* boiled noir down to its existential essence: This is the way the world works—make your choice and be prepared to live or die by it.

Champion (UA) was also made in 1949 and until a lawsuit sorted things out, it too was called *The Set-Up*. In this film, the savagery of fighter Midge Kelley (Kirk Douglas) is never ennobled. He's a rotten son of a bitch with no compunction about letting the mob grease the skids for him, cynically discarding his wife and brother when they try to reform him. It's a relief when Midge finally dies of a brain hemorrhage in the locker room. The Mark Robson–directed film is scathing in its depiction of the public and media making Midge a hero when he's just a thug.

Robson also directed Budd Schulberg's *The Harder They Fall* (Columbia, 1956), a loose account of the career of heavyweight champion Primo Carnera, a lumbering circus strongman from Italy who was ushered to the title by conniving promoters in the early '30s. Once his backers earned sufficient lucre from their freak attraction,

Body and Soul: Shorty Pulaski (Joe Pevney) is killed after challenging his boyhood pal, boxer Charley Davis (John Garfield) to break from his corrupt promoter, Roberts (Lloyd Gough). Everybody knows Roberts had Shorty killed but only Peg (Lilli Palmer) has the integrity to walk away from the high life and easy money.

ABOVE: **Robert Ryan about to pay the price for a hard-fought victory in** *The Set-Up* **BELOW: Humphrey Bogart hates himself for abetting gangster Rod Steiger in** *The Harder They Fall.*

he was left on his own to be cruelly exposed: Max Baer knocked him down eleven times in their 1934 title fight. Schulberg, who always wrote with moral indignation, centered the story around jaded sportswriter Eddie Willis (Humphrey Bogart, in his final performance), who sells his soul to gangster Nick Benko (Rod Steiger) by taking a PR job for an operation he knows is crooked. The film ends with Willis calling for a congressional investigation into the mob's influence on boxing.

One of the most famous films to wrestle with sports rackets was *Night and the City* (Fox, 1950). Its protagonist wasn't a boxer, but a scrappy combatant nonetheless. Harry Fabian (Richard Widmark), an expatriate Yank living in London, longs for his piece of the action and hatches a plot pitting him against Kristo, kingpin of pro wrestling. Despite all his frenzied promoting and emoting, cajoling and buttonholing, Fabian meets the fate that Charley Davis and Stoker Thompson escaped: murdered and dumped in the river.

GAMBLING, OF COURSE, WAS THE UMBILICAL CORD between boxing and organized crime. While fight films of the '30s and '40s took the "fix" as a fait accompli, it wasn't until the peak of the noir movement that movies actually showed the inner workings of gambling rackets. The best of these was *711 Ocean Drive* (Columbia, 1950), in which noir's Everyman, Edmond O'Brien, climbs from sad-sack workingman to sleek-suited kingpin.

Columbia PR flaks raved about how the studio had valiantly pressed on with this groundbreaking film despite constant threats of sabotage and violence. Insurance policies with Lloyd's of London were taken out to guard against the kidnapping of the film's stars. "It can now be revealed that key Los Angeles police officers, instituting security measures that recalled the top-secret activities of the government in wartime, guarded the filming of *711 Ocean Drive* against repeated threats of violence."

The truth: *711 Ocean Drive* was one of the first movies Columbia made—and definitely the best—in a new subgenre of 1950s noir: the exposé picture. Televised congressional hearings into organized crime had captured the public's imagination, and Hollywood sensed a craving for reenactments of what was revealed. A pair of enterprising writers, Richard English and Francis Swan, cozied up to LAPD Lieutenant William Burns, part of the department's legendary Gangster Squad, cops given carte blanche to keep organized crime outside the county line. Their renegade exploits could only be properly depicted decades later, in films such as *Mulholland Falls* (MGM, 1996), *LA Confidential* (WB, 1997), and *Gangster Squad* (WB, 2013).

In 1950, while the squad was still in action, it was a big deal for Burns to give these two writers the scoop about interstate gambling rackets. But instead of turning the inside dope into a show about crusading cops, English and Swan told the tale of an ordinary guy—an electronics whiz played by Edmond O'Brien—rising through the ranks to become Mr. Big in an illegal West Coast gambling empire.

This was the biggest show veteran director Joseph Newman had ever handled, and he confirmed that there *were* obstacles facing the production when the company tried to shoot in Vegas, where a film exposing how the mob bilked suckers was, as you might imagine, unwelcome. The Vegas scenes were moved to Palm Springs. But when the producers staged the film's climax at Boulder Dam, only thirty-seven miles from Vegas, "discouraging" phone calls were placed to the producers.

Columbia turned the situation to its advantage, making it seem as if production of *711 Ocean Drive* was only slightly less daring than the landing of troops at Normandy. Today, of course, gambling is a multibillion-dollar *legal* racket, making *711 Ocean Drive* and films like it seem like much ado about nothing. It is, however, a terrifically entertaining movie, one that gave Edmond O'Brien a rare chance to play the lead—and have enough wardrobe changes to make Claire Trevor jealous.

SARTORIAL ELEGANCE IS A MAJOR PART OF THE GANGSTER LIFE. Most mobsters had fled the squalor of the slums and were therefore compulsive about displaying panache around the swells who'd made their piles legitimately. That's why nightclubs figure prominently in Dark City's datebooks. Fronting the typical city speakeasy was a boy born to the booze business, who'd missed last call at the recruiting office but emerged on the other side of the war with an up-and-up establishment, well-equipped to host victory parties. Welcome to Slim Dundee's Round-Up, the

TOP: Pressbook for *711 Ocean Drive* BOTTOM: One-time working stiff Edmond O'Brien lives the lush life as a gambling kingpin in *711 Ocean Drive*.

EXTRA 711 OCEAN DRIVE EXTRA

Copyright 1950 Columbia Pictures Corp. ★ COLUMBIA PRESSBOOK SUPPLEMENT ★ Printed in U.S.A.

"711" MAKES NEWSPAPER HEADLINES!

Guard Film Studio From Gang Terrorism!

Chicago Herald American

Armed guards patrolled the sets when "711 Ocean Drive" was filmed in order to protect players and production personnel from gang threats directed against the film. Edmond O'Brien, shown at right, stars in the expose of the $8,000,000,000 gambling racket.

Charge Underworld Halted Bookie Movie!

New York Post

Senator Alexander Wiley, of Wisconsin, a member of the Special Senate Committee to Investigate Interstate Gambling, referred to hoodlum threats directed against "711 Ocean Drive" as "a shocking commentary." He is shown here with film producer Frank N. Seltzer in Washington.

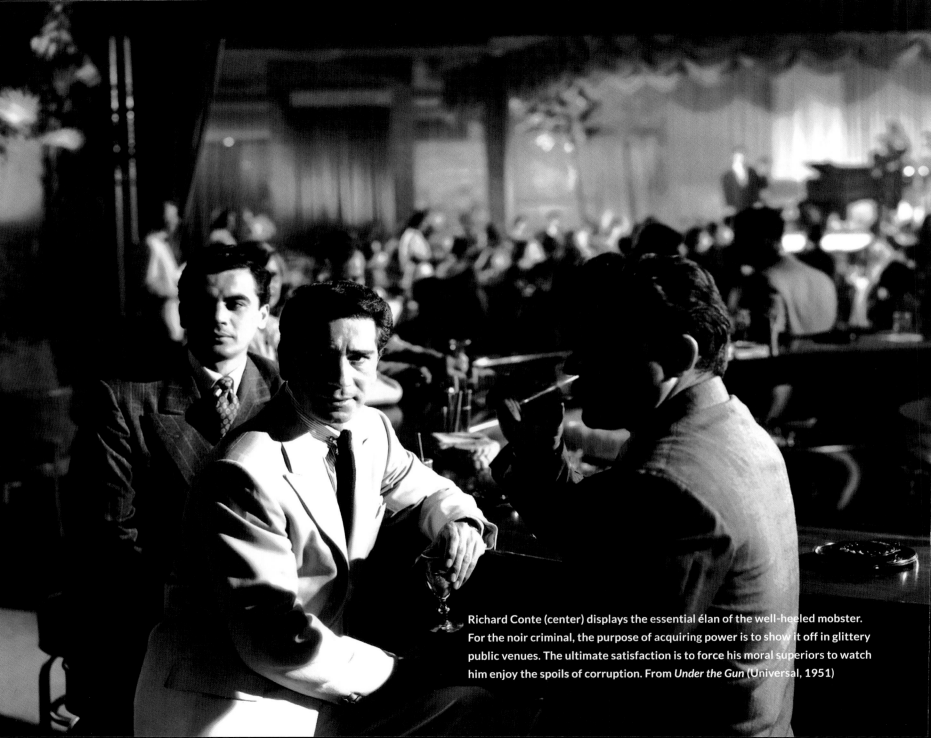

Richard Conte (center) displays the essential élan of the well-heeled mobster. For the noir criminal, the purpose of acquiring power is to show it off in glittery public venues. The ultimate satisfaction is to force his moral superiors to watch him enjoy the spoils of corruption. From *Under the Gun* (Universal, 1951)

Sanctuary Club, the Regent Club, the Blue Dahlia, the Kit Kat—ask about the veterans' two-for-one special.

The club owner's juice within the city's power structure was built on savoir faire and seating strategy: a discreet booth for the shady contractor buying a highball for the district alderman; a stage-side table for the judge who likes an unobstructed view of the seductive chanteuse. It's all showbiz. The bistro boss and his maître d' choreograph a nightly mating dance in which lowlifes and upper crust mingle, their schemes and secrets spilling out amid top-shelf bourbon and torchy ballads.

The nightlife impresario is a fixture in noir: Peter Lorre in *Black Angel* (Universal, 1946), Robert Alda in *The Man I Love* (WB, 1946), Kirk Douglas in *I Walk Alone* (Paramount, 1947), Morris Carnovsky in *Dead Reckoning* (Columbia, 1947), Zachary Scott in *Whiplash* (WB, 1948), Dan Duryea in *Criss Cross* (Universal, 1949) are only a few memorable examples of the barroom brotherhood. These potentially dangerous nightspots symbolize the halfway point in a criminal's rise from illicit to legitimate business.

The gray area between old-school hoodlum and "organization man" was fertile turf for noir fables. *The Racket*, released by Howard Hughes's RKO studio in 1951, was a remake of the second film Hughes produced, back in 1928. Its central figure, Nick Scanlon (Robert Ryan), is a Prohibition-era enforcer, all grease and muscle and boiling rage. He's a thorn in the side of the cops (represented, in true melodrama fashion, by his boyhood pal), and a liability to the boardroom boys who have moved from running numbers to buying judges and fixing elections.

Scanlon's deeper motives are familial. His younger brother must be given the opportunity to succeed in legitimate endeavors. "I even kept him out of the rackets," Scanlon explains to his nemesis, Captain McQuigg (Robert Mitchum). "He could marry anybody in this town—society people even!" Emulating the snooty gentry they despised was a full-time job for mob bosses.

Scanlon has a spiritual kinship with Shubunka, a self-made racket man played by Barry Sullivan in *The Gangster* (Monogram, 1947). Shubunka runs a protection dodge in a nameless East Coast beachfront district. A puffed-up peacock presiding over his two-bit territory, Shubunka believes he's the second coming of Scarface. In truth, he's a paranoid psychotic, his judgment clouded by obsessive jealousy over his beautiful mistress (Belita). As the encroaching syndicate puts the screws to him, Shubunka's insecurities spew out: "I came up from the sewer. Out of the muck and the mud, I came up by myself. I went to work when I was six—six years old! I was doing jobs for gangsters when I was nine. Bootlegging on my own when I was fourteen. Did anybody worry about me? Did anybody cry his eyes out over me? What do you want me to do—worry about the world? Let 'em rot, every one of them. They don't mean a thing to me. Don't flinch at me, don't you dare look down at me. I'm no crumb—I made something out of myself and I'm proud of it!"

Shubunka is confessing not to the chief of police, but to a teenage girl whose condescending gaze rips him apart. Like Scanlon, he'll be dead before the night is out, removed by tidier "businessmen" parceling out his turf.

VIRILITY IS AS CRITICAL TO DARK CITY'S CROOKS as respectability. In *The Big Combo* (Allied Artists, 1955), the gangster picture is distilled into a sexual battle between saturnine Mr. Brown (Richard Conte) and dogged flatfoot Leonard Diamond (Cornel Wilde). Both men covet the appetizing Susan Lowell (Jean Wallace), whom Diamond has been stalking for months as part of his investigation of Brown's illegal combination.

The themes are insinuated from the start: David Raksin's score bumps and grinds like a burlesque band summoning forth a stripper. Susan flees a boxing match and is pursued through shadowy alleys before being collared by Brown's henchmen. The scene is a visual expression of Brown's sexual dominance. Possession of a beautiful woman is at the root of his quest for power.

Brown and his yes-man McClure (Brian Donlevy) visit the dressing room of Brown's boxer, Bennie (Steve Mitchell), who's lost his bout. Brown gives Bennie a philosophical crash course, using the whipped McClure as case in point. "We eat the same steak, drink the same bourbon. Look—same manicure, cuff links. But we don't get the same girls. Why? Because women know the difference. They got instinct. First is first and second is nobody. . . . What makes the difference? Hate. Hate is the word, Bennie. Hate the man who tries to kill you. Hate him until you see red and you come out winning the big money. The girls will come tumbling after. You'll have to shut off the phone and lock the door to get a night's rest."

Brown then slaps Bennie across his already bruised face. When the fighter takes it, Brown says, "You should've hit me back. You haven't got the hate. Tear up Bennie's contract. He's no good to me anymore."

Sartorial superiority is essential to crook Alec Stiles (Richard Widmark).
Undercover underling Gene Cordell (Mark Stevens) helps dress the boss

The Big Combo was a different kind of boxing film, with Brown and Diamond, twentieth-century cavemen, slugging it out for possession of the trophy blonde. Diamond may genuinely want to stanch the spread of Brown's corruption, but he'd rather castrate him than incarcerate him. Sexual perversity runs rampant. Susan has sacrificed all her ambitions, held captive by the way Brown lavishes his bankroll, and tongue, on her. Brown gets an erotic charge out of bracing her in a hidden room filled with money and munitions. Brown's enforcers Fante (Lee Van Cleef) and Mingo (Earl Holliman) are depicted—through surreptitious suggestion, of course—as gay lovers who use beatings and torture as foreplay. Rita (Helene Stanton), the cop's girlfriend, gives him the lay of the land: "Women don't care how a man makes his living, only how he makes love." Brown scores points against Diamond even by proxy.

"You'd like to be me," Brown tells Diamond. "You'd like to have my organization, my influence, my fix. You think it's the money. It's not—it's personality." He also dominates the verbal sparring match, clipping off some of the best racketeer chatter ever, courtesy of writer Philip Yordan:

"That's *Mister* Brown to you. Only my friends call me Brown."

"I'm going to break him so fast he won't have time to change his pants."

"You're a little man with a soft job and good pay. Stop thinking about what might have been and who knows—you may live to die in bed."

"If they take you to police headquarters, shoot yourself in the head. It'll make things simpler."

Yordan's tale was the most stripped-down rendering of gangsterism yet. It benefits from the austere direction of Joseph H. Lewis, who plays it like Robert Bresson, if Bresson swung a shot-loaded sap. The poverty of the production is artfully masked by the photography of John Alton. The three had a good time pushing the limits of what was permissible on-screen. In one scene, Conte kisses Jean Wallace's shoulders, then sinks out of the frame as she moans, giving a strong suggestion of oral sex. When the buddy-buddy button men are in hiding, Fante implores his stir-crazy roomie to eat something. "I can't swallow no more salami," mumbles Mingo, subtly enough to evade the censor's radar. For many writers and directors, crafting subtle and suggestive detours around the Production Code was a clever and defiant game, one that added extra spice to genre programmers.

ABOVE: "It was for her I began to work my way up. All I had was guts. I traded them for money and influence. I got respect from everybody but her. . . . This is my bank. We don't take checks, we deal strictly in cash. There isn't anybody I'd trust with so much temptation—except myself. Or maybe you."—Mr. Brown (Richard Conte) to Susan (Jean Wallace) in *The Big Combo* BELOW: Robert Ryan as Nick Scanlon in Howard Hughes's *The Racket*

JOHN GARFIELD
HE RAN ALL THE WAY

C rime dramas produced in the years following World War II projected a political battle on the nation's movie screens. The hot-button issue in virtually every crime story was the Haves versus the Have-Nots. The distribution of wealth in America was an unresolved bête noire from the Depression and a chief ingredient in noir postwar.

The "naturalist" school took hold in Hollywood. Its politics were knee-jerk leftist, steeped in the Utopian Socialism that swirled around New York's influential Group Theater in the 1930s. Crime stories emerging from this creative cauldron saw criminals as products of a flawed system.

No artist exemplified the "naturalist" approach more than John Garfield. While directors and cinematographers are always lauded for developing the noir style, it was Garfield, as much as anyone, who gave the early noir ethos its defiant face and voice. One of his first was the aptly titled *They Made Me a Criminal* (WB, 1939).

On-screen, Garfield was the first true rebel, a Bowery boy who took no guff and hit with the impact of underdog boxing heroes Benny Leonard and Barney Ross. Born in 1913 as Jacob Julius Garfinkel, John Garfield would become for another underclass the kind of larger-than-life symbol Jimmy Cagney was for the shanty Irish. He brought to Hollywood a fiery desire to Make a Difference. In his wake came a caravan of writers, directors, and actors from the New York stage. If the initial wave from Ellis Island who developed the movie business were dedicated to making money, the second wave, of which Garfield was the point man, were committed to making Art. The ideological and economic clash that ensued was a gangland turf war that influenced the angry, pessimistic screenplays of film noir.

As a Warners contract player, Garfield combed the Dark City limits with offerings such as *Out of the Fog* (1941) and *The Fallen Sparrow* (on loan to RKO, 1943). But it was his attitude, his way of struggling with moral ambiguity, that would prove most influential. Once operating as an independent, Garfield's projects adopted a darker hue and a heavier weight, including the one-two combination in which he gave his best performances back to back: *The Breaking Point* (WB, 1950), a version of Hemingway's *To Have and Have Not*, grimmer and more wrenching then Howard Hawks's flippant 1946 version; and *He Ran All the Way* (UA, 1951), a neglected noir classic that's a harder, more hellish version of a '30s Warner Bros. street-kid crime meller.

In *The Breaking Point*, Garfield plays "boat jockey" Harry Morgan, a war hero struggling to make ends meet. He agrees to smuggling schemes that go horribly wrong. Garfield put everything he had into it, even acting as de facto producer. He showed progressive credentials by dumping Hemingway's casually tossed-off racial epithets and turning Harry's shipmate and best friend Wesley Park (Juano Hernandez) into an African-American; he fleshed out the roles of wife Lucy (Phyllis Thaxter) and "other woman" Leona Charles (Patricia Neal), making them two of the most fully realized female characters in noir. Under Michael Curtiz's commanding direction, *The Breaking Point* was the best Hemingway adaptation ever, its emotional gut-punch putting the source novel's meandering musings to shame.

Warner Bros. rewarded Garfield by dumping the film and its star when he was labeled "Red." His next film would be independently produced, made with loyal collaborators. *He Ran All the Way* is a crime drama that effectively cauterizes its bleeding heart. Nick Robey (Garfield), still living with his spiteful shrew of a mother, is unable to pull himself above a life of petty crime. When a cut-and-dried robbery gets scrambled, Nick panics and shoots a cop. He hides out among the sweltering masses at a public swimming pool, where he latches onto Peg Dobbs (Shelley Winters). Nick charms her into taking him home, where he'll be safe from the manhunt.

Nick ingratiates himself with Peg's folks, but before the night is over he goes berserk and takes them hostage. While the Dobbses sweat out whether they'll survive, Nick veers between envy and derision of their complacent domestic life. He tries on roles as patriarch, big brother, benefactor, and, ultimately, Mr. Right for Peg. He gives her the holdup cash, so she can get

John Garfield drifts into deep water with Patricia Neal and Juano Hernandez in *The Breaking Point*.

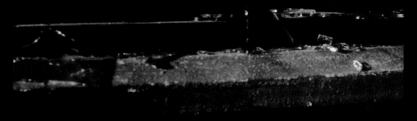

John Garfield infatuates and terrorizes Shelley Winters in *He Ran All the Way*.

them a car in which they can elope. The plan, of course, goes haywire. Peg winds up with the .38 and must choose between her dad and Nick.

He Ran All the Way was Garfield's last film and he made it—defiantly—with screenwriters Hugo Butler and Guy Endore and director John Berry, all of whom would be hounded out of Hollywood by the HUAC witch hunt. But of all the Hollywood artists scarred by the blacklist, John Garfield may have suffered the most.

Abraham Polonsky explained Garfield's triumph and tragedy in the introduction to Howard Gelman's *The Films of John Garfield*: "Garfield was a star who represented a social phenomenon of enormous importance for his times and, perhaps, ours too. He lived as a star without contradiction in the imagination of those who loved him for something that lay dormant in themselves, and this was tuned to the social vigor of the time that created him. Naturally, when those times became the political target of the estab-lishment in the United States, Garfield, whose training, whose past were the environment of the romantic rebellion the Depression gave birth to, became a public target for the great simplifiers."

Those simplifiers, Senator Joe McCarthy, Red-baiting attorney Roy Cohn, FBI boss J. Edgar Hoover, HUAC chairman J. Parnell Thomas, and the rest of his Commie-hunting crew were convinced that Garfield was help-ing Commie vipers infiltrate Hollywood. Garfield, who was never a fellow traveler—and had done more than any other Hollywood actor to aid the war effort on the home front—was invited to clear his Red-stained reputation by publicly turning fink before the committee. He ratted out no one.

As a result, his star was irreparably tarnished and he was exiled to the New York stage that spawned him. Angry and embittered, Garfield died of a heart attack in New York at the age of thirty-nine. Abe Polonsky, who would also lose his career, if not his life, to the blacklist, said that Garfield "defended his street boy's honor and they killed him for it."

If it takes a "soldier's mentality" to survive in a corrupt world, as Abe Polonsky maintained, then Samuel Fuller produced the basic training manual for Dark City's dogfaces.

More than any other writer or director, Fuller espoused a philosophy for coping with the creeping venality that, in his view, stretched beyond the city's limits. During the prime years of film noir, 1948–1952, while other directors exposed the underbelly of our urban nightmare, Fuller made westerns and war films that revealed the same criminal element on the frontier and the front lines. Crime was nothing new to Fuller, just another depraved aspect of human nature. Civilization was a pretense: Society is constantly at war, and war, according to Fuller, is "organized lunacy." The challenge is to survive in the cross fire.

Sinister Heights was one more battleground to Fuller. His late noir–era gangster picture *Underworld USA* (Columbia, 1961), presents the Feds and the mob as warring clans of equal resources, firepower, and ruthlessness. Fuller offers no moral judgment, just bitter irony: The hit man who murders a witness's child is also the lifeguard at a public swimming pool the mob runs for PR purposes. As Earl Connors, the syndicate boss, says: "There'll always be people like us. As long as we keep the books and subscribe to charities, we'll win the war. We always have."

Fuller's real concern is for Tolly Devlin (Cliff Robertson), his vengeful protagonist. As a teenager, Tolly sees his father murdered by small-time hoodlums. Orphaned, he falls into a life of crime and ends up in prison, where he connives to meet one of his father's killers. He squeezes from him the names of the others. Paroled, Devlin embarks on a crusade to execute them all.

By this time, the culprits are pillars of the community—as well as syndicate directors. Tolly infiltrates their mob *and* manipulates the Feds, using each to his own advantage. Spreading disinformation, he sows paranoia among the gangsters. He escorts his father's killers to their deaths, while keeping his own hands clean. Mission accomplished.

But when Connors, the big boss, has Tolly's informant girlfriend beaten, things go sideways. Tolly bursts into the big man's lair, throws him into the swimming

Newspaperman, novelist, filmmaker, storyteller, and indefatigable soldier Samuel Fuller

pool, and stands on him until he's dead. Connors's button man shoots Tolly, who staggers to the same alley where his father died. Love, fatefully, has loused up his mission.

Fuller spins this saga in the bombastic cinematic equivalent of tabloid journalism—lurid, punchy, and sensational—ideas and emotions smacking the viewer in 200-point type. It's a style Fuller grasped early, as a teenage crime reporter for the *New York Graphic*, Manhattan's preeminent "scandal sheet" during the Roaring Twenties. That's where Fuller learned to deliver hard facts with a fill-up of "creative exaggeration."

In 1960 Fuller declined an offer from John Wayne to produce Fuller's dream project, a war film called *The Big Red One*. His reasoning reveals the "soldier's mentality" at the heart of noir: "[Wayne] is a symbol of the kind of man I never saw in war. He would have given it a heroic touch that I hate in war movies. In real combat situations, everyone is scared, everyone is a nervous animal. You can't determine the heroes from the cowards in advance.

"A lot of those John Wayne–type characters came through in combat and a lot of them fell apart. The ones you didn't expect anything from, you'd be surprised what they could do in that situation, when you're cornered. I saw things men did— they might have been called heroes later, but we didn't call them that. You were doing your job. Or you were saving your ass. If you got spotted—an officer has to be one of your witnesses—you got a medal. . . . If you weren't spotted—*nothing*."

That credo of self-preservation got a full airing in *Pickup on South Street* (Fox, 1953), Fuller's first full-fledged crime drama and one of the best ever produced. It's another war story—a battle between America and undercover Communists—but Fuller's loyalties were with the grunts trying to survive in the margins while the ideological loonies struggle for power.

Skip McCoy (Richard Widmark) lives on the periphery of society—in a shanty teetering over New York harbor, content to eke out a living picking pockets and pilfering purses on the subway. One day he unwittingly lifts stolen microfilm off Candy (Jean Peters), a luscious tart being used, unknowingly, as a courier by her Commie boyfriend (Richard Kiley). Just like Tolly Devlin, Skip plays both ends against the middle, as they frantically bid for the prized strip of celluloid. When a federal agent accuses him of treason, Skip gives the guy a hearty laugh and a "Who cares?" in response.

Skip winds up aiding the FBI out of love and loyalty to Candy, not patriotism. For Fuller, allegiance to your fellow soldiers is all that matters. When his compatriot, elderly grifter Mo (the fabulous Thelma Ritter), is killed by a Communist agent, Skip retrieves her pine coffin from a barge headed to Potter's Field and pays for a proper burial with his own hard-stolen money. No unmarked graves for Fuller's valiant dogfaces.

Under the enthusiastic auspices of Darryl F. Zanuck and 20th Century-Fox, Fuller shot the seventy-minute *Pickup* in only ten days. Within those limitations, he packed in more storytelling pizzazz than some directors muster in a lifetime. In one scene, Widmark knocks Jean Peters out cold with a right cross, then revives her by pouring beer on her face. She comes to, and as he's fingering her bruised lips, they embrace and kiss. In the climactic fight, Widmark yanks Richard Kiley down a flight of stairs, banging his chin on every step. Love scenes or fight scenes, Fuller gave them the lurid gusto of someone born to the crime beat.

Like any good muckraking journalist, Fuller also stirred up controversy. FBI boss J. Edgar Hoover was mortified by *Pickup*'s disdain for flag-waving ideology. From the left, Fuller was criticized for joining Hollywood's anti-Communist bandwagon, which was reeling out such things as *I Married a Communist* (RKO, 1949), *The Red Menace* (Republic, 1949), and *I Was a Communist for the FBI* (WB, 1951).

Sam Fuller was Hollywood's equivalent of Skip McCoy: scuffling in the margins, picking his marks carefully, striking quickly, staying light on his feet, and living to work another day. And, like Skip, Fuller faced the world's brutality with a cynical laugh and an eagerness to keep forging ahead like a good soldier, one foot in front of the other. He proved to be the ultimate noir survivor, making crazy independent potboilers into his eighties, all loudly declaring: The world is a madhouse, but *goddamn* it's a thrilling ride.

Richard Widmark and Jean Peters meet "noir" in *Pickup on South Street*.

THE PRECINCT

THE CAPTAIN'S STACK OF UNSOLVED CASES TOPPLES OFF THE DESK, INTO THE DEAD CHRISTMAS TREE. HE'LL DEAL WITH IT NEXT YEAR. FOUR HOURS LEFT ON THIS SHIFT; THE COFFEE'S BURNED BLACKER THAN TAR. HE TRIES NOT TO THINK OF THE NEW FOLDERS BEING CREATED THIS MINUTE, TOMORROW, ALWAYS. HIS WIFE WANTS TO DANCE IN THE NEW YEAR AT THE GLASS SLIPPER. HE WANTS TO SPEND THE NIGHT BUSTING THE MOBBED-UP OWNER AND KNOCKING THAT SLIMY SMILE OFF HIS FACE. COME MIDNIGHT, HE'LL BE DREAMING THE USUAL: OPEN HOUSE IN THE WEAPONS ROOM AND A FREE DAY IN THE STREETS TO SETTLE UP.

The chore of riding herd on Dark City's crime rate fell to either harassed, burned-out cops, or clean-cut, upright federal agents. Distinctions between the two went deeper than their shoeshines and expense accounts. The local boys were only trying to keep their heads above water until the pension kicked in. The Feds were on a political crusade.

Any picture that involved the actions of the Federal Bureau of Investigation had J. Edgar Hoover, figuratively, as its executive producer. He'd been installed as the Bureau's acting director in 1924, presiding over an obscure agency that did little more than chase car thieves who crossed state lines. But, in 1932, national obsession with the Lindbergh baby kidnapping upped the profile of the FBI forever. Fear of kidnappers and bank robbers led, in 1933, to a broadening of the FBI's activities and its arsenal. The tommy gun was soon as synonymous with the "G-man" as it was with Pretty Boy Floyd.

Hoover was a better propagandist than he was a crime buster. He stooped

Scott Brady and Roy Roberts lead a team of LAPD officers into the city's sewers to hunt down a clever killer in *He Walked by Night*.

to rewriting facts to bolster the image of the FBI—and of himself as the nation's greatest lawman. Melvin Purvis, the agent whose pursuit of John Dillinger resulted in the postmatinée execution of Public Enemy No. 1, was extricated from official accounts of the case. In the sanctioned version, an army of G-men dropped the noose on Dillinger, under Hoover's guidance. Purvis quit the Bureau in disgust.

Hoover mythologized the FBI to counteract outlaw folk legends retold in tabloid newspapers and on the screen. His publicist, Louis Nichols, helped J. Edgar hone his image as the eunuch of justice, able to resist every temptation but one: using the latest gadgetry—surveillance cameras, wiretaps—to lay bare the lives of suspected wrongdoers.

For years, Hoover withheld his imprimatur from crime movies. He wouldn't grant the Bureau stamp to *G-Men* (WB, 1935) because undercover agent Jimmy Cagney patronized a nightclub. But once Hoover saw Hollywood's impact on the World War II propaganda machine, he recruited filmmakers to aid his mythmaking.

Louis de Rochemont had produced the successful *March of Time* documentary series and came with the financial backing of 20th Century-Fox. Hoover figured de Rochemont's facility with factual material would add authenticity to the Bureau's product. Their collaboration, *The House on 92nd Street* (Fox, 1945), was the first

film to take a "semi-documentary" approach to crime. Based on several cases in which Nazi spies were undone by undercover FBI agents, the film was shot in actual locations, using the type of clandestine camerawork celebrated in the film. The Bureau loaned Fox the same surveillance vehicles it employed in the field.

Throughout the film, we see the use of hidden cameras and microphones, two-way mirrors, and microphotography. Americans saw the immensity of the Fingerprint Collection that Hoover hoped would one day contain thumbprints of every citizen. Reaction, to say the least, was mixed. Some marveled at this new level of security. Others saw the foundations of a fascist state.

As the film was readied for release in 1945, the Allied triumph in Europe was imminent. To stay current, de Rochemont transformed the Nazi spy ring into nebulous subversives, easily interpreted as the nation's next enemy, Communists. The secret at the script's core, Project 97, wasn't identified, but when A-bombs dropped on Nagasaki and Hiroshima weeks before the film opened, the soundtrack was altered to refer specifically to the atom-smashing scientists who had developed those bombs.

This ersatz-documentary approach would influence other crime pictures as well, such as *Boomerang* (Fox, 1947), *Call Northside 777* (Fox, 1948), *The Naked City* (Universal, 1948), *Walk a Crooked Mile* (Columbia, 1948), and *Walk East on Beacon!* (Columbia, 1952), the latter pair finally calling a Red a Red.

More central to the development of film noir were low-budget films released by Eagle-Lion Studios (an outgrowth of Producers Releasing Corporation), which thrust government agents into a grim night-world, devised by director Anthony Mann and cinematographer John Alton.

The best of the federal-agent noirs is *T-Men* (Eagle-Lion, 1948), in which Treasury agents (Dennis O'Keefe and Alfred Ryder) go undercover to bust a ring of counterfeiters. It opens with Treasury official Elmer Irey reciting—with startling

TOP: FBI agent Lloyd Nolan briefs a group of government and military personnel on the bureau's counterespionage tactics in *The House on 92nd Street*. BOTTOM: Dennis O'Keefe engages in one the FBI's favorite activities—wiretapping—in *Walk a Crooked Mile*, one of the first anti-Communist films from a Hollywood studio.

ineptness—statistics proving the effectiveness of the Department's crime-busting tactics. Viewers expecting a stiff federal dog-and-pony show were about to be surprised.

As the narration (courtesy of stentorian gasbag Reed Hadley) drones on about the dedication T-men display for the people of the United States, the agents descend into an underworld of horrifying brutality unlike anything Hoover's G-men had faced on-screen before. When O'Keefe, who's infiltrated the crooks' inner circle, must stand by silently as his partner is murdered, crime films hit a new level of cold-bloodedness. Mann and Alton were so adept at rendering the agents' life of loneliness and dread, the jingoistic narration comes off as disrespectful.

The surprising success of *T-Men* influenced the FBI. Its next sanctioned film was *The Street with No Name* (Fox, 1948), directed by William Keighley, who'd done *G-Men* in the '30s. It eschewed the semi-documentary look for more stylized noir elements, but kept the bogus narration and *92nd Street*'s Lloyd Nolan as a federally funded father figure.

The same year saw the release of *Walk a Crooked Mile*, the first true Cold War film. It fed the growing anti-Communist hysteria with a tale of enemy spies infiltrating atomic testing laboratories. Producer Edward Small was cashing in on his own *T-Men*, which also starred Dennis O'Keefe. Small started in show business as a talent agent, and O'Keefe remained his primary client. *T-Men* had transformed O'Keefe from a lightweight comedic actor to a square-jawed tough guy, and Small wasted no time exploiting his new persona. Prior to *Walk a Crooked Mile*, O'Keefe played an *homme fatal* in another Small production, the phenomenal 1948 noir *Raw Deal*, created by the same duo—director Anthony Mann and DP John Alton—who made *T-Men* such a revelation.

Small intended to title it *FBI vs. Scotland Yard*, but he dropped *FBI* from the title after learning how meddlesome Hoover could be. Unlike Louis de Rochemont, Small had no interest in Hoover lurking over his shoulder as a coproducer. When he refused to let the FBI vet George Bruce's screenplay, Hoover demanded all references to the Bureau be removed from the film. Small persisted, asserting that, as a public agency, the FBI was fair game for fictional treatment. In the end, the only change was to the title. Hoover wrote a letter to the *New York Times* complaining that the FBI had not sanctioned the film.

Standing up to Hoover came easily to Eddie Small, who'd had lots of practice

Charles McGraw, who had previously made a striking impression as a hit man in *The Killers* (1946), raised movie cruelty to a new level as Moxie, the counterfeiting ring's torpedo in *T-Men*. Whether threatening to break off Dennis O'Keefe's fingers or nonchalantly frying Wallace Ford in a steambath, McGraw's ruthlessness plumbed frigid depths. Here he watches impassively as Jack Overman throttles O'Keefe.

squaring off with the major studios. In 1942 he threatened a strike against United Artists if the studio failed to meet his terms on a distribution deal. Small served as president of the Society of Independent Motion Picture Producers, formed in 1941 to protect independent producers from domination by the majors. His strategy was to make low-budget films with a loyal cadre of talent—*Walk a Crooked Mile* screenwriter George Bruce wrote many scripts for him, and actors O'Keefe, Louis Hayward, and Louise Allbritton were part of his stock company. Small was no slouch when it came to noir. In addition to the classics *T-Men* and *Raw Deal*, his credits include *99 River Street* (UA, 1953), *Wicked Woman* (UA, 1953), *Down Three Dark Streets* (UA, 1954), *New York Confidential* (WB, 1955), and *The Naked Street* (UA, 1955).

While never reaching the heights of *T-Men*, *Walk a Crooked Mile* is an exciting procedural enlivened by location photography in San Francisco and Los Angeles, the hulking menace of a goateed Raymond Burr, and the charm of Dennis O'Keefe. His interplay with costar Louis Hayward makes it something of a "buddy film" as well, with a surprising undercurrent of gay innuendo. Despite his contentious feelings about the film, one can assume that the ending—in which FBI agent and Scotland Yard operative stroll off arm in arm—met with the approval of J. Edgar Hoover and his longtime "companion" Clyde Tolson.

The anti-Communist film Hoover always wanted was finally issued in 1952. *Walk East on Beacon!* is based on a *Reader's Digest* article ("The Crime of the Century"), written by Hoover himself. His trusted movie colleague Louis de Rochemont paid Hoover $15,000 for the rights to the story and set a team of writers to work adapting it into a remake of *House on 92nd Street*, with Communist spies stealing Manhattan Project secrets. Leo Rosten had written original stories for several noirs—*The Dark Corner* (Fox, 1946); *Lured* (UA, 1947); *Sleep, My Love* (UA, 1948); *The Velvet Touch* (RKO, 1948); *Where Danger Lives* (RKO, 1950)—but the other writers, Virginia Shaler and Yale classmates Leonard Heideman and Emmett Murphy—were neophytes.

Walk East on Beacon! is a Cold War artifact, having little to do with noir. For real noir, consider the story of coscreenwriter Leonard Heideman. This picture gave him a leg up in the movie business, and Heideman made the move to Hollywood. In the mid-'50s he wrote regularly for television, including the anti-Commie series *I Led Three Lives*. In 1955 he married schoolteacher Dolores Hearn and by the end of the decade they had two sons and were living the high life. By 1963, however,

BROUGHT THRILLINGLY TO LIFE BY THE MAKERS OF "CANON CITY"!

Savage TRUTH! Stronger than Fiction!

In the watery darkness of the massive sewers that wind tortuously beneath Los Angeles a man flees for his life. Now he stops — waiting, listening, his finger tense about the trigger of his gun. Suddenly — he whirls — fires blindly into the blackness!

Savage, brutal—this is the killer who has struck again and again — the killer the police have hunted, patiently, skillfully, courageously — relentlessly tying each tiny clue, every shred and strand of evidence into an evertightening net.

Now it's closing . . . they have him cornered again, fighting desperately for his life . . . deadly, defiant, unafraid!

FROM THE
HOMICIDE FILES
OF THE
LOS ANGELES
POLICE

A BRYAN FOY Production
Presented by EAGLE LION FILMS

"HE WALKED BY NIGHT"

Heideman was beset by financial problems. One morning, in the midst of a raging argument, Heideman stabbed his wife to death. An evaluation by psychiatrists found him legally insane and unfit to stand trial. He was committed to Atascadero State Hospital for the criminally insane.

Fourteen months later, doctors declared him cured. Two years later, under the name Laurence Heath, Heideman resumed his television career, writing scripts for *Mission: Impossible*, *Mannix*, *Hawaii Five-O*, *Dynasty*, and *Murder, She Wrote*. He remarried twice, and under the name "John Balt" wrote a grueling autobiography—*By Reason of Insanity*—recounting the mental breakdown that led him to murder his wife. Heideman lived until 2007, when, at the age of seventy-eight, he committed suicide by hanging himself. You want noir? *That's* noir.

The director of *Walk East on Beacon!*, Alfred Werker, had previously directed a genuine and influential noir, 1948's *He Walked by Night* (Eagle-Lion). Richard Basehart plays a killer who uses his brilliance with electronics to evade a police manhunt. It was based on the true story of Erwin Walker, a police dispatcher who had served with distinction in World War II. He'd been traumatized when his signal corps unit was massacred, for which he assumed blame. After discharge, his survivor's guilt worsened. He dwelled in a secret workshop, obsessed with an electronic "project." In 1945, still a stateside Army first lieutenant, Walker began a robbery spree in support of his secret mission, during which he fatally shot a highway patrolman. He later explained he was developing a ray gun that would turn metal into dust, which would force the government to raise soldiers' pay; that would make it too costly to fight wars. The press sniffed an insanity plea and dubbed him "Machine Gun" Walker.

The case captured the attention of writer-producer Crane Wilbur, who'd been writing crime and prison pictures since the early 1930s. He saw a fresh wrinkle in Walker's sad saga—a police procedural ("Ripped from the Files of the LAPD") that focused on the disturbed loner, a one-time cop, lost on the dark side. Wilbur was intrigued by Walker's use of the county's sewer system as a means of transit and escape. *He Walked by Night* ends, after seventy-nine minutes of shadowy foreboding, with Basehart killed like a rat in the city's sewers (brilliantly photographed by John Alton, with several sequences directed by a pinch-hitting Anthony Mann).

Playing a small role as a police technician was Jack Webb, who co-opted much of this material to create *Dragnet*, the archetypal TV police procedural, which combined the righteous attitude of the crusading Feds with the daily grind of lowly flatfoots.

T-Men's influence was still being felt at the end of the decade, in such low-budget crime dramas as *Trapped* (Eagle-Lion, 1949) and *Southside 1-1000* (Allied Artists, 1950), which both featured Treasury agents going undercover to bust up counterfeiting rings. Per usual, the villains were the more compelling characters, with Lloyd Bridges livening up the Richard Fleischer–directed *Trapped* and, in a rare twist, Andrea King playing a female crime boss in *Southside*.

All these films shared a Republican view of crime, at odds with the more Democratic Warners-style film that saw crooks as wayward offspring of a corrupt environment. Whenever the Feds were heroes, criminals were rogue parasites, hunted down and exterminated to protect taxpayers from infection.

Now step into authentic noir terrain: *T-Men*, *He Walked by Night*, and the 1949 prison-break yarn *Canon City* were all financed through a silent partnership between Eagle-Lion production chief Bryan Foy and Johnny Roselli, who'd started his show business career as a liaison between the Chicago mob and the Hollywood craft unions. They hired Joseph Breen Jr., son of the Production Code Administration boss, to grease their skids. Roselli had once worked in the Hays office and he reunited with Breen after a federal stretch for extortion. He'd been sent up by Willie Bioff and George Browne, former heads of the corrupt IATSE union, who, as noted back in Sinister Heights, enjoyed several years getting rich off studio payoffs.

Roselli eventually left Hollywood to help the Chicago boys establish a foothold in Vegas. He later was a middleman in negotiations between the Mafia and the CIA to assassinate Fidel Castro. His career ended on a yacht off Miami, when he was butchered, stuffed into an oil drum, and set adrift by, it's assumed, his criminal colleagues.

FEDS ONLY TROOPED INTO DARK CITY on the heels of interstate racketeers, or other footloose miscreants deemed a threat to national security. Solving crimes perpetrated in the burg itself was left to local lawmen, and, by the early 1950s, the city's station houses were lousy with disgruntled detectives, embittered that their decision to patrol the straight and narrow earned them less than a hundred bucks a week, paltry benefits, and a calloused heart.

Jim Wilson (Robert Ryan), protagonist of *On Dangerous Ground* (RKO, 1951), was once a decent cop. Eleven years on the beat have hardened him into a marauding thug, doling out fierce punishment to Dark City's denizens. His uncontrollable violence threatens both the department's image and his own career.

"So I get thrown off the force," he barks. "What kind of job is this anyway? Garbage, that's all we handle. Garbage! . . . How do you live with yourself?"

"I don't," his more levelheaded partner responds. "I live with other people. This is a job just like any other. When I go home, I don't take this stuff with me. I leave it outside."

Wilson doesn't have a wife or a family, or the prospect of one. His contempt for the easily corrupted is so strong he acts as solitary judge, jury, and—if he doesn't get sorted out—executioner. Sensing that Wilson is a bomb with a smoldering fuse, his boss sends him upstate to cool off and bring some city savvy to a manhunt in the sticks. In tracking down a young girl's murderer, Wilson meets his doppelgänger: the victim's father, Walter Brent (Ward Bond), an ignoramus bent on vigilante justice.

The trail leads to the farmhouse of Mary Walden (Ida Lupino), a blind spinster devoted to her mentally ill brother, Danny—who is the killer. Wilson sees in Mary a reflection of his lonely soul. Her trust and faith give him a shred of hope. He promises Mary he'll protect her brother from Brent. But Danny falls to his death in the climactic chase, and, when Wilson guiltily tries to reconcile with Mary, she sends him away, back to Dark City.

On Dangerous Ground injected Eastern philosophy into the cop drama. The duality of nature, both physical and spiritual, is the theme of A. I. Bezzerides's script. To find connectedness to life, the unbalanced man, a destroyer, must shed his armor and accept vulnerability and compassion. Although Mary, the nurturer, spurns him, Wilson returns to duty with a more Zen-like perspective. At least that was the script's ending. RKO told director Nicholas Ray to tack on a new finish, Wilson racing back to Mary for an embrace at the fade-out. Ray refused to shoot it, and Lupino and Ryan blocked out the final scene themselves.

LEFT: Cop Dana Andrews ponders a suspect he has accidentally killed in *Where the Sidewalk Ends*. TOP RIGHT : Kirk Douglas takes sudden retirement in *Detective Story*. BOTTOM RIGHT: Robert Ryan routinely abuses suspects in *On Dangerouis Ground*.

On Dangerous Ground considered the spiritual crisis at the core of police brutality.

A deeper crisis of faith—and a worse fate—confronts Detective Jim McLeod (Kirk Douglas) in *Detective Story* (Paramount, 1951). Like Jim Wilson, McLeod has been made a heartless bastard by police work. He presides over his precinct like a courthouse judge, meting out punishment to everyone—crooks and suspects alike.

He reserves his most hateful third degree for a suspected abortionist (George Macready). The doctor's attorney turns the tables on McLeod, however, claiming the cop is on a personal vendetta: McLeod's wife (Eleanor Parker) received an abortion from the doctor the previous year. Devastated, McLeod refuses to forgive his wife. Instead, he commits suicide by walking into the firing line of a scared punk trying to escape arrest.

In *Where the Sidewalk Ends* (Fox, 1950), cop Dana Andrews beats a suspect to death, then pins the murder on a gangster he despises. It was among the earliest of dozens of 1950s noirs that showed the police not only as fallible and fatigued, but as bust-out sociopaths. Two decades later, the deranged cop would reemerge, unrepentant, as "Dirty Harry" Callahan. By then there were twice as many rats in the cage, and the public, pissed-off and powerless, embraced him as a savior, not a psycho. Where noir typically treated psychopathology as a sad condition, by the 1980s Clint Eastwood's "Dirty" character was worth millions.

The Big Heat (Columbia, 1953) featured a clean-cut version of Dirty Harry, but one just as angry. Uptown critics dismissed it at the time as just another crime potboiler, signifying Fritz Lang's demise as an A-list director. They missed the cold brilliance that electrified genre conventions, an exhilarating union of Germanic fatalism and Wild West ass-kicking.

When corrupt cop Tom Duncan blows his brains out, he leaves a suicide note exposing the death-grip gangster Mike Lagana (Alexander Scourby) has on the city's power elite. Duncan's wife stashes the note, keeping it to blackmail Lagana and keep herself in a style she never enjoyed as a cop's wife. Sergeant Dave Bannion (Glenn Ford), a blue-collar bulldog, gets suspicious and turns up Duncan's mistress, Lucy Chapman, a B-girl who knows where the bodies are buried. Next thing Bannion knows, Lucy's one of those bodies.

Despite warnings from his bosses to back off, Bannion barges into Lagana's mansion. There's art, servants, music: It sickens Bannion. "Cops have homes, too. Only sometimes there isn't enough money to pay the rent, because an honest cop gets hounded off the force by you thievin' cockroaches for tryin' to do an honest job." He vows to bring the big heat down on Lagana.

Insulted, Lagana returns to his roots: His thugs plant a bomb in Bannion's car, killing the cop's wife (Jocelyn Brando). When his boss doesn't go after Lagana, Bannion flips off his badge and loads up his .38. "That doesn't belong to the department," he seethes. "I bought it."

Locked and loaded, *The Big Heat* gallops into the concrete frontier: There

Bringing down *The Big Heat*: with a shot heard, one hopes, in all the barrooms and brothels of Dark City, Debbie Marsh (Gloria Grahame) settles a score for all the town's B-girls. Confronting corrupt Bertha Duncan, who's living high on the hog off racketeer Mike Lagana's blood money, Debbie informs her, "You know, Bertha, we're all sisters under the mink." She then lets Dave Bannion's borrowed service revolver finish the thought.

are showdowns in saloons, rustlers biding their time with endless hands of poker, a robber baron devouring territory while tin stars look the other way. And, most critically, there's the whore with the heart of gold.

Debbie Marsh (Gloria Grahame) is the moll of Lagana's troglodyte torpedo, Vince Stone (Lee Marvin). She's a sexy, smart-mouthed, material woman, adrift amid all the macho posturing. After Vince, in a jealous rage, scars her face with boiling coffee, Debbie throws in with the cop. Bannion, true to his moral superiority, never gives in to murderous temptation. But Debbie, already in the gutter, redeems herself by wasting their tormentors. First she blows the lid off Lagana's empire by blasting Mrs. Duncan—allowing Bannion to retrieve the incriminating suicide note. Feeling her oats, Debbie settles up with Vince, administering her own hot java facial.

Debbie dies in the climactic shoot-out. As she longingly looks to Bannion for approval, he eulogizes his dead wife. In the epilogue, Bannion is back on the force, Marshal of Metropolis, waiting for the next Lagana to ride into town.

The film's power is mainly due to two men: author William P. McGivern, a former crime reporter who wrote as many crackerjack crime yarns as anyone, and Lang, whose work is synonymous with noir. His early German films, *M* (Nero-Film AG, 1931) and *The Testament of Dr. Mabuse* (Nero-Film AG, 1933), etched the blueprints of Dark City: omnipotent forces dictating the fate of innocent people, uncontrollable urges leading to self-destruction.

Lang fostered the legend that he had stared down the demon in 1933, when Hitler and Goebbels anointed him the "man who will give us the big Nazi pictures." He claims to have immediately fled Germany, his riches repatriated by the Reich. Later research revealed him a master of embellishment: In truth he'd displayed little resistance to the Nazis' rise to power. It was the promise of Hollywood—mixed with fear that the Nazis would betray him, due to his mother's Jewish heritage—that led Lang to surrender his preeminence in the German film industry. Once on Hollywood production lines, Lang became the movies' official Minister of Fear, dusting his studio confections with the doom he felt was at the heart of the universe.

ON THE OTHER SIDE OF THE STATION HOUSE from upright, uptight cops like Bannion and Wilson was another kind of lawman. Brogans propped on the desk,

worrying a toothpick, figuring his angles. This guy could easily be one of the perps cooling his heels in a holding cell. He's from the same neighborhood scrap heap, just figured a badge was the better percentage play. But somewhere along the line, he saw the game was rigged, leaving him a flatfooted schmuck, holding nothing but low cards. So he'd fix the game, determined to beat the house.

"So I'm no good," snaps Webb Garwood, one of the dirtiest boys in blue. "But I'm no worse than anybody else. You work in a store, you knock down the cash register; a big boss, the income tax; ward healer, you sell votes; a lawyer, you take bribes. I was a cop—I used a gun."

Webb (Van Heflin) is rationalizing the Machiavellian scheme he perpetrates in *The Prowler* (UA, 1950). It begins when he answers a distress call from an affluent married woman reporting a Peeping Tom. Webb's more interested in her, and her ritzy home.

Pretending it's in the line of duty, Webb insinuates himself into the life of Susie Gilvray (Evelyn Keyes). They have an affair while her disc jockey husband does his nightly broadcasts (the voice that of uncredited and blacklisted screenwriter Dalton Trumbo).

Susie's no femme fatale. She's levelheaded but lonely, unable to resist the cocky advances of the overly attentive cop. When Webb learns she's depressed because her husband is sterile, he hatches a nefarious plan. He reappears as the prowler, coaxing Susie's husband out of the house. He murders him and makes it look like a tragic accident.

An inquest upholds Webb's version, yet Susie's still convinced he's a murderer. But Webb has big plans for their future. He quits the force and sets out to win Susie's trust, persuading her he's a decent guy who just never got a break in this world. He promises to marry her and give her the baby she desperately wants. In exchange, he'll tap her late husband's life insurance windfall, so he can buy a motel in tax-free Nevada and escape the rat race.

Susie caves in and Webb squires her away to his dusty little dream "resort." But on their wedding night she stuns Webb by announcing she's four months' pregnant. He panics—the timing of the baby's birth will be proof of their affair, giving him a motive for killing Gilvray.

In a mockery of the domestic bliss they craved, Webb and Susie set up a bizarre domicile in a desert ghost town, so the baby can be born in secrecy. Complications

Dirty cop Webb Garwood (Van Heflin) executes his lover's husband and makes it look like an accident in *The Prowler*.

The Prowler: Webb's dreams of material success evaporate when he and Susie (Evelyn Keyes) are forced to hide out in an abandoned mining town to avoid the scandal of her unexpected pregnancy.

force Webb to bring in a doctor. Susie finally turns on Webb when she realizes he'll kill the doctor to preserve their secret. She slips the doctor the car keys and her newborn. Webb's in hot pursuit, but the cops are already on the way. His former blue brethren corner Webb and waste him like a wild dog.

Webb Garwood was different from other loony lawmen: His wild scheme was based on an impatient desire for middle-class ease, more than a need to set the world straight. A swaggering sports hero in high school, Webb figured himself a world-beater. He'd done everything by the book, but the book turned out to be a cheap paperback. If a badge doesn't give you a leg up on a better life, what the hell good is it?

In his first features, *The Boy with Green Hair* (RKO, 1948) and *The Lawless* (Paramount, 1949), director Joseph Losey attacked bigotry and prejudice. He'd been honing his social conscience since the 1930s, when he'd worked in the Red-hued Federal Theater project in New York. In Hollywood he cut his teeth directing shorts for MGM's *Crime Does Not Pay* series (one of which, "A Gun in His Hand" [1945], was the genesis of *The Prowler*).

In 1950–1951, Losey worked exclusively in noir, combining gritty crime with a "subversive" intellectualism, a combustible mixture typical of many artists in Dark City. His 1951 remake of *M* transposed the criminal underworld of Berlin to Los Angeles, and *The Big Night* (UA, 1951) treated a young boy's passage to adulthood as a noir nightmare. But it was *The Prowler* in which Losey's political antagonists saw an anti-American sentiment: Pursuit of a middle-class materialist lifestyle could lead to derangement. The film's working title, *The Cost of Living*, made such allusions obvious. Today, the "subversive" message seems barely discernible. Garwood's modern-era equivalent is a garden-variety nutcase, as played by Richard Gere in *Internal Affairs* (Paramount, 1990) and Ray Liotta in *Unlawful Entry* (Fox, 1992), cop-from-hell remakes of *The Prowler*. To the anti-Communist crowd in

1951, the filmmakers were undermining American values.

Screenwriter Hugo Butler and Joseph Losey were both named as Communist sympathizers—"Comsymps" in the argot of the day—and blacklisted. Losey's incrimination oddly paralleled that of *The Prowler*: His career was derailed by an informer who, Losey learned later, once had an affair with his wife.

WEBB GARWOOD'S USE OF HIS BADGE AS A SHIELD FOR MURDER was echoed in a 1954 film titled, appropriately enough, *Shield for Murder* (UA). Based on another novel by William (*The Big Heat*) McGivern, the story reverberates with the same motivations found in *The Prowler*.

Barney Nolan (Edmond O'Brien, who also codirected with Howard Koch) wants to swap his roller and revolver for a two-car garage and a backyard barbecue. Realizing it will take years of saving—and that he might stop a bullet in the meantime—Barney opts for an easier route: He kills a bagman carrying a $25,000 payoff and pockets the loot. All in the line of duty, he testifies—neglecting to mention the dough. What busts his play is a deaf-mute who witnessed the murder and sucks up the guts to report it. Nolan assigns himself to the investigation and ends up murdering the guy to cover his tracks.

All sweaty, frantic Barney wants is a suburban oasis for him and his fiancée (Marla English). While Nolan is conning his peers, gangster Packy Reed is tracking his missing twenty-five Gs. Soon, Barney is on the lam from both crooks and colleagues. After shooting his way out of a public swimming pool, Barney hides out in the unfinished tract home he covets, and ends up riddled with police slugs, dying facedown on the yet-to-be planted front lawn.

There were lots of other dirty cop noirs, from high-end studio products like *Rogue Cop* (MGM, 1954), based on yet another McGivern novel, in which Robert Taylor plays a bull who'd rather take mob payoffs than solve crimes, to mellers like *The Man Who Cheated Himself* (Fox, 1951) and *Pushover* (Columbia, 1954), about cops abandoning ethics for erotic prizes (Jane Wyatt and Kim Novak, respectively).

One of the best was *Private Hell 36* (Filmakers, 1954), in which the bond between two cops (Howard Duff and Steve Cochran) comes unglued after Cochran steals a dead gangster's strongbox of loot and swears Duff to secrecy. Cochran wants to launder the swag in Mexico, then hightail it to the good life with his torch singer

girlfriend, played by Ida Lupino (who also produced and cowrote the script).

When the dead gangster's partner tries to blackmail them, the pair decides to pull the money from the mobile home where it's hidden (the trailer-park slot of the title). Turns out the blackmailer is their suspicious boss (Dean Jagger), and Cochran is gunned down after wounding his partner, who he thinks ratted him out. Don Siegel directed with typical punch and panache.

THE MOST UNSCRUPULOUS COP in Dark City wasn't unearthed until 1958. By then noir had been whitewashed and transplanted to television shows like *The Lineup* and *Dragnet*. But lying low on the outskirts, wallowing in his foul fiefdom, was Hank Quinlan, whose reign as the "police celebrity" of Los Robles, a pestilent little border town, is tainted by a *Touch of Evil* (Universal).

Directed, starring, and adapted by Orson Welles (from Whit Masterson's novel *Badge of Evil*), the film follows the final days of Quinlan's life, when the car-bomb murder of contractor Rudy Linnekar explodes long-buried conspiracies. Passing through town when the fireworks start is Miguel Vargas (Charlton Heston), a narcotics investigator from Mexico City, on honeymoon with his American wife, Susie (Janet Leigh). Vargas, to Quinlan's chagrin, takes an interest in the bombing, since the victim had crossed the border from Mexico. Meanwhile, Uncle Joe Grandi (Akim Tamiroff), Los Robles' drug lord, plots to ruin Vargas, who plans to send Grandi's brother to prison in Mexico.

Vargas is appalled by Quinlan—a three-hundred-pound pustule of hubris, arrogance, and racism. Part of the big man's duty has been to absorb the sins of the district attorney and the police chief. Quinlan does their dirty work, leaving them clean and dignified while he bloats with venality. In exchange, they follow him like a covey of quail, marveling at his intuitive powers, chuckling in amusement at every affront to proper police procedure.

All the stray plotlines, tangled double crosses, and lurid tortures of Susie Vargas by the Grandi clan are embellishments to the core story: how Vargas drives a fatal wedge into the relationship of Hank Quinlan and his partner, Pete Menzies (Joseph Calleia). The cops are like an old married couple who've been together forever. Pete's always doted on Hank, who's never forgiven himself for failing to catch his wife's killer. Hank once stopped a bullet for Pete, and he claims that it's his game leg that

ABOVE: Barney Nolan (Edmond O'Brien) squanders his pension in *Shield for Murder*. OPPOSITE: Cops Howard Duff and Steve Cochran succumb to temptation in *Private Hell 36*.

helps him divine solutions to crimes. Out of loyalty to Hank, Pete has been an accomplice to years of bogus police work, helping plant evidence and buying into Quinlan's rationalization that "I never framed anybody—unless they were guilty."

In the rogues' gallery of rotten cops, Hank Quinlan is the most pathetic. He didn't betray the badge for money or social status, as Webb Garwood or Barney Nolan did. He justifies his corruption by *not* accepting the spoils, preferring to look down his nose at the DA and police chief, as he provides the fast convictions that keep the voters happy. As he and Menzies pass through the shadows of Los Robles' pumping oil derricks, he reminds his friend how rich he *could* have been, amid that black gold, if he'd *really* been corrupt—"Instead, all I've got to show for my thirty years is that lousy turkey farm."

Touch of Evil is noir as a three-ring circus. There are high-wire acts (the dazzling

Janet Leigh and Charlton Heston confront the *Touch of Evil*.

moving camera shot that opens the film), sleight-of-hand tricks (the single-take interrogation of Manolo Sanchez), outrageous clowns (Akim Tamiroff and Dennis Weaver), scary animal acts (the Grandi boys' torture of Susie), and clever disguises (Joseph Cotten, Mercedes McCambridge, Zsa Zsa Gabor, and Marlene Dietrich all have masquerade cameos). Welles capably plays both ringleader and elephant.

Welles pulled out all the stops to prove that he was still a viable artist and commercial filmmaker. After years of self-destructive shenanigans and creative stutter-steps, this lowly "B" thriller cleared him a path back to the movie business. Here was a man whose first film, *Citizen Kane* (RKO, 1941), changed the grammar of motion picture storytelling and set the cinematic syntax for film noir: the quest for truth in morally ambiguous terrain, the cynical take on the corrupting influence of power, the off-kilter visual style. With *Touch of Evil*, the most influential director of modern times had ended up working for Albert Zugsmith, who would soon move on to such masterworks as *Sex Kittens Go to College* and *The Incredible Sex Revolution*.

After spending most of the '50s in European exile, Welles had returned to America paranoid, alcoholic, and with the IRS at his heels. He worked as an actor for survival pay. Zugsmith offered him the Quinlan role in what was a starring vehicle for Charlton Heston. In fact, Heston only agreed to make the film because he mistakenly believed Welles was directing. When the actor made that a condition of his acceptance, Welles agreed to direct while taking only his actor's salary.

Quinlan's debasement mirrors Welles's own fall from grace. Like Quinlan, Welles made a career of half-baked convictions, with wild intuition and flagrant grandstanding often passed off as determined work. Like Quinlan, he surrounded himself with toadies who worshipped his brilliance no matter how jerry-rigged. Like Quinlan, he made up outrageous lies about anyone who criticized his work methods or personal habits.

Watching *Touch of Evil* is like drinking vintage wine before it turns to vinegar. The flavor, pungency, and headiness are there, but so is a queasy aftertaste. The filmmaking is intoxicating, at times magnificent, but as the coda of Orson Welles's Hollywood career, it leaves a hangover. Welles could have been the most original talent of the century, but his ego and appetites left his legacy squandered on exhilarating but disappointing productions. He was a hell of a man, but then, what does it matter what you say about people?

"C'mon, read my future for me."
"You haven't got any."
"Whatd'ya mean?"
"Your future is all used up."
—Former flame Tanya tells Hank Quinlan
(Orson Welles) the bad news in *Touch of Evil*.

GLORIA GRAHAME
THE FALLEN QUEEN

Whenever a cop or a crook needed solace, he'd trot the Retreat, a bluesy nightspot in the red-light district where a guy could savor thirty-five-cent beer and visions of more intimate diversions. In the rear, in the red leather banquette, waiting for a single kept promise, sits the fallen queen of this demimonde, Gloria Grahame.

Born Gloria Hallward in Los Angeles in 1923, she was descended from British and Scottish royalty. Louis B. Mayer bestowed the new name upon her, perhaps hoping to cast her in the same regal realm as Greta Garbo. Gloria, however, preferred to be a more accessible empress.

In *Blondie Fever* (MGM, 1944), she was introduced with the line, "You're destined to make wise men foolish." Prophetic. Her early specialty was sultriness, tempered by a silly streak. She learned Shakespeare chapter and verse, but if they wanted her to swing her hips and bat her vampish eyes, why not?

Her first foray into Dark City came in *It's a Wonderful Life* (RKO, 1946), the only time director Frank Capra set foot inside the city limits (if only for a frightened fifteen minutes). She played Violet Bick, a sweetly sexy girl who, in Jimmy Stewart's angel dust–inspired nightmare, becomes the whore of Pottersville.

She secured her position—as actress and B-girl—with an Academy Award nomination for *Crossfire* (RKO, 1947), playing a call girl ensnared in a murder investigation. Director Edward Dmytryk described her as "a serious kind of kooky." You'd be kooky, too, if you'd trained in classical theater, had a wicked sense of humor, a ravenous intellect, and a longing to portray Lady Macbeth—but always ended up in some crib with greasy wallpaper.

Gloria's ticket to the top was the coveted role of Billy Dawn in Columbia's version of the hit Broadway comedy *Born Yesterday*. It fell through when Howard Hughes, tinkering around as the head of RKO, refused to release her from her contract. Judy Holliday won an Oscar in the role; Gloria settled for playing a slinky gambling house girl in the debacle *Macao* (RKO, 1951).

Although she had success with supporting parts in major films—*The Bad* and the Beautiful (MGM, 1952), *The Greatest Show on Earth* (Paramount, 1952) and *Oklahoma!* (Fox, 1955)—breakthrough roles eluded her. Dark City became her permanent address: *A Woman's Secret* (RKO, 1949), *In a Lonely Place* (Columbia, 1950), *Sudden Fear* (RKO, 1952), *The Big Heat* (Columbia, 1953), *The Glass Wall* (UA, 1953), *Human Desire* (Columbia, 1954), *Naked Alibi* (Universal, 1954), *Odds Against Tomorrow* (UA, 1959)—a gallery of screw-loose but seductive women, aching to break out of the margins of a man's world, but always tripped up by their own compulsions and insecurities.

In her personal life, Grahame was married and divorced four times, with a list of lovers longer than her film credits. Producer George Englund, an early suitor of Gloria's, explained her promiscuity: "Have you ever seen a litter of kittens feeding at their bowls? There's always one who lifts her head and looks around at the other bowls in curiosity, nudging her head into them to see different things they might have to offer. That was Gloria."

Her life began to take on the noir overtones of her films. Her first starring role, opposite Humphrey Bogart in *In a Lonely Place*, should have made her a star. But in Hollywood, the performance was secondary to the strangeness surrounding its creation. Her marriage to the film's director, Nicholas Ray, was disintegrating and to preclude production problems, Grahame had to sign a contract stipulating that she would accede to all of Ray's demands. The finished film, a bitter meditation on doomed relationships, was a veiled portrait of their hopeless union.

The marriage crashed in 1951, when Gloria's feline curiosity resulted in a sexual liaison with Anthony Ray, her husband's thirteen-year-old son by a previous marriage. Fallout from the incident gave her a reputation for being professionally engaged but personally unhinged. (In his early twenties, Anthony Ray became Gloria's fourth and last husband.)

As producers continued to trade on her sex appeal, Gloria became increasingly insecure about her looks. She had several plastic surgeries on her upper lip, trying to enhance the lush pout she thought essential to her allure. She lifted weights in hopes of enlarging her breasts, which, unlike her mouth, she refused to have surgically altered.

Despite her best efforts, time took its toll. The boys prowling the Retreat began passing her by for younger game. She staved off the inevitable onstage, but by the 1970s she was discounting the remnants of her sexiness in tawdry horror films.

During her last years, she battled cancer in a holistic, narcissistic way, refusing any treatment that would alter her physical appearance. In 1981, terminally ill, she suffered septic shock after a procedure intended to relieve her pain backfired. She survived a grueling flight from Liverpool back home to New York, where she died in a hospital at age fifty-six.

It was a sad ending, but not a tragic life. In the Dark City district she inhabited, Gloria Grahame left a unique legacy, which included being the subject of noir's most heartbreaking lines (from *In a Lonely Place*):

I was born when you kissed me
I died when you left me
I lived a few weeks while you loved me

As a nightclub singer hiding out in a border town, Grahame tempts another renegade cop (Sterling Hayden) in *Naked Alibi* (Universal, 1954).

HATE STREET

Hot wind shakes the sycamores. Leaves dance on the dry lawn. Dad sits at the wheel of the Hudson, staring at their dream house. Room 619 of the Embassy, that's his dream house now. He can feel her heat on his fingertips. His lips still ache. How can he go back? Mortgage, insurance, scrimping for some new thing, always more *things*. The ball 'n' chain is waiting inside with her list. He checks his eyes in the rearview: She'll never know. Mom sees him through the kitchen curtains, coming up the walk. She thumbs the edge of the kitchen knife: It's good and sharp.

In Dark City, crime isn't solely the province of professionals. Between the picket fences and the manicured hedges of the city's residential enclaves, death is sown daily. Little white lies sprout into deceit, grow into dreadful secrets, and bloom into fateful gunblasts and knife slashes. In this part of town, it's passion, not profit, that's at stake.

When dark deeds were done by amateurs, usually the case on Hate Street, the tales were known in the trade as "murder dramas," distinct from the "crime thrillers" that were the province of crooks and cops. Murder dramas weren't as male-dominated. In fact, many were what exhibitors called "women's pictures." But the distinction was as much one of geography as gender. Crime thrillers took place in the streets and offices where men fought to conquer the city. Murder dramas unfolded in bedrooms and gardens and kitchens, and women wielded their own weapons.

During the hardscrabble 1930s (post–Production Code), Hollywood sold American women an ideal of domestic complacency and economic security. Hang

tough, girls—the perfect man, the right neighborhood, and two darling kids were the answers to any soul-searching that tossed you in your sleep. Men had cops and crooks and cowboys to distract and inspire them. For women, films of the 1930s were Sears catalogs of middle-class gratification.

Noir tore the catalog apart. It suggested that domesticity was a suffocating trap. Somewhere amid the laundry and shopping and bill paying, life's passion had been snuffed out. Noir is about what happens when the fuse is reignited: when a devoted husband takes a new woman in his arms, or a bored wife admits that the life she's cherished will never satisfy her.

If you can blame one man for screwing up Hollywood's master plan for matrimonial harmony, it's James M. Cain. In his tales, the sacred conjugal bed is soaked with the sweat of illicit sex. Before long, the gleaming kitchen tiles are spattered with blood. In Cain's stories, death and sex are inseparable.

The foundation for Dark City was laid in 1934, when Alfred Knopf published Cain's first novel, *The Postman Always Rings Twice*. A fierce tale of adultery and murder, it scored a critical and popular success. Its bluntness and desperation tapped into Depression-era consciousness with prose so spare and vivid it demanded

Gloria Grahame and Glenn Ford in *Human Desire*

critical appraisal. Its popularity was based on two things: sex rawer than was typical in mainstream novels, and a style so terse it compressed a complex plot into a very slim volume. Mom and Dad could read it fast and hide it easily in a purse or a bureau drawer.

RKO and Columbia saw sparks jump from the manuscript when it was still in galley form. But the newly rejuvenated Production Code Administration—Hollywood's censorship entity—provided a cold shower. Boss censor Joseph Breen vowed that *Postman* would never reach the screen. Undaunted, MGM bought the rights. Nothing came of it. No screenwriter could tame Cain, so tightly was the depravity woven into his plots.

Cain followed with a story in *Liberty* magazine called *Double Indemnity*. Five studios panted after it, driving up the price to $25,000—even though the PCA declared such amorality off-limits. Meanwhile, Cain kept hammering away. In '37 he published *Serenade*, an even more unfilmable concoction of rough sex, homosexuality, murder, and opera.

It wasn't until 1943 that Billy Wilder, working at Paramount, was able to raise Cain on to American movie screens. (Two versions had already been made in Europe: *Le Dernier Tournant* [France, 1939] and *Ossessione* [Italy, 1942], directed by Pierre Chenal and Luchino Visconti, respectively). After Wilder's writing partner, Charles Brackett, begged off touching such tawdry material, Wilder adapted *Double Indemnity* with popular detective-story novelist Raymond Chandler. They dealt the censors a miraculous hand of three-card monte, earning approval for the script by cutting Cain's more debased notions, substituting wicked innuendo for smash-mouth sex, and stressing the moral that even the "perfect crime" would not go unpunished.

Double Indemnity marked the first time a Hollywood film explicitly explored the means, motives, and opportunity

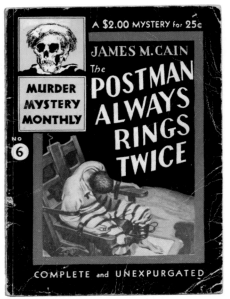

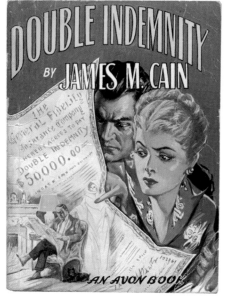

of committing murder. Like every story from Hate Street, it's about people risking their lives on one big chance, in hopes of transcending their mundane existence.

Insurance salesman Walter Neff (Fred MacMurray) takes his risk with Phyllis Dietrichson (Barbara Stanwyck), a client's dangerously sexy wife. They plot to murder her husband and trick the insurance company into paying double on the "accidental death" clause in his policy. Neff dives into Phyllis's black pool, intoxicated by her glossy lips, tight sweaters, and flesh-pinching anklet.

But Neff isn't merely being led around by his libido. Beneath the cavalier manner and playboy patter lurks a terrorist, eager to blow up society's rigid structures. He longs to refute the constipated worldview of his mentor, claims investigator Barton Keyes (Edward G. Robinson), who believes that human behavior is reducible to statistical demographics and empirical probabilities. So Neff commits murder—just to throw a wrench into the gambling wheel over which Keyes proudly stands watch.

The critical and commercial success of *Double Indemnity* was due to Wilder's wizardry in coordinating brilliant collaborators. Chandler goosed Cain's clipped dialogue into whipcrack sass traded by the stars: *There's a speed limit in this state, Mr. Neff—forty-five miles an hour / How fast was I going, officer? / I'd say around ninety / Suppose you get down off your motorcycle and give me a ticket? / Suppose I let you off with a warning this time / Suppose it doesn't take / Suppose I have to whack you over the knuckles / Suppose I bust out crying and put my head on your shoulder / Suppose you try putting it on my husband's shoulder / That tears it.*

MacMurray and Stanwyck handled the hard-boiled banter and provocative glances with panache, making murder wickedly entertaining. The PCA may have accepted that *Double Indemnity* was ultimately about the punishment of

The infernal and eternal triangle: Insurance salesman Walter Neff (Fred MacMurray) has an affair with Phyllis Dietrichson (Barbara Stanwyck) under the nose of her husband (Tom Powers) in James M. Cain's seminal tale, *Double Indemnity*.

immoral people, but Wilder knew its appeal was in the vicarious excitement of participating in a murder, then stepping out of the killers' shoes and watching the nooses tighten around their necks.

"That gloomy, horrible house the Dietrichsons lived in, the slit of sunlight slicing through those heavy drapes—you could smell that death was in the air, you could understand why she wanted to get out of there, away, no matter how," Barbara Stanwyck later reflected. "And for an actress, let me tell you—the way those sets were lit, the house, Walter's apartment, those dark shadows, those slices of harsh light at strange angles—all that helped my performance. The way Billy staged it and John Seitz lit it, it was all one sensational mood."

Stanwyck, Wilder, and company had turned Cain's slender novel into the primer for dozens of future noirs, influencing writers and directors for decades to come. *Double Indemnity*'s success rejuvenated sales of Cain's earlier books and solidified his (erroneous) reputation as a novelist of the hard-boiled school. His success as an author was a twist worthy of one of his credulity-stretching plots.

JAMES M. CAIN WAS REARED in the affluent upper-middle-class environs of Maryland. His parents were Irish Catholics, and, despite his lapsing at age thirteen, vestiges of sin, guilt, and retribution remained. Those formed the backbone of his books. Opera, not literature, was Cain's love. His mother, a coloratura whom he worshipped, dissuaded him from a singing career. She had, in the tenor of the times, quit her own career to marry a businessman. Cain had little regard for his father, perhaps explaining why he'd write so many stories about ambitious women who murder their way out of unfulfilling marriages.

During the teens and '20s, Cain struggled at work and marriage. His wife, Mary Clough, was too highbrow for his taste and he cheated on her regularly. He claimed that God's voice directed him to be a writer, although, by his own admission, he had little aptitude for it. He caught on as a newspaperman, which is how he described himself for the rest of his life. In 1924, his writing career kicked in with acceptance of an article for *The American Mercury*, H. L. Mencken's witty journal of American letters.

Cain divorced his wife, moved to New York, and hobnobbed with luminaries like Mencken and Walter Lippmann, kings of elite journalism. He had an affair with Elina Tyszecka, a Finn whom he called "the great love of my life." Once they married, in 1927, the flame died: "It was gone, that old black magic we had." Rediscovering passion would be a core motivation for Cain's characters.

When Cain moved to Hollywood with Elina, he made boatloads of money as a script doctor, without being able to float a salable script of his own. In fact, Cain hated movies. But the discipline of screenwriting, and the sultriness of Southern California, had a profound impact on him.

Bar-B-Q, the manuscript that would become *Postman*, was lashed out in a blast of May-September desperation before Cain returned East, as if he were spewing out demons in a to-hell-with-it kiss-off of his literary ambitions. Sparking his imagination were impure thoughts about a "bosomy-looking thing" who pumped his gas at the local filling station: "Commonplace, but sexy, the kind you have ideas about." Cain gave those ideas free rein, shoehorning in details from the case of Ruth Snyder, who had murdered her husband in 1927 and tried to poison her lover/accomplice.

Almost unwittingly, Cain had become surveyor and architect of Hate Street. The terrain is morally unstable and there is no outlet. When its residents grab their darkest wish, choosing ecstasy over civility, their lives literally climax. Guilt and suspicion slam the lovers head-on into the big black cul-de-sac. You can only hope the sex was worth it.

Cain became so identified with sexually charged murder dramas that he believed Hate Street was his exclusive domain. Monogram's 1945 release *Apology for Murder* was such a blatant Cain knockoff industry wags called it *Single Indemnity*. Despite disdain for any kind of political activism, Cain campaigned within the Screen Writers Guild to create the American Authors Authority, a union that would own its members' work, negotiate better subsidiary deals, and guard against copyright infringement. It didn't float, and Cain returned to Maryland, bitterly, continuing to produce novels that tried, with various degrees of success, to replicate the thrill, and popularity, of *The Postman Always Rings Twice* and *Double Indemnity*.

While *Double Indemnity* deserves full credit for jump-starting the noir movement, another tale from Hate Street might have that distinction if not for real-life plot twists. *Conflict*, directed by German émigré Curtis Bernhardt, from a story by

ABOVE: John Garfield and Lana Turner start a fire in *The Postman Always Rings Twice*. **BELOW:** Dr. Karen Morley's unrequited love for colleague John Loder leads to murder in the obscure and eccentric 1945 release *Jealousy*. **RIGHT:** Humphrey Bogart returns to the scene of the crime in *Conflict*.

Robert Siodmak, was made at Warners in 1943, but not released until June 1945. Critics called it a knockoff of *Double Indemnity* when, in fact, it had beaten Billy Wilder to the punch.

The delay was caused by a lawsuit brought against Warners by two writers, claiming the script plagiarized their story. Litigation dragged on for two years before a settlement allowed the film to be released.

Its star, Humphrey Bogart, wished it never had been. Even after he'd captured the public's imagination as a romantic antihero in hits like *High Sierra* (1940), *The Maltese Falcon* (1941), and *Casablanca* (1942), studio boss Jack Warner couldn't believe this second banana was now the studio's top draw. To test the public's fascination with Bogart, Warners followed *Casablanca* with *Conflict*—in which his character is far removed from the savoir faire of Rick Blaine.

Richard Mason (Bogart) is an unhappily married engineer so fixated on his young sister-in-law (Alexis Smith) he arranges an "accident" to kill his wife—after he's faked an injury that gives him a wheelchair-bound alibi. The accident, on a mountain road, is lifted from *The Postman Always Rings Twice*, which was yet to be filmed. A load of cut timber tumbles down the mountain and covers the crashed car—so Kathryn Mason (Rose Hobart) is *feared* dead; the wreck, let alone her corpse, is never found. But Richard is haunted by hints that Kathryn is alive—shades of yet-to-come *Diabolique* (Filmsonor, 1955)—and he is driven, madly, to confirm his wife's demise by returning to the scene of crime, which, as we know, is *never* a good idea.

It was a role Bogart didn't want to play, as the on-screen marriage was uncomfortably close to his own hellish union with actress Mayo Methot. They were known around town as the "Battling Bogarts," due to ugly arguments fueled by boatloads of booze. Jack Warner forcing Bogart to play a man who murders his wife seemed like a cruel joke at the actor's expense.

Robert Siodmak concocted the story with the help of fellow German émigré Alfred Neumann. Siodmak and Curt Bernhardt were friends and colleagues from Berlin, where they'd learned moviemaking in the 1920s before escaping from the Nazis. Bernhardt had a reputation as one of Germany's finest directors, held in higher regard than Siodmak, who only established himself after several years in Hollywood's B units. Then the tables turned—Siodmak became an A-list director, rivaling Hitchcock as the "master of suspense," while Bernhardt never had

the cachet, or scripts, that came to his fellow countrymen, like Fritz Lang, Otto Preminger, or Fred Zinnemann. It wasn't for lack of talent, as Bernhardt showed with his direction of *High Wall* (MGM, 1947) and *Possessed* (WB, 1948). If not for a twist of fate, it could have been Curtis Bernhardt, not Billy Wilder, who was the German émigré credited with igniting the film noir movement.

Another 1945 noir, *Jealousy* (Republic), was one of the odder offerings to emerge from Hate Street. What could have been a dryly cut tale of marital murder is spun every which way by writers Dalton Trumbo and German émigré Arnold Lipp, and Czech director Gustav Machaty. It's a brooding B about a frisky female cabbie, Janet Urban (Jane Randolph), mired in a marriage to alcoholic writer Peter Urban (Nils Asther), a cantankerous Czech émigré. Janet drives an affluent doctor (John Loder) home one day and her knowledge of Brahms wins his heart. A chaste romance ensues, which doesn't sit well with Peter or the doc's longtime colleague, Monica (Karen Morley). When Peter is found dead from a point-blank gunshot, Janet is the prime suspect. So far, so noir.

The film's raison d'être, however, is its depiction of European intellectuals displaced to a strange new land. As Peter, Nils Asther, a gay Swede whose best days were behind him (back when he played the title role in Capra's *The Bitter Tea of General Yen* [Columbia, 1932]), curses the plight of European artists adrift in America after fleeing the Nazis, treated like peons by intellectually inferior Americans. His lone friend is another Czech refugee, played by actual Czech refugee Hugo Haas.

Gustav Machaty had soared to notoriety when he directed *Ecstasy* (Slavia Film, 1933), a provocative film about female sexuality in which future star Hedy Lamarr (yet another Euro-émigré) caused a global sensation by appearing nude. Her exposed derriere was Machaty's ticket to Hollywood. Once there, he toiled unhappily at MGM, where his experimental approach to cinema was squelched; mostly he directed pickups and retakes, sweeping up after other directors. *Jealousy*'s most striking moments display Machaty's distinctively weird style: jagged montages full of Dutch angles and handheld camera moves, abrupt fade-outs, slow-motion close-ups, prowling POV shots, elliptical passages of shadowy dread. The passagework—dialogue-heavy scenes advancing the plot—revealed Machaty's discomfort with the English language and basic narrative storytelling. He was more poet than storyteller.

If *Jealousy* was the bottom of the Hollywood barrel circa 1945, *Mildred Pierce* was the dark crème on top. This Warner Bros. concoction, based on the James M. Cain novel, unveiled one of the legendary dames of Dark City.

People came from miles around to strap on the feedbag at Mildred's bustling diner, where she served heaping portions of all-American chow. Some guys—if they looked useful—got the special dessert, after hours. Mildred Pierce (Joan Crawford) was a lower-class woman obsessed with conquering the material world. Like the gangsters of Sinister Heights, she wanted to ensure that her offspring—especially her spoiled daughter Veda—would be welcomed in the swankiest salons.

In her rise from hash slinger to businesswoman, Mildred left a succession of husbands and lovers emasculated. Her true love was Veda, for whom she'd make any sacrifice. In the novel, Veda showed her gratitude by stealing Mildred's husband, following her bliss to an opera career, and leaving her mother with the solitary crush. On-screen, Veda didn't run away with lecherous Monte Beregon (Zachary Scott)—she killed him (for spurning her matrimonial desires). Mildred, the matriarchal martyr, took the rap for her precious daughter.

Cain loved Crawford's version of Mildred, inscribing a leather-bound copy of the book "To Joan Crawford, who brought Mildred to life as I always hoped she would be and who has my lifelong gratitude." Crawford deserves the credit, and how. But her Oscar-winning portrayal of this woman—mother, moneymaker, homemaker, lover—tapped only a few drops from the dark vein that ran through Crawford herself.

JOAN CRAWFORD
ACTRESS AS AUTEUR

Joan Crawford was a classic rags-to-riches story. Born dirt-poor in San Antonio as Lucille Fay LeSueur, she was abandoned by her father in childhood. She changed her name to Billy Cassin after moving to Kansas City with her remarried mother. After toiling as a phone operator, launderer, and waitress, she won a Charleston contest and danced her way to New York stages, then to Hollywood, parlaying her big eyes and shapely legs into a series of "flapper" roles in silent pictures.

Like Mildred, she was ruthless in her quest for the brass ring. She trained diligently to improve her body, mind, acting, and savoir faire. A publicity campaign staged by Louis B. Mayer changed her name to Joan Crawford, signifying MGM's commitment. Columnist Louella Parsons said, "She is the only star I know who manufactured herself . . . She drew up a blueprint for herself and outlined a beautiful package of skin, bones and character and then set out to put life into the outline. She succeeded, and so Joan Crawford came into existence at the same time an overweight Charleston dancer, born Lucille LeSueur, disappeared from the world."

If this sounds like the plot of a film noir—it gets thicker. Crawford's ascension from chippie to princess culminated in marriage to Douglas Fairbanks Jr., scion of the famous acting family. Joan's mother-in-law, Mary Pickford, was the biggest star of the silent era. (Joan never spoke of her marriage to New York sax player James Welton, whom she left when Hollywood called.) Soon Crawford was coronated herself, able to pick plum roles and leave that cheap party girl Lucille behind forever. Joan's wide-shouldered costumes, tailored by Gilbert Adrian, started fashion trends; she demanded approval of her close-ups; she refused to work during her period, claiming she didn't photograph as well. She controlled her career and stood up to the biggest shots with a tough-talking demeanor Mildred Pierce would have envied.

Such ball-breaking bluntness proved a rough go for her husbands. She required them to walk two steps behind her in public, and in private often made them submit to her on their knees. Once she gained entrée to the Dream Factory firmament, she dropped Fairbanks. She had affairs with many of her leading men, most famously Clark Gable, but she picked stage actor Franchot Tone as husband #3. One day she caught him in his dressing room, "rehearsing" with a young extra. She demanded to know how long he'd been cheating. "Every day," he replied. "I have to prove to myself that I am still a man, before I go home to you."

Husband #4, Phil Terry, was functional. "I knew what kind of marriage it was going to be when she walked on the set," recalled John Wayne. "First came Joan, then her secretary, then her makeup man, then her wardrobe woman, then finally Phil Terry, carrying the dog."

Crawford with Steve Cochran in *The Damned Don't Cry*

Crawford had had an abortion in the late 1920s, so as not to derail her accelerating career. Once she wanted children, things got difficult: seven miscarriages while married to Tone. By 1939 she had abandoned hope of conceiving. One attempt at adoption was pure noir: She secretly ordered a newborn from a Tennessee baby mill, but when the child's mother learned who had adopted her, she showed up at Crawford's door angling for more money. Instead, Joan just gave the baby back.

She adopted a baby girl who endured infancy as Joan Crawford Jr., before Mother gave her a break and renamed her Christina. Last break the kid got. The maternal Crawford careered out of Dark City into horror film terrain. According to the grown-up Christina, exacting revenge in the poison memoir *Mommy Dearest*, Crawford would routinely beat her and her

three adopted siblings, lock them in closets, publicly humiliate them, lash them to their beds all night—a form of psychotic motherly domination to challenge the world's finest headshrinkers.

When *Mildred Pierce* came along, Crawford was on the skids. MGM dumped her, convinced that her brassy style was tarnished by encroaching middle age (she was in her early forties). Moving to Warner Bros., she entered a professional partnership with producer Jerry Wald, who, after the departure of Hal Wallis, became the most ambitious producer on the Burbank lot. Wald sensed the coming darkness in Hollywood. He helped Crawford mold a new image, forsaking the glamour for a tougher, more self-revelatory persona. Despite the airs she affected, Crawford had a gutter mouth and always toted a short dog of booze in her velvet clutch. Noir was the perfect fit; it let a little Lucille LeSueur resurface.

"From *Mildred Pierce* onward, a show of innocence was impossible," wrote her biographer, Bob Thomas. "Her portrayals could no longer be complementary to men, they were competitive with men. She sought to destroy them, not to entice them."

In *Possessed* (WB, 1947), she destroys Van Heflin, even though he's the love of her life. The film opens with Crawford wandering, catatonic, through Los Angeles at dawn, asking strangers if they've seen "David." Taken to a hospital, she is induced—through "narcosynthesis"—to relate her story (in tried-and-true flashback fashion): Joan is, yet again, a poor working woman, nurse Louise Howell, who falls in love with engineer David Sutton (Heflin). She cares for rich industrialist Dean Graham's bedridden wife, Pauline. She introduces David to her employer (Raymond Massey), who gives him a job—in

Possessed

Canada. Louise is crushed. Pauline imagines that her husband and Louise are having an affair; she commits suicide. Now Graham does make a play for Louise. Having lost true love, she opts for security. But David shows up at their wedding reception, this time more interested in Louise's stepdaughter, Carol (Geraldine Brooks).

Confused and jealous, Louise has a mental breakdown. Thus impaired, she murders David.

Possessed is a classic "woman's picture," tinted noir by the application of murder, madness, and the brooding Expressionistic direction of Curtis Bernhardt. For the first time Joan's huge eyes displayed more craziness than sexiness. She was nominated for another Oscar. Joan had reclaimed the brass

ring and would from this point on be the de facto producer of her films. The oddly masculine animus beneath those fine cheekbones came pouring out. Exerting control over her projects and all the people around her, Joan Crawford plowed through Hollywood's double-standards and became a genuine auteur.

The Damned Don't Cry (WB, 1950) came closest to Joan's own noir vérité soul. She plays Ethel Whitehead, White trash sharing an oil field shack with a bitter husband. After the death of her young son, she takes off for a new life in New York as a dress model. She quickly learns there's faster cash in private fittings with the buyers. She lures a naïve accountant, Martin Blackford (Kent Smith), into doing her bidding, even arranging for him to handle the books of a syndicate boss, George Castleman (David Brian).

Once Castleman realizes Ethel's eggs are as brassy as his own balls, he takes a cue from Louis B. Mayer, transforming her into "Lorna Hansen Forbes," his high-society mistress. Martin is left high and dry. Castleman sends Lorna to Nevada to spy on Nick Prenta (Steve Cochran), a regional crime boss who's getting mutinous. She falls for Prenta, and all kinds of double-dealing and gunplay erupt amid the ranch houses and saguaro cactus. Lorna lams to Ethel's old oil field shack, still swaddled in her cherished mink. Castleman hunts her down, looking to terminate their contract.

The film was entertaining, but not a huge hit. The public may have been catching on to the Wald-Crawford formula. Once again, the climactic murder opened the proceedings, and the story spilled out in the "where did I go wrong" confession of a cast-iron gold digger.

In the early 1950s Joan's star dimmed as she and Warner Bros. butted heads over how to maintain the forty-six-year-old actress's luster. Arch melodramas (*Harriet Craig* [1950], *Goodbye, My Fancy* [1951], and *This Woman Is Dangerous* [1952]) were not the answer. But in 1952, once free of Warners, noir rescued Crawford again. In *Sudden Fear* (RKO, 1952) she played Myra Hudson, a successful playwright romanced by Lester Blaine (Jack Palance), an actor she'd rejected for her latest play. He may be flaccid on the boards, but in the sack he's just the ticket. They marry. This being Dark City, Lester's really interested in Myra's estate. He's got a greedy little gal (Gloria Grahame) on the side and together they script an "accidental" curtain for the wealthy playwright. The lovers concoct the plot, however, in Myra's study, where a built-in dictaphone records their scheme. Myra cunningly counterplots their demise. *Sudden Fear* was a big hit, and Crawford earned a third noir-stained Oscar nomination.

It was Joan's last hurrah in Dark City. She clung tenaciously to her imperiousness, but producers looked elsewhere for box-office allure. When the big contracts dried up, she married husband #5, Alfred Steele, an executive with Pepsi-Cola. Joan became a director and ambassador for the soft-drink company, and she and Al lived the high life on Pepsi's tab. When he died suddenly of a heart attack in 1959, it was a one-two punch for Joan: After debts and taxes were tallied, Steele had died flat broke.

Joan went back to work, but now as she moved through middle age, the parts offered parodied her image. She and Bette Davis picked themselves to pieces in Robert Aldrich's horrific black comedy *Whatever Happened to Baby Jane?* By the 1960s, Crawford was a monstrous joke, bulging her famous eyes in horror shows such as *Straight-Jacket* (Columbia, 1964), *I Saw What You Did* (Universal, 1965) and *Berserk* (Columbia, 1967). She was treading vodka by the time she did her last picture, *Trog* (WB) in 1970.

After that, her public appearances were boozy, bleary, and embarrassing. Pepsi distanced itself from its most famous stockholder. A serious fall almost killed her, and scared her into drying out. Unfortunately, her withdrawal induced paranoia. She spent her last years a virtual prisoner in her apartment, afraid to venture out for fear she'd be murdered. By May 1977, she'd withered to a shell of her once vital self, bedridden, attended by two nurses. But she had one great Joan Crawford moment left. When she overheard one of the nurses praying for her soul in her final moments, she raised her head and seethed: "Damn it—don't you *dare* ask God to help me!"

The perfect Dark City exit line.

Crawford exacts her vengeance in *Sudden Fear*.

If not for Ann Sheridan's mile-wide independent streak, movie history—and Joan Crawford's career—might have been different. The Texas-born beauty queen, christened by Warner Bros. "The Oomph Girl" (to her chagrin), was also the studio's "Suspension Queen" for refusing roles she felt didn't suit her . . . like *Mildred Pierce*.

How could Sheridan have passed on a role that fit her like her glove? After a rocky start in the '30s, she found a niche at Warner Bros. as a smart-mouthed dame sashaying through a rugged man's world. In *Castle on the Hudson*, *They Drive by Night*, *City for Conquest*, and *Torrid Zone* (all 1940), she was foil to the studio's most popular male stars: Jimmy Cagney, Humphrey Bogart, John Garfield, George Raft, Pat O'Brien. Her screen persona was Sheridan being herself: worldly wise and self-sufficient.

"They always thought of me as 'The Oomph Girl,' never as an actress," she complained. "I could never convince them that I could act." But when she passed on *Mildred Pierce*, Jack Warner put her on long-term suspension; Sheridan called it a "strike"—for better scripts, more money, and a guaranteed multipicture deal. The stalemate kept her off-screen for eighteen months during the prime of her career. But in 1947 Jack Warner granted her wish: a pay raise, a six-picture deal, and script approval. Her first two projects were tailor-made by director (and lover) Vincent Sherman: *Nora Prentiss* (1947) and *The Unfaithful* (1948) were forays into the rising noir tide. The studio sold them on her sex appeal, but she's not a femme fatale in either. She plays complex women, not manipulative villainesses.

Nora Prentiss is especially bleak, a darker version of Warners' 1946 hit *The Man I Love*. It could have been called *The Man Who Shouldn't Love Me*. Kent Smith portrays milquetoast San Francisco MD Richard Talbot, who meets gorgeous cabaret singer Nora when he patches her up after a traffic accident. Telling her he's writing a paper on "ailments of the heart," she cracks, "A paper? I could write a book."

The doc falls hard. To escape his loveless marriage, Talbot slips his wedding ring on a "John Doe" and dumps the corpse off a cliff in his car. Presto: a new life with Nora in New York. Except Talbot can't show his face anywhere. Saintly

---

TOP: Ann Sheridan in *Nora Prentiss* **BOTTOM:** Sheridan can't shake wily reporter Dennis O'Keefe in *Woman on the Run.*

Nora tries to make it work—but jealousy consumes the doc when she goes back to singing in clubs. He almost kills her boss and beats Nora senseless. Ashamed, he flees—crashing his car and getting horribly burned. Now unrecognizable, he's arrested for murder—of *himself*, back in San Francisco! The spectacular improbability goes down easier thanks to the gloomy but glamorous cinematography of James Wong Howe and Sherman's sensitive direction.

Nora Prentiss was a hit, vindicating Sheridan's campaign for better roles. Writer David Goodis, hot off the success of *Dark Passage*, reworked W. Somerset Maugham's *The Letter* (WB, 1940) into *The Unfaithful*, a California-based murder mystery about wartime infidelity. Ironically, both films were marketed with virtually the same ad campaign used to successfully sell *Mildred Pierce*.

After three films under the new contract, Sheridan feared the six-picture deal was a trap. She bought her way out. Fidelity Pictures' Howard Welsch, casting his low-budget thriller *Woman on the Run*, felt Sheridan's specialties—weary wisecracks and snide side-eyes—were perfect for the lead role. He sweetened the offer by making her the de facto coproducer, with say-so on cast and crew.

Woman on the Run is modest, but unique: a love story told in reverse. The romance once shared by Frank and Eleanor Johnson has crashed and burned. Walking his dog one night, Frank (Ross Elliott) witnesses a killing. Interviewed at the scene by inspector Martin Ferris (Robert Keith), Frank learns the victim was to testify against a local mobster. Fearing for his life, Frank takes a powder. But he needs medicine for a heart condition; without it, he'll die. The cops turn to Frank's wife for help. Surprise: Flinty Eleanor *wants* her husband to croak. A wily newspaper reporter, Danny Leggett (Dennis O'Keefe, charming *and* obnoxious), offers Eleanor $5,000 to lead him to Frank, giving his paper a scoop. The cops, of course, are hot on their heels.

The manhunt takes a back seat as subtext surfaces: Hunting her husband, Eleanor learns how their love went sour—and falls in love with Frank all over again. The suspense is ratcheted up when Leggett, coming on to Eleanor the whole time, is revealed as the killer. When she reunites with Frank, Leggett intends to kill him.

It's a pungent depiction of spoiled marriage, and a clever use of detective-story structure to rekindle the ruined romance. Cowriter Alan Campbell drew on his tumultuous thirteen-year union to legendary author Dorothy Parker. The pair had married in 1934 and soon after moved from New York to Hollywood, trading the Algonquin Round Table for nightclubs on the Sunset Strip. Campbell, fourteen years younger than his rapier-witted wife, struggled to escape the perception that he was the untalented half of the team, and here his bitter wit crackles.

Director Norman Foster was a protégé of Orson Welles, who'd recruited him in 1941 to direct a segment of his proposed Latin American anthology film *It's All True*. Welles was impressed by the Charlie Chan and Mr. Moto B movies Foster made at Fox in the late 1930s, where he showed flair for mise en scène on a shoestring—something Welles greatly admired. Foster's kinship with Welles is evident, especially in a dazzling finale on a rickety roller coaster.

How did *Woman on the Run*, superior to some more heralded noirs of its era, end up in obscurity? It was produced by an upstart outfit, with none of the long-term protection afforded studio-financed films. It became an orphan once Fidelity's distribution deal with Universal ended. It was made by a director with no critical cachet; if Raoul Walsh or Joseph H. Lewis or Don Siegel had made it, it would've long ago been rediscovered and heralded as a minor masterpiece.

ONE BALMY EVENING IN THE MID-'30S you'd have sworn Hate Street was Bristol Avenue, a tony boulevard in the exclusive LA enclave of Brentwood. That night Joan Crawford's neighbor, Barbara Stanwyck, scrambled over the wall separating their palatial homes, fleeing the punches of her drunk husband, Frank Fay. Crawford knew where Stanwyck was coming from. She used a thick base to hide bruises doled out by her own tanked-up spouse, Franchot Tone.

Lousy husbands weren't all the two stars had in common. Both had been chorines in New York. Both survived bleak, impoverished childhoods. Both ranked career over marriage and played second fiddle to no man. Neither could bear children. Both chose to adopt; both were atrocious mothers. Between them, they left an indelible impression—a new cinematic image of iron-willed, independent women.

If any actress came to epitomize noir, it was Barbara Stanwyck. Her memorable turn as the scheming temptress in *Double Indemnity* was only her initial contribution to "murder dramas." Stanwyck reeled out an array of ferocious females, both "good" and "evil," slugging their way through the riskiest parts of Dark City. Real life had offered her plenty of experience to draw from.

Born Ruby Stevens in Brooklyn, 1907, the youngest of five kids, she was three years old when her mother, stepping off a streetcar, was killed by a drunk. Her devastated dad abandoned the children and fled to Panama, finding work as a ditchdigger. When Ruby ran away from foster homes, her siblings always found her on the stoop of their old house, waiting for Mom.

By fourteen, Ruby was on her own, working menial jobs and forgoing formal education. She had no illusions about the world or her place in it. She was wounded and angry and talented and disciplined. The perfect soldier. (A pity she and Sam Fuller only made one picture together, the loaded-for-bear western *Forty Guns* [Fox, 1957].)

By sixteen, Ruby had a home in the Deuce, hoofing in the chorus of the Strand Roof nightclub, the first of her many shake-and-shimmy joints. Working the roaring all-night shift, she no doubt rubbed shoulders with fellow jazz baby Lucille LeSueur in one glittery speakeasy or another. She became tight with Oscar Levant, piano-playing Pied Piper of Manhattan's smart set. She was pals with gangster Owney Madden.

Broadway impresario Willard Mack gave Ruby, at nineteen, her boost to the legit stage, a showcase role in his production of *The Noose*, starring Rex Cherryman. He also changed her name to Barbara Stanwyck. "Ruby Stevens sounds too much like a stripper," he said.

Wise to the ramble but unschooled in affairs of the heart, Stanwyck fell in love with the rakish Cherryman. Simultaneously, their careers got legs: Stage work and film offers poured in. They talked of marriage once things settled down. Suffering from exhaustion, Cherryman was advised by doctors to book a restorative voyage to Europe. Barbara bid him adieu on the New York wharf, pledging her love. Cherryman didn't need a round-trip ticket. He died aboard ship, from septic poisoning.

The lonely orphan learned her lesson. From then on, she would be invulnerable.

Levant introduced her to vaudeville star Frank Fay, New York's King of Comedy. His Irish bluster and roguish arrogance busted the Big Apple open for her.

Barbara Stanwyck in court in 1935, for divorce proceedings against husband Frank Fay.

Stanwyck said Fay was the father she never had. One month after Cherryman's ill-fated cruise, Stanwyck and Fay married. Louis B. Mayer, in town to find performers he could exploit in those newfangled talkies, saw and *heard* Stanwyck in the stage show *Burlesque* and offered a screen test.

Fay and Stanwyck progressed in opposite directions. In Hollywood, she zoomed to prominence, while Fay's pugnacious tomfoolery fizzled. Their rocky relationship is the basis of the regularly remade *A Star is Born*.

Stanwyck was always different. She projected a steely self-reliance that had as much to do with her ingrained identity as with acting ability. With no formal training, she became the most reliable, protean actress in the business. She appeared in challenging films by Frank Capra and William Wellman, waded to an Oscar nomination in the tear-drenched *Stella Dallas* (UA, 1937), and was a smashing comedienne in two classics, *Ball of Fire* (RKO, 1941), as slang-spewing Sugarpuss O'Shea, and the Preston Sturges romance *The Lady Eve* (Paramount, 1941).

Stanwyck feared her initial descent into Dark City, *Double Indemnity*, would coldcock her career, pushing her toughness to the extreme—remorseless murder. To her surprise, audiences relished her cruelty. Mrs. Dietrichson became legend. In 1944, the Internal Revenue Service revealed that the former dime-a-dance dame was the highest-paid woman in the United States, outworking and outearning her nearest rival, Bette Davis.

Postwar, Stanwyck parked permanently on Hate Street, starting with *The Strange Love of Martha Ivers* (Paramount, 1946). Written by Robert Rossen, it's a delirious "woman's picture," in which the fear and guilt of youth plague the protagonists throughout their adult lives.

Walter O'Neil is witness as orphaned Martha kills her evil aunt. Martha's cover story blames the killing on a robber, and she gets Walter to back her play. Walter's father, a greedy lawyer, realizes Martha stands to inherit her late father's fortune, so he uses her fraudulent testimony to frame an innocent man, who is executed for the murder. Walter and Martha then marry, bound forever in conspiracy. They dominate Iverstown, Martha (Stanwyck) as a hard-charging industrialist, Walter (Kirk Douglas, in his movie debut) as the Scotch-sodden district attorney.

The guilt-edged union turns into a volatile triangle when Sam Masterson (Van Heflin) comes home. Sam had been Martha's childhood chum; they were running away together the night Martha iced her aunt. Now a nomadic ne'er-do-well, Sam

rekindles Martha's deferred desires, provoking Walter's suspicion. He's convinced Sam is out to blackmail them and hires local muscle to work over his former pal and deposit him beyond the city limits. But Sam won't quit. He's determined to uncover the secret keeping the mismatched couple together. He also wants to humiliate Walter by flaunting Martha's attraction to him. It works.

"You know what's on my mind, Martha? About Sam, I mean," says Walter. "I think I do," she responds, "And that's where it will stay. On your mind. Unless, of course, I tell you differently." Definitive Stanwyck.

Once Sam and Martha consummate their passion, guilt rains down. Walter drunkenly confronts Sam with self-loathing fury, but tumbles down the master stairway. Sam is stunned when Martha implores him to finish off her unconscious husband, so they can be "free." But just like twenty years earlier, Sam flees from the house—this time taking their secret with him.

In the feverish finale, Walter embraces Martha. "I love you," he tells her, as she watches her true love, Sam, walking away. "And don't cry. It's not your fault . . . It's not anyone's fault. It's just the way things are. It's about what people want, and how hard they want it. And how hard it is for them to get it."

Martha and Walter kiss, and she vows they'll start over, "Just like nothing happened." Walter pulls a gun from his pocket and pushes it into Martha. He hesitates, still looking for her to lead. She guides his trigger finger. *Blam!*—an end to all her fear and loathing. Walter then obliterates his own pain with a single shot to his heart.

WHILE THIS GRIM FAIRY TALE was being concocted on Paramount's painted sets, real-life dramas flared outside the lot. A power struggle between rival labor unions, the entrenched IATSE and the growing Conference of Studio Unions (CSU), erupted in chain-swinging melees. The CSU, promising to chase racketeers out of Hollywood's unions, had loosened IATSE's grip on a number of craft unions. Pressing its advantage, it threw picket lines around several major studios, trying to intimidate IATSE members into defecting. Studio heads, caught in the middle,

Lovers Van Heflin and Barbara Stanwyck drive her husband (Kirk Douglas) to drink, and the brink, in *The Strange Love of Martha Ivers*.

called in the cops—and mob-sponsored goon squads—to break things up. This street warfare was ground zero in the coming anti-Communist frenzy. Hollywood honchos and IATSE bosses preserved their uneasy alliance by casting the CSU as a Communist front organization, thereby marshaling federal forces against them. (There was more than a tinge of pink to the fledgling conference, but it was cleaner than graft-tainted IATSE.)

Lewis Milestone, director of *The Strange Love of Martha Ivers*, often ceded the helm to assistant directors Robert Aldrich or Byron Haskin while attending CSU strategy sessions at a restaurant across the street. Milestone was among the first group of "unfriendly" witnesses targeted by the original HUAC hunting expedition in 1947.

Barbara Stanwyck had no qualms about crossing the picket lines. She disdained the political battle around her, trampling anyone who tried to cheat her out of work. Long ago she'd traded political and religious beliefs for career compulsion. When the witch hunt burned through Hollywood, Stanwyck swung to the right, aligning herself with those who'd safeguard her career.

The "real" Stanwyck was a legendary cipher, obsessively private, with a small circle of friends. Her second marriage, to actor Robert Taylor, was studio-arranged and many people suspected it was "lavender," intended to camouflage the partners' rumored homosexuality. While Taylor's dalliances with Lana Turner, Ava Gardner, and other ingénues proved him at least bisexual, Stanwyck remained faithful, propping up the façade of "the perfect Hollywood marriage."

Throughout her twelve-year arrangement with Taylor, which ended in divorce in 1951, Stanwyck was actually closer to her veteran publicist, Helen Ferguson. Their bond spawned decades of gossip that Stanwyck was a closeted lesbian—despite liaisons with Farley Granger (who *was* gay) and Robert Wagner, revealed later by both men in their memoirs. While the innuendo swirled, Stanwyck marched on, submerging loneliness in a torrent of work, much of it emanating from that nasty residential cul-de-sac in Dark City.

In *Sorry, Wrong Number* (Paramount, 1948), she's wealthy invalid Leona Stephenson, who through crossed telephone wires overhears the plotting of a woman's murder. Confined to her bed, Leona is terrified to realize *she* is the intended victim. Scenarist Lucille Fletcher fleshed out her famous twenty-two-minute radio play, infusing it with a theme endemic to many noirs—the resentful underclass

Stanwyck in the rare role of victim in *Sorry, Wrong Number.*

scheming to undermine the rich. In this case the culprit is her dimwit husband (Burt Lancaster), rebelling against his wife's mental and monetary domination.

The Lady Gambles (Universal, 1949) begins with a shock: Stanwyck beaten senseless when she's caught cheating in a back-alley dice game. While the rest of the film never matches the intense opening, it's a compelling study of addiction, cannily directed by Michael Gordon. If you read a little extra into Roy Huggins's script, you might infer Stanwyck's gambling addiction is actually code for an insatiable sex drive.

The File on Thelma Jordon (Paramount, 1950) put Stanwyck back in Cain territory. She lures gullible DA Cleve Marshall (Wendell Corey) into an affair, so she can use him in a plot to rob and murder her rich aunt. Although her sleazeball lover Tony Laredo (Richard Rober) actually hatches the crime, Thelma is arrested and tried. Hopelessly in love, Cleve intentionally loses the case, expecting to win Thelma's devotion. Thelma dumps him to run away with Tony, but, displaying the sudden remorse that often overwhelms culprits in Dark City (thanks to the PCA), she yanks the steering wheel from Tony as they're leaving town, sending them plummeting over a cliff.

No Man of Her Own (Paramount, 1950) may be the ultimate "woman's noir." Mitchell Leisen, a wizard at "weepies," directed this adaptation of Cornell Woolrich's *I Married a Dead Man*, fashioning a combination tearjerker and backstabber. A pregnant woman (named Helen Ferguson, in honor of Stanwyck's closest friend) is dumped by her cad boyfriend and tearfully heads cross-country, seeking a fresh start. She's befriended on the train by a pregnant newlywed, traveling with her husband. The train crashes and Helen, through a wild fluke (Woolrich's hallmark), is mistaken for the other woman and eventually accepted into her "late husband's" affluent family. Needless to say, the cad comes out of the past, threatening Helen's newfound happiness.

Clash by Night (RKO, 1952), based on Clifford Odets's play, like most of his work, was borderline noir of a verbose variety. Mae Doyle (Stanwyck) returns to her hometown and takes a shot at complacency by marrying a sweet, simple fisherman (Paul Douglas). Motherhood can't ease her ennui; she ruins her marriage by having an affair with her husband's scary pal, Earl (Robert Ryan). The actors are all great, but by the tenth self-revelatory Odets monologue you're itching for somebody to grab a gat and start blasting.

Jeopardy (MGM, 1952) featured the queasy spectacle of Stanwyck allowing herself to be raped by escaped con Ralph Meeker, in exchange for his helping save her husband (Barry Sullivan), who's drowning under a collapsed pier. Stanwyck literally dukes it out with Meeker: She pops him with a wicked right cross, only to be decked by a countering left. *Witness to Murder* (UA, 1954) was a distaff *Rear Window*, beating Hitchcock's film into theaters, but lacking its brilliantly polished angles. Scenes of Stanwyck complaining that men never listen to women—especially when they're outing murderous Nazis in the building next door—showed prescience.

Stanwyck's last saunter down Hate Street came with *Crime of Passion* (UA, 1957). A feisty San Francisco newspaper advice columnist, Kathy Ferguson (!), upstages an out-of-town cop by using her column to reel in the fugitive he's pursuing. Lieutenant Bill Doyle (Sterling Hayden) falls for her, and they get hitched. Kathy drops her career and moves to the drowsy suburbs of Los Angeles. The thrill of the newsroom is replaced by endless cocktail parties, where the men talk pensions and the wives blather about clothes and canapés. Kathy's suddenly mundane existence induces psychosis: She foists all her thwarted ambition onto her passive husband, vying to win him the promotion that will place them above the peers she detests.

Unfortunately, her plan involves sex with Tony Pope, the chief of homicide (Raymond Burr). When Pope balks at naming Bill his successor, Kathy swipes a gun from the precinct's evidence room and gives Pope six good reasons he should have promoted her husband. Bill pieces things together, collars his wife, and carts her off to jail.

Jo Eisinger's script isn't bold enough to portray Kathy as much more than a sociopathic harpy, but it does suggest that she was better off as a career woman than an unhappy homemaker. Stanwyck's transformation from tart-tongued reporter to a lapdog in her own house was a none-too-subtle condemnation of women's subordination—trapped in a conventional murder drama. It was a solid, if unspectacular, finale to Stanwyck's reign as the Queen of Noir.

Stanwyck commits a *Crime of Passion*.

Pat O'Brien and the boys in the pressroom in the 1931 film version of *The Front Page*

THE CITY DESK

THE HOT SHOTS HAVE ALL FILED COPY, LATE SPORTS SCORES MADE THE BULLDOG EDITION, NOTHING'S COOKING FOR THE FRONT PAGE'S FUDGE BOX. IT'S 3 A.M. AND THE NEWSROOM IS A TOMB. THEY WARNED HER THE LOBSTER SHIFT WAS STRICTLY FOR BACHELORS, ONES WITHOUT A LOVE LIFE. BUT SHE WANTED TO BE A REPORTER, HOT ON A SCOOP, THE NEXT NELLIE BLY. THIS IS PURGATORY. *RIIIIING!* "CITY DESK." *WANNA KNOW WHERE THE GOVERNOR IS RIGHT NOW?* "WHO IS THIS?" *SOMEBODY WITH DOPE TO ALTER THE ELECTION. I'M AT THE PICKWICK HOTEL.* "I'LL BE THERE IN TWO SHAKES OF A LAMB'S TAIL!" *BRING A CAMERA.*

August 14, 1928 is an overlooked date in the development of film noir. That's the night a stage play called *The Front Page*, written by newspapermen Ben Hecht and Charles MacArthur, premiered at the Times Square Theatre on Broadway. The mordant comedy takes place entirely in the pressroom of Chicago's Criminal Courts Building, where a gaggle of jaded reporters await the execution of Edwin Williams, a purported Communist accused of killing a Black police officer. Star reporter Hildy Johnson (Lee Tracy), eager to begin his honeymoon, drops in to bid his colleagues adieu. But a scoop falls in Hildy's lap when the condemned man breaks custody; the reporter hides him in the pressroom's rolltop desk and scores an exclusive. He learns Williams is being railroaded to the gallows by the mayor, who's anxious to win over Black voters in the upcoming election. This perfectly noir premise was delivered as uproarious comedy, thanks to Hecht and MacArthur's ribald rat-a-tat dialogue, which instantly created a new American archetype—the fast-talking, hard-drinking newshound who'll do anything for a scoop.

Hecht and MacArthur were part of a fraternity of newspapermen—H. L. Mencken, Damon Runyon, Paul Gallico, Gene Fowler, Herman Mankiewicz, Mark Hellinger, and Walter Winchell, among the more celebrated—who would change American vernacular speech during the rise of talking pictures. They didn't all become screenwriters, but their gift for lively lingo—syndicated nationally—would influence the *sound* of noir as much as German Expressionism inspired its look.

The popularity of *The Front Page* inspired a slew of newspaper movies in the 1930s: *The Finger Points* (WB, 1931), *Five Star Final* (WB, 1931), *The Final Edition* (Columbia, 1932), *Blessed Event* (WB, 1932), *Hold the Press* (Columbia, 1933), *Picture Snatcher* (WB, 1933), *The Murder Man* (MGM, 1935), *Adventure in Manhattan* (Columbia, 1936), *Libeled Lady* (MGM, 1936), *Behind the Headlines* (RKO, 1937), *News Is Made at Night* (Fox, 1939), and *many* more. Reporters were depicted as unscrupulous but irresistible hustlers, savvy to a rigged system. Most squared themselves in the last reel, rediscovering their ethics and exposing the truth—typically the hypocrisy of the rich and powerful. Some of those honorable newsmen were still around in the post–World War II noir era, reporters like P. J. McNeil (Jimmy Stewart), who uncovers a plot that put an innocent man on Death Row in *Call Northside 777* (Fox, 1948), or Jim Austin (John Forsythe), single-handedly rooting out organized crime in *Captive City* (UA, 1952), or Jerry McKibbon (William Holden) a jaded reporter who pays full price for exposing corruption in *The Turning Point* (Paramount, 1952).

WITH THE RISE OF NOIR, however, the irascible reporters, editors, and publishers who'd charmed audiences in the 1930s slipped over to the dark side. Lee Tracy, who after his turn as Hildy Johnson in *The Front Page* played nothing but garrulous ambulance chasers, epitomized this change. In *High Tide* (Monogram, 1947), an older, booze-ravaged Tracy recycled Hildy Johnson as Hugh Fresney, editor of the *Los Angeles Courier*. Threatened by a local gangster he's investigating, Fresney hires an old pal, tight-lipped detective Tim Slade (Don Castle), as his bodyguard. The switchbacking plot ultimately reveals Fresney as the culprit. It must have pained fans of *The Front Page* to see effervescent Hildy turn rancid. *High Tide* also features the greatest framing device in noir: The speeding sedan Fresney and Slade are riding in crashes onto a rugged shoreline; the entire story is reeled out in flashback as the rising tide threatens to drown them. Director John Reinhardt packed lots of creativity into this seventy-two-minute B, made on the cheap by fledgling producer Jack Wrather.

By contrast, Paramount spared no expense bringing Kenneth Fearing's 1945 best seller, *The Big Clock*, to the screen in 1948. George Stroud (Ray Milland), editor of popular *Crimeways* magazine, has a dalliance with the boss's girlfriend. When she turns up dead, Stroud realizes he was the last to see her alive—and he probably saw her killer. His boss, media magnate Earl Janoth (Charles Laughton), puts Stroud in charge of the investigation. It's a race against time as Stroud hunts the real killer as evidence mounts framing *him*.

The publishing world was familiar turf to Fearing. He had worked at *TIME*, crown jewel in the media empire of Henry Luce, a devout Christian and anti-Communist whose self-proclaimed mission was to spread democracy and open markets worldwide. In the early '40s, when Fearing was one of his minions, Luce gave his empire a black eye by supporting Mussolini's fascist government in Italy and downplaying in print Hitler's threat to our European allies.

So it was no surprise Luce became grist for Fearing's imagination. *The Big Clock*'s Earl Janoth was the writer's caricature of the great man, and Charles

Lee Tracy, the archetypal newshound

Laughton had a field day portraying him as a larger-than-life megalomaniac, a more diabolical version of Charles Foster Kane. As his foil, Milland is perfectly cast. It's squirmy pleasure watching the suave actor come apart at the seams as the walls close in—but still go toe-to-toe with Laughton in a razor-sharp game of cat-and-mouse.

The film's visual élan came courtesy of director John Farrow, a one-time screenwriter who, in the mid-'40s, honed his style in noir's shadowy terrain. He's abetted by Paramount's maestro of chiaroscuro, John F. Seitz, who'd previously shot two watershed noirs—*This Gun for Hire* (1942) and the definitive *Double Indemnity*—as well as *The Lost Weekend* (1945) and Farrow's darkly exotic *Calcutta* (1947). Paramount's Art Department crafted an actual "big clock" as centerpiece of Janoth's monolithic office tower. The title of Fearing's novel is merely metaphor—homage to Raymond Chandler's influential *The Big Sleep*. Making the clock literal was Hollywood at its most absurd and brilliant—an artistic metaphor transformed, at immense cost, into a structure in which much of the third act takes place.

Beyond the marvelous acting and visual pyrotechnics, the success of *The Big Clock* was due largely to the former newspapermen who wrote the book and its film version. Kenneth Fearing was an unlikely writer of crime yarns—even if he had been a police reporter in Chicago in the 1920s. His fiction career began in pulps like *Tattle Tales* and *Paris Nights*. But in the '30s Fearing turned into one of the nation's foremost poets, vividly evoking Depression-era America. His colleague, Kenneth Rexroth, said, "No other poet of the time so closely identified himself with the working class, with the impoverished stratum of the underworld, with hustlers, grifters, nifties, yeggs, and thirsties, and no one else so completely immersed himself in the lingo of the mass culture." Reading Fearing's poetry, he said, was like "a taxi driver reading a billboard while fighting traffic."

Fearing was also film critic for *New Masses*, a Marxist magazine aligned with the Communist Party of the United States. He described his readers as "genuine, dyed-in-the-wool movie hop-heads," and while he claimed Hollywood's "dream powder" was "the lowest form of opiate on earth," Fearing admitted he "couldn't get enough of it."

At the time Fearing wrote *The Big Clock*, he was married to artist Nan Lurie. He wrote the manuscript in her Greenwich Village studio, where the couple lived the hand-to-mouth existence of most poets and artists. Sale of *The Big Clock* to a major publisher, and then the movies, brought a windfall that Fearing—unaccustomed to financial security—did his best to drink away. His newfound notoriety also earned the attention of the House Un-American Activities Committee. Called to testify under oath as to whether or not he was a Communist, Fearing replied—"Not yet"—the most sardonic response ever to that question. Despite his alcoholism, Fearing wrote more novels and poetry during the 1950s, before dying in 1961, at fifty-nine years of age.

The Big Clock's screenwriter, Jonathan Latimer, was undaunted in adapting a book that was clever, complex, and beyond the bounds of the Production Code (only hints of the book's adultery and homosexuality remain in the film). While Fearing's novel divides the narrative between four first-person voices, Latimer tells it all from Stroud's point of view, in noir-ubiquitous flashbacks. He dropped Fearing's social commentary, replacing it with the offhanded wit that was his hallmark. Like Fearing, Latimer began as a reporter, working the crime beat for Hearst's *Chicago Herald-Examiner*. He specialized in "gangland slayings, kidnappings, more or less routine homicides, race riots, bank embezzlements and such," Latimer noted in a 1983 interview. "I knew Al Capone, George 'Bugs' Moran and assorted other gangsters, as well as whorehouse madams, pimps, dope peddlers and con men."

In the '30s, Latimer channeled this knowledge into a series of mystery novels featuring detective Bill Crane, who did as much boozing as sleuthing. On that score, he and Fearing shared common, if unsteady, ground. By the 1940s, Latimer found a comfortable niche in Hollywood as an ace screenwriter. He adapted Dashiell Hammett's *The Glass Key* for Paramount in 1942, although his screen version of Hammett's *Red Harvest*, also written for Ladd and Lake, was never produced. Farrow was so pleased with Latimer's reworking of *The Big Clock* he demanded

For the film version of Fearing's novel, Paramount actually built a big clock, in which Milland hides from his pursuers. In the book, it is merely metaphor.

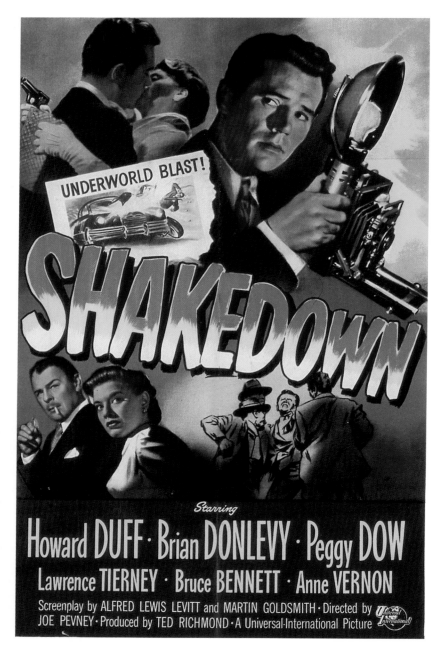

UNDERWORLD BLAST!

SHAKEDOWN

Starring

Howard DUFF · Brian DONLEVY · Peggy DOW
Lawrence TIERNEY · Bruce BENNETT · Anne VERNON
Screenplay by ALFRED LEWIS LEVITT and MARTIN GOLDSMITH · Directed by
JOE PEVNEY · Produced by TED RICHMOND · A Universal-International Picture

him as writer on most of his films. In all, Farrow and Latimer made ten pictures together, including the 1948 Cornell Woolrich adaptation *Night Has a Thousand Eyes* (Paramount) and 1949's fantastic *Alias Nick Beal* (Paramount) a passion project for the über-Catholic Farrow, in which Milland portrays a suave and debonair devil.

By the end of the decade, hard-bitten, wisecracking reporters were as ubiquitous in noir as seedy PIs and seductive femmes fatales.

Chicago Deadline (Paramount, 1949) was an ink-stained variation on *Laura*, with Alan Ladd portraying a cityside reporter obsessed with learning the secrets of a young woman he finds dead in a brothel. Connecting the dots all around Chicago, he cobbles together the sad history of a good girl (Donna Reed) gone wrong.

In *Abandoned* (Universal, 1949), Dennis O'Keefe is a smart-mouthed Los Angeles reporter who helps a fresh-off-the-bus Midwesterner (Gale Storm) search for her missing sister. The pair navigate around heavies Raymond Burr and Mike Mazurki to expose a black-market baby ring. Featuring crackling dialogue by one-time newspaperman William Bowers, *Abandoned* is an overlooked gem that doesn't soft-pedal its unsettling theme.

Shakedown (Universal, 1950) offers Howard Duff as Jack Early, an ethics-free San Francisco news photographer who sells his incriminating photos to the highest bidder, whether they're editors or mobsters. The story by Don Martin and Nat Dallinger, originally called "The Magnificent Heel," was modeled on legendary New York street photographer Arthur "Weegee" Fellig. The script by Alfred Lewis Levitt and Martin (*Detour*) Goldsmith is so relentlessly cynical it spirals into black comedy. *Shakedown* marked the directorial debut of Joe Pevney, reliable character actor in several noirs, notably *Nocturne*, *Body and Soul*, and *Thieves' Highway*. Pevney became Universal's most dependable contract director in the 1950s, maintaining a vestige of noir in some of his best films: *Iron Man* (1951), *Meet Danny Wilson* (1952), *Flesh and Fury* (1952), *Playgirl* (1954), *Female on the Beach* (1955), *Six Bridges to Cross* (1956), and *The Midnight Story* (1957).

The Underworld Story (UA, 1950) disappointed moviegoers expecting a typical gangster movie. The title is ironic, since it's set in a New England town filled with decent folks and one affluent clan of blue bloods presided over by publishing magnate E. J. Stanton (Herbert Marshall). Into town blows disgraced city reporter Mike Reese (Dan Duryea), blackballed out of New York for his ties to racketeer Carl Durham (Howard da Silva). Reese buys half-interest in the struggling local paper, the *Lakeville Gazette*, and plans to show its naïve editor Cathy Harris (Gale Storm) how things are done in the big city. When the murder of Stanton's daughter-in-law makes Lakeville the center of a media circus, Reese manipulates the story to bargain his way back into the big leagues.

The Underworld Story was based on a story by Craig Rice—not a well-known name today, but in 1945 *she* was the first mystery writer ever featured on the cover of *TIME*. Craig Rice was Georgiana Ann Randolph Craig on her birth certificate, and one of the best-selling mystery novelists of the era, on par with Agatha Christie, Erle Stanley Gardner, and Rex Stout. Her specialty was the screwball mystery: *Having Wonderful Crime*, *Home Sweet Homicide*, and *My Kingdom for a Hearse*, among others. Few of her books remain in print, but once she was known as the "Dorothy Parker of mystery fiction."

There's nothing funny, however, about the adaptation of her story by Henry Blankfort, who'd recently written the tough B *Open Secret* (Eagle-Lion, 1948), about Nazis conspiring to run Jews out of a small American town. Director Cyril Endfield, also a writer, added a racial angle to *The Underworld Story*—making Molly Rankin, the murder suspect, African-American. Reese discovers that Molly, the Stantons' maid, is being framed. The real killer is E. J. Stanton's son, Clark, who convinces his father to railroad Molly to save the family's reputation—and because no one cares about "a nigger." Endfield, a died-in-the-wool progressive, pushed the hottest buttons. Unfortunately, producer Hal E. Chester had less guts: He caved to distributors' demands that a white actress play Molly, so as not to hurt business in the South. Anderson's blackface is so subtle she has to declare several times, "I am a Negro," to assuage the audience's incredulity. An inexcusable blunder in a film that otherwise is close to a minor masterpiece.

The Underworld Story had much in common with Billy Wilder's *Ace in the Hole* (Paramount, 1951), which came out the following year. Both revolve around crafty and cynical reporters whose questionable tactics get them bounced from a big city paper. Both men try to outdistance their disgrace, starting over in small towns filled with folks they see as naïve know-nothings and gullible rubes. Both stumble

Alan Ladd is a reporter obsessed with the death of a young prostitute in *Chicago Deadline*.

Disgraced newsman Chuck Tatum (Kirk Douglas) uses trapped prospector Leo Minosa (Richard Benedict) as his ticket back to the big time in Billy Wilder's savagely cynical *Ace in the Hole.*

on a hot story that could be their ticket back to the big time. Wilder's film may have less noir iconography than *The Underworld Story*, but it's a far more savagely cynical film.

Reporter Chuck Tatum (Kirk Douglas), hoping to revive his credibility at a newspaper in New Mexico, learns of a local prospector trapped in the caverns of an ancient Native American dwelling. He manipulates the rescue effort, prolonging it to serve his own ends, and cannily placing himself in the media spotlight he engineers. This includes tutoring the guy's estranged wife, Lorraine (Jan Sterling)—who couldn't care less if her husband survives—to deliver the platitudes the public craves. When Tatum suggests she be photographed in church, praying for her husband's salvation, Lorraine tosses off the most cynical line in noir: "I don't pray—kneeling bags my nylons."

The script, by Wilder and Lesser Samuels, is based on the true story of Floyd Collins, a spelunker who was trapped in a Kentucky cavern in 1925. The rescue effort became a national sensation not only in newspapers but on radio—Americans could actually hear Collins's voice during his captivity. During the first four days, rescuers got water and food to him, but a cave-in cut off the passageway, stranding Collins in the earth for more than two weeks. He died before rescuers could reach him. Twenty-five years after Collins's death, Wilder had the temerity to reframe the story so the media, embodied by the venal Tatum, was responsible for his death. Wilder had bitterness to spare, also ridiculing the rubes who flock to tragedy, gawking like it's a carnival attraction.

A box-office disaster on release, *Ace in the Hole* fared little better when reissued by Paramount as *The Big Carnival.* Years later, its prescience was recognized, but it was long after the film's warning had been resoundingly ignored. By the time *Ace in the Hole* was lauded as one of Wilder's finest movies, cheap sensationalism was the standard for American mainstream media.

Ace in the Hole wasn't the only borderline noir released in 1951 based on a true story of entrapment. *The Well* (UA), written by Russell Rouse and Clarence Greene (they'd written *DOA* just prior), was based on the 1949 story of Kathy Fiscus, a three-year-old who fell into an abandoned well in San Marino, California. The rescue attempt, broadcast by Los Angeles station KTLA, was early "must see" TV. Unfortunately, it wasn't scripted. Kathy Fiscus died. Rouse and Greene turned her story into a provocative take on racism by reimagining Kathy as a Black child, whose tumble into the well is witnessed by no one. When a White drifter is suspected of having killed her, the tenuously integrated town threatens to erupt into a race riot. *The Well* is tough and suspenseful, with an exhausting climax clearly intended to relieve the public's memory of Kathy Fiscus's miserable fate.

THE BOOK THAT INSPIRED *The Big Clock*, Samuel Fuller's 1944 thriller *The Dark Page*, didn't make it to the screen until 1952, retitled *Scandal Sheet* (Columbia). It's a classic Fuller yarn: Mark Chapman (Broderick Crawford) is a veteran newspaperman challenged to reverse the sagging circulation of the tabloid *New York Express*. He'll resort to any kind of publicity stunt, including "Lonely Heart" mixers. At one of these, he encounters his long-gone ex-wife, who threatens to expose Chapman's shady past. They tussle and she winds up dead. Chapman covers his tracks but then—unable to resist the allure of a juicy circulation booster—he assigns a wet-behind-the-ears reporter (John Derek) to track down the "Lonely Hearts Killer." Big mistake.

This socko premise was so good Howard Hawks bought the film rights for $15,000 while Fuller was still fighting overseas with the 1st Infantry Division. Back home—having survived wartime experiences he'd later pour into his 1982 World War II epic *The Big Red One*—Fuller turned *The Dark Page* into a script, with help from screenwriter Sidney Buchman. But it was never produced and Hawks—a very savvy operator—sold it to producer Edward Small for a hefty $85,000 profit. Small wanted to make it with John Payne in the lead. He and the actor had a profit-sharing production triad with Phil Karlson, who had a style as exciting and dynamic as any director in the business. When it came to the rough stuff, nobody was better than Karlson. But it's Fuller's fingerprints all over *Scandal Sheet*, especially its depiction of the cutthroat allure of the newspaper business. Fuller had been one of the nation's youngest crime reporters, proving his newshound cred on the beat in 1929 when, working for the *New York Graphic*, he discovered the body of silent film star Jeanne Eagels, dead from a drug overdose. "My front page article on the mysterious death of Jeanne Eagels in the morning edition of October 4, 1929, scooped every other daily paper in New York," Fuller later recalled. "I was damn proud . . . but, at the same time, deeply saddened by the death of the young actress, only thirty-five when she died."

Broderick Crawford is a newspaper editor who commits murder in *Scandal Sheet*, based on Sam Fuller's novel *The Dark Page*.

BEN HECHT
SCRIBE OF THE CENTURY

Ben Hecht came to Hollywood in 1926 at the behest of colleague Herman Mankiewicz, another hotshot reporter with literary ambitions. "Mank" extended the invitation in a telegram, which concluded, "Millions are to be grabbed out here and your only competition is idiots. Don't let this get around." For newspapermen of the Roaring Twenties, writing for pictures was seen as slumming. Very profitable slumming.

Ensconced in an office at Paramount, earning a fast $300 per week, Hecht got a crash course in picture writing from his sarcastic pal. "I want to point out to you," Mankiewicz advised, "that in a novel a hero can lay ten girls and marry a virgin for a finish. In a movie this is not allowed. The hero, as well as the heroine, has to be a virgin. The villain can lay anybody he wants, have as much fun as he wants cheating and stealing, getting rich and whipping the servants. But you have to shoot him in the end. When he falls with a bullet in his forehead, it is advisable that he clutch at the Gobelin tapestry on the library wall and bring it down over his head like a symbolic shroud. Also, covered by such a tapestry, the actor does not have to hold his breath while he is being photographed as a dead man."

Hecht added his own spin: "The thing to do was skip the heroes and heroines, to write a movie containing only villains and bawds [broads]. I would not have to tell any lies then." In his 1954 autobiography, *A Child of the Century*, Hecht explained that "As a newspaperman I learned that nice people—the audience—loved criminals, doted on reading about their love problems as well as their sadism. My movie, grounded on this simple truth, was produced under the title of *Underworld* (Paramount, 1929). It was the first gangster movie to bedazzle movie fans and there were no lies in it—except for a half-dozen sentimental touches introduced by its director, Joe von Sternberg."

Hecht thought so little of the director's additions that, upon seeing the film, he sent von Sternberg a telegram: "You poor ham. Take my name off the picture." Paramount kept Hecht's name on the credits. *Underworld* won the first Oscar given for Best Original Story.

Howard Hughes then hired Hecht to write a movie based on the exploits of Al Capone. Hecht agreed, with conditions: He had to be paid $1,000 per day, cash, the money delivered precisely at six o'clock. "In that way I stood to lose only a day's labor if Mr. Hughes turned out to be insolvent." The finished script for *Scarface* (UA, 1932) incorporated many elements Hecht had used in *Underworld*. It also brought a pair of midnight visitors to his hotel. Hecht described the scene:

"They entered the room as ominously as any paid movie gangsters, their faces set in scowls and guns bulging in their coats. They had a copy of my *Scarface* script in their hands. Their dialogue belonged in it.

"You the guy who wrote this?" I said I was.

"We read it." I inquired how they had liked it.

"We wanna ask you some questions." I invited them to go ahead.

"Is this stuff about Al Capone?"

"God, no," I said. "I don't even know Al."

After some back-and-forth about mutual associates back in Chicago, the gangsters prepared to leave, satisfied that the script was about "them other" Windy City crooks. But they stopped in the doorway.

"If this stuff ain't about Al Capone, why are you calling it *Scarface*? Everybody'll think it's him."

"That's the reason," I said. "Al is one of the most famous and fascinating men of our time. If we call the movie *Scarface*, everybody will want to see it, figuring it's about Al. That's the part of the racket we call showmanship.

"My visitors pondered this, and one of them finally said, 'I'll tell Al.' A pause. 'Who's this fella Howard Hughes?'

"'He's got nothing to do with anything,' I said, speaking truthfully at last. 'He's the sucker with the money.'

"'OK. The hell with him.'"

Ben Hecht's fingerprints are all over some of Hollywood's greatest movies, including early prototypes of what would become film noir. Unimpressed with Hollywood's approach to filmmaking, Hecht made independent films of his own in the 1930s, mostly at Astoria Studios in New York, in collaboration with cameraman Lee Garmes. Pictures like *Crime without Passion* (Paramount, 1934), *The Scoundrel* (Paramount, 1935, another Oscar winner for Best Story), and *Angels over Broadway* (Columbia, 1940) all contain a dark streak Hecht would plumb in such noirs as *Kiss of Death* (Fox, 1947), *Ride the Pink Horse* (Universal, 1947), *Whirlpool* (Fox, 1950), and *Where the Sidewalk Ends* (Fox, 1950). He also served as a top-dollar script doctor and dialogue polisher on dozens more. His pal Herman Mankiewicz would write (with Orson Welles) the most important newspaper movie ever made, *Citizen Kane* (1941).

Hecht (seated) at work with frequent collaborator Charles Lederer

STAR-STUDDED IS A TERM RARELY used in relation to film noir. You don't find *Grand Hotel*s in this part of town, no A-list pictures brimming top-to-bottom with big-name stars. Around here it's usually a flophouse on some rainy street, with a couple of losers playing out the string. But *While the City Sleeps* (RKO, 1956) was the exception that proved the rule. It featured a star-studded cast, many of whom had made an indelible impression in noir: Dana Andrews, Ida Lupino, Vincent Price, Rhonda Fleming, George Sanders, Howard Duff, Thomas Mitchell, Sally Forrest, and John Barrymore . . . Junior. Unlike most noir films, there is no protagonist—it's an ensemble piece, something Robert Altman might have made twenty years later.

This 1956 offering was a signpost marking the end of the road in America for director Fritz Lang. His early German films garnered him a reputation as the world's most important film director, but that rep evaporated in Hollywood, where Lang's career was a rough road of peaks and valleys. Like Orson Welles, Lang had talent and ego in equal measure and, like Welles, he constantly butted heads with studio executives he considered his inferiors. By the mid-'50s Lang was an aging autocrat with too many burned bridges behind him.

Luckily, a neophyte producer offered him a two-picture deal. Bert E. Friedlob was the ex-husband of actress Eleanor Parker who, through a previous marriage, had tapped into the Annenberg publishing fortune. Lang, of course, hated him, considering him a man of poor taste. But he loved Friedlob's maiden project—an adaptation of a novel called *The Bloody Spur*, about the manhunt for a serial killer. For Lang, it had echoes of his 1931 masterpiece *M*. And, like *M*, based on the actual case of Düsseldorf child killer Peter Kürten, *The Bloody Spur* was also based on fact.

For an entire year between 1945 and '46, Chicago had been terrorized by the grisly killings of several young women. The culprit used the victims' lipstick to scrawl a plea for his capture at one murder scene. As months wore on and the hunt for the "Lipstick Killer" led nowhere, the press went wild with gambits of its own, spurring the public's bloody imagination. Hence the novel's title, written by one of those Chicago newshounds, Charles Einstein.

The book was adapted by Casey Robinson, a veteran screenwriter, but one who'd never been a newspaperman. His script had little of the verisimilitude of a picture like *Deadline–U.S.A.* (Fox, 1952). What Lang relished was the tale's cynicism; how the journos backstab each other in pursuit of the killer—not because

ABOVE: Ida Lupino appears to be directing Fritz Lang and Dana Andrews in rehearsal for a scene in *While the City Sleeps*. BELOW: Writer Dana Andrews and publisher Sidney Blackmer concoct a ration of circumstantial evidence to get Andrews wrongly convicted of murder in *Beyond a Reasonable Doubt*.

they want justice, but because the one who nabs the murderer will win a promotion.

The film is not as dark as it sounds—tonally or visually. The focus is on the shenanigans of reporters, not the psychosis of the young killer. Parts of it are even played for laughs—risky, given that humor was not Lang's strong suit, but it was nowhere near as caustic as *Ace in the Hole* in depicting the media at its worst. A lighter tone is also apparent in the film's look, which has little of the familiar noir mood. Ernest Laszlo's cinematography is flat—TV lighting that didn't need to be reset for each shot. Probably a good idea with a cast that drank as much as this one—the less time spent in dressing rooms, nursing a bottle, the better. Lang recalled one scene—Andrews, Lupino, and Mitchell hoisting a few in the corner saloon—in which the actors were actually three sheets to the wind. Sadly, by 1956, this was common for Andrews, who couldn't work before 11 a.m. due to the severity of his hangovers. He'd eventually enter rehab to maintain his career and his life.

A galling wrinkle added to the script was the killer's motivation—comic books are blamed for his derangement. In Einstein's 1953 novel, the killer was obsessed with the Bible—but that would never get past the largely Irish-Catholic Production Code office. Blaming comic books, however, was topical, inspired by the 1954 book *Seduction of the Innocent* by Dr. Fredric Wertham, which spurred congressional hearings on comics' role in juvenile delinquency. The chairman of those hearings, Senator Estes Kefauver, was even hired as a consultant on *While the City Sleeps*, a stunt orchestrated by producer Friedlob.

Given the subject and the story's bitter perspective, it's surprising how little *While the City Sleeps* feels like noir. Yet for decades it's been considered one of the preeminent noirs on Lang's résumé. That's because much early scholarly writing on film noir cited Lang as its primary practitioner. Which made sense, given that German Expressionism had been credited as the progenitor of the visual style, and Lang, during his days in Berlin, created many of those Expressionist films. His relocation to America coincided so neatly with the rise of film noir he became, to critics constructing those first studies of noir, the movement's figurehead. In the process, several Lang films were tagged "noir," that, at least in my opinion, don't fit the bill. *While the City Sleeps* is one of them.

Far more noir was the story of the actual "Lipstick Killer" on whom the book and movie was based. Apprehended after a six-month manhunt and media circus, he was revealed as seventeen-year-old University of Chicago student William Heirens, a popular kid with excellent grades who dabbled in petty burglaries. After he was arrested breaking into a house near the site of one of the killings, police charged him with murder, declaring that his fingerprints were on a ransom note left in the victim's home. In an era before Miranda rights, Heirens was beaten by the cops and repeatedly injected with "truth serum"—until he finally cracked and signed a confession. He was charged with all three Lipstick Killer murders, and, on the advice of lawyers, he pled guilty, getting three consecutive life sentences instead of the chair. He recanted almost immediately. "I lied so I could live," Heirens told the press. All requests for a review of his case were denied, multiple times, and Heirens spent the rest of his life—sixty-five years—in an Illinois prison, where he died in 2012 at the age of eighty-three, maintaining his innocence until the end.

Fritz Lang's final American film was also a newspaper noir. In *Beyond a Reasonable Doubt* (RKO, 1956), based on an original script by Oscar-winner Douglas Morrow (*The Stratton Story* [MGM, 1949]), writer Tom Garrett (Dana Andrews) agrees to be framed for a murder and sentenced to death—all an elaborate ploy on his publisher's part to prove the pitfalls of capital punishment. There are plenty of twists and turns in the film's brisk eighty-minute running time, and there's a daring climactic surprise that either leaves viewers slack-jawed or pulling out their hair at its preposterousness.

While Lang always expressed satisfaction with *While the City Sleeps*, remarking in some interviews that it was the favorite among his American films, he recalled *Beyond a Reasonable Doubt* as nothing but misery. He and producer Bert Friedlob were constantly at odds, especially when it came to the film's ending, in which Garrett is revealed to actually be the killer; his participation in his boss's scheme is only a ruse to camouflage the killing of his ex-wife (more shades of *The Dark Page*).

Whether or not a viewer buys the big twist or not, Douglas Morrow, Bert Friedlob, and RKO Pictures deserved credit for an ending that spit in the eye of the "happily ever after" normalcy creeping back into Hollywood product in the mid-1950s. By most accounts Lang didn't try to rewrite this script, as he did in his halcyon days. But he and Friedlob locked horns on how far to go with the shocking finish. The producer argued that if they were going downbeat, go all the way—strap Garrett in the electric chair and give him the juice. Lang refused, daring Friedlob to direct the scene himself. Then he walked off the picture—his last decision on a Hollywood set.

One can't help but think *Beyond a Reasonable Doubt* was difficult for Lang because of ghosts Morrow's script resurrected. Like Tom Garrett, Lang had a first wife whose demise was the subject of much speculation. Her name was Lisa Rosenthal. Sometime in early 1921, she caught her husband having sex in their apartment with his new scriptwriter, Thea von Harbou. Minutes later, Lisa Rosenthal was dead from a bullet to the chest, fired by Lang's gun. As there were no witnesses beyond Lang and von Harbou, the authorities believed their version of events—that Rosenthal committed suicide—despite suspicions raised by the lovers waiting more than an hour before notifying the police. It was an incident Lang buried once he came to America. But given the final twist of *Beyond a Reasonable Doubt*, it's hard not to imagine Rosenthal's death preying on Lang's conscience while making what turned out to be his final American film.

BY THE LATTER HALF OF THE 1950s, television was surpassing newspapers and radio as Americans' main source of news. "Columnists," whether in print or on the airwaves, were losing their superstar status. During the 1930s, Walter Winchell, the nation's biggest media star, had more than fifty million people—almost two-thirds of American adults—reading his syndicated daily column and listening to his regular Sunday night broadcasts. Winchell relished power and was ruthless in taking vengeance on people he felt had crossed him. In his autobiography, Winchell said, "I'm not a fighter. I'm a 'waiter.' I wait until I can catch an ingrate with his fly open, and then I take a picture of it."

Writer Ernest Lehman, fearing retribution from the most powerful man in American media, stressed that the main character of his novella "Sweet Smell of Success," J. J. Hunsecker, was *not* based on Winchell, but was a composite of people he'd worked with as a young PR agent in New York. Its publication used up the goodwill Lehman had banked in the Big Apple—everybody in his professional coterie thought he was writing about *them*. So when Paramount offered him a job, Lehman jumped coasts and hit Hollywood running, writing on *Executive Suite* (MGM, 1954), *Sabrina* (Paramount, 1954), *Somebody Up There Likes Me* (MGM, 1956), and *The King and I* (Fox, 1956) during his first two years in town.

Riding high, Lehman sold the rights to "Sweet Smell of Success" to an upstart production company formed by Harold Hecht (no relation to Ben), James Hill, and

Burt Lancaster. He instantly regretted it, describing the partners' business style, and their lives, as "corrupt" and "evil." Shooting was scheduled for Manhattan in the winter of 1956—before Lehman had even finished a script. Working on the project had made him sick; his doctor wouldn't allow him to accompany the crew in New York. Lancaster accused the writer of faking illness to get away from him.

According to everyone who worked on the film, it was utter chaos. Composer Elmer Bernstein, who would contribute a fantastic jazz score, called the production "a snake pit." Yet from this maelstrom emerged one of the best movies of the 1950s, a corrosive take on ambition, fame, and power.

As fearsome columnist J. J. Hunsecker, Lancaster gives his most unexpected performance—and most unforgettable. Originally, he'd wanted Orson Welles for the part. Welles had returned from self-imposed European exile and was taking acting jobs to replenish his barren coffers. But after the success of *Trapeze* (UA, 1956), in which Lancaster and Tony Curtis costarred as circus acrobats—the actor-producer decided to don horn-rimmed specs and play Hunsecker himself—and give Curtis his best role yet. As Sidney Falco, a hustling press agent who shamelessly sucks up to the all-powerful Hunsecker, Curtis reverted to the New York street kid Hollywood was polishing into a matinee idol. Bernie Schwartz gave, by his own estimation, the performance of his career.

To direct, Lancaster chose Alexander "Sandy" Mackendrick, a Scotsman who'd made a few classic comedies at Ealing Studios, including *Whiskey Galore!* (1949), *The Man in the White Suit* (1951), and *The Ladykillers* (1955). When Ealing was sold to the BBC in 1955, Mackendrick came to America, seeking work. He signed a deal with Hecht-Hill-Lancaster after Lancaster promised he'd get to direct another of the company's projects, *The Devil's Disciple*. Lancaster thought he was hiring a director he could dominate. He'd learn different.

It was Mackendrick's idea to bring in playwright Clifford Odets to spice up Lehman's script. Odets had written *The Big Knife* (UA, 1955), a vicious excoriation of Hollywood; the producers hoped he had bile left to sling at the New York media. Odets did not disappoint. *Sweet Smell of Success* bristles with nasty dialogue:

J. J. Hunsecker (Burt Lancaster) looks ready to take a bite out of Sidney Falco (Tony Curtis), his "cookie full of arsenic" in *Sweet Smell of Success*.

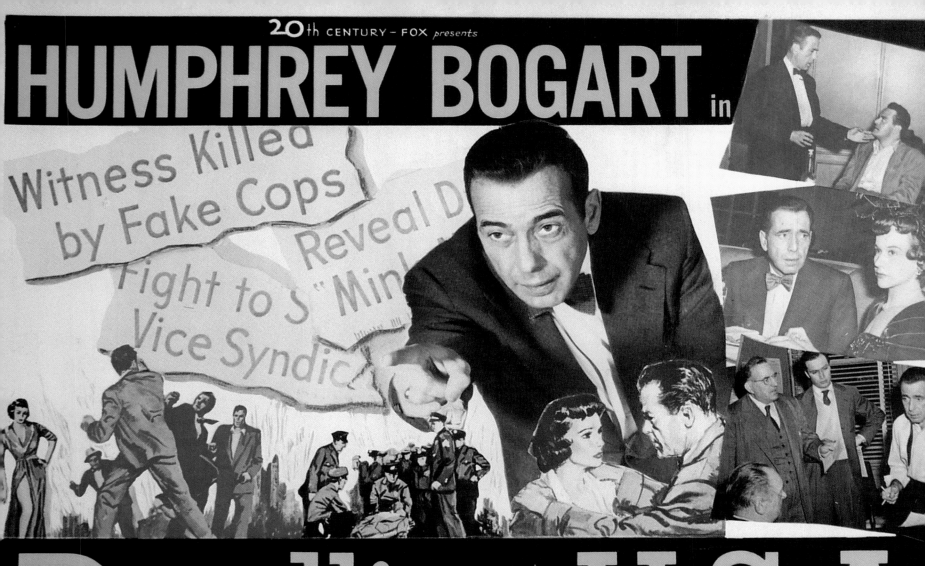

"You're dead, son—get yourself buried." / "I don't relish shooting a mosquito with an elephant gun. Why don't you just shuffle along?" / "I'd hate to take a bite out of you, Sidney—you're a cookie full of arsenic."

Mackendrick worried the language would come off as exaggerated and implausible. But Odets told him: "Play it fast—stage scenes not for the words but for the situations. Play it all 'on the run' and it'll work just fine." The actors, especially the stars, make the purple prose believable; their characters are, after all, *writers*—acting out their own streetwise mythology. The flashy language fits them perfectly.

Production in Manhattan was a shoot-by-night improvisation, an exhilarating but excruciating experience for a perfectionist director who sometimes called for twenty or thirty takes of a scene, which infuriated Lancaster. Mackendrick had only worked within the safety of a studio. Now he was shooting on the fly with big stars in Times Square, in freezing conditions, with Clifford Odets squished in the prop truck banging out new dialogue for scenes to be shot minutes later.

Mackendrick and Lancaster came close to duking it out. Lancaster was an intimidator who exerted his will over everyone, but Mackendrick didn't back down—though in later interviews he admitted he feared Lancaster would attack him. Cast and crew recalled the film shot in a state of hysteria, with no one sure what was happening moment to moment. What happened was that all this nastiness, hostility, and bitterness was imbued in every foot of film. *Sweet Smell of Success* (UA, 1957) emerged from the cutting room a perverse, unpleasant, brilliant, and profound film. Arguably the best work of everyone involved.

By the time the picture was released, Walter Winchell's influence was waning. His support of Senator Joe McCarthy's anti-Communist grandstanding backfired when public opinion turned against McCarthy in 1954. By '59, Winchell was a parody of himself, selling his famous rat-a-tat delivery as narrator of *The Untouchables* TV series. His only public references to *Sweet Smell of Success* were to note, gleefully, its dismal failure at the box office. And make no mistake—it was a bomb. After a preview screening, one viewer said, "Don't change a thing—just burn all the prints." This was not the Burt Lancaster and Tony Curtis the public wanted to see. Lancaster wrote it off as a failure and moved on.

Some may doubt the film's credibility as noir. No murders, no femme fatales, no blatant or punishable crimes. But if you're hip to a noir "ethos"—a jaundiced view of the world and the nature of the people who inhabit it—*Sweet Smell of Success* is as noir as it gets. And as a wild ride through the neon jungle, the movie satisfies like no other, thanks to cinematographer James Wong Howe. It's the definitive depiction of Manhattan after dark; the camerawork visual corollary to the film's verbal sensationalism, a cinematic equivalent of the tabloid style the movie both relishes and rips apart.

THE BEST NEWSPAPER MOVIE of the film noir era wasn't really a film noir. *Deadline–U.S.A.* (Fox, 1952) was one of the first films to exploit the televised congressional hearings on organized crime that transfixed the public in 1950–1951. Twentieth Century-Fox sold it as a topical exposé, but for writer-director Richard Brooks, the mobster at the core of his story was a stalking horse. Brooks cared less about threats posed by organized crime than threats posed to a free press.

The plot ostensibly revolves around a campaign by *The Day*, a metro daily in financial straits, to expose the underworld connections of "bidnizman" Tomas Rienzi (Martin Gabel), linking him to the death of his chorine mistress. The more passionate plotline concerns sale of the venerable paper by its indifferent heirs. Brooks based it on the true story of Joseph Pulitzer's three sons, who, in 1931, sold their late father's flagship, the *New York World*, to his archrival, the Scripps-Howard newspaper chain.

Pulitzer's life had been a genuine American saga, in which a homeless immigrant became a titan of American media. His papers competed head-to-head with William Randolph Hearst's and the two publishers changed newspapers forever. Pulitzer's sons petitioned the court to break their father's will, which stipulated that his paper never be sold to a competitor. The *World*'s staff banded together to oppose the sale. They lost in court, and, as they feared, lost their jobs when Scripps-Howard shuttered the *World*, keeping only its legendary name on the new masthead, the *New York World-Telegram*.

Deadline–U.S.A. prophesied how consolidation of newspapers and their owners' preference for personal gain over public good would erode the foundations of democracy. The publisher's greedy heirs are depicted as a public menace, more dangerous than racketeers.

Brooks worshipped the newspaper business, and his film nails the details of a paper's nervous system: the composing room where copy is set, the pneumatic tubes shuttling copy between departments, the thrill of deadline pressure, the quake of presses rumbling to life. Brooks depicted the daily paper as the nerve center of the American metropolis, and he was determined to depict it with "honesty and dignity."

The newspaper business had allowed Brooks to survive the Depression. After dropping out of Temple University in 1931, he bummed around the country, freelancing human interest articles about the lives of folks left homeless in hard times. He had sporadic employment as a sportswriter, a rewrite man, and a cityside reporter. He was never the "star reporter" his PR bio touted, but he worked for dailies in St. Louis, Philadelphia, and New Jersey, and served his last stint as a reporter at the *New York World*—after it had been folded into the *Telegram*—the bitter saga he recounts in *Deadline—U.S.A.*

Brooks wrote the character of managing editor Ed Hutcheson for Humphrey Bogart, but he had to battle studio boss Darryl Zanuck to cast him. Zanuck felt Bogart was no longer a box-office draw. Coming off the legendarily arduous production of *The African Queen*, the actor was adamant that his next project be shot on climate-controlled sets. *The African Queen* hadn't been released, however, and Zanuck couldn't know that an Oscar awaited Bogart. He wanted either Gregory Peck or Richard Widmark—both under contract to Fox—but Brooks, showing spine on only his second film (he'd been a Marine), wouldn't budge off Bogart, who was perfect for the part, due to his inimitable way of projecting cynicism and idealism simultaneously, his stock-in-trade since *Casablanca*.

Bogart had been a Brooks supporter since the writer arrived in Hollywood, having loved his 1945 novel *The Brick Foxhole* (eventually filmed as *Crossfire* [RKO, 1947]). Bogart gave the book to Mark Hellinger, and although Hellinger passed, the producer gave Brooks's career a boost by hiring him to work with John Huston on the script for *The Killers*, made in '46. Instead of giving Brooks screen credit, Hellinger gave him a percentage of the profits, which worked out well when the movie hit big. Brooks then wrote the script for Hellinger's prison yarn *Brute Force* (Universal, 1947), which put his tendency toward preachiness on full display. As an artist, Brooks did not tread lightly—to borrow a Huston analogy, "He was hunting big game," making films with big themes and big ideas. Brooks also wrote the screenplay for Bogart's *Key Largo* (WB, 1948), so he and the actor were compatriots by the time they made *Deadline—U.S.A.* Bogart cared enough for his pal's pet project to spend a week at the *New York Daily News*, studying the editors and reporters.

Much of the film was shot in the *Daily News*'s plant.

The script deploys reporters from every department to dig up dirt on Rienzi, giving plum roles to Audrey Christie ("sob sister" Mrs. Willebrandt), Jim Backus (entertainment columnist Jim Cleary), and Paul Stewart (sportswriter Harry Thompson). All have memorable scenes, as does Ethel Barrymore as the nominal owner of *The Day*, taking Hutcheson's side when she's betrayed by her children. But the heart of *Deadline—U.S.A.* belongs to the victim's mother, Mrs. Schmidt (Kasia Orzazewski), who agrees to turn over evidence against Rienzi, but only to "the boss," the newspaper's editor-in-chief. This character, essentially, is Brooks's mother, Esther. His parents were Russian Jewish immigrants who didn't speak a word of English when they arrived in Philadelphia. They learned the language by studying the daily paper, while they scrimped and saved to cover their son's college tuition. Mrs. Schmidt's speech about the newspaper teaching her to become a good American is Brooks at his best.

Deadline—U.S.A. was released not long after Billy Wilder's *Ace in the Hole*, which was roundly criticized for cynically deriding the media. Both films were made at the midway point of the twentieth century, and while *Deadline—U.S.A.* offered a cautionary take on the potential decline of an independent press—"A free press, like a free life, is always in danger," warns Ed Hutcheson—it is also a valentine to the glory of the newspaper business. *Ace in the Hole*, on the other hand, excoriated the press's sensationalist tendencies, and offered a spot-on prediction of the media circus that would soon permeate the culture.

Despite a rousing finish, in which Bogart gets out one last edition in the face of death threats from Reinzi—"That's the press, baby! And there's nothing you can do about it!"—*Deadline—U.S.A.* ends as a bittersweet eulogy, the sun setting on *The Day* despite the heroic rescue efforts of its editor and loyal staff.

The dominoes are still falling. Richard Brooks's worst fears have come true.

Managing editor Ed Hutcheson (Humphrey Bogart) visits the composing room while getting out the final edition in *Deadline-U.S.A.*

Dick Powell turned in his dancing shoes for a .38 revolver in *Murder, My Sweet*, adapted from Raymond Chandler's novel *Farewell, My Lovely*.

SHAMUS FLATS

ALF THE RYE IN THE BOTTLE HAD DISAPPEARED SINCE I'D SAT BACK TO WATCH THE SUN DROP BEHIND THE ROOFTOPS. IT WAS NO TIME TO HEAR FOOTSTEPS ECHOING IN THE CORRIDOR. ESPECIALLY JANGLING FOOTSTEPS, LIKE SOME COWBOY FORGOT TO DOFF HIS SPURS. I SAW A HULKING SHADOW ON THE PEBBLED GLASS. THE DOOR SLOWLY SWUNG OPEN. BENEATH THE STETSON, HIS FACE WAS CRACKED LIKE SHOE LEATHER. DECADES OF PRAIRIE DUST CLUNG TO HIM. HE DREW HIS COLT, SPUN IT TWICE, AND SLAPPED THE BUTT IN MY OPEN PALM. "YOUR TURN," HE WHISPERED. THEN HE FOLDED OVER, DEADER THAN LAST NIGHT'S FOUR-STAR FINAL.

Somewhere in the mid-1940s the lonesome rider on the range passed the iron to a new icon of macho American independence—another alienated, yet incorruptible lone wolf: the private eye.

Here was a guy who knew all the ins and outs of Dark City. Usually a former cop, he became a thorn in the side of the boys at the precinct when he decided to go solo. Most of his clients drove downtown from Hate Street, seeking some streetwise savvy to locate a lost relative or stray sibling. Without fail, the trail led to Sinister Heights. The retainer: $25 bucks a day, plus expenses. For all the getting around this guy did—especially during wartime rationing—the gas bill must have been a doozy.

Our man was born in *Black Mask*, in the early '20s. You can paddle around in the dark waters of Edgar Allan Poe, panning for antecedents to film noir, but you needn't venture further back than this rough-edged magazine of "pulp" fiction. It was created in 1920 by H. L. Mencken and George Jean Nathan as a lowbrow bookend for the pair's witty and urbane *Smart Set*. They sold their interest prematurely, not anticipating the lode of significant popular fiction that would fill the pages of the tawdry little publication. Joseph T. Shaw, "The Captain," took over as editor in 1926, and became the primary prospector of what would become

known as "hard-boiled" fiction: spare, pull-no-punches fantasies of city-dwelling masculinity and moxie.

In its pages the philosophical underpinnings of noir took root, principally in the work of Dashiell Hammett. Like most writers of the period who slashed verbiage to the lean essentials, Hammett would be compared to Hemingway. No sale. Hammett was his own man, a decidedly original writer. His stories crackled with an aura of immediacy, perfectly targeted to a new type of urban reader. His prose snapped straight at the proles, headed to work on the subway or relaxing after a killer shift. An instinctive storyteller, Hammett never failed to entertain. But he also wove a worldview into the flow, without waxing didactic.

His tales of crime and detection weren't diversions, penned by the "classic" authors of drawing-room intrigues. In old-fashioned mysteries, egghead investigators engaged in games of clever reasoning: Spot the liar. In Hammett's world, deducing the "truth" was a war of attrition; the detective had his work cut out for him, outlasting all the liars. *No one* spoke the truth. There may not have been much "realism" in Hammett's contrived plots, but readers responded to his authentic voice and his cold, clear, cynical ethos.

Hammett's protagonists could have been descendants of James Fenimore Cooper's Natty Bumppo or Mark Twain's Huckleberry Finn. Loners on a quest, men in a sprawling landscape, seeking private vindication in the wilderness, telling their tales in rugged New World vernacular. By the 1920s, the vast frontier had been squeezed off, paved over, forever cheapened. The pathfinder was now relegated to a spare third-floor office in an anonymous downtown walk-up. Randomness, not destiny, became the overriding theme and a code of honor, however quixotic, was all that kept the "hero" afloat. The hard-boiled gumshoe was a soldier in a one-man army.

Hammett's background added weight to his writing. He left home in Maryland at fourteen, scuffling through his "tender years" as a stevedore, railyard freight agent, stock clerk, and cannery worker. In 1915 he answered a classified ad in a Baltimore tabloid, taking a job with the local branch of the Pinkerton National Detective Agency. By twenty-one, he was adept at tradecraft, shadowing suspects, packing heat and using it. A long knife scar on his leg and the indentation of a brick in his skull were lasting mementos of some slipshod technique that helped spur his imminent career change.

Pinkerton's clients were a far cry from Brigid O'Shaughnessy. The agency was mostly involved in industrial work, protecting corporations from employee conspiracies. Pinkertons were often hired as moles and strikebreakers. In a pivotal event in his life, Hammett was assigned to infiltrate the Industrial Workers of the World, which was trying to unionize Anaconda Copper miners in Montana. At first, Hammett exhibited the professional zeal and buried conscience he'd later give his nameless shamus, the Continental Op. He'd adopt alternative identities and pull information out of duped "colleagues." But when Hammett was offered five grand by an Anaconda official to kill IWW organizer Frank Little, he suddenly developed a code of ethics. Little was murdered anyway—by a company-supported lynch mob—and Hammett's worldview snapped into focus. So did his politics: Hammett became a staunch Marxist.

Diagnosed as tubercular when he volunteered for military duty in World War I, Hammett spent the next several years checking in and out of hospitals before finally settling down in San Francisco after marrying one of his nurses, Josephine Annis Dolan. It was largely by the Bay, during the '20s, that the fragile, alcoholic Hammett hammered out his small but influential body of work.

The Continental Op stories for *Black Mask* were vigorous exercises in which Hammett seemed to be limbering up for a big vault. His first novel, *Red Harvest*, serialized in *Black Mask*, was a fast-paced exposé of political corruption that drew heavily on his experience with the Montana copper miners' uprising. The style remains remarkably fresh. Its follow-up, *The Dain Curse*, was an occult-tinged domestic drama that didn't coalesce its serialized origins quite as well.

His third book, *The Maltese Falcon*, was the McCoy. The stuff legends are made of.

Amazingly, for a book emblematic of a whole genre, *The Maltese Falcon* is more character study than whodunit. It revolves around detective Sam Spade's entanglement with a gaggle of double-crossing dervishes, all pursuing the elusive, jewel-encrusted "black bird." Plot takes a back seat to Hammett's exploration of deceit and avarice. The question of "Who done it?" is moot (the murder of Spade's partner, Miles Archer, kick-starts matters and casts a menacing pall, but Archer's already forgotten fifty pages in).

Most detective stories that emerged from Dark City followed this pattern. They had less to do with feats of deduction than they did with the tarnished chivalry and jaundiced attitude of the detective. This was a character trait Hammett made immortal when he penned Spade's kiss-off to the desirable but duplicitous Brigid, or Ruth, or whoever she was that day: "I won't play the sap for you. . . . If I send you over, I'll be sorry as hell—I'll have some rotten nights—but that'll pass."

Warner Bros. paid $8,500 for the movie rights to the *Falcon* but mustered only a pair of smirky offerings from Hammett's masterwork: *Woman of the World* (aka *Dangerous Female*, 1931) and *Satan Met a Lady* (1936). The industry in the 1930s was more in tune with the author's final novel, *The Thin Man*. Full of the boozy banter Hammett exchanged with paramour Lillian Hellman, it generated a remarkably lucrative franchise: comedy capers starring William Powell, Myrna Loy, and a spunky terrier named Asta. (The novel is as overserved as Hammett himself; downing it in one gulp can induce a contact high.)

In 1940, when screenwriter John Huston told Jack Warner that he wanted to

remake *The Maltese Falcon* as his directorial debut, the first spark in a cultural phenomenon was struck. Huston decided not to tinker with a good thing: The director's secretary, Meta Carpenter (who'd later become William Faulkner's Hollywood mistress), put the novel into script form without major changes, and Huston sent it to the boss for approval. Although he had twice demanded tangled reworkings of the same material, Warner now inexplicably commended Huston on "a great script." (Allen Rivkin was given a cowriter credit to keep young Huston from getting too big a head.)

For the first time, Hammett's words were in the care of someone with an affinity for them. "The story was a dramatization of myself, of how I felt about things," Huston said. "Hammett's mentality and philosophy were quite congenial to me." By hewing faithfully to the writer's crisp exposition, Huston crafted the most significant landmark in the development of Hollywood noir.

No small measure of the film's success can be attributed to the ego of actor George Raft. As Warners' top gangster star, Raft had right of first refusal on tough-guy roles. He disdained doing *Falcon* because it was a remake, unbecoming a star of his magnitude. He also begged off because the budget was paltry and Huston was a tyro. Only four days before the cameras were to roll, Warners told Huston he'd have to settle for a leading man from the second tier: Humphrey Bogart. Of course, it was Huston's plan all along to cast his pal and drinking buddy. The director later noted that "If Raft had appeared on the set, I'd have beaten him with a pair of brass knuckles."

Bogart = Spade. Huston caught lightning in a bottle. Bogart had been waiting his whole career for a role like this. He'd transcended his blue-blood birthright, playing menacing gangsters in an assortment of '30s melodramas, but he'd always been left of center, leering in the shadow of Cagney, Robinson, and Raft. And he always died, snarling. Spade was his first bona fide leading man role. He was an antihero now, not an outlaw.

Dashiell Hammett, father of American detective fiction

In his critical appraisal of Bogart, *Take It and Like It*, Jonathan Coe put his finger on the spot where Hammett and Bogart meshed to create a new archetype: "What the audience senses here is not an absence of feeling, but a distant suggestion of feelings so complex that Spade sees no point in bringing them to the surface." Beneath that, he notes, was "a deeper tension, fundamental to the Bogart persona, between an ironic fatalism (his belief that life does not count for much) and an indisputable courage (his will to persevere at all costs, nevertheless)."

Huston cut Bogart a swath through which Spade could swagger. Much of it involved keeping producer Hal Wallis at bay. Throughout production Wallis complained that Bogart had "adopted a leisurely, suave form of delivery [that has] a tendency to drag down the scenes and slow them up too much. Bogart must have his usual brisk, staccato manner and delivery, and if he doesn't have it, I'm afraid we're going to be in trouble." Mary Astor, like Huston, was thrilled by Bogart's fresh approach. "He kept other actors on their toes because he listened to them, he watched them, he looked at them." She recalled that he "related to people as though they had no clothes on. If they grabbed at their various little hypocrisies for protective cover, his laugh was a particularly unpleasant chortle."

Even as the film launched Huston and Bogart on successful careers, Sam Spade's creator was virtually finished. Hammett lived off royalties from his novels and film adaptations, while illness and alcohol drained his creative well. What little energy remained in his tall, elegant frame was channeled into politics, not writing. Various directors offered him assignments, almost out of pity. But Hammett could no longer muster the muse. William Wyler handed him ten grand in 1950 to pass a blue pencil over Sidney Kingsley's play *Detective Story*, but Hammett, clinging to his ethics, returned the advance when he couldn't produce real work.

The witch hunt provided Hammett a stage for a Spade-like final stand. Haggard and spindly, he stood up to the inquisitors, declaring, "I don't let cops or judges tell me what democracy is." Found in contempt of Congress, he served six months at the federal pen in Ashland, Kentucky, where the old man was given light duty: cleaning toilets. Every Friday he'd gather with other inmates to listen to *The Adventures of Sam Spade* on the prison radio.

HAMMETT'S SUCCESSOR AS DEAN of the hard-boiled school had little in common with its founder. Raymond Chandler was a cranky, ill-tempered milquetoast, American-born but English-bred, working as a midlevel oil company executive until he was fired for problem drinking. At the late age of forty-five, Chandler took his first pecks at the typewriter keys, following Hammett's path through the pages of *Black Mask*. In a series of evocative short stories, Chandler molded the golem-like alter ego who would avenge all the humiliations of his life.

Philip Marlowe was a more romanticized vision of the private eye. To Chandler, he was a hero, not just a professional. His code of honor was more rigid than Spade's, and, unlike Hammett's taciturn protagonists, Marlowe tended to erupt in florid soliloquy. Their respective gumshoes were reflections of both men. While Hammett endured life's pain stoically, Chandler ranted over its indignities. If the energy he expended in bitchy letter-writing had been redirected to his fiction, Chandler's canon would be even more impressive.

Over the course of seven novels, Marlowe became Dark City's great soapbox orator. "We've got the big money, the sharpshooters, the percentage workers, the fast-dollar boys, the hoodlums out of New York, Chicago and Detroit," he vents in *The Little Sister*. "We've got the flash restaurants and nightclubs they run, and the hotels and apartment houses they own, and the grifters and con men and female bandits that live in them. The luxury trades, the pansy decorators, the lesbian dress designers, the riffraff of a big hard-boiled city with no more personality than a paper cup."

Despite his contempt for the place, Chandler/Marlowe was in thrall to his perfumed and perverse city. Chandler's Los Angeles was an alluring femme fatale that crushed his heart each time he came back for more. His vision of the sprawling artificial paradise, in which corruption was camouflaged by the glare of sunlight and neon and the fragrance of blooming jacaranda, was so vivid it became the world's adopted perception of Los Angeles, long after the place had all the style leached from it.

A Philip Marlowe Mystery

212

FAREWELL, MY LOVELY

RAYMOND CHANDLER

POCKET BOOK EDITION COMPLETE AND UNABRIDGED

Hollywood could never translate the best of Chandler: the rhythm of his prose, the vulpine verbiage of his descriptive passages, his uncanny ability to paint moods at once exciting and dreadful. Instead, adaptations leaned on his flair for gaudy patter, while trying to cope with the shortcomings of his plots. (Chandler assembled novel-length mysteries by cobbling together elements from his short stories. His plots had none of Hammett's momentum. It was the élan of his prose that made his novels compelling.)

The first two attempts to film Chandler were as bogus as the first two Hammett adaptations. RKO purchased his second novel, *Farewell, My Lovely*, to serve as source material for a film called *The Falcon Takes Over*, one of a series of hour-long programmers based on Leslie Charteris's effete investigator, the Saint. (Charteris groused so loudly about the lousy films made from his books that RKO finally changed the character's name to the Falcon, prompting a lawsuit by the author.) In 1942, Fox bought Chandler's *The High Window* to provide a story line for *Time to Kill*, the last installment of its Michael Shane detective series. Paying Chandler for his plots made as much sense as hiring Rita Hayworth to do voice-overs. Eventually, *someone* had to recognize Chandler's distinctive vision.

That turned out to be Adrian Scott, a theatrical producer from New York just beginning his movie career at RKO. The studio owned the rights to *Farewell, My Lovely*, so it didn't have to pay Chandler another cent. Enlisting the aid of fledgling screenwriter John Paxton and director Edward Dmytryk, a bulwark of the studio's B features, Scott set to work making the first faithful Chandler movie.

Murder, My Sweet, released in late 1944, pruned Chandler's plot to within a mile or two of coherence, and smartly played up his strengths: attitude and ambience. Dmytryk and cameraman Harry Wild displayed many of the visual motifs that would become noir staples: deep shadows, cut by key light; unsettling angles (many lifted from *Citizen Kane*); a dreamy, hypnotic pace accelerating toward inevitable disaster. Scott and Paxton understood that it was the reflective nature of the detective's first-person narration, weary with regret and resignation, that made these stories you could take personally.

Following hard on the heels of *Double Indemnity* (which Chandler coscripted), *Murder, My Sweet* was the back end of a one-two punch that knocked filmgoers—and even more so, filmmakers—for a loop. After those two, things would be done a little differently around town.

Following the success of *Murder, My Sweet*, Jack Warner gave director Howard Hawks $50,000 to buy the rights to Chandler's first novel, *The Big Sleep*. Hawks called up Chandler and asked if he'd like to see Bogart as Marlowe. Chandler was as tickled as a kid at Christmas. Hawks paid him five grand for the rights and pocketed the rest, probably to underwrite one hell of a hunting trip. Chandler and Hammett, like their hard-boiled alter egos, were soft when it came to money. Hammett got a decent payday for the rights to *The Maltese Falcon*, but then spent years wrangling to regain control of Sam Spade, not wanting to believe he'd sold off the name forever. When Chandler signed on as a studio writer in the '40s, he was so overwhelmed by the weekly retainer it never dawned on him to ask for what lesser writers were earning.

Although Dick Powell did a fine job in *Murder, My Sweet*, he couldn't quite conceal his bouncy hoofer's energy beneath a rash of stubble and a rumpled suit. He came off more petulant than world-weary, closer to Chandler perhaps, but wide of the author's romantic ideal. On the other hand, "Bogart was the genuine article," as Chandler bubbled in anticipation of his Marlowe incarnation.

Howard Hawks's film was not, however, as true to Chandler as Dmytryk's. Blame Lauren Bacall. Both Hawks and Bogart were infatuated with the twenty-year-old starlet, whom Hawks had Svengalied into a sexy, self-possessed woman in her debut, *To Have and Have Not* (WB, 1944). It was Bogart who would Have, and Hawks who'd Have Not. Bacall fell hard for the man Bogart had created on the set of *The Maltese Falcon*, and they lived out a romance that seemed to exist in the Hollywood ether. (Mayo Methot was compensated for stepping aside; Bogart was lucky to escape with only flesh wounds.) Hawks overcame his envy of the lovey-dovey stars. His consolation prize was a durable marriage to beautiful, adventurous Nancy Roe Gross—nickname "Slim"—a real-life version of the take-no-guff dames Hawks made his silver screen signature.

While Bogart and Hawks lived large with women half their ages, Chandler doted on his frail wife Cissy, more than twenty years his senior. The code of honor

---

Marlowe (Bogart) has his hands full with the sexy Sternwood siblings, enigmatic Vivian (Lauren Bacall) and her nymphomaniac sister Carmen (Martha Vickers) in Howard Hawks's adaptation of Chandler's *The Big Sleep*.

LEFT: Robert Montgomery's Marlowe had eyes only for Audrey Totter in *The Lady in the Lake.* A lugubrious exercise in subjective camerawork, the film was smug and jokey in ways the blithe *The Big Sleep* avoided. Totter was the main attraction. **RIGHT:** Secretary Lucille Ball gets her boss, PI Mark Stevens, out of numerous jams in *The Dark Corner.*

It's become legend that no one involved in making *The Big Sleep* could make heads or tails of its Byzantine plot, and that Howard Hawks couldn't have cared less. His intuition was dead on. Keeping pace with the PI as he puts his underpaid ass on the line in dangerous settings is what detective fiction is all about. If it somehow hangs together, all the better. But this wasn't film noir. Howard Hawks was too cocksure, too unfettered by doubt and anxiety, to give a damn about the citizens of Dark City. *The Big Sleep* is a terrific piece of tomfoolery, a fantasy that has little to do with Chandler's vision.

Just an aside: The actor best suited to play Marlowe was William Holden. As *Sunset Boulevard.* and *Stalag 17* showed, he could be caustic yet charismatic, and it's easy to picture him smoking a pipe and working out chess problems, like the Marlowe of the novels.

Instead, we're left with actor-director Robert Montgomery's off-base *The Lady in the Lake* (MGM, 1947), in which he attempted a corollary to Chandler's first-person narration by presenting the story entirely from Marlowe's visual viewpoint. This meant awkward scenes of actors playing to the camera's roving eye, while Montgomery, showing no flair for smart-mouth dialogue, cracks wise in voice-over. Cameras were cumbersome in 1947, which meant everything unfolded slowly, a fatal flaw in a detective yarn. A bright spot is Audrey Totter, whose character, Adrienne Fromsett, is beefed up from the novel. She carries the whole affair with an endless repertoire of expressions. Conforming to Hollywood scripture, Marlowe's ascetic pose is dropped for a holiday frolic with Miss Fromsett.

By the time Montgomery sank *The Lady in the Lake*, the tough-talking private dick had already veered into satire. *The Dark Corner* (Fox, 1946) got excitement, and laughs, out of contrasting lowly gumshoe Bradford Galt (Mark Stevens) with society gadfly Hardy Cathcart (Clifton Webb). The original screenplay by Jay Dratler and Bernard Schoenfeld combined the private eye formula with the

the author ingrained in Marlowe had a streak of sexual repression. During his Hollywood years, Chandler was torn between loyalty to his elderly wife and the temptation of beautiful young women as bountiful as wild berries on the backlots. Chandler's libidinous conflicts seeped into poor, unmarried Marlowe.

By contrast, breezy sexual byplay was the stock-in-trade of Hawks's men and women. *The Big Sleep* was made to cash in on the chemistry of its stars, and their badinage became the core of the film. Chandler's supporting characters hung around the periphery while Bogey and Bacall swapped insinuating bon mots, some scripted by William Faulkner and Jules Furthman, brought in to spice up Leigh Brackett's adaptation. Release of the film was delayed a year after Warners decided it wanted even more innuendo slung between the two. When Bogart wasn't back-chatting Bacall, he made time with women who went into heat at the sight of him. This Marlowe would have snorted at the one in the novel—the one who tore apart his bed after Carmen Sternwood had the temerity to lay her nude body on his pure sheets.

upper-crust milieu depicted in *Laura* (Fox, 1944), in which Webb played the exact same character. Surveying the crowd at his gala, Cathcart remarks with practiced disdain that it's "a nauseating mixture of Park Avenue and Broadway—it proves I'm a liberal." Meanwhile, down in the flats, Galt tells his smitten secretary Kathleen (Lucille Ball), "If you're sharp you'll get out now. Fast. I got a feeling I'm behind the eight ball. Something's gonna happen. And when it does, you'll end up right in the corner pocket." It had been only five years since *The Maltese Falcon* made the private dick an icon, but *The Dark Corner* already felt like a parody. There would be a blast of transcendence, however.

Out of the Past (RKO, 1947) burst the bonds of the PI formula, favoring a head-long plunge into the self-destructive psyche of its private eye. Daniel Mainwaring (as Geoffrey Homes) constructed an involuted tale that owned up to what most films in the genre only hinted at: These are tales about the protagonist's quest for solutions to his own problems, not his client's. And *Out of the Past* presented one of the sexiest, and most vulnerable of detective heroes.

Jeff Markham (Robert Mitchum) is half of a two-man, nickel-and-dime detective agency. He's called to Sinister Heights by glib gangster Whit Sterling (Kirk Douglas), who wants his girlfriend, Kathie Moffatt (Jane Greer), tracked down. Seems she lifted forty grand, leaving Whit a deposit of two low-caliber slugs. Markham tells partner Jack Fisher (Steve Brodie) that they'll split the skip-trace fee, but he'll chase the skirt solo. The trail leads to Mexico, and as soon as Jeff spots Kathy gliding from punishing sunlight into the languid dimness of La Mar Azul cantina, it's hasta la vista.

"I went to Pablo's that night," he sighs. "I knew I'd go every night until she showed up. I knew she knew it. I sat there and I drank bourbon and I shut my eyes, but I didn't think of a joint on 56th St. I knew where I was and what I was doing. What a sucker I was."

Kathy's wise to Jeff, figuring he's come to arrest her. If Jeff provides her protection, she proposes, they can parlay their affair into full-time bliss. So Jeff

TOP: Private eye Jeff Markham (Robert Mitchum) walks willingly into the web of duplicitous Kathie Moffatt (Jane Greer) in *Out of the Past*. BOTTOM: . . . but Jeff and Kathie can't escape racketeer Whit Sterling (Kirk Douglas).

sandbags Whit and he and Kathy hightail it to a new life. "I opened an office in San Francisco. A cheap little rathole that suited the work I did. Shabby jobs for whoever would hire me. It was the bottom of the barrel and I scraped it. But I didn't care—I had her."

Their idyll comes to an end when Jeff is spotted by his old partner, Fisher: "He just stood there with our lives in his pocket, because I knew if he ever saw her he'd sell us both for a dollar-ninety-five." So the lovers split up, Jeff taking his shadow on a wild goose chase around Southern California. When Fisher catches up, Jeff tries to persuade his partner he's all wrong about Kathy. They promote rights and lefts off their respective chins. Kathy doesn't fancy long arguments: one pop from the handgun in her purse and Fisher's finished. While Jeff fires up a smoke to collect his thoughts, Kathy takes a powder, leaving Jeff to bury the body.

And that's barely the halfway point. Whit comes back in the picture, he and Kathie reunite, Jeff is seduced by her again, Jeff pulls a switcheroo on Whit—there's three movies' worth of plot crammed into the last half. It shouldn't work. But . . .

Out of the Past was the most spellbinding film yet to emerge from Dark City. It invigorated genre clichés with depth and style. Mainwaring's serpentine story is all about mood and movement, dreamily winding its way through various locations, shifting rhythms, seducing the audience toward the black hole at its heart. It nailed the bull's-eye and its reverberations linger after repeated viewings: guilt, duplicity, self-deception, and the lonely hero's need to push it to the bitter end, tempting fate once too often.

For director Jacques Tourneur and director of photography Nicholas Musuraca, *Out of the Past* was a career high point. Tourneur was so suited to this material, it's a crime he only made one other bona fide noir, *Nightfall* (Columbia, 1957). Born in Paris but raised in the States, Tourneur was the son of French director Maurice Tourneur, who'd made hundreds of films in his homeland and Hollywood. Jacques grew up on soundstages and by the early '40s he was directing for innovative RKO producer Val Lewton. The duo made a remarkable series of visually inspired, low-budget horror films: *Cat People* (1942), *I Walked with a Zombie* (1943), and *The Leopard Man* (1943). Tourneur could have been another Robert Siodmak, excelling at crime dramas, but instead he specialized in period costume dramas, such as *Stars in My Crown* (MGM, 1950), *Anne of the Indies* (Fox, 1951), and *Way of the Gaucho* (Fox, 1952).

In *Out of the Past*, Tourneur's mise en scène is extraordinary. No film better realized the swirl of shifting locations that made pulp fiction intoxicating: New York to Mexico to Frisco to Tahoe. Ritzy penthouse to smoky cantina to moonlit beach to opulent apartment to roadside filling station to swank nightclub to lakefront lodge. With each new scene, we share the rush of excitement drawing Mitchum deeper into limbo. Musuraca painted light and shadow on the settings with the touch of a master. Rather than casting stark swatches of light and dark, à la John Alton, he used soft fill lights to reveal a set's details, then played dramatically with the key lights on the actors. It's the richest chiaroscuro in any noir.

The actors also showed up ready to play. Kirk Douglas was never better than when his brash hamminess was channeled into nasty villains, and he electrifies whenever he appears, a squirmy portrayal of a man too rich, too handsome, too ruthless. Jane Greer's cunning eyes betray a venality not apparent in her angelic face. She vamps into the ranks of cinematic Circes, second to none.

Then there's Mitchum—the rolling piano theme beneath Kirk's insistent bass and Jane's sexy saxophone. He hit the set with fresh wounds from real-life crime. His business manager and "best friend," Paul Behrmann, had siphoned the actor's bank account down to fifty-eight bucks, while doling out a weekly $20 stipend to his stake horse. Mitchum didn't press charges. When Behrmann was nailed for more fiscal malfeasance, he tried to hang the rap on Mitchum.

To medicate his woes, Mitchum fired up more reefer—as if he needed to get more languorous. After being busted for pot possession in 1948, it looked like *Out of the Past* would remain Mitchum's most memorable star turn. At the booking, he gave his occupation as "former actor." But RKO stood by him; it had three more of his films in the can. Mitchum's 'tude in jailhouse photos, swabbing a cell block, got him over. The public loved him like the black sheep of the family. On release, reporters asked the actor what he'd thought of jail. "Just like Palm Springs," he cracked, "Without the riffraff."

The actor's greatest gift was his way with language, his own or the writers'. Consider this exchange from *Out of the Past*: "Don't you see," Greer tells Mitchum after dispatching Kirk Douglas, "you'll only have me to make deals with now."

"Then build my gallows high, baby." Only Mitchum could toss off such a deliriously stilted line and make it as fluid as hard bop.

DARK CITY'S
BEATNIK COWPOKE

I t's fitting that Robert Mitchum started out in westerns. The saunter in his gait and languor of his speech branded him a cowboy, worn out from a hard day's work, hankering for a roll in the hay or a quiet, thoughtful smoke.

It was an image that came easily to him. Mitchum spent his fatherless youth wandering America, working as a deckhand, coal miner, roustabout, whatever got him down the road. "In those days motion itself seemed an adequate philosophy for me," he'd later say. "Moving around like I did, though, I could be just any place, not high maybe but somehow alone and free." His take-it-as-it-comes attitude assumed larger-than-life proportions once he became a leading man.

Not everyone was impressed. "You can't act," Katharine Hepburn told him on the set of *Undercurrent* (MGM, 1946), her lone trip to noir territory, "and if you hadn't been good-looking you would never have gotten the picture. I'm tired of playing with people who have nothing to offer." Mitchum loved to recount the moment, with a dead-on impersonation of haughty Miss Hepburn.

For a guy who couldn't act, Mitchum made some memorable movies in the '40s: *When Strangers Marry* (Monogram, 1944); *The Story of G. I. Joe* (UA, 1945), which earned him an Oscar nomination; Raoul Walsh's noir western *Pursued* (WB, 1947); and *Blood on the Moon* (RKO, 1948), another revisionist sagebrush saga.

When Mitchum drifted into Dark City, where the prairie was paved over in asphalt, his eyes betrayed a wariness that any chance for a free life was lost. In *Out of the Past* (RKO, 1947), he was the quintessential noir protagonist: neither hero nor crook, just a guy trying to go his own way, at his own pace. His pose was rough as bark, hiding the sap at his core. He surveyed

Jean Simmons leads Mitchum straight to hell in *Angel Face*.

moral wreckage with a jaundiced gaze, but you sensed compassion stashed in his hip pocket, on the off chance he'd find a woman easy to love.

Such dames were rare at RKO, where Mitchum described himself as "a tall dog on a short leash." Once in a while he'd find *His Kind of Woman* (1951)—a lusty, laid-back doll like Jane Russell. But studio head Howard Hughes liked pictures about demented women with gorgeous faces and diseased souls who toppled the toughest studs. Maybe Mitchum was Hughes's fantasy image of himself.

The zenith—or nadir—of Mitchum's susceptibility to feminine wiles came with *Angel Face* (1953). Screenwriters Frank Nugent and Oscar Millard reduced Chester Erskine's unpublished story into a black roux. Otto Preminger, working with a crafty veteran crew, took only nineteen days

to concoct a film that's suffocating in its morbid sense of entrapment and futility.

Mitchum plays ambulance driver Frank Jessup, another cowboy out of time. Frank meets twenty-year-old heiress Diane Tremayne (played with a touch of narcolepsy by dreamy Jean Simmons) when he is called to her family's hilltop mansion in response to the near-fatal asphyxiation of Diane's stepmother. Accident or attempted murder?

The question is moot as soon as Frank lays eyes on Diane, spookily playing the piano while the life-and-death commotion transpires. Word that

her mother will survive brings a tearful overreaction from Diane, and Frank applies his limited medical know-how—he slaps her across the face to stem the hysteria. She slaps him right back, hard and unhesitating, her depthless black eyes brimming with an eroticized instability.

Start making up a room in hell for these two.

Frank accepts a job as the Tremaynes' chauffeur, sampling the largesse of their affluence and the illicit charms of their daughter. He's soon in thrall to the lazy and spoiled Diane, even after he tips to the twisted truth: Diane and Daddy are the real lovebirds, and Stepmom must go. And go she does, hurtling backwards over the cliff in the couple's land-yacht convertible. But Daddy goes too, in a twist that fate wedges into Angel Face's devious scheme.

At every turn, Frank has the chance to return to the good graces of his girlfriend Mary, the hardworking, sensible mother-in-waiting. But Frank thinks he can have his cake and eat it, too. He's the prize over whom Mary and Diane battle, and Frank makes the fatal mistake of thinking his insouci-ance will let him slip the worst punch any woman can throw. Diane pays a steep price to teach him otherwise.

Jean Simmons came hot on the heels of Faith Domergue, who had

Faith Domergue shows Mitchum *Where Danger Lives.*

previously shown Mitchum *Where Danger Lives* (1950). Domergue was a Howard Hughes "project," which meant she spent almost a decade as a well-kept captive in his Hollywood harem. The mogul had notions of molding her into another Jane Russell, whom he'd hyped to sex-bomb status in *The Outlaw* (1941).

In *Where Danger Lives*, Domergue is Margo Lannington, a full-figured fruitcake wed to wealthy San Franciscan Frederick Lannington (Claude Rains). She seduces Dr. Jeff Cameron (Mitchum), convincing him that Rains is her father. Learning he's been duped, Dr. Jeff accidentally knocks Lannington out in a brief scuffle. While he seeks first aid, Margo polishes off her husband, then talks her new beau into taking it on the lam. Jeff follows, concussed but obedient. He eventually turns on his master in a sleaze pit near the Mexican border. Margo administers the doctor a hot lead injection and tries to make the border alone. Staggering after her in the street, Jeff fingers her for the Federales; she gets riddled. After that, you'd think he'd have wised up.

By the mid-'50s, Mitchum was done playing the sap. He'd show the liars and double-crossers how bad it could really get. As psychotic evangelist Harry Powell in *Night of the Hunter* (UA, 1955), he tortured women and children without remorse. As sadistic rapist Max Cady in *Cape Fear* (Universal, 1962), the cowboy drifted all the way into darkness, brandishing his lazy carnality as a weapon—sly smile still in place, conscience completely gone.

Mitchum enjoyed a revival in the '70s, starring in *The Friends of Eddie Coyle* (Paramount, 1973), one of his best films, and *The Yakuza* (WB, 1975), an intriguing hybrid of gangster, western, and samurai genres. It was, however, too late for him to effectively portray Philip Marlowe in remakes of *Farewell, My Lovely* (Avco Embassy, 1975) and the disastrous British version of *The Big Sleep* (ITC, 1978). He kept his career going deep into the 1990s, showing how far a little insolence can take you in this town, even when you make a habit of succumbing to temptation.

By the early '50s, the American gumshoe was weary to the bone. Chandler's last two major novels, *The Little Sister* and *The Long Goodbye*, were masterful in their prose, but Marlowe was more likely to be bellyaching over a chilled gimlet than chasing a hot lead. Chandler nosed around in the legit literary landscape he'd always wanted to explore, but his drinking tightened the tap on his output.

Hastening him to pasture was the success of Marlowe's evil twin, Mike Hammer. As Chandler struggled to work without a net—forced to craft original story lines once his lode of short stories was fully mined—Mickey Spillane started churning out detective novels that pushed hard-boiled around the bend, toward psychotic. The dilemma of a chivalrous hero acting honorably in a corrupt world was disassembled by Spillane: His Hammer was a righteous killing machine. If Mike felt you'd done him—or his country—wrong, he'd stomp a mudhole in your chest and walk it dry.

Brooklyn-born Spillane wrote comic books, served in the Army Air Corps in World War II, and pumped out his first potboiler in nineteen days. They came at a brisk clip after that, each fat advance making him among the highest-paid authors in the world.

The title of the first Hammer novel, *I, the Jury*, cut to the heart of the Spillane phenomenon. It was published in 1947, as the anti-Commie crowd fueled "patriotic" hysteria. Hammer rode the reactionary wave, pummeling anyone who didn't conform to conservative, berserk, misogynist values. A far cry from the apolitical knights-errant of Hammett and Chandler, Hammer wallowed in half-baked ideology. "So I was a sucker for fighting a war," he bellows in *One Lonely Night*. "I was a sap for liking my country. I was a jerk for not thinking them [the Reds] a superior breed of lice!"

Marlowe was a misfit; Hammer was a misanthrope. He hated everybody. Where Spade pitted his antagonists against each other, and Marlowe wearily

Sometimes you *can* judge a book by its cover.

prescribed himself another shot of wry, Hammer waded in and busted heads. The violence is like pornography. To quote from *My Gun Is Quick*: "I rolled on top of him and took his head like a sodden rag and smashed and smashed and smashed and there was no satisfying, solid stomp, but a sickening squashing sound that splashed all over me."

Dash and Ray had been doppelgängers of their detectives. So it seemed was Mickey: a mercenary at the typewriter, pounding out prose the way Hammer pounded out Commie teeth. Spillane sported a jarhead's flattop. Promo stills showed him smacking dames around. It was all a put-on, but the vast audience hungry for this sex and blood smorgasbord was *not* in on the joke. In sales, Spillane beat the pulp out of both Hammett and Chandler, selling by some estimates as many as sixty million books by 1953.

The movies couldn't keep up. Producer Victor Saville tried to make a splash with a 3-D version of *I, the Jury* (UA, 1953), starring Biff Elliot and Peggie Castle. The only thrill was seeing DP John Alton's glorious black and white cinematography in three dimensions. Yet the hype of Hammer's misogyny was shameless. PR flacks quoted Elliot saying, "Women readers go for Mike Hammer because they like the way he handles his girls. He'd as soon hit them as kiss them, and somehow that sort of treatment appeals to the latent atavism in women."

But fireworks never ignited on-screen. There was no way Hollywood's Production Code would allow theater screens to be splashed with the bodily fluids Spillane enthusiasts craved—although a wild scene of sadomasochistic bondage in Saville's Hammer-less follow-up, *The Long Wait* (UA, 1954), came damn close.

It wasn't until 1955 that a memorable movie would be built around America's favorite unglued gumshoe. *Kiss Me Deadly* (UA, 1955) held surprises for Hammer's diehard fans. Adapted by writer A. I. Bezzerides and director Robert Aldrich, the film both exploited and lampooned Spillane's casual sadism and breakneck

momentum. As Hammer, Ralph Meeker shattered the detective's code of honor as cavalierly as he snaps one informant's cherished 78 of Caruso's *Pagliacci*. This Hammer was the thickest and most vain dick ever.

Mr. Hammer's wild ride begins when he nearly runs down a barefoot woman (Cloris Leachman) bolting in terror down a desolate highway. She's on the lam from the nuthouse and begs Hammer to shepherd her to safety. Mystery men waylay them, and the woman is tortured to death in a roadside shack. Hammer, unconscious, is crammed in the car with her body, and they're sent over a cliff.

Once recovered, Hammer grudgingly pursues the mystery of the dead woman. He'd rather be squeezing big fees from husbands and wives in ugly divorce cases, using loyal aide Velda (Maxine Cooper) to set up philandering guys while he handles the wives. Mike and his moll are no better than all the other scumballs. But their dodge keeps Hammer outfitted with all the latest perks of American manhood: fast cars, vintage booze, electronic gizmos.

Hammer's not a textbook investigator. He meanders around indiscriminately intimidating people. His efforts spin threads of a plot, but he's too numbskulled to stitch it together. Undercover operators tire of his tenacity and take a few more cracks at killing him. This makes Hammer madder, but no smarter. But when they execute his mechanic—*the* essential person in his life—it becomes a vendetta. The trail leads to a locker at the Hollywood Athletic Club. Hammer scopes a strapped-up strongbox. Its seething contents burn his wrists. Turns out it's a batch of nuclear material swiped from the Los Alamos Nuclear Test Site. This really makes Mike's head hurt.

None of this was in the novel. Spillane's original climaxes, like most, with a jolting juxtaposition of sex and death. Sexpot Lily Carver emerges as the villain, and, as she pumps a couple of slugs into Hammer, she tantalizingly doffs her robe to reveal that *There was no skin, just a disgusting mass of twisted, puckered flesh from her knees to her neck making a picture of gruesome freakishness that made you want to shut your eyes against it.* Hammer lights a Lucky to soothe his nerves, then zaps Lily with his Zippo, igniting her. Did I forget to mention she'd "brought the sharpness of an alcohol bath in with her, so that it wet her robe . . ."?

Bezzerides coaxes this crazy climax to apocalyptic heights. Lily (Gaby Rodgers), an unscarred, pixieish Pandora, can't resist a peek inside the strongbox everyone's died to get their hands on. Hissing like a harbinger of hell, the incendiary contents swallow her whole. Hammer tries to pull Velda to safety as Lily flares up like the Human Torch. Then everything blows sky high and THE END zooms out of the firestorm. Viewers could only interpret it literally, nuclear annihilation being at the core of the Cold War paranoia that defined the 1950s.

It would be learned, decades later, that this shocking ending was a mistake, executed—purposefully or accidentally—without the director's knowledge. The scripted ending, in which Mike and Velda escape the explosion, was discovered and restored—diluting hundreds of critical dissertations that heralded *Kiss Me Deadly* as a subversive depiction of America on the brink of Armageddon.

FEDORAS WERE OUT BY THE EARLY '60S; the new hero sported a crop of thick hair, à la President Kennedy. Even he was a fan of the new macho icon, James Bond. Once America became obsessed with the space race, and the Cold War's flashy technologies, the rumpled shamus was trampled by a stampede of Matt Helms, Derek Flints, Men from U.N.C.L.E.—suave playboys saving a cool op-art world from tractor beams and death rays.

A couple of '60s films took the old-school shamus out for one more lap around the track. Paul Newman loaned his laconic cool to the archetype in *Harper* (WB, 1966), based on a novel by Chandler's successor as the quintessential California mystery writer, Ross Macdonald. Screenwriter William Goldman and director Jack Smight created an updated version of *The Big Sleep*, right down to casting Lauren Bacall as one of Harper's female foils. The lead was originally intended for Frank Sinatra, who then tried to replicate Newman's success by shifting the setting to Florida and imitating his idol, Bogart, as *Tony Rome* (Fox, 1967). Sinatra enlisted some stalwarts from the original noir era—director Gordon Douglas, writer Richard L. Breen, and costar Richard Conte—and the film was solid enough to rate a sequel, *Lady in Cement* (Fox, 1968). Sinatra was trying to revive the hard-boiled humor of '40s noir for a new generation, but the mix of sass, sauce, and sex made for an out-of-date and unappetizing cocktail.

It wasn't until 1974 that a film finally made good on the cinematic promise of Dashiell Hammett and, especially Raymond Chandler. But *Chinatown* (Paramount) was no mere homage. It extended their bleak vision. Woven into its plot is a bitter rumination on human progress, how the rapaciousness that drives a father to corrupt his own daughter is also what erects majestic cities in the desert.

Screenwriter Robert Towne spent two years fashioning a narrative that combined a detective story with the sprawling fact-based history of the Owens Valley water scam, central to the development of Los Angeles. An LA vice cop who'd worked Chinatown told him, "You don't know who's a crook and who isn't a crook. So in Chinatown they say, 'Just don't do a goddamn thing.'"

The resulting 180-page script was ambitious and unwieldy, but producer Robert Evans sensed a hit in the tangled narrative. He was eager to deliver another huge success like *The Godfather*, without having to share credit with coproducers. Evans's smartest move was hiring director Roman Polanski, whose familiarity with evil would bring black depths to a project most participants considered a dip in the Hollywood nostalgia pool. Polanski and Towne collaborated for two combative months, emerging with a shooting script that charted a brilliant course toward an uncertain destination—they couldn't agree on an ending. Filming commenced nonetheless.

The production was pure alchemy. Running feuds and temper tantrums tested each participant's mettle, but everyone produced gold. Cinematographer John Alonzo and production designer Richard Sylbert conjured the spoiled paradise of Chandler's LA, avoiding the curse of retro-nostalgia that dragged down the florid version of *Farewell, My Lovely* (Avco-Embassy) released the same year. Polanski's elegant direction evoked Chandler's first-person prose without resorting to gimmicks or voiceover.

J. J. "Jake" Gittes (Jack Nicholson) is a fastidious PI who manages to keep his natty suits cleaned and pressed while rummaging through clients' dirty laundry. A former cop, he gloats about escaping the beat, and basks in the reflective glow of glittery Hollywood, where he never runs out of divorce cases. But then he's played as a pawn in a plot to discredit Hollis Mulwray, an official in the Department of Water and Power who's blocking a massive dam project crucial to the city's growth. Gittes thinks he's handling another simple, sordid case of adultery. But as he wades

deeper into the lives of Mulwray and his mysterious wife, Evelyn (Faye Dunaway), he uncovers a flood of conspiracies—personal and political. At the mouth of the polluted stream lies civic power broker Noah Cross (John Huston, whose presence fuses the noir circuit). Gittes realizes that solving the case means laying bare the ugly truth about one of the city's most powerful and respected founding fathers. The amoral Cross has raped more than a bunch of Okie orange growers; for decades he's committed crimes of both power and passion.

"Most people never have to face the fact," Cross says, "that at the right time, in the right place, a man is capable of just about *anything*." Engrave *that* on a plaque outside the Dark City Hall of Justice. Gittes struggles to untangle the web of corruption Cross has woven across the arid basin, gamely trying to prove that a couple of little pups can somehow survive in a world of heartless predators.

Nicholson's performance is crafty and deep. He displays subtle allusions to noir avatars: Bogart's sass-mouth delivery and flourish with a cigarette, Mitchum's flirtatious insolence, Alan Ladd's overcompensating sartorial splendor—references painting a melancholy portrait of a guy propping up his low-rent reality on crutches of wish fulfillment.

Like the Hollywood hero he wants to be, Gittes falls for Evelyn and risks all in an attempt to save her. In Towne's original script, Evelyn exacts her revenge, shooting her incestuous father to death in a rainstorm that ends LA's drought. She and Gittes cling to each other in a rousing, old-fashioned fade-out. Evans and Towne could hear the audience's applause for such a richly evocative piece of pure entertainment. A throwback to the classics. But this was to be Roman Polanski's film. Few filmmakers are as darkly cynical. Fewer still have earned the attitude as painfully.

Polanski wrote the finale the night before it was shot. All the main characters converge on a Chinatown street. Gittes hopes to pull off a parlay: Sneak Evelyn and her daughter Katherine off to Ensenada, while handing over the murderous Noah Cross to the cops. But everything goes horribly wrong. The police arrest Gittes

Jake Gittes (Jack Nicholson) and Evelyn Mulwray (Faye Dunaway) in *Chinatown*, the film that finally cashed in on the cinematic promise of Raymond Chandler's novels.

instead. The distraught Evelyn tries to flee. A trigger-happy flatfoot squeezes off a lucky shot. Dark City holds its collective breath as the horn on Evelyn's Packard convertible starts to wail. A crowd gathers around the car. Evelyn slumps from the driver's seat, shot through the head. Katherine screams uncontrollably, unable to look away from her dead mother. Cross wraps his massive paw across her eyes; she's now in the clutches of the monster who spawned her. Gittes stares slack-jawed, engulfed by futility. "Forget it, Jake. It's Chinatown."

Towne hated Polanski's ending, calling it "The tunnel at the end of the light." Polanski responded: "I thought it was a serious movie, not an adventure story for the kids." The final version of this great film belongs to a man who survived a childhood of punishment by Nazis in a Warsaw ghetto, and used artistic ambition

and talent to work his way from Poland to the sunny splendor of Hollywood—only to have his wife and friends slaughtered by the Manson family. Then the "victim" became the predator, with Polanski's rape of an underage model adding an additional layer of nihilism to his brutal life story. Yet it's his scarred vision that transformed *Chinatown* from a beautifully crafted diversion into the ultimate noir detective story.

VIXENVILLE

DON'T BOTHER LOOKING FOR A CHURCH IN THIS PART OF TOWN. THE AIR'S TOO HOT AND HEAVY FOR HYMNS. NOT THAT YOU CAN'T FIND HOUSES OF WORSHIP. CHECK OUT THE WINDOWS, FLICKERING IN THE NIGHT LIKE OFFERTORY CANDLES. WITHIN THE ROOMS ARE SUPPLICATORY MEN, ON THEIR KNEES, PRAYING FOR A DIFFERENT KIND OF SALVATION. THEY BRING TO THE ALTAR GIFTS OF FRAGRANCES AND LACE, HOPING THEY'LL BE JUDGED WORTHY. MOST WILL END UP CRUCIFIED, FOR BELIEVING THAT HOLINESS COMES WRAPPED IN SEAMED SILK, REDEMPTION STRETCHED SHEER AROUND A SHAPELY CALF.

Welcome to the spiritual center of our community. Home to dozens of luminescent, enigmatic goddesses. Some concerned citizens tried to quarantine this part of town, claiming what went on here was degrading and immoral. Tales emanating from these parts, they charged, were an insult to the fairer sex, making all females seem manipulative, coldhearted, and evil. Not all, exactly—just the interesting ones.

Naysayers believe that because women are nurturers, responsible for the propagation and care of the species, they aren't capable of the same terrible behavior as men. Tell it to the victims of Livia, Augustus Caesar's scheming wife. She bumped off scores of friends and countrymen, tightening her hold over ancient Rome, the original Dark City. Power-mad women are smart enough not to bloody their own hands. That's what men are for.

"Women encourage killers," says scientist and philosopher Howard Bloom, in *The Lucifer Principle*. "They do it by falling in love with warriors and heroes. Men know it and respond with enthusiasm. The Crusaders marched off to war with ladies' favors in their helmets. . . . The heroes sliced up adults and baked infants on spits, all the while thinking of how the damsels back home would admire their bravery."

In every species in the animal kingdom, Bloom argues, females develop a craving for a certain kind of guy, and males compete to live up to that ideal. "And what have human females gone for in nearly every society and time? 'Courage' and 'bravery.' In short, violence."

In a civilized society, women want a man who provides security. But who's talking about a civilized society? The Second World War had just killed seventy-five million people and left the surviving soldiers shaken by the extremity of human savagery. They'd seen grunts in the trench who'd said their prayers every night still take a round flush in the face. Back home they peered through the windows of restaurants they couldn't afford, watching councilmen and criminals order off the same menu. These guys needed something to believe in, something more immediately attainable than the everlasting kingdom of heaven. They found it, or so they thought, in the glorious peaks and valleys of Vixenville.

This is no place to raise a family—although you'll find plenty of fathers coming crosstown from Hate Street, blowing the kids' tuition on diamond earrings and champagne cocktails. Some of the women here started out as gawky kids in

A face to die for: noir glamour-puss Lizabeth Scott

Hoboken, but they learned that a little rouge and a lot of attitude can make a deity of a simple dame. What they're offering isn't straight-laced, soldier-for-the-church sex. It's a chance at transcendence.

Stella (Linda Darnell), a gorgeous hash slinger who worked in a crummy café in a little town off the highway, knew all about that. Men saw her as a *Fallen Angel* (Fox, 1945). One of the smitten, a transient grifter named Eric Stanton (Dana Andrews), hatched a cruel plot to win her love. Since Stella was only interested in men who could pay her way out of this jerkwater, Stanton courted the monied and virginal June Mills (Alice Faye). After he'd tapped her family fortune, he planned to drop June and run off with Stella. But Stella ended up murdered. There's no shortage of suspects: They worshipped daily at her Formica altar, sipping coffee and dreaming of how they might sample the delights within her snug uniform. Stella was only one of many women in Dark City sacrificed on the slab of a man's thwarted desire.

But women weren't always the victims. Although the times dictated fables in which the renegade double-X chromosome must be vanquished before the fade-out, noir allowed women to savor for themselves the acrid nectar of unleashed power and violence. "A dame with a rod is like a guy with a knitting needle," cracks Jack Fisher (Steve Brodie) in *Out of the Past*. Of course, that's before he gets an extra orifice blown open, compliments of Kathie Moffatt (Jane Greer), one of Vixenville's empresses. There's no greater kick in this town than when a woman finally wraps her delicate fingers around the trigger of a .38 Lingham and blasts

The erotic heart of noir: Sensuous Stella (Linda Darnell) drives men to murder in *Fallen Angel* (Fox, 1945). Darnell was another example of a young woman, pushed by her mother, chosen by the priests of her tribe to serve as exalted movie star. At twenty-one, she married the man who shot her screen test. The union fell apart as Darnell struggled to maintain her image as a two-dimensional goddess. She was infertile, and unable to sustain long-term relationships. She pondered suicide. Watching one of her old films, Darnell fell asleep while smoking. The resulting fire burned her to death. She was forty-three. "My problems were not those of my real self," she once said, "but a sort of synthetic, unreal self known as 'Linda Darnell.'"

A very much alive Laura Hunt (Gene Tierney) ends up competing with her own dreamy image in the mind of Mark McPherson (Dana Andrews), the detective assigned to investigate her "death."

away every bit of genetic encoding and cultural repression in a roaring fusillade of little lead forget-me-nots.

IN AN OPULENT FOURTH-FLOOR APARTMENT at a swank East Side address lives Laura Hunt. She's the heart of the most famous murder case ever to unfold in this neighborhood. The protagonist of *Laura* (Fox, 1944) isn't a schemer or a calculating bitch, just a naïve beauty whose only crime was a determination to live by her own free will. But she inspired a devotion in others that led to obsession and murder.

When Laura (Gene Tierney) is found dead in the entryway of her apartment, her face obliterated by a shotgun blast, Detective Mark McPherson (Dana Andrews) is assigned the case. He encounters suspects a world apart from the usual street rabble. There's fey columnist Waldo Lydecker (Clifton Webb), who runs Wilde: "In my case self-absorption is completely justified. I have never found any other subject quite so worthy of my attention." There's also Southern playboy Shelby Carpenter (Vincent Price) and jealous society woman Ann Treadwell (Judith Anderson). Even Laura's servant, Bessie (Dorothy Adams), seems unnaturally devoted to the young beauty.

McPherson's in no hurry to solve the crime. In fact, the case conjures in him a bewildering vision of the late enchantress. He secretly makes arrangements to buy the portrait of Laura that hangs above her mantle. "You better watch out, McPherson, or you'll end up in a psychiatric ward," chides Lydecker. "I don't think they've ever had a patient who fell in love with a corpse."

But when Laura walks back into her apartment—still alive and none the worse for wear—McPherson is spurred to action. Not only does he have to uncover the identity of the faceless corpse, he has to compete for Laura's affections in a league where he's way out of his depth. In a battle of wits with Waldo, McPherson's unarmed.

Although it's little more than a succession of dialogue scenes, *Laura* mesmerizes, due, in no small measure, to a quick-witted script and the erotic tension pulsing beneath the high-gloss surfaces. Sexual drives are strong, but orientations are ambiguous. Waldo appears decidedly gay, and even Shelby's manner seems lushly lavender. Lydecker's love of Laura is ascetic, but there's a spark of something in the way he sizes up McPherson. Most of the film's messages are couched in sidelong

Early rushes stank, so Zanuck buried the hatchet (in Mamoulian), passing the directorial reins to Otto. Aided by brilliant cinematographer Joseph LaShelle, who'd win in Oscar for his work, Preminger crafted what he felt would be his breakthrough film. An advance screening was held for Zanuck and his yes-men. They all hated it. Too confusing, they said. Zanuck demanded a new ending, filmed to his specs. Preminger, not yet the autocrat he'd become, consented. Weeks later, another preview. All assembled panned it anew—except a visitor in the back row. Walter Winchell, the most powerful newspaper columnist and radio broadcaster in the nation, raved to Zanuck. "Darryl, that was big time—*big time*—great, great, great! But are you going to change the ending? What's happening at the end? I don't understand." Zanuck let Preminger restore his finale. Another classic managed to steal its way out of the Dream Factory.

The film's eighty-eight minutes of elegant moodiness still beguiles viewers. *Laura* cast a spell on its players, as well. For the rest of his career, Clifton Webb would play some variation of Waldo Lydecker, most famously the cantankerous "Mr. Belvedere" of the 1950s film series. Dana Andrews's acting style would become so tightly wound only a steady infusion of Scotch could loosen the screws. But it was Gene Tierney who would be most haunted by Laura's theme.

A Brooklyn debutante who came west to fashion a career from her extraordinary face, Tierney lived a life that, short of a shotgun blast, was as compelling as Laura's. She was pursued by two of America's leading men—Howard Hughes and John F. Kennedy (but then, who wasn't?). Aly Khan, son of Pakistani spiritual leader Aga Khan, eventually preferred Tierney's beauty to that of his wife, Rita Hayworth. Men were more captivated by what Tierney's ravishing beauty did for *them*, than by genuine love.

Tierney shocked her family by eloping with couturier Oleg Cassini—Waldo Lydecker's real-world twin. The ferret-faced Cassini was of White Russian heritage, and wielded a rapier wit worthy of Waldo. Like Waldo, Oleg treated Tierney as his great creation, applying a lacquer of sophistication and dressing her in magnificent

glances. The interplay between droll columnist and taciturn cop is legendary. "Have you ever been in love, detective?" Lydecker asks. "A dame in Washington Heights once got a fox fur out of me," offers McPherson.

It's remarkable that the film was even made, let alone that it became a timeless classic. Darryl Zanuck, head of 20th Century-Fox, despised Preminger, and swore that, though under contract, he'd never direct at the studio. But Zanuck grudgingly allowed Otto to produce, on a short leash, this adaptation of Vera Caspary's novel (which was inspired by Steve Fisher's novel *I Wake Up Screaming*, made at Fox three years earlier). Three writers labored over the script, which everyone but Otto hated. Zanuck hired Rouben Mamoulian to direct, and fought Preminger's desire to cast relative unknowns Dana Andrews and Clifton Webb. Zanuck wanted John Hodiak and Laird Cregar, with Jennifer Jones as Laura.

In *Leave Her to Heaven*, Tierney's lush beauty made her psychotic jealousy all the more shocking.

fashions. Unlike Waldo and Laura, the relationship was not platonic. In 1943 the couple had a child, born drastically premature. Weighing only two-and-a-half pounds, Daria needed eleven blood transfusions, but miraculously survived.

The complications were due to Tierney's contraction of rubella (German measles) early in the pregnancy. Daria was discovered to be brain-damaged; in a decision that would forever prey on her, Tierney had her daughter institutionalized for the rest of her life.

A year after Daria's birth, a woman introduced herself to Tierney at a party, claiming they had met before, when Tierney was doing her bit for the war effort, glad-handing with the troops. "Did you happen to catch the German measles after that night?" the woman asked, smiling. "The whole camp was down with the German measles. I broke quarantine to come to the Canteen and meet the stars. Everyone told me I shouldn't go, but I just had to go. You were my favorite."

IN THE WAKE OF *Laura*, Gene Tierney would score her critical triumph, playing the most deranged femme fatale ever. In *Leave Her to Heaven* (Fox, 1945), based on the best seller by Ben Ames Williams, she was Ellen Berent, a Technicolor princess with pathological jealousy lurking in her luminous green eyes. Ellen is the flower of her wealthy clan. But she's never been quite right since her beloved father died, and in their concern for protecting Ellen, the family is blind to the damage inside her. "There's nothing wrong with Ellen," says her mother. "She just loves too much."

Ellen captivates and weds novelist Richard Harland (Cornel Wilde), who shrugs off his resemblance to Ellen's late father. It should have been a big hint. Richard squires her to his woodsy retreat in Maine. She promptly dismisses the caretaker. Ellen doesn't believe in sharing her paradise with anybody. This leads to a pair of the most notorious scenes in noir. First, she decides her husband's crippled brother, Danny (Darryl Hickman) is too much of a rival for Richard's attention. When Danny tries to impress Ellen with how he's learned to swim, she turns his pubescent eagerness against him, enticing him beyond his limits. As he sinks below the lake's surface, struggling for his life, Ellen watches implacably from behind her fashionable sunglasses.

Later, when she fears the baby she's carrying will purloin her husband's affection, she stages an "accidental" tumble down a flight of stairs, killing the unborn child. When Ellen's husband gets too friendly with her sister, Ruth (Jeanne Crain), she delivers the coup de grâce: She poisons herself, arranging it to implicate her husband and sister as her murderers. There was no precedent for the morbidity of these scenes, somehow made all the more malignant by the lushness of Leon Shamroy's deliriously ripe color cinematography.

"As much as any part I played," Tierney said in her memoirs, "Ellen has meaning for me as a woman. . . . She believed herself to be normal and worked at convincing her friends she was. Most emotionally disturbed people go through such a stage, the equivalent of an alcoholic hiding the bottle." Tierney's real life would outstrip her Oscar-nominated performance. Starting in the mid-'50s she suffered a series of mental breakdowns, convinced—among an avalanche of delusions—that

Scarlet woman: As the languorous Kitty "Lazy Legs" March in *Scarlet Street*, Joan Bennett displayed as much raw sexuality as Hollywood's Production Code would allow.

---

every book, everywhere, was filled with cataclysmic Communist ravings. Twice she was escorted from her posh Sutton Place apartment, in déclassé straitjackets, to the soft rooms of the Menninger Clinic in Topeka, Kansas. There, Hollywood's greatest beauty was strapped to a gurney and bound in ice-cold wet sheets, an Ike-era attempt at shock therapy. On the outside, she pondered a suicidal leap from her 57th Street balcony. Only her vanity cut through the despair. "If I was going to die," she'd write later, "I wanted to be in one piece, a whole person, and look pretty in my coffin."

Tierney's saga ended triumphantly, however. Released from Menninger's in 1959, she took a steady job as a clerk in a Topeka dressmaking shop. Throughout her recovery she was gently courted by, and eventually wed to, Texas oil millionaire Howard Lee, an ex-husband of actress Hedy Lamarr.

Gene Tierney never returned to Dark City.

SEE THAT OLD FELLA OVER THERE, shuffling through the park? His name's Christopher Cross, and though you'd never know it to look at him, he once was a respectable citizen. Worked as a cashier, punched in and out at the same time every day. Mr. Reliable. His wife, Adele, was pure misery. Chris always came up short when she compared him to her late husband, a cop who drowned heroically in a rescue attempt. But Chris could tolerate her indignities; his Sunday hobby, oil painting, was all the distraction he needed.

Then one night, feeling blue after a testimonial dinner at which twenty-five years of servitude earned him only a lousy watch, Chris Cross (Edward G. Robinson) strays onto *Scarlet Street* (Universal, 1945). He comes across a man and a woman, fighting. With a lucky swat of his umbrella, Chris fends off the attacker. It earns him a drink with the gal, Katherine "Kitty" March (Joan Bennett). He thinks she's an actress, still dressed up from a show. She laughs, and deals him a fresh hand: "I'll bet you're an artist!" He plays those cards, becoming, for this gorgeous woman only, the man he always wanted to be. Tumescence makes him oblivious to the dismissive twinkle in Kitty's eyes.

The poor sap doesn't know that Kitty's sparring partner was her pimp, Johnny (Dan Duryea). When Johnny learns this daffy geezer has fallen for his punch, he encourages Kitty to fleece the rube for all he's worth. Chris rents Kitty a spacious apartment, where he comes each Sunday to paint, her presence rekindling his ardor for life, love, and art. When he leaves, Johnny shows up to debauche "Lazy Legs," the goddess Chris worships.

When Johnny unloads one of Chris's paintings, it starts a buzz on the street. He convinces Kitty to sign her name to Chris's canvases, which he sells to a prestigious uptown gallery. Katherine March is soon lauded as the art world's latest discovery. Even this doesn't phase Chris. He's a happy acolyte, content to serve his priestess. But soon she's demanding greater offerings, and Chris must embezzle to keep her—and, by extension, Johnny—satisfied.

Even catching Kitty and Johnny in the act doesn't deter Chris. He rationalizes that Johnny must've forced himself on her. He forgives her, says they can start over as husband and wife.

"How can a man be so dumb," Kitty spits at him. "I've been wanting to laugh in your face ever since I met you. You're old and ugly and I'm sick of you!" Chris picks up a discarded ice pick and punctures Kitty through her satin bedcovers.

But it's Johnny who is arrested for the murder, tried, and convicted. He insists that Chris Cross murdered the renowned painter Katherine March, but who takes the word of a pimp against a respectable citizen? Chris rides the train to Sing Sing with a pack of journalists to witness the execution. "Nobody gets away with murder," says one of them. "No one escapes punishment."

Scarlet Street, the darkest sexual roundelay to emerge from Vixenville, was based on *La Chienne*—*The Bitch*—a 1931 Jean Renoir film adapted from Georges de la Fouchardière's novel. Its immediate antecedent was *The Blue Angel*, in which the infatuated Emil Jannings humiliates himself for the woman of his desires, Marlene Dietrich. *La Chienne* was originally purchased by Paramount, with the expectation that Ernst Lubitsch would create an Americanized version. But after Hollywood implemented its Production Code, Lubitsch felt the material wouldn't survive a watered-down rendition. It remained untouched until Fritz Lang resurrected it as the initial project of Diana Productions, a company he formed with producer Walter Wanger and actress Joan Bennett (Wanger's wife). *Scarlet Street*'s screenwriter, Dudley Nichols, was also a board member.

Upon release, *Scarlet Street* reaped more controversy than praise. It was one of the first Hollywood films since the imposition of the Code in which a guilty killer went free, while an innocent man was executed. It could have been that, by 1945, Hollywood was no longer as eager to insult the intelligence of its customers, figuring they could handle an adult story that concluded with a jolt of irony. Or chalk it up to Dan Duryea's detestable sleaziness: Everybody wanted him dead.

Most critics considered *Scarlet Street* identical to Lang's *The Woman in the Window* (RKO, 1944), released the previous year. Both feature the same main players and concern meek men smitten by beautiful connivers. In the earlier film, Robinson plays a professor who meets a fabulous femme (Bennett), accepts her offer of a nightcap, and ends up putting the shears to her brutish boyfriend when he barges in on them. They dispose of the body, but it's discovered by the police. The noose tightens when the dead man's bodyguard (Duryea), who knows the truth, blackmails them. Robinson sees no way out and mixes himself a poison cocktail. But Duryea dies in a gun battle with the cops, and they conveniently pin his boss's murder on him. Bennett calls to tell Robinson they're in the clear. The camera pulls back to reveal him slumped in his chair, apparently dead. But then he bolts up—*it's all been a dream*. Audiences loved the film; many critics slammed the cop-out ending.

Lang felt the two films were thematically distinct. *The Woman in the Window* was a cautionary tale of how a person "must always be on guard." He believed that a "logical" ending to the film, in which a man's life is destroyed by a brief flirtation, would have been too "defeatist." Victimized merely by coincidence, Robinson's punishment would have outweighed his crime. But Chris Cross was different: He willfully pursued his misery, begging to be hurt. A slim but not insignificant distinction.

Starting with *Scarlet Street*, Lang claimed all his films "wanted to show that the average citizen is not very much better than a criminal." We must always be on guard from ourselves, and our deepest desires. Lang's early films displayed a fascination with the vagaries of fate. After *Scarlet Street*, that changed. In 1974, accepting a tribute, Lang declared, "I don't believe in fate anymore. Everyone makes fate for himself. You can accept it, you can reject it and go on. There is no mysterious something, no God who puts fate in you. It is you who must make fate yourself."

BELITA, ICE QUEEN OF NOIR

One more example of noir's pervasiveness in postwar Hollywood is the career of Belita, an Olympic figure skater touted as the next Sonja Henie, who in a trio of crime thrillers—*Suspense*, *The Gangster*, and *The Hunted*—was more like Audrey Totter on ice.

Belita wasn't like full-figured actresses of the time—she had an athlete's sinewy shape and legs more muscular than any actor. Her speech was oddly stilted because she was hiding a British accent. Unschooled as a thespian, she displayed a confidence and charisma, almost a haughtiness, that lifted her above the cheapness of her B-level productions.

The "ballerina on blades," as PR guys called her, was born Maria Gladys Olive Lyne Jepson-Turner in Hampshire, England. The name *Belita* (Spanish for "Little Beauty") was bestowed by "Queenie," her ambitious stage mother. At age three Belita was studying ballet. Ice skating began at four, with instruction from a Swiss champion. Queenie convinced famed dancer-choreographer Anton Dolin to take on her six-year-old daughter as a pupil. Five years later, she was Dolin's dance partner. Her ballet debut was at age eleven, a solo event in Cannes. Her accompanist was Noël Coward, who remarked with typical panache, "I was told I was to play for a little girl. Had I realized I was playing for an artist, I would have practiced." Months later she competed in the World Figure Skating Championships. At thirteen, she represented Britain at the 1936 Olympic Games in Berlin.

Still a teenager, Belita had a ballet/skating show conceived for her by Jean Cocteau, Cecil Beaton, and Salvador Dalí. Unfortunately, by that time she was having trouble walking, let alone dancing and skating. She'd suffered a back injury being knocked offstage in a show at Covent Garden. The injury brought her to America, her mother having learned of a back specialist in

Los Angeles. The legit doctor was a bust—but Peter Lorre recommended a veterinarian who hung Belita heels-over-head from a meat hook, a remedy the vet used for animals. She was skating again weeks later.

Monogram signed her to a multipicture deal and made her the star of its first "million dollar" production, *Suspense* (1946). The picture, costarring Barry Sullivan, was a James M. Cain murder-triangle knockoff that shoehorned in several skating numbers, one of which features Belita in a skimpy dominatrix outfit doing "death-defying" axels through a ring of swords. More mundane was her role in *The Gangster* (Monogram, 1947), again with Sullivan, as his (nonskating) trophy girlfriend.

Her best is *The Hunted* (Allied Artists, 1948), in which she's a paroled jailbird who, of course, happens to be a figure skater. Preston Foster—twenty-five years older than his costar—plays Johnny Saxon, a cop who's sent Laura Mead (Belita) to prison on a robbery charge—even though he's in love with her. Laura swears revenge and four years later, out on parole, she drops back into Saxon's life. Steve Fisher's script crackles with tension between the two.

Laura Mead is a character on thin ice, and the audience, like Johnny, is kept guessing as to her motivations. The "is-she-or-isn't-she" handling of the femme fatale, and the notion of love as a form of persecution are the core of this gem, directed by Jack Bernhard with evocative camerawork by B-movie workhorse Harry Neumann. Close-ups of Belita revealed for the first time a scar, running the length of her face, a nasty souvenir from a skating accident. One more ordeal she overcame.

The worst was marriage to aspiring actor Joel Riordan, a move made in 1946 to escape her mother. Free of Queenie, Belita revealed herself in interviews to be a smart, sophisticated woman. Her upbringing made her approach life as a competition, she explained. She played violin and spoke four languages. She was an expert skier and swimmer. She had a mind and body capable of anything.

Yet her intelligence and ambition made her husband jealous. In the divorce petition, she testified he "drank heavily" and "beat her frequently." She paid Riordan 40 percent of her earnings to be rid of him.

She fled Hollywood to skate again in Europe. In Paris she met Charles Laughton, shooting an adaptation of Georges Simenon's *The Man on the*

Eiffel Tower (1949). She became his protégé and performed in revivals of *The Cherry Orchard* and *Twelfth Night*, taking a pay cut in favor of acting for her new mentor.

In 1956, she hung up her skates, never to hit hard water again. She retired to England and married actor James Berwick. She opened a gardening center in West London and watched her fame disappear. She remained with Berwick until his death, then spent her last years alone in the south of France. "I have a lovely time doing absolutely nothing," she noted happily in a rare interview in 2003.

Back in '56, immediately after her retirement from skating, Belita declared: "I hated the ice. I hated the cold, the smell, everything about it. I only did it for the money." Spoken like the one and only Ice Queen of Noir.

In *Suspense*, Belita amazed ice show boss Eugene Pallette and Barry Sullivan by leaping through a ring of swords.

"YOU'RE A LITTLE MAN WITH A BRIEFCASE," says a beautiful Mona Stevens (Lizbeth Scott). "You go to work every morning and you do as you're told. Today they told you to go to such and such an address and pick up some stolen goods. So here you are. Tonight, when you're sitting around with the boys, you'll say, 'You should've seen the babe I ran into today. Not bad. But you know me—strictly business when I'm on the job.'"

"Is that the way I impress you?" counters insurance agent John Forbes (Dick Powell).

Mona: "That's the way."

Forbes: "How *should* I be?"

Mona: "If you were a nice guy, you'd cry a little bit with me, and feel sorry for a girl whose first engagement ring was given to her by a man stupid enough to embezzle, and stupid enough to get caught."

Before you know it, it's three o'clock in the afternoon and Mona's sobbing into Johnny's gin at a dimly lit cocktail lounge. Any other day, Forbes would be dutifully filing claim reports. But today, his by-the-book life has encountered a *Pitfall* (UA, 1948). He's supposed to confiscate for Olympic Mutual Insurance the gifts showered upon Mona by her lover, Bill Smiley. Just like Chris Cross, Smiley swiped company funds to pay for his tokens of devotion. But Smiley got pinched and is doing a year, wondering if Mona will wait.

Mona fesses up about the motorboat Smiley gave her. She even takes Forbes for a ride. The dizzying skips over the waves, the sea spray, the closeness of this gamine—Forbes's façade of fidelity starts crumbling. Mona doesn't need to beg to have the boat left off his report. Johnny wants some more. He wants to tempt fate.

But Forbes has a bigger problem in his guilty conscience. Mac MacDonald (Raymond Burr), the PI he hired to find Mona, is also obsessed with her. Shadowing Mona has stoked his already evident psychosis. When he spies Forbes leaving Mona's house after hours, he sandbags his "rival," threatening to reveal his omission of the speedboat from the recovery report. When that fails, he treats Forbes to a beating.

To her credit, Mona drops the femme fatale act when she learns Forbes is married: "Aren't you a little relieved to get out of it this easily? This is a setup. This is the kind of girl you always dreamed about, and I'm going to let you off without an angle. I could be nasty but I'm not going to be." Forbes takes the hint and returns home, chastened.

MacDonald sees a clear field. He hounds Mona, driving her nuts. She cracks and asks Forbes for help. To regain his pride, he gives MacDonald a payback pummeling, which allows him to face the wife and kid a stronger man. But MacDonald visits Bill Smiley in jail, only a month before his parole. He says Forbes is moving in on Mona. Jealousy festers. On his release, Smiley goes looking for revenge. When he breaks into Forbes's home, he gets shot dead.

Having orchestrated the demise of both his rivals, Mac pounces on Mona. "People are born to have certain things," he smugly tells her, as he forces her to pack up for a Reno wedding. "Smiley didn't have the nerve, Forbes didn't have the chance—so it's me you end up with." He caresses her stilettos as he lays them in her suitcase. "The only reason I did all this is because I really love you." Mona breaks off the elopement with a couple of love notes from a snub-nosed .38—another undocumented gift from the late Bill Smiley.

The ending jerks no tears. Forbes's masters—the law and his wife—muscle his libido into place and send him back to his cubicle. "If a man has always been a good husband, except for twenty-four hours," says his wife, Sue (Jane Wyatt), "how long should he be expected to pay?"

Mona, however, gets the rawest deal. She's arrested for MacDonald's murder, and the last Forbes sees of her, she's being carted off to prison. He can't even muster a "Tough luck, kid." This was how Hollywood typically dealt with the "other woman." They carried all the emotional power, but were never offered the escape hatch reserved for the man. The real noir story here is Mona's, having to cope with the fixation of a horny married man, the return of a vengeful ex-con, and the obsession of a psychotic stalker.

The script, credited to Karl Kamb but actually written by the brilliant William Bowers (based on the novel by Jay Dratler), is noteworthy for its realistic depiction of this femme fatale. Which makes it all the more disappointing when she's banished from the plot after blowing away MacDonald.

The extramarital dalliance with model Mona Stevens (Lizbeth Scott) by insurance man John Forbes (Dick Powell) becomes doubly dangerous when he's threatened by her psychotic stalker (Raymond Burr) in *Pitfall*.

"THE THREAT"

izabeth Scott, one of the stalwart dames of Dark City, was no stranger to Vixenville. She even worshipped at the same temples of the flesh. Born in Scranton, Pennsylvania, with the decidedly un-vixenish name Emma Matzo, she was discovered by producer Hal Wallis in 1942, understudying Tallulah Bankhead in a stage version of *The Skin of Our Teeth*. History didn't record the backstage lessons Lizabeth may have absorbed from the legendary Tallulah.

Scott made her debut as Van Heflin's romantic interest in *The Strange Love of Martha Ivers*. She's stilted and awkward, but for a neophyte, just holding her own opposite Van Heflin, Barbara Stanwyck, and Kirk Douglas (also *his* debut) was enough to ask.

Soon she was a noir fixture: *I Walk Alone*, *Dead Reckoning*, *The Racket*, *Stolen Face* (Lippert, 1952), *Two of a Kind* (Columbia, 1951), the astoundingly bizarre *Desert Fury*, and *Dark City* (Paramount, 1950). Even sexier than her sultry eyes, the husky, bedroom voice was her signature—soaked in gin and burnished by endless cigarettes, hung over from long nights of laughing or crying too hard. It could talk you into things you never dreamed of. The PR mill, noting similarities to Lauren Bacall, nicknamed Scott "The Threat."

Her defining role was as rapacious housewife Jane Palmer in *Too Late for Tears* (UA, 1949). Alan Palmer (Arthur Kennedy) and his wife Jane have $60,000 tossed into their convertible while cruising Mulholland Drive. He wants to turn it in, but she won't hear of it. When a shady operator (Dan Duryea) comes to claim the dough—sex, deception, and murder ensue. Roy Huggins's screenplay (from his novel) is complicated, breezy, and black-hearted, but a meager budget forced most of the action indoors, giving it the feeling of a bedroom farce.

Liz Scott was known within the industry as producer Hal Wallis's mistress. But rumors ran rampant that she reserved the real pillow talk for other women. Today, she'd be the toast of the town. But in 1952, *Confidential* magazine flattened her career, claiming she was "prone to indecent, illegal, and highly offensive acts in her private and public life." Even this was witch-hunt hysteria, which overflowed from political crusade into a campaign for conformity. "You can hardly separate homosexuals from subversives," brayed Cornhusker Senator Kenneth Wherry.

Scott hired attorney Jerry Geisler to sue *Confidential*, but the petition was dismissed on a technicality. In '57 she recorded an album, *Lizabeth*, that defiantly declared she should have done her own singing in all those noirs where she was a nightclub canary. One track, featuring the refrain "I've got a deep dark secret," showed she had a sense of humor. By the '60s, Scott was living in seclusion in the Hollywood Hills, returning only once to Dark City in Michael Hodges's witty spoof *Pulp* (1972).

Jane Palmer (Liz Scott) is excited by a satchel of cash tossed into her car in *Too Late for Tears*. Her husband (Arthur Kennedy) will fall victim to her murderous materialism.

AT ONE TIME MEN CREATED SPIRITUAL ICONS from marble or stained glass. Things were trickier in the movies, where actual flesh and blood was a necessary intermediate step. Hollywood's "love goddess" was born in Queens in 1918. Margarita Carmen Dolores Cansino was the introverted daughter of dancers Eduardo and Volga Cansino. When her father realized she'd inherited a passion for dance, he scotched the schooling and put her in the act. She was only twelve, but puberty had its way with her early. Her joyful abandon not only entertained audiences, it fired the dark parts of some imaginations—including her father's. Before going off to drink and gamble, Eduardo would lock Margarita in her room, for her own protection. She had no protection when Dad returned, purportedly hammered and amorous.

The Cansinos moved to Los Angeles in 1930, Eduardo already grooming his daughter as his stake horse. Studio scouts saw her performing at the Agua Caliente Jockey Club, a retreat north of the Mexican border where gangsters and picture folk swapped dangerous glamour. She was fifteen. Fox exec Winfield Sheehan was the first of Margarita's "mentors." He shortened her name to Rita and plugged her into numerous trifles as the Dancing Latina. Edward Judson, a shifty operator of uncertain means, asked Rita's parents for permission to squire their daughter around town, hinting that he could make her a star. The Cansinos consented, though the guy was old enough to be Rita's father. Judson drove to a chapel in Nevada, where naïve and helpless, Rita said the necessary words.

Enter Harry Cohn. Hollywood's most unrepentantly vulgar boss—a portrait of Mussolini was displayed in his office—Cohn took Columbia Pictures from Poverty Row to major status by devouring cash-poor rivals. He knew how to sell this new girl: Whitewash her. Rita's black hair was dyed auburn and the studio made her endure electrolysis to raise her hairline, making her look less ethnic. Her last name was changed to Hayworth.

The public loved her. Cohn couldn't get over creating such a gorgeous fantasy figure. He felt she belonged to him—the ultimate gangster's moll, even though he was married. He pursued her the way Raymond Burr stalked Liz Scott in *Pitfall*—spying on her, haranguing her, wiretapping her house. He assigned one of his producers, Virginia van Upp, to create a star vehicle for his show pony. Then an unexpected stranger entered the picture: Orson Welles.

The enfant terrible was at a crossroads. *Citizen Kane* made him the most influential director since D. W. Griffith, but he'd veered off track with the fiasco of

Margarita Cansino in 1935, before Hollywood erased her ethnicity and renamed her Rita Hayworth.

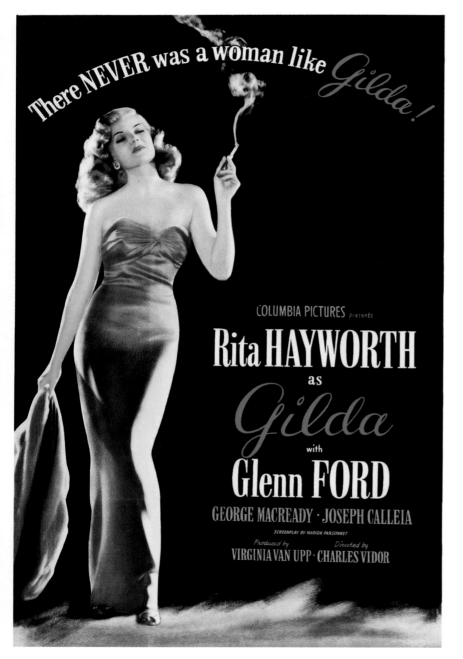

There NEVER was a woman like *Gilda!*

COLUMBIA PICTURES presents

Rita HAYWORTH

as

Gilda

with

Glenn FORD

GEORGE MACREADY · JOSEPH CALLEIA

SCREENPLAY BY MARION PARSONNET

Produced by VIRGINIA VAN UPP · *Directed by* CHARLES VIDOR

The Magnificent Ambersons (RKO, 1942). He'd tried to right himself at the studio with the more workmanlike *Journey into Fear* (1943) and *The Stranger* (1946), but to show that he was a true Hollywood player, Welles decided to marry a movie star. Without having met her, Welles said intended to marry Rita Hayworth. It was no surprise when he backed it up. He was, after all, an accomplished magician. He and Hayworth lived the high life for two years. Meanwhile, van Upp constructed a vehicle for Hayworth that propelled her into the crucible of public consciousness.

Gilda (Columbia, 1946) is more tango than movie. The script is pretext for watching overheated players enact a dance of sexual passion. It's also very kinky for PCA-dominated Hollywood.

Johnny Farrell (Glenn Ford), a gambler living off his wiles in Buenos Aires, is spared from a stickup by the intervention of suave and sinister Ballin Mundson (George Macready). Johnny then shows up at Mundson's casino, angling for a job. Even bowing to Production Code constraints, Mundson and Johnny are clearly bisexual. Munson "buys" Johnny, and the vagabond quickly warms to life as a tuxedoed punk. But one day Mundson brings home his latest acquisition—the ravishing Gilda (guess who). She and Johnny once were lovers. They shower sparks all over the place, lashing at each other with tantalizing and corrosive insinuations.

Halfway in, *Gilda* douses the sexy fireworks and sets about constructing a plot. Things fizzle. Nazi agents skulk around. One is murdered in the club. Mundson fakes his own death to evade the police. In honor of his late lover, Johnny marries Gilda but locks her away—apparently to sap the sexual ardor he can't tap. A fraudulent ending reunites Johnny and Gilda, cooing like teenagers. The vengeful Mundson reappears to kill them both, but he's stabbed by a washroom attendant.

Not that plot mattered. It was all about the way Rita looked, spoke, and moved. Her first appearance, tossing back her mane of fiery hair as she kneels on Mundson's bed, made blood pressures rise the world over. Her "Put the Blame on Mame" striptease . . . well, you know. *Gilda* was a phenomenon. When an A-bomb was tested in the Bikini atoll in 1946, it was nicknamed "Gilda" and adorned with a painting of Hayworth in a négligée. She was a bombshell, literally.

Hayworth's popularity exacerbated the estrangement from Welles. His dream project, *It's All True*, was in shambles, his career scattered all over cutting-room floors. Cohn offered Welles a shot at redemption—creating a follow-up to *Gilda*

The last passage from the labyrinth is always guarded by a woman. Sometimes it's the spirituality of Beatrice; other times it's the sorcery of Circe. Here it's the dangerous duplicity of Elsa Bannister (Rita Hayworth) in *The Lady from Shanghai*, Orson Welles's delirious home movie pipe dream of his marriage to, and murder of, the '40s greatest sex symbol.

that would keep the public's ardor for her burning. Cohn was determined to *own* these two, just as Mundson owned Johnny and Gilda.

Welles rewrote *If I Die Before I Wake*, a trim potboiler by Sherwood King, turning it into a globetrotting affair retitled *The Lady from Shanghai*. Cohn gave the erratic genius a $2 million budget and complete control—letting him write, produce, direct, and play the lead. Right off, Welles had Hayworth's famed coppery coiffure cut short and bleached platinum. The war with Harry Cohn was underway.

From associate producer William Castle's diary entry in Mexico: "*November 17. . . Cloudy and the heat oppressive. First day of shooting on Lady from Shanghai. The dark clouds seemed like an evil omen . . .*" Prescient. On the first take, assistant cameraman Donald Cory keeled over dead from a heart attack. The arduous production would become Hollywood legend, akin to the journey upriver in Joseph Conrad's *Heart of Darkness*.

The tale concerned Irish sailor Michael O'Hara (a blarney-filled Welles), hired by famed lawyer Arthur Bannister (Everett Sloane) to skipper his yacht from New York to the West Coast. O'Hara is a gullible fish, hooked by the lawyer's glamorous wife, Elsa (Hayworth). George Grigsby (Glenn Anders), Bannister's partner, offers O'Hara five grand to sign a confession stating he accidentally killed him, so Grigsby can vanish into a new life. The wily Bannister will then exonerate O'Hara. But Grigsby turns up *really* dead and O'Hara is cuffed for the murder—confession and all. Bannister, savvy to the affair between Michael and Elsa, provides his client vaudeville shtick in place of a defense. Realizing he's cooked, O'Hara breaks from custody. Several disjointed scenes later, Elsa is revealed as the real culprit. She and her husband ("I'm aiming at you, lover!") shatter all remaining illusions in a Hall of Mirrors shoot-out that climaxes the film. O'Hara leaves Elsa bleeding out on the funhouse floor, crying, "I don't want to die!"

It makes sense in a pared-down retelling. But when Welles delivered the

rushes to Columbia, it was a sprawling mess. Cohn yanked control from Welles and assigned editor Viola Lawrence to whip it into shape. She fashioned a bumpy 88-minute ride out of what Welles envisioned as a 155-minute epic. Watching the final cut, Cohn bellowed, "I'll give a thousand dollars to anyone who can explain this thing to me!" He was so incensed with the desecration of his star that he shelved *The Lady from Shanghai* for more than a year, eventually leaking it out on the bottom half of double bills just to recoup some of the budget. Welles was finished in Hollywood as a director.

Sadly, Hayworth was pretty much done herself. She formed her own production company and valiantly tried to crack the femme fatale mold, but the public had hardened her into an icon. Cohn presented her as *Salomé* (1953) and *Miss Sadie Thompson* (1953), refusing to let her shed the Love Goddess image. Just as Welles abandoned her after his initial excitement wore off, so did her legions of fans, once Marilyn wiggled into town and slipped into the form-fitting role of the newly minted sex goddess.

SAPS. FOOLS. MARKS. FLUNKIES. DUPES. CHUMPS. Call 'em what you will, women in Vixenville needed foils, men they bent to their will. The handsomer, the better. Any tramp could hook a geezer like Chris Cross. More satisfying was bringing a thoroughbred to heel.

Take this guy, for example—striding through Slim Dundee's nightclub, turning every head. He coolly cases the joint, nonchalantly sniffing the play. Women imagine their hands roving in his thick wavy hair, across his broad, muscled shoulders. Men know what their dates are thinking. Geez, he could have any dame in the place. But virility gets you only so far in Vixenville.

Just ask Burt Lancaster—the guy in Slim's. He'd had his heart broken here before, but he always came back for more. He was ruined by so many women, so often, it was obvious there wasn't much spine supporting all that beefcake.

Lancaster's screen debut revealed an indelible image of vanquished masculinity.

The imperious Rita presides over Ted de Corsia's demise in *The Lady from Shanghai*.

Burt Lancaster's steaming virility was turned into thin gruel by Ava Gardner in *The Killers* (Universal, 1946). Gardner was the real thing: Hollywood's earthiest femme fatale. She married Mickey Rooney, Artie Shaw, and Frank Sinatra. She had affairs with, among others, Clark Gable, Robert Taylor, David Niven, Robert Walker, John Huston, Peter Lawford, Howard Duff, Robert Mitchum, and—of course—Howard Hughes.

Yvonne De Carlo is an old flame who burns down Lancaster's defenses in the 1949 noir classic *Criss Cross*.

In *The Killers* (Universal, 1946), a pair of assassins track down boxer Ole "The Swede" Anderson (Lancaster). Although he's warned, the Swede doesn't run. He lies back and awaits deliverance. The rest of the film explains, in flashbacks, how the Swede got entangled with a bunch of crooks and had his heart cut out by two-faced Kitty Collins (Ava Gardner).

Lancaster was cast by Mark Hellinger, a Damon Runyan–style newspaperman and short story writer–turned–producer. He knew Lancaster was the real thing as soon as he laid eyes on him. So did the public. Born in East Harlem in 1913, Lancaster was a young man with a mind as limber and well-developed as his body. He'd acted a bit growing up, but disdained it as "sissified." He earned a meager living—but a world of experience—as a circus acrobat. A hand injury forced him to fall back on odd jobs. During military service in Europe, he met his future wife, Norma, a USO entertainer. Back in New York, he was meeting Norma at her office when a theatrical producer spotted him. One audition later he was the lead in *A Sound of Hunting*. It ran only three weeks, but Lancaster hooked seven Hollywood offers. He was *that* obvious.

Starting with *The Killers*, Lancaster appeared in a series of noirs where the main attraction was seeing this chiseled Adonis mercilessly flogged by brutal authority or treacherous women. In *Brute Force* and the even more aggressively titled *Kiss the Blood Off My Hands* (Universal, 1948), Lancaster bared his torso to endure the lash of savage captors. Women swooned over his swell build.

But there was more to Burt than beef. From day one, he soaked up filmmaking technique and business acumen, becoming a behind-the-camera contributor as well. By his eighth film, *Kiss the Blood*, he was coproducing. The following year he made *Criss Cross* (Universal, 1949), capping a three-year run through Dark City in which he starred in *The Killers*, *Desert Fury*, *Brute Force*, *I Walk Alone*, *Sorry Wrong Number*, *Kiss the Blood Off My Hands*, and a noir-stained adaptation of Arthur Miller's *All My Sons* (Universal, 1948).

Criss Cross culminated this fecund cycle. It reunited the brain trust from *The Killers*, with one exception: Mark Hellinger, only forty-four, died of a heart attack just as the deal came together. He'd recently scored his biggest success with *Naked City* (1948) and seemed headed for a long career as Dark City's dominant storyteller.

Hellinger was inspired by Don Tracy's 1933 novel about a racetrack robbery complicated by sexual passions. Daniel Fuchs (with additional dialogue by Bill

Dan Duryea corners lovers Burt Lancaster and Yvonne De Carlo in *Criss Cross*.

Bowers) fashioned the screenplay for pinch-hitting producer Michael Kraike. *Criss Cross* may not have been the home run that *The Killers* was, but like a ball off the top of the fence, daringly legged into a triple, it might be even more exciting than the long ball.

Steve Thompson (Lancaster) is an armored car guard who has it bad for his ex-wife, Anna (Yvonne De Carlo). He's drawn back to Slim's, the club where their passion burned brightest. Only she's now in thrall to Slim Dundee (Dan Duryea), a slick and crooked operator. Anna sparks a firefight between the two. When Dundee catches him with Anna, Steve blurts a cover story: He's willing to act as inside man so Dundee can knock over one of his company's armored cars. Steve plans on

Ida Lupino as Lily Stevens in *Road House*.

double-crossing Slim, grabbing his cut, and running off with Anna. Slim plans to kill Steve in the heat of the heist.

One of the lasting pleasures of *Criss Cross* is its amazing style. Robert Siodmak, who also directed *The Killers*, had a flair for compositions and camera movements ominous yet elegant. Images simultaneously enticing and foreboding are essential to noir, and Siodmak crafted them like nobody's business. From the first shot—the camera swooping out of the sky like a nightbird to catch Lancaster and De Carlo in an embrace in the parking lot of Slim's club—Siodmak infuses the drama with a dreaminess that gets under your skin like a narcotic.

During its eighty-eight minutes, *Criss Cross* shoots out slivers of art that will never leave your head. The lanky Duryea dangling like a jackal in a zoot suit; Lancaster's lovelorn face as he watches De Carlo rumba 'round the dance floor; robbers in gas masks firing blindly through a smoke haze. Vivid, dynamic imagery—and vivid, dynamic acting—stick in the mind long after "naturalism" has evaporated. Modern noir plays like real life. Classic noir plays like fevered memory.

Burt Lancaster earned his greatest tribute from Louis Malle, who cast him as the aging two-bit gangster in *Atlantic City* (Paramount, 1980), writer John Guare's take on old-style romanticism juked up by modern mores. When Lancaster strolls the Jersey boardwalk and pauses to sigh, "You should've seen the Atlantic back then—now *there* was an ocean," it was the perfect capper to his Dark City career. Susan Sarandon was a nice retirement present.

BEFORE WE ANKLE OUT OF VIXENVILLE, there's one last person you need to meet. You hear a lot about folks being "one-of-a-kind." In Ida Lupino's case, it wasn't just blowing smoke. Unless you didn't take her seriously—then she'd blow it right in your face.

Born in London, Ida was in the show as soon as she could walk. Her father, Stanley Lupino, was the most venerable comedian on the British boards. Her family's theatrical roots reached back to the seventeenth century, so there was little doubt of Ida's calling. At fourteen she projected womanly confidence in several British films.

Director Allan Dwan "discovered" her and invited her to Hollywood. She was herded into the overflowing starlet stable, where her distinctiveness was hidden beneath a Jean Harlow bleach job. Ida bristled and wasn't afraid to warn movie magazines, "I cannot tolerate fools, won't have anything to do with them. I only want to associate with brilliant people." Harry Cohn, the town's most brilliant fool, told Ida, "You are not beautiful, but you've got a funny little pan," then inked her to a two-picture deal.

Barely twenty, Ida became a popular Hollywood figure: a sweet-faced ingenue who dispensed straight talk with a tart tongue. In early 1936, she gained notoriety as the star witness at the media-saturated inquest into the death of Thelma Todd. The actress had been found dead in her garage after a party at the Trocadero, thrown by Ida and her family. Later that year, Ida developed "blind devotion" to actor Louis Hayward, even though she told interviewers that "I never expect anything to last . . . neither success nor love . . . I can't be hurt." Hayward and Lupino became one of the town's highest-profile married couples, presiding over a sprawling household filled with family, friends, music, dance, and the arts.

Her breakthrough came in William Wellman's *The Light That Failed* (Paramount, 1939), in which the funny little pan served up a startling menu of emotions. The one-time student of the Royal Academy of Dramatic Arts was then whisked into the rugged man's world of producer Mark Hellinger. He cast Ida as the nail-tough broad between George Raft and Humphrey Bogart in *They Drive by Night* (WB, 1939). Ida's courtroom breakdown ("The doors made me do it!") stole the show. Although possessed of a porcelain delicacy, Ida had a streak of raucous humor, a hair-trigger temper, and a no-bullshit demeanor that made her a favorite of the tough guys. She could hold her hooch and crack wise with any of them.

She also carried her own water, bearing the rigors of making *High Sierra* (WB, 1940), Hellinger's rough and romantic outlaw saga. Initially wary of each other, she and costar Humphrey Bogart became compadres (while Bogey's jealous wife Mayo, lurking off-set, tried to intimidate her). Ida's popularity earned her top billing over Bogart. She followed *High Sierra* with the socially conscious *Out of the Fog* (WB, 1940), costarring John Garfield. She and Garfield reunited later that year for *The Sea Wolf* (WB), cementing a lifelong friendship that proved to be, for him, tragically short.

She then astounded everyone by playing, at twenty-three, a severe middle-aged murderess in *Ladies in Retirement* (Columbia, 1941). It should have propelled her onto the "A" list. But having shed the ingenue tag, she now found herself typecast as a villainess.

She rejected so many scripts Warner Bros. put her on suspension. Mark Hellinger, also disgruntled with Warners' ways, had moved over to 20th Century-Fox and he took Ida with him. They made *Moontide* (1942), a heaping helping of hash-house melodrama, costarring French import Jean Gabin. To prepare for their roles, Gabin and Lupino waded through the fetid underbelly of downtown Los Angeles. Ida never forgot what she saw there.

The Hard Way (WB, 1942) followed, a mean-spirited movie depicting the single-minded drive of an obsessed stage mother (in this case, a stage *sister*). Lupino hated making it; burned out by the histrionics, she suffered frequent "spells" during shooting. Not that it mattered: The film was a big success, and she pulled rave notices.

Then her life came apart. In 1943, husband Hayward was serving as a Marine captain, supervising a photography corps in the South Pacific. Responsibility for making a visual record of the infamous assault on the Tarawa atoll nearly destroyed him. During a four-day frenzy of artillery shelling, sniper fire, and hand-to-hand combat, Hayward documented the slaughter of more than six thousand soldiers, Americans and Japanese, battling for the strategic landing strip. He came home shell-shocked. Movies meant nothing to him any longer. Ida watched the love of her life descend into depression. They divorced, and Ida joked that she was now the town's leading "bachelor girl." In truth, she was devastated.

She struggled through *The Man I Love* (WB, 1947) as torch singer Petey Brown, the embodiment of resilient feminine spirit; a talented, smart-mouthed gal with a tender spot waiting to be pierced. She returns from the road to discover her family has become a catalog of wartime crises: too many babies, not enough money, an angry shell-shocked vet, a nephew straying into crime, a floozy neighbor cheating on her husband . . . and so on. Ida whirls through them, the Lone Ranger in gold lamé, belting out ballads and tossing off wisecracks ("Well, well . . . the people you run into when you're not carrying a gun").

Single-handedly, she straightens everyone out—except herself. To save her no-good nephew from a murder rap, she submits to the affections of crook Nicky Toresca (Robert Alda). Her true love, alcoholic pianist Sam Thomas (Bruce Bennett), sails out of her life on a freighter. Two moments are indelible: When distraught Johnny (Don McGuire) threatens to kill Toresca, Ida steps in, knocks the gun loose, and slaps him silly. Moments later, after kissing Sam goodbye for the last time, she strides up the wharf, tears streaming down her face. She musters a tight little grin: *Yeah, life's cruel*, it says, *but I'm going to play out the string*. The ending tugged at and toughened heartstrings, of women and men alike. *The Man I Love* was the peak of Ida's Movie Star phase.

She tired of acting and decided to pursue other creative impulses, seeking fresh scripts to produce—and crafting her own. At twenty-nine, she formed a production company with Benedict Bogeaus. She favored stories about "poor, bewildered people. That's what we all are." Ida met Italian director Roberto Rossellini, who complained to her that "In Hollywood movies, the star is going crazy, or drinks too much, or he wants to kill his wife." His observations were an inspiration to Ida, who'd soon embark on a second career (discussed in detail later) as the industry's only female director.

In the meantime, agent Charles K. Feldman tried to win Ida's affection by purchasing and tailoring a property for her, a novel titled *The Dark Love*. Renamed *Road House* (Fox, 1948), it was one of the biggest hits of the year. Playing a whiskey-voiced chanteuse, Ida proved she could do anything: For the first time, her own voice was heard in a film's musical numbers. "One for My Baby," written by Johnny Mercer and Harold Arlen, and performed by Lupino, went to the top of the Hit Parade.

As "Lily Stevens," Ida was the subject of two of the sharpest cracks ever uttered in this burg. Her first night on the job, a regular gives her the once-over and says, "She reminds me of the first woman who ever slapped my face."

After she's shot Jefty (Richard Widmark), the screw-loose rich boy who can't accept losing her to his old buddy Pete (Cornel Wilde), he looks up at her, smiling as he dies, and says, "I told you she was different."

Jefty knew. He was nuts, but he knew.

Lupino at the height of her stardom, with Robert Alda in *The Man I Love*. The gown was so tight Ida passed out on the set; it had to be cut off so she could be resuscitated.

The Stranger on the Third Floor

BLIND ALLEY

WHAT DID I DO? WHERE DID THINGS GO WRONG? WAS IT STOPPING FOR THAT DRINK LAST NIGHT? ANSWERING THE PHONE IN THE HOTEL LOBBY? I SHOULDN'T HAVE PICKED UP THAT WALLET. BUT I DID—AND NOW I CAN KISS OFF EVERYTHING I THOUGHT WAS IMPORTANT. FORGET THE RAISE—HELL, FORGET THE JOB. FORGET THE FUR FOR CATHY AND OUR TRIP OUT WEST. NONE OF IT MATTERS. THE FUTURE MAY NOT STRETCH ANOTHER TEN MINUTES. WHY DID THIS HAPPEN? OUT OF ALL THESE PEOPLE ON ALL THESE STREETS IN ALL THESE BUILDINGS—WHY AM I THE ONE BEING PUNISHED? TELL ME, GOD—IF YOU CARE AT ALL—WHY ME?

Once upon a time, movies were all about order. If your train ran off the rails in real life, a quarter would still buy you a double dose of reassurance at the Rialto. But on September 1, 1940, doubt and dread snaked into cinemas across the land. RKO released a sixty-four-minute programmer called *The Stranger on the Third Floor*.

Fledgling newspaperman Mike Ward (John McGuire) earns a front-page byline after witnessing the grisly murder of a shopkeeper. He fingers jittery cabbie Joe Briggs (Elisha Cook Jr.) as the culprit. His courtroom testimony makes him a "star" reporter, the envy of his pressroom pals. His fiancée, Jane (Margaret Tallichet) is the only one unimpressed. She can't stomach how Briggs—crying innocence—is so swiftly convicted. While Mike thinks of his $12 raise helping rent a ritzier place uptown, Jane wonders if he's not consigning the wrong man to the hot seat.

Mike soon waivers: "What if he isn't guilty?" he asks a crony—"What if they fry an innocent man?" His colleague, clearly a Dark City native, replies, "So what? There's too many people in the world as it is."

Back in his gloomy tenement, Mike spies a stranger entering a neighbor's apartment. His newfound angst sparks paranoia: Mike lurks in the stairwell, suspecting some dreadful deed. When the stranger skulks out, Mike gives chase.

Skittering like a hermit crab, the weird little guy escapes into the night. Mike goes to bed convinced his neighbor has been murdered, and his guilt about Briggs spurs bad dreams: *He* is arrested for murdering his neighbor. Witnesses attest to his hatred of the victim. Motive is established. Evidence mounts. Mike is strapped, screaming, in the electric chair.

Awaking, Mike breaks into the neighbor's apartment. The guy's throat is slashed, just like the shopkeeper's. Mike is certain the stranger killed them both. He tries to halt Briggs's execution. But the cops like Mike for the second murder. The nightmare turns real. Only Jane believes Mike's tale of the stranger. She prowls the streets in search of the shifty homunculus while Mike stews in stir. The film's abrupt ending may flick on the lights and clean things up, but by then *The Stranger on the Third Floor* has broadcast more fear and paranoia than can be stowed away in a tidy wrap-up.

The vagaries of fate are a venerable subject, but this was the first American movie to depict the theme with a hallucinatory style straight from the German Expressionist school of filmmaking, which favored audacious artifice over quotidian naturalism. Mike's guilt is made palpable through dramatic lighting, exaggerated set design, and surreal directorial flourishes. *The Stranger on the Third Floor* was the first Hollywood film to fully display the look later described as noir.

In truth, it was more historical footnote than trendsetter. *Citizen Kane*, released the following year by RKO, used similar techniques, more subtly and influentially, in service of a grander story. No one would mistake *Stranger*'s director, Boris Ingster, for Orson Welles. Yet both films changed the grammar of cinematic storytelling. A major part of *Kane*'s vision can be traced to art director Van Nest Polglase, fresh off his extraordinary design of *The Stranger on the Third Floor*. And with his lighting of night-shrouded streets, ominous corridors, and shadow-stabbed rooms, cinematographer Nicholas Musuraca established visual motifs that would become noir staples.

The film's other essential ingredient was Laszlo Loewenstein, a diminutive Hungarian with the stage name Peter Lorre. As the Stranger, he epitomized an unnerving weirdness loose in the big city. "The squat, wild-eyed spirit of ruined Europe," as film historian David Thomson put it. Indeed, Lorre's un-American visage was iconic: He was Old World darkness incarnate, an ogre from Eastern European fairy tales about to infect American movies.

Lorre had already made an anguished impression as the child killer in Fritz Lang's *M* (1931), showing the derangement of a man trampled at the bottom of the pecking order—beneath even the most corrupt criminals. Lorre put a sad, scary—and human—face to the most heinous crime. As the *New Republic* noted on the film's American premiere: "It . . . could not under any circumstances have been made in Hollywood—indeed, any American director who suggested such a thing would probably find his own sanity suspected. Nevertheless, Hollywood will make better pictures after seeing this one."

While never plumbing the depths of *M*, *The Stranger on the Third Floor* expressed the grimmest theme in noir: the cruelty of fate. Doesn't matter if you're innocent. Justice truly is blind, but not because she's impartial: Either God's poked

Peter Lorre

her eyes out or she's taking a payoff to look the other way. This is Blind Alley, the cruelest part of a merciless town. Don't bother with a map. You're on your own.

IT'S THE LITTLE GUYS who always take it in the shorts—bank tellers, teachers, truckers, letter carriers. The juiceless citizens of Dark City. They don't *know* anybody who can grease the skids or bail them out. Consider *Quicksand* (UA, 1950), which could have been called *Andy Hardy Goes to Hell*. It starred America's rapidly maturing Boy Next Door, Mickey Rooney. Danny Brady (Rooney) is a hot rod–loving grease monkey. Caught flat broke after lining up a date with dishy waitress Vera (Jeanne Cagney), Danny lifts a double sawbuck from his garage's till. He plans to cover it the next day with twenty bucks a pal owes him. Following morning, the bookkeeper shows up ahead of schedule. To restock the register, Danny buys a fancy watch for a dollar down, then hocks it for thirty. Next thing he knows, a cop is down on him. The jeweler figures Danny will skip on the bill. A grand theft charge now looms, if Danny doesn't pay for the watch in twenty-four hours.

So Danny rolls a guy at an amusement park who's loaded with gin and fifties. Except everybody on the boardwalk knows the victim, ancient gashound Shorty—including Nick, an arcade operator (Peter Lorre!) who carries a torch for Danny's gal Vera (she's tramped the promenade a few times). Figuring Danny as the amateur who mugged Shorty, Nick forces the kid to steal him a new car off the lot. Danny's boss, mean old Mr. Mackey (Art Smith), calls him on the theft. If the car's not returned Danny will be stuck for its three-grand price tag. Vera encourages Danny to rob Nick's arcade—then swipes half the dough to buy herself a fur coat! Old man Mackey accepts Danny's payback—but still calls the cops! Danny goes nuts and strangles him. He takes it on the lam, running for his life. *Whew!*

Directed by Irving Pichel from an original screenplay by Robert Smith, *Quicksand* is the archetypal Blind Alley thriller, revolving around the pursuit of money and its pitfalls. Although fate plays a part in his downfall, it's the naked greed shown by everyone Danny encounters that pulls him down. This naïve kid learns the hard way that everyone is more corrupt than he ever imagined.

Twist of fate scenarios are fright shows, showing us the horrors that await if we succumb to the temptation of easy money. The "moral" was no more sophisticated than the message of highway safety films like *Red Asphalt* or *Signal 30*, screened in high schools from the dawn of Driver's Ed: If you value your life don't get in a car with the bad boys.

Side Street (MGM, 1950) offers one of those dangerous rides. Farley Granger, the quintessential innocent, plays Joe Norson, a veteran struggling to support his pregnant wife (Cathy O'Donnell) as a fill-in letter carrier. He dreams of opening a service station (guys in noir all wanted filling stations). Desperate, Joe steals an envelope he thinks contains $200 from an office on his route. When he discovers that it holds $30,000, his dreams blow up in his face.

Written by Sydney Boehm and shot by MGM's premier cinematographer, Joe Ruttenberg, *Side Street* was the grandest production yet from director Anthony Mann. Born Emile Anton Bundsman in San Diego, Mann was hired by David O. Selznick in 1939 as an all-purpose underling. Within a couple of years, having rechristened himself, Mann was helming imaginative B pictures for Republic. His strong style could turn a daffy lark like *Strange Impersonation* (1946) into an engrossing diversion. His breakout came with *Desperate* (RKO, 1947), which he cowrote. It showed a full-throttled command of the medium. Mann benefited from the collaboration of DP George Diskant, one of the great light painters. With Ruttenberg, Diskant, and John Alton behind the camera on his noirs, Mann's films were always visually arresting.

In *Desperate*, freshly hitched trucker Steve Randall (Steve Brodie), drives into a blind alley when he agrees to a spur-of-the-moment hauling job. It's a heist, staged by evil Walt Radak (Raymond Burr). The job blows up, a cop gets shot, and Randall cuts out, leaving Walt's brother to be cuffed as a cop-killer. Randall and his bride (Audrey Long) go on the run, pursued by the law and Walt's gang. Another honest Joe whose life is ruined by the pursuit of easy cash.

In *Side Street* and *Desperate*—as well as *Railroaded* (PRC, 1947), *Raw Deal* (Eagle-Lion, 1948), and *Border Incident* (MGM, 1949)—Mann's storytelling is as swift and seamless as a seasoned shakedown. He gave pulp material a fresh

ABOVE: Mickey Rooney tussles with Peter Lorre in *Quicksand*. In the early '50s, Rooney would play lovelorn innocents mixed up in crime in *The Strip* (MGM, 1951) and *Drive a Crooked Road* (Columbia, 1954). BELOW: Joe Norson (Farley Granger) isn't sure he can trust Helen Sinton (Jean Hagen) as he searches for a way out of a possibly lethal *Side Street*.

Director Anthony Mann meters out the tension as psycho Georgie (James Craig) takes Joe for the climactic ride in *Side Street*.

urgency through a visceral, at times brutal, style. Unlike, say, Robert Siodmak, who empathized with his characters from a dignified distance, Mann dragged viewers headfirst through violence that, for its time, was unrivaled in its intensity.

Loophole (Allied Artists, 1954) also offers stolen money as the ruination of a man's life, although its poor sap is in no way responsible for his downfall. Mike Donovan (Barry Sullivan) is a bank clerk victimized by an "inside job." Another teller at a crosstown bank poses as a federal inspector. He slips fifty grand into his briefcase during reconciliation. Donovan is so stunned by the shortage in his drawer he's afraid to report it at the Friday total-up. When Monday rolls around, he's the lone suspect.

The bonding company has six months to retrieve the money before it has to reimburse. Investigator Gus Slavin (Charles McGraw) dogs the suspect, shadowing Donovan's every move, spreading the word that he's a thief, costing him jobs—and his sanity. Donovan is squeezed between the real crook's thievery and Slavin's ferocity to exact punishment.

Made at the tail end of the McCarthy era, *Loophole* replaced fear of criminals with fear of authority run amok. McGraw exemplified the scary establishment torpedo, whether it's an insurance investigator, a Commie-hunting Fed, or a self-righteous cop. There was no distinction between "law-abiding" McGraw and the ruthless torpedo he played in *T-Men*: Either way, he's cruel for the hell of it, relishing the license he's granted to torture citizens, guilty or not.

Money, of course, isn't the only thing that leads Dark City naïfs down blind alleys. As we've seen in Vixenville, plenty can go wrong when trolling for pleasures of the flesh. In *The Accused* (Paramount, 1949), Wilma Tuttle (Loretta Young) is a spinsterish psychology professor whose knowledge of the human mind has caused her to retreat to the sanctuary of a lonely apartment—until she's lured out by the randy blandishments of precocious student Bill Perry (Douglas Dick). He's got the book on the prim teacher: Between the tight bun and the square-toed sensible shoes is a woman longing for sexual release. Perry takes Wilma for a moonlit swim, then forces himself on her. She defends herself with a tire iron, busting Bill's skull. She dumps him in the ocean, making it look like he slipped on the rocks and drowned.

Murder does wonders for Wilma's pheromones. She's pursued, romantically, not only by Perry's legal guardian Warren Ford (Robert Cummings), but also by Lieutenant Ted Dorgan (Wendell Corey), the cop investigating Perry's death. As

Mann's World: *Raw Deal* (Eagle-Lion, 1948) managed to pack every noir theme and bit of iconography into one eighty-minute movie. Marsha Hunt (top left) plays the good girl who competes with moll Claire Trevor for *homme fatal* Dennis O'Keefe. It looks like no contest—until Hunt proves her mettle by blasting O'Keefe's nemesis, John Ireland.

Wilma desperately tries to hide her guilt, the men battle for her. Ford learns the truth and tries to protect her; Dorgan suspects the truth and tries to break her. A bitter lawman with no love life, Dorgan takes pleasure in exposing what lies beneath Wilma's frigid façade. He wants her in the muck with him, as guilty as everybody else.

Adapted from June Truesdell's novel *Be Still, My Love*, *The Accused* was tricky subject matter for a 1949 film. Although Ketti Frings had sole screenwriting credit, five writers had a hand in softening a story of rape, in which men fall for a murderess. The story is exceptional for putting the screws to a *woman*. It was common for them to be engineers of a man's demise, but it was considered bad form to hang

them with the same noose that ensnared the men of Dark City.

For comparison, consider the case of Frank Bigelow, another citizen who can't feature why life doesn't dish him some fleshier pleasures. In *D.O.A.* (UA, 1950), this sad sack is saddled with a destiny no dame would be made to suffer. One of our town's wildest stories starts with Frank (Edmond O'Brien) trudging into the Homicide Department of an LA precinct to report a murder—his own. The cops are expecting him; Frank has left a trail of carnage during the preceding forty-eight hours. The doomed man reels out his testimony:

A bean counter in the one-horse town of Banning, Bigelow wanted a breather from his fiancée, Paula, who is eager to clamp on the matrimonial bridle. Frank's not ready to sacrifice the carefree bachelor life—especially since he's never lived it. So it's off to San Francisco to sow his wild oats. Paula lets him go, confident Frank will return all the wiser.

Buddying up with pub-crawling conventioneers, Frank casts his net at the Fisherman, a juke 'n' jive joint on the Embarcadero. As he's reeling in a blonde at the bar, a mysterious man in overcoat and slouch hat enters. He sneakily swaps Frank's bourbon for a luminous toxin cocktail. Frank returns to his hotel a little queasy; the lush life isn't all it's cracked up to be. Waiting is a bouquet and a loving note from Paula. Frank tears up the blonde's phone number and hits the sheets, alone and content.

Come morning, Frank's topsy-turvy inside. A visit to an MD delivers startling news: He's been poisoned. A second opinion confirms the worst. This doctor even produces a beaker of glowing liquid we must assume is Frank's radiant urine. Frank demands instant remedies. The doc, with blunt bedside manner, says, "I don't think you understand, Bigelow. You've been murdered."

As Bigelow races through the streets in a panic, *D.O.A.* leans toward atomic age allegory: the radioactive man, out of time, inventorying daily activities that might be annihilated in the blink of an eye. He stares into the sun, bright as a bomb blast, and contemplates his own Armageddon: "A day, two, maybe a week at the most," according to the doctor.

The trail leads back to LA, through a plot as twisted as *The Big Sleep*. Something about the ominous mineral iridium and nefarious characters who've bought it, sold it, and stolen it from each other. And just like when Marlowe goes snooping, people start dropping dead. But Bigelow, determined to reason out his demise, is more frantic than Marlowe: "Why'd Eugene Phillips kill himself? Who's George Reynolds? Where do I find this Raymond Rakubian? Who are you? Majack! Who's Majak? What's Halliday got to do with this? You mean he's having an affair with Mrs. Phillips?!"

Searching for his fatal piece of the iridium puzzle, Bigelow recognizes his love for Paula, but spares her news of his imminent death. It turns out Bigelow notarized a bill of sale that was evidence that could have foiled a plot to make a murder look like suicide . . . or something like that. Trapped in a blind alley with no outlet, Bigelow clutches Paula and moans, "All I did was notarize one little paper—one paper out of hundreds!"

Frank concludes his investigation in LA's atmospheric Bradbury Building, having tracked down the man who slipped him the lethal cocktail. He reciprocates with several shots, straight up.

Concluding his statement to the cops, Bigelow keels over. "Better call the morgue," says a hardened homicide dick. "What'll we tell 'em?" comes the off-screen prompt. "Tell 'em—*Dead on Arrival*."

Most cases from Blind Alley aren't whodunits, but Houdinis—as in "How will they get out of this?" As such, they have built-in entertainment value, the equivalent of the old banana peel gag. It's fun as hell to watch somebody else take the fall. In films of this type the victims, bruised and chastened, usually dust themselves off and walk away at the fadeout. *D.O.A.*'s most memorable quality, by contrast, is its downbeat finish.

Some critics go all-in on the atom bomb analogy; others assert that Bigelow is punished by higher powers for ranking casual encounters over marriage vows. Lighten up. *D.O.A.* is as close as any noir got to being a live-action cartoon. Realizing the plot is little more than a succession of gab-happy interrogations, director Rudolph Maté gave Edmond O'Brien free rein to push things to a fever pitch. He responded with more animation than Daffy Duck. As he frantically

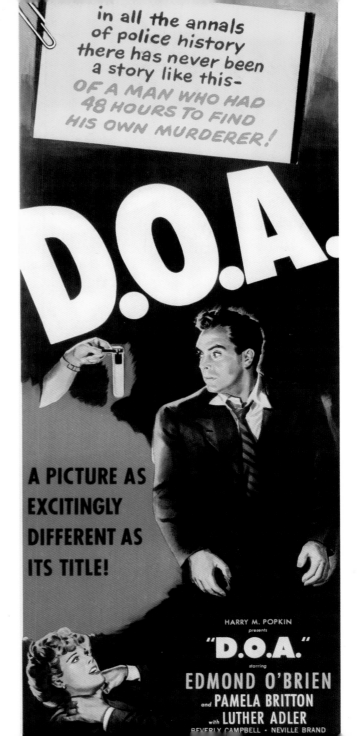

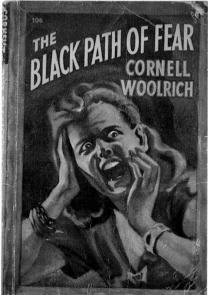

lunges in and out of scenes, you almost see cartoon motion lines *poof* from slammed doors. When he ogles a passing skirt, a comic wolf-whistle sounds off-screen. He skitters and slides through streets and hallways, outrunning his feet in the best Chuck Jones tradition.

This isn't a complaint. Directed to play it straight, as in *The Killers* and *White Heat* (WB, 1949), O'Brien was the ideal Everyman. But when material threatened to go stiff, O'Brien could shake things up. Faster than any actor, he'd go from Average Joe to whirling dervish, flapping his prodigious pompadour like an overgrown coxcomb. His noir resume is lengthy: *The Web* (Universal, 1947), *A Double Life* (Universal, 1947), *711 Ocean Drive* (Columbia, 1950), *Between Midnight and Dawn* (Columbia, 1950), *Backfire* (WB, 1950), *Two of a Kind* (Columbia, 1951), *The Hitch-Hiker* (RKO, 1953), *Shield for Murder* (UA, 1954), and *A Cry in the Night* (WB, 1956). In all, O'Brien was never less than entertaining—sometimes outrageously so.

DRAMAS OF TWISTED COINCIDENCE were to most viewers—and creators—nothing more than diversions. For overly sensitive souls, they were the modern equivalent of consigning Christians to the lion's den. Life or death as entertainment. Thumbs-up or -down, if one man was the Bard of Blind Alley, it was Cornell Woolrich.

The preeminent scribe of noir suspense, Woolrich sampled success in the '20s, when two of his early novels gained notoriety. But Easy Street turned into Rough Road during the Depression. Woolrich retooled his craft as a "penny-a-worder," pumping out stories for the pulps.

Sales of those stories to movies, radio, and television would make him the most financially rewarded "pulp" author ever. It was meaningless to Woolrich, who lived like a pauper and toted his own booze, in a paper bag, to the few literary fêtes he'd attend. "All I was trying to do was cheat death" is how he described his writing. No amount of cash can buy that safe passage.

In 1944's *Phantom Lady*, "Kansas" (Ella Raines) puts herself at risk tracking down the *woman* who can alibi her boss for murder. After stalking a shifty bartender (Andrew Tombes), the amateur sleuth becomes possible prey.

The Window, based on Woolrich's story "The Boy Cried Murder." Audiences were on the edge of their seats when innocent Bobby Driscoll was terrorized by his murderous upstairs neighbors (Paul Stewart and Ruth Roman). Everyone breathed easier when Driscoll survived a climactic fall in an abandoned, crumbling tenement. The film was a smash and Driscoll received a special miniature Oscar for his performance. In 1968, at age thirty-one, his career long since fizzled, Driscoll flamed out with a methedrine overdose in a vacant Greenwich Village tenement not far from where *The Window* was shot.

Woolrich spent his youth in Mexico, dragged around by his father after his parents divorced. The old man, Genaro, bounced around south of the border, managing construction projects with his son in tow—a gangly, carrot-topped wraith. The insecure kid needed to come off as macho. He bribed a local bully into withstanding harmless beatings within sight of Señor Woolrich. Only when his father took him to a touring company's Mexico City performance of *Mme. Butterfly* did the young man feel a stirring of direction—a desire to tell (and escape into) dramatic stories. But his ambition always squirmed beneath Damocles's sword. In his autobiography, titled *Blues of a Lifetime*, Woolrich revealed how "when I was eleven and, huddling over my own knees, looked up at the low-hanging stars of the Valley of Anahuac, and I knew I would surely die finally, or something worse. . . . I had that trapped feeling, like some sort of poor insect that you've put inside a downturned glass, and it tries to climb up the sides, and it can't, and it can't, and it can't."

His biographer, Francis Nevins, says facts of the man's life are as elusive as smoke. Woolrich was a pathological liar, rewriting the truth for the sake of a better story. We may only know him by what's on the pages left by a writer who assembled his neuroses into breathless communiqués from the loneliest outskirts of Dark City.

For most of his life, that outpost was an apartment in the Hotel Marseille, Broadway at 103rd, in Manhattan, which he shared with his mother, Claire. From his upper-floor room, he'd survey the roofs and alleys and fire escapes, imagining the myriad terrors that befell souls streaming through the city's clogged arteries. Every time a siren wailed, he must've started pounding the typewriter—that's how prolific he was.

Taken individually, these tales are masterful excursions of nail-biting suspense.

As a life's work, they are unrelentingly bleak, each story a brick in a wall of malevolence Woolrich spent his life building. Nevins's epitaph: "He had the most wretched life of any American writer since Poe."

It didn't start out so bad. Woolrich prospered during the '20s, when his Jazz Age novel *Children of the Ritz* brought comparisons with F. Scott Fitzgerald and a trip to Hollywood to assist with the First National screen adaptation. In Los Angeles, the mercurial writer met and impulsively married Gloria Blackton, daughter of J. Stuart Blackton, founder of Vitagraph Studio and one of the industry's pioneers.

According to Blackton's half-sister, Marian, Woolrich professed a "reverence" for his wife that precluded physical consummation. Three months after they'd exchanged vows, Woolrich disappeared. Gloria came across a diary in which Woolrich had penned graphic accounts of homosexual encounters on the docks. Maybe that explained the sailor suit she discovered in a valise he usually kept locked and stowed. Even more shocking to his wife was Woolrich's mocking revelation that he'd married her as a joke.

Woolrich returned to Manhattan, and his mother, with whom he lived until her death in 1957. He was a morose recluse, a guy who'd fit any serial killer profile. Fortunately, his mayhem was confined to a Remington portable typewriter, with which he mastered the art of injecting pathos and despair into stories of exhilarating excitement.

His specialty was layering a razor-edged latticework of coincidence over the dreary lives of beleaguered Americans (in Woolrich novels, the Great Depression never ended). Those frantically looking for a break took fate's bootheel square in the kisser. People raced the clock, and unbeatable odds, to avert disasters, murders, and executions. Sweat-soaked nightmares were reenacted during waking hours, driving the dreamer mad. The love of someone's life might be an evil imposter—or might one day vanish without a trace, as if they never existed. When dazed souls turn to the law for help, they encountered cops like the one in Woolrich's "Dead on Her Feet"—a sick flatfoot who forces the innocent boyfriend of a dance-hall murder victim to tango with the corpse until he goes insane.

In the '40s, Woolrich was the perfect writer to provide source material for the confluence of stylish European existentialism and gritty urban crime drama that was seeping into the shooting schedules at every picture factory. Studios snapped up Woolrich's novels and short stories.

Street of Chance (Paramount, 1942), based on *The Black Curtain*, was the first to capture the Woolrich spirit. Burgess Meredith played an amnesiac struggling to make sense of three missing years. The follow-up novel, *Black Alibi*, was transformed by Val Lewton and Jacques Tourneur into a spellbinding film, *The Leopard Man* (RKO, 1943), in which something—man or beast?—is killing folks at random.

In 1944, the pivotal year for film noir, Universal issued *Phantom Lady*, adapted from a novel Woolrich wrote under his pseudonym, William Irish. It's a classic Blind Alley thriller. A husband angrily ditches his wife and spends an evening with a woman he picks up in a bar. He returns home to find his wife murdered and cops waiting with the cuffs. His companion that evening, all that stands between the sap and his unjust doom, has vanished into thin air. A loyal coworker races against time to uncover the needle in a haystack, her only clue an extravagant hat worn by the mystery woman.

Phantom Lady was the breakout film for its producer, Joan Harrison, and its director, Robert Siodmak. They sacrificed some of the screw-tightening suspense in favor of a waltz into Woolrich's particular strain of darkness. In addition to the inky menace brushed over desolate locations, they amplified sounds of urban dread: the screeching of elevated trains, footsteps echoing on wet pavement, and, most famously, the scary abandon of an after-hours jazz club.

In 1946, three Woolrich-inspired films were released: *Black Angel* (Universal), *Deadline at Dawn* (RKO), and *The Chase* (UA). *Deadline at Dawn* was an intriguing attempt by luminaries of New York's Group Theater to elevate the book's moist pulpiness into something loftier. Producer Adrian Scott, fresh from *Murder, My Sweet*, hired compatriots Clifford Odets and Harold Clurman to adapt the tale of a man who has from midnight until dawn to find the perpetrator of a murder for which he'll be charged. The sweaty frenzy of Woolrich's novel was a poor match for artists as mannered as Odets and Clurman; they seem to lose interest around 3 a.m. (In fact, art director William Cameron Menzies finished directing the film). The reliable atmospherics of Nicholas Musuraca and Susan Hayward's turn as a prickly taxi dancer enliven this stilted adaptation.

The Chase (UA, 1946) was a wilder ride. Screenwriter Phil Yordan threw out the map (*The Black Path of Fear*) in the middle and arbitrarily shifted destinations thereafter. Director Arthur Ripley, who had subversive notions about narrative cinema, didn't bother with the brakes. As a result, *The Chase* is as spellbinding as a

car wreck. Downtrodden vet Chuck Scott (Robert Cummings) gets a chauffeur's job with Miami gangster Eddie Roman (Steve Cochran) after returning the guy's lost wallet. While Eddie and his aide Gino (Peter Lorre) trade sinister non sequiturs, Chuck falls in love with Roman's French wife, Lorna (Michelle Morgan), whom Eddie keeps a virtual captive. She talks Chuck into arranging their escape via freighter to Havana.

Once Chuck and Lorna flee, things advance at a languid pace, as if they're moving on shifting sand. When the lovers embrace in a bustling Havana nightclub and Chuck breathes, "I love you" into Lorna's rapt face, it's like a death sentence. Seconds later, she slumps to the floor, dead, a knife jutting from her back.

The Woolrich fever is perfectly captured: The police hound Chuck; menacing witnesses pop up to lie about his actions that night; the exoticism of Havana is frightening in itself. There is a palpable feeling that the world—or maybe Chuck's head—has come loose from its moorings. The audience certainly feels that way when Gino reappears and *kills* Chuck as he's about to solve Lorna's murder.

But hold on—we're only halfway there. Chuck wakes up in his chauffeur's uniform, back in Miami. It's all been a fever dream, induced by malaria Chuck contracted in the Pacific. If things weren't confusing enough, Chuck suffers amnesia, a side effect of the disease. Eddie and Gino bow out in a train wreck, and Chuck and Lorna *do* escape to Havana—only to be greeted by characters from Chuck's ominous dream.

Critics called *The Chase* a hopeless mess. But director Ripley had real flair for evoking off-kilter dream scenes; this is as close as any '40s film came to the subconscious cinema of David Lynch, adroitly evoking Woolrich's world of doomed romance and terrifying helplessness.

At the height of the noir era, studios grand and grimy mined Woolrich's tales. *Night Has a Thousand Eyes* (1948) was a prestige offering from Paramount, directed by A-lister John Farrow and starring Edward G. Robinson as a vaudeville "mentalist" cursed by the actual gift of prophecy. It's a moody but sluggish affair that, despite Robinson's best effort, fails to generate a genuine sense of impending doom.

At lowly Monogram, fledgling producer Walter Mirisch (a major Hollywood player by the 1960s) made a trilogy of low-rent second features from Woolrich stories: *Fall Guy* (1947, from the story "Cocaine") starred Sean Penn's father Leo doing a frazzled John Garfield impression; *I Wouldn't Be in Your Shoes* (1948) was a re-do of *Phantom Lady*, with Elyse Knox as the amateur sleuth trying to save her fiancée from a trumped-up murder rap. The best at capturing the writer's fetid milieu was *The Guilty* (1948), in which Don Castle, taking "tight-lipped" to extremes, navigates the treachery of twin sisters played by Bonita Granville. Director John Reinhardt captured the threadbare desperation of the source material ("Two Men in a Furnished Room") and pulled off clever misdirection with an unreliable narrator. *The Guilty* rewards repeat viewings, to appreciate Reinhardt's directorial sleight of hand.

The most commercially successful Woolrich adaptation of the era was *The Window* (RKO, 1949), based on the story "The Boy Cried Murder." It's a Dark City version of Aesop's fable about the little shepherd with a big imagination. Tommy Woodry (Bobby Driscoll) eases the misery of tenement life by telling tall tales to his family and friends. When he takes his pillow onto the fire escape one night to beat the summer heat, he witnesses a murder in the apartment above. No one believes him. He persists, so his fed-up mom teaches him a lesson—she marches him upstairs to the Kellersons' apartment and makes him confess his fibs. The Woolrich paranoia is even more wrenching when entangled with a child's vulnerability—Tommy's own mother (Barbara Hale) leads him to the slaughter!

No character seemed as close to Woolrich as Tommy Woodry, a boy trying to overcome his fear of the dark, in the world and in himself. Claire Woolrich was eighty-three, struggling with the effects of a heart attack, when she died in 1957. Woolrich believed the nurse who cared for his mother killed her when he went for a walk. True to form, he was inconsolably guilty for leaving her side. He then spent ten lonely years after that as a dead man walking. He scared off admirers with his penchant for marathon stints of ill-tempered imbibing. The prodigious wellspring of fiction evaporated; he tapped out only a few meager efforts a year. One of those, "A Story to Be Whispered," published in 1963, offered a window into Woolrich's self-loathing. A man picks up a floozy in Prohibition-era San Francisco and accepts an invitation to her dingy crib. Poised for his sexual release, he instead beats his lover to death. The surprise ending: ". . . It wasn't as though I had killed another man. Or even (God forbid) as if I had killed a woman. Or yet (banish the thought) killed a little child. All I had killed was a queer."

As Woolrich's days dwindled, his life and fiction merged. He was convinced another resident of the Sheraton-Russell Hotel was covertly searching his room,

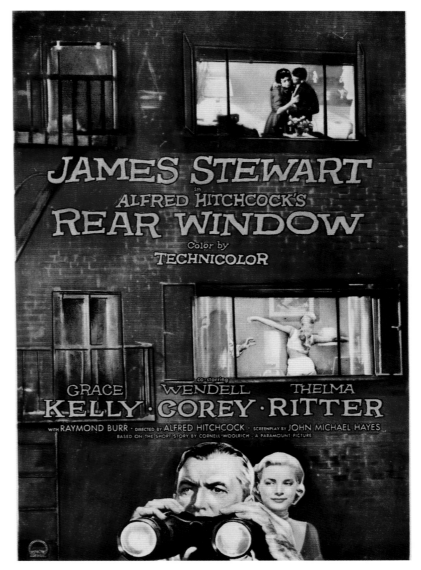

The most highly regarded Woolrich adaptation of all time was made by a kindred spirit in 1954, Alfred Hitchcock's Technicolor version of the writer's short story "It Had to Be Murder." James Stewart's voyeur seemed like little Tommy Woodry all grown up.

trying to assume control of his life. A chafing shoe caused an infection. Left untreated, it turned gangrenous. Now a prisoner in his rented room, Woolrich watched his leg rot. He may have found this appropriate, for it was a foot infection that had incapacitated him decades earlier, leading him to write his first short story.

His leg was amputated and Woolrich told people this "miracle" led him to return to the Catholic church, which he'd abandoned as a boy. Could several months of prayer actually stave off the terror Woolrich spent a lifetime anticipating? Woolrich was found passed out in his hotel room on September 19, 1968. He died six days later without regaining consciousness.

ONE OF THE FEW WHO COULD HAVE COMMISERATED with Woolrich in his final days was his artistic and spiritual brother, Alfred Hitchcock. Like Woolrich, Hitchcock was a populist, a maker of escapist entertainments who carried a chip on his shoulder about not being accepted as an artist. Like Woolrich, his specialty was the Blind Alley thriller. But unlike the wordy recluse, who rarely let his characters skip town, Hitchcock had a well-stamped passport: His expansive imagination was not trapped within the boundaries of Dark City. It roamed the globe, where he found the same fear and guilt lurking everywhere.

These two sensibilities meshed most famously in *Rear Window* (Paramount, 1954), Hitchcock's gripping adaptation of Woolrich's 1942 story "It Had to Be Murder." Its premise captured the essence of both men: physically "incapacitated" voyeurs who viewed the world from a distance—one that is never safe enough. Broken-legged photographer L. B. Jeffries (Jimmy Stewart) enjoys observing the passion plays enacted within the windowframes of neighboring apartments, until he spies what he's convinced is a gruesome uxoricide. The killer (Raymond Burr) knows Jeffries is a witness, and steadily pulls the spectator into the game.

It's the same story as *The Window*, but unlike that noir fable, *Rear Window* exists wholly in Hitchcock's manufactured studio world. Its calculated artifice is a perfect example of the engrossing, but unchallenging thriller. In fact, most of Hitchcock's trips down Blind Alley were like bad vacations, ones full of hair's breadth brushes with disaster. But sometimes the journeys were laden with guilt. When he combined the two, as in *Shadow of a Doubt* (Universal, 1943) and *Strangers on a Train* (WB, 1951), Hitchcock produced noir masterpieces.

Shadow of a Doubt's Uncle Charlie (Joseph Cotten) is Hitchcock's alter ego—the charming dinner guest who unnerves the family with frank talk about man's innate evil. Charlie's devoted niece (Teresa Wright) discovers her idol is a peripatetic psychopath. Although she slips his assassination attempts, she'll never shake the shame of finding him so desirable. Transference of guilt is also the theme of *Strangers on a Train*, in which dangerously demented Bruno Anthony (Robert Walker) acts out the secret desire of Guy Haynes (Farley Granger) to get rid of his wife. Hitchcock relished stories in which morally confused innocents were tortured by morally bankrupt predators.

"He considered all life unmanageable," declared Hitchcock biographer Donald Spoto. "The paradox of Alfred Hitchcock was that his delight in his craft could never be liberated from a terrible and terrifying heritage of desire and its concomitant guilt."

Sounds like an innately fearful child educated by Jesuits. The Catholic church instilled in Hitchcock all the terrors that await the tempted but gave him no earthly weapons to defend himself. What peace is there for anyone who believes their dark imaginings will result in next-world punishment? As screenwriter Arthur Laurents noted, "It was obvious to anyone who worked with him that he had a strong sense of sin, and that whether he was a regular churchgoer or not, his Victorian Catholic background still affected him deeply. He might have been indirect in dealing with sexual things in his films, but he had a strong instinct for them. He thought everyone was doing something physical and nasty behind every closed door—except himself."

The success of *Strangers on a Train* curiously left Hitchcock creatively offtrack, unsure of his next destination. With the stabilizing influence of his wife Alma (like Mrs. Raymond Chandler, as much a mother as a spouse), Hitchcock undertook a project he'd had on the back burner for years, an adaptation of the 1902 play *Nos Deux Consciences (Our Two Consciences)* by Paul Bourde. The result, *I Confess* (WB, 1953) is one of Hitchcock's most brooding films, one that directly confronts the mystery of faith. A priest is forbidden by the sanctity of the confessional to reveal the identity of a murderer. Father Michael Logan (Montgomery Clift) chooses to adhere to his spiritual principles even when *he* is tried for the crime. Guilt has a field day, especially given that the murder victim was blackmailing a woman with whom Logan had an affair years earlier. As in *Strangers*, an innocent man is consumed by guilt over a crime he may have *wanted* to commit, but did not.

The Wrong Man was based on the true story of Emmanuel Balestrero (Henry Fonda), a bass player at New York's Stork Club, who, in 1952, was arrested for a string of holdups around his Queens neighborhood. So many witnesses identified Balestrero at his trial that it prompted one juror to blurt out, "Do we have to listen to any more of this?" A mistrial was immediately declared. During the defendant's excruciating wait for a new trial, the real culprit was serendipitously arrested for another petty robbery, clearing Balestrero.

I Confess raised to metaphysical heights Hitchcock's perennial theme of unjust fate. It pitted a system of fallible human justice against the conceit of God's divine plan. It's the conundrum at the heart of every Blind Alley thriller: Is there hope of cosmic balance, or is chaos the only true god? The dread this question inspired in Hitchcock twitched beneath even his most diverting escapades.

Hitchcock's films, like most Blind Alley stories, are about fate. By extension, they ponder the existence of God. These stories revolve around the lost and impoverished—in short, the Chosen.

Take the Jews, for example, dominated by the original Dark City power brokers, the Romans. Pontius and the boys showed how savagely challenges to the status quo are dealt with, nailing the Jews' most influential storyteller. But the disciples knew the value of a good story, and their collected works made for "the greatest story ever told." The battle between those wielding earthly might and those claiming the kingdom of heaven has always been the catalyst of theological belief—in a word: faith. In Dark City, it's a given that the Romans' descendants will always be in charge, because around here muscle counts for more than heavenly dispensation. For the powerless, belief in God is the essential survival tool.

Hitchcock grappled with this theme in *The Wrong Man* (WB, 1956), another departure for him. He eschewed the studio for location shooting, to more effectively convey the real-life terror of Emanuel Balestrero, accused unjustly and ushered unceremoniously into Kafka's worst nightmare. The story combined several Hitchcock obsessions: fear of the police, transference of guilt, and the mystery of divine intervention. The director always maintained that the seminal event in his youth (and art) occurred when he was locked in a jail cell—his father's way of shocking him onto the straight and narrow. Hitchcock's production designer, Robert Boyle, thought that chestnut was apocryphal: "Hitch told it so often, and it was convenient for the press, that he probably came to believe it himself." Another bond with Woolrich.

Whether drawing on experience or not, Hitchcock created in *The Wrong Man* a sinking sense of despair as innocent Manny Balestrero (Henry Fonda) is sucked into the bowels of an indifferent justice system. Fonda plays Manny as the ultimate victim. He barely raises his voice to protest his treatment, and when he does it embarrasses him. Manny doesn't rail, he doesn't fight. He just goes gentle into that cruel night.

Kim Novak, in her guise as "Madeleine," beguiles investigator Scotty Ferguson (James Stewart) in Hitchcock's masterpiece of sexual obsession, *Vertigo*.

Emotionally, the film couldn't be further from colorful, cavalier spectacles like *To Catch a Thief* (Paramount, 1954), from the director's fertile mid-'50s period. But neither was it the dispassionate example of cinema verité Hitchcock initially intended. The direction and cinematography are calculated noir, nothing like the flat, documentary images Hitchcock claimed he was after. *The Wrong Man* is full of stylistic flourishes; but it's stripped of all romantic pretense.

The muted climax comes when Manny's devout mother tells him his only recourse is to pray. "I don't need a miracle," he sighs. "What I need is some luck." But Manny, who has muttered rosaries throughout his trial, stares at a picture of Christ and gives prayer one last shot. Hitchcock superimposes a street over his face, and another man—almost a twin—slowly walks up to the camera, his face fitting perfectly beneath Manny's. The guy then tries another stickup but he's collared and ID'd for the crimes hanging over Manny. Miracle or luck?

Hitchcock regretted his handling of the scene, claiming it destroyed the "authentic" nature of the film. In hindsight, Hitchcock always seemed uncomfortable with films in which he didn't hide his insecurities behind a prankster's façade. He confessed to "miscalculations" when the public didn't warm to *I Confess* and *The Wrong Man*, the two films where he exposed his fearful confusion over how true believers can be abandoned—or rediscovered—by their God.

Hitchcock put his sexual insecurities at the heart of his next and arguably his greatest film, *Vertigo* (1958). Based on the novel *D'entre les morts* (*Among the Dead*) by Thomas Narcejac and Pierre Boileau, it's about a man remaking a woman into the image of his dead lover. The convoluted scheme at the core of the story doesn't demand our attention, nor the director's, as much as the spellbinding depiction of a man made psychotic by longing and regret. Hitchcock tailored the film for Vera Miles, whom he was intent on grooming into his ideal actress. When she evaded his ambitions, Kim Novak—more practiced at dealing with men's compulsions—stepped into the dual role of Madeleine Elster/Judy Barton, giving a profound earthiness to the director's trademark "cool blonde."

The status of *Vertigo* has steadily grown since its disappointing initial release.

Long forgotten in the wake of the director's subsequent blockbusters *North by Northwest* (MGM, 1959), *Psycho* (Paramount, 1960), and *The Birds* (Universal, 1963), the movie reemerged, Phoenix-like, to be hailed by many cineastes as the greatest film ever made. Equally debatable is its status as noir. Rather than rehash the plot, searching for noir bona fides, or arguing whether it's disqualified by a sumptuous color scheme, consider this: *Vertigo* is not only the story of an acrophobic former cop who becomes obsessed with an old friend's "wife" when he's hired to follow her around San Francisco. It's also the tale of young Judy Barton, down on her luck, who agrees to participate in a rich man's crazy scheme, impersonating his wife for the cop's benefit so her employer can arrange the murder of said wife. What she doesn't count on is the dupe spotting her again, in her real identity, and his ravenous desire to reclaim "Madeleine" at all costs—including Judy's life.

Vertigo is noir any way you look at it—but if viewed as Judy's story, rather than that of lovelorn Scotty Ferguson (Jimmy Stewart), it is 150 proof, the tragic tale of a beauty from Salina, Kansas who can't escape the berserk manipulations of men. Kim Novak had no problem understanding the role: "Madeleine was me," she said in a 2014 interview with the author.

The darkness inside Alfred Hitchcock has been grist for critical interpretations and biographies. Like Woolrich, he was fortunate to have an outlet for his fears and desires. Unfortunately, he was heir to all the terrors of the Catholic church and none of the balm its rituals of faith are supposed to provide. "I was born a Catholic," Hitchcock told an interviewer late in his life. "I went to Catholic school, and now I have a conscience with lots of trials over beliefs." When he was dying, going about the pretense of work at the studio, he told his aides, "Don't let any priests on the lot. They're all after me. They all hate me." Hitchcock turned tremulous as the end neared. There were maudlin scenes in which he regressed into his childhood fears. According to Spoto, he declared not long before his death: "One never knows the ending. One has to die to know exactly what happens after death, although Catholics have their hopes."

As Kafka's friendly cops said in *The Wrong Man*: "Just remember, Manny—an innocent man has nothing to fear."

THE MISTRESS OF SUSPENSE

When Alfred Hitchcock arrived in Hollywood in 1939, he had an ace up his sleeve, a female protégé who would become a crucial figure in noir—Joan Harrison. She made waves as one of only three female producers in a male-dominated business (Virginia Van Upp and Harriet Parsons were the others), and industry scribes worked themselves into a lather describing how this "feminine fireball" challenged the status quo while "wearing an evening gown with the same eye-filling éclat as Lana Turner."

Harrison's rise was related as a fairy tale in which a British lass went from shopgirl to secretary to screenwriter to shot-caller (". . . but for a trick of fate, she might today be one of millions tending babies in English cottages," claimed one hack). But the bottom line is that Joan Harrison was essential to development of the film noir movement. Her sensibility was attuned to psychological thrillers and she crafted them with a keen story sense and a strong guiding hand, every bit the equal of her counterparts Mark Hellinger, Hal Wallis, and Jerry Wald. Over the entirety of her professional life, Harrison rarely strayed from the shadows—her career arc tracing, precisely, the trajectory of noir in the culture's bloodstream.

In 1933 Harrison had answered an ad Hitchcock had placed, looking for an assistant. The director, working at Gaumont British studios, was won over by her intellect, charm, and taste for the macabre. Her fascination with crime was fostered by her uncle, Harold Harrison, a "keeper" of the Old Bailey, in charge of scheduling cases in London's criminal court: "He was one of those uncles young girls adore," Harrison said. "He not only took you to lunch, he knew the grisly details of all the most shocking crimes."

Joan Harrison became Hitchcock's "reader," and soon collaborated in meetings, not merely taking notes but offering suggestions. The female lead in *The Lady Vanishes* (Paramount, 1938), played by Margaret Lockwood, bears a significant resemblance to Harrison. If Hitchcock's wife, Alma Reville, was threatened by her husband mentoring this young woman (Harrison was twelve years younger than the Hitchcocks), she betrayed no jealousy—even when Harrison got a cowriting credit (with Sidney Gilliat) for 1939's *Jamaica Inn* (Paramount). Despite collaborating on every facet of her husband's films, Alma never earned a credit more significant than "Continuity."

When the Hitchcocks sailed to America to discuss adapting Daphne du Maurier's *Rebecca* for producer David O. Selznick, Harrison traveled with them as family. The registry listed her as "Joan Hitchcock." Friends and associates called them the "Three Hitchcocks."

On *Rebecca* (UA, 1940), Harrison received coscreenwriting credit (with Robert Sherwood)—and an Oscar nomination. She was now integral to the development, scripting, and preproduction of Hitchcock's films: earning cowriter credit on *Foreign Correspondent* (UA, 1940), *Suspicion* (RKO, 1941), and *Saboteur* (Universal, 1942). Rumors arose: Harrison was the real talent behind Hitchcock, or an especially "personal" assistant. The "Three Hitchcocks" ignored the gossip, but before *Saboteur* was in the can, Harrison opted to forge out on her own.

Her search for an appropriate project led to a novel by Cornell Woolrich—the type of story she'd previously have taken to her mentor. Her first-draft adaptation convinced Universal to let her build it as a feature. Being a woman, she was granted only "associate" producer status—even though there were no other producers.

Lunching at a bistro favored by European émigrés, Harrison encountered a director who shared her interest in crime stories. Despite an accomplished career in Germany, Robert Siodmak's Hollywood years had been spent freelancing on B movies. It was his 1942 *Fly-by-Night*, made for Paramount's B unit, in which Harrison recognized a variation on Hitchcock's approach—the

Hitchcock's one-time secretary, scenarist, and protégé Joan Harrison would become one of the essential producers of noir, both on the big screen and on television.

Robert Young and Susan Hayward are illicit lovers enjoying a romantic idyll before tragedy strikes in *They Won't Believe Me*, a Hitchcockian thriller with more fully realized female characters than Harrison's mentor ever managed.

elegant commingling of shadowy mystery, whipcrack pace, and sly sexuality, as well as a flair for dynamic set pieces. She signed Siodmak up as director of her breakout project, *Phantom Lady*.

With this 1944 release, Harrison not only helped foster the film noir movement, she set the course of Siodmak's career. Some critics, such as *The Nation*'s James Agee, intrigued by the possible emergence of a female Hitchcock, considered *Phantom Lady* entirely Harrison's handiwork. His

review discussed "Harrison's use" of light and sound—never mentioning the actual director.

Harrison and Siodmak reunited for a film version of Thomas Job's daring 1942 Broadway hit *Uncle Harry*. The heavy hints of perversion in its three-way romantic triangle appealed to them both. They also reunited with actress Ella Raines, who'd starred as "Kansas" in *Phantom Lady*. *Uncle Harry* was Raines's third film with Siodmak in less than two years. In each she played a self-sufficient and bracingly modern young woman. Raines noted in interviews that she gleaned the persona from her producer, Joan Harrison.

Production of *Uncle Harry* was a blissful affair—but things soured when Universal altered its ending. When it was announced that (retitled) *The Strange Affair of Uncle Harry* would be test-screened, Harrison sniffed defeat. The test audience of "bobby-soxers" led to Universal creating *five* endings—none good. Harrison walked off the lot, burning a major bridge behind her. "If my standards as a producer and writer were to be subject to the whims of the front office," she declared, "then the only thing for me to do was leave."

Dore Schary, RKO's chief of production, welcomed Harrison to his studio. They shared a desire to make edgy, tightly scripted thrillers on modest budgets. Her first RKO effort, 1946's *Nocturne*, saddled her with an incompatible leading man—George Raft—and his "personal" director, the prodigiously untalented Edwin L. Marin. Harrison still crafted a nifty noir, buoyed by a clever Jonathan Latimer script, a colorful supporting cast, and the evocative cinematography of Harry Wild.

They Won't Believe Me (1947) was a more serious affair. Developed by Harrison and Latimer from a story by Gordon McDonnell, it's the producer's finest film. For this Cain-style saga, she deep-sixed genre conventions. Instead, she crafted a story about an *homme fatal* (Robert Young) whose behavior ruins three women. As played by Rita Johnson, Jane Greer, and Susan Hayward, these are the most authentic jilted wife and "other women" in noir—no femmes fatales or Pollyannas here. Real people die, not plot devices—a rarity for the genre.

Harrison's new studio-home was ransacked in late '47 when it was purchased by Howard Hughes; following Schary's lead, Harrison bolted for less volatile environs. Ironically, she landed back at Universal—where Robert

Montgomery (another pal from the Hitchcock days) asked her to produce his follow-up to *The Lady in the Lake*. Harrison strode straight into hard-boiled terrain—adapting a novel by Dorothy B. Hughes, self-admitted devotee of Hammett and Chandler.

Ride the Pink Horse is a picaresque revenge thriller as well as a despairing take on the sprawl of American corruption. For the screen version—drafted by always reliable Ben Hecht—Harrison again ran up against the intractable adolescence of the Production Code. Its mandated changes (such as transforming the villain from a homicidal senator into a garden-variety gangster) diluted the book's profound bitterness into petulant sourness. The novel's vicious antihero, known only as "Sailor," emerges on-screen as truculent "Lucky" Gagin (Montgomery). The movie has an off-kilter energy and enough trapdoors and funhouse mirrors to make it unique. Although he'd have been wise to cast someone with more gravitas as Gagin, *Ride the Pink Horse* is unquestionably Montgomery's finest work as a director.

While Harrison's collaboration with him was fortuitous, the allegiance she showed Montgomery—one of her most admirable traits—was ill-advised. Two more films with him (*Once More, My Darling* [Universal, 1949], an unfunny comedy, and *Eye Witness* [Eagle-Lion, 1950], an intriguing but listless courtroom drama) squandered Harrison's talent at the height of the noir era. *Circle of Danger* (RKO, 1951) followed, a whodunit with a few Hitchcockian moments. It's no lost classic, but it let Harrison cap her movie career with something worthier than those Montgomery misfires.

Joan Harrison's career, however, was far from over. If anything, she was about to have a renaissance. By the early '50s, her mentor was the most recognized movie director in the world, and his

agent, Lew Wasserman, suggested Hitchcock double-down on his popularity by conquering TV as well. Hitchcock was wary, afraid of stretching himself too thin. Wasserman suggested he bring Joan Harrison back into the fold.

Their reunion resulted in one of the greatest television shows of all time. *Alfred Hitchcock Presents*, the thirty-minute anthology series, ran for seven years before morphing into *The Alfred Hitchcock Hour* in its final seasons, 1962–1965. Harrison produced 266 installments of *Alfred Hitchcock Presents*, hiring veteran directors (John Brahm, Robert Stevenson, Paul Henreid, Robert Florey) as well as newcomers (Arthur Hiller, Stuart Rosenberg, Boris Sagal, Robert Altman). Ida Lupino directed two episodes, even though Harrison once said, facetiously, that women don't make good directors: "To be a director you sometimes have to be an S.O.B. It is much harder for a woman to be this." In interviews, Harrison deployed dry British wit, giving expected answers a droll twist.

In a 1957 interview, realizing she'd forever be linked with Hitchcock, Harrison expounded upon her own approach to suspense, dropping all ladylike pretense: "Let 'em suffer," she said, referring to the viewers. "Let 'em become participants in the show and twist and turn with every twisting and turning. That's why I'd rather make shows with ordinary persons for characters—secretaries, housewives, a man in an ordinary job. Not the so-called upper classes. They lead a *particular* kind of life. Hitch is a member of the great middle class and he knows these people. When he thinks about stories of the ordinary person, he's absolutely wonderful. . . . The most interesting murderers are the most mild-seeming men. Inside, the most extraordinary things are happening to them."

THE PSYCH WARD

THE RADIATOR SIZZLES LIKE RAIN OFF THE HOT BARREL OF A HOWITZER. THE FLASHING NEON MAKES HIM TWITCH; MUSCLE MEMORY OF THE MUZZLE'S FLASH. THE CEILING FAN SPINS LIKE THE PROP BLADES ON THE STRIPPED-DOWN BOMBER THAT BROUGHT HIM BACK. HE'D TRIED TO BURST THE GURNEYS STRAPS AND SPRINT ONBOARD—COULDN'T WAIT TO GET HOME. BUT THEN THERE WAS THE WARD: THE DAILY STENCH OF DISINFECTANT AND FESTERING DREAMS. AND BIG BLANK GAPS IN HIS THOUGHTS, FILLED UP WITH THE FACES OF THE DOGGIES LEFT BEHIND, DEAD ON SOME CRATERED ROAD IN FRANCE.

Far from the tourist spots of Dark City is the Veterans Hospital, packed with men who fought their best but left pieces of themselves in places they'd never imagined visiting. This cold gray building stands in a neighborhood most citizens never see. Screenwriters, on the other hand, made frequent visits. For them, discharged and disoriented dogfaces offered a new spin on the bewilderment and betrayal the Great Depression had inspired in earlier crime dramas.

Even before the war ended, some producers looked past the imminent victory galas to the trauma vets lugged back home. *The Best Years of Our Lives* (RKO, 1946) and *Pride of the Marines* (WB, 1945) dealt with disabled vets in sensitive fashion—stoic GIs did their patriotic duty by shaking off tragedy, adjusting to their misfortune, and not asking inconvenient questions of their country. Everyone could feel better about armless and sightless soldiers after a trip to the movies.

The nation's concern for its vets was codified by enactment of the GI Bill,

which provided benefits to soldiers for education and vocational training. The federal largesse of the bill assuaged Americans about the fortunes of its brave returning soldiers. But in the musty wards of the Dark City VA hospital are some old-timers with a different story to tell.

One of their favorites is a real-life crime saga that outdoes anything from Sinister Heights. Back in 1921, President Warren G. Harding appointed a personal friend, Charles Forbes, to run the fledgling Veterans Bureau, as the VA was initially called. A Marine Corps deserter, Forbes was an odd choice for the position. He'd had no stomach for combat, but Forbes had no problem brownnosing Washington power brokers. He raised pork-barrel chicanery to nefarious heights. He controlled the sale of all surplus Army supplies and wangled jurisdiction over all new hospital construction. He fraudulently resold pristine goods as "damaged" supplies, pocketing millions.

"Forbes' quarter-billion dollars in accumulated graft, corruption, and inefficiency was to become a landmark by which a succession of VA administrators could be measured," wrote Robert Klein in his history of the VA, *Wounded Men, Broken Promises.* When Harding learned of Forbes's criminal impunity, he tried to strangle his appointee in the Red Room of the White House. Forbes did a two-year stretch

In *High Wall*, Dr. Lorrison (Audrey Totter) uses narcosynthesis to help brain-damaged serviceman Steve Kenet (Robert Taylor) learn the truth about his wife's murder.

in Leavenworth and was given a $100,000 fine—less than a tenth of 1 percent of what he'd stolen from American taxpayers.

Forbes's successor, Brigadier General Frank T. Hines, was a New Deal opponent who shoveled funds back into federal coffers, rather than squander them on veterans. On his leash the VA became a bureaucratic boondoggle incapable of meeting the needs of discharged servicemen. A congressional probe proved the depth of the problem, but its only solution was to appoint popular Omar Bradley, the "GI's General," to take over the agency. Bradley forged alliances with medical schools to take up the slack, but it didn't stem the wave of needy veterans.

Hollywood got in the act, albeit in melodramatic fashion. Within a year of the atomic bombing of Japan that brought an apocalyptic finish to Pacific combat, movies for the first time touched on the disillusionment of combat vets. Least mawkish of these films were noirs. When dislocated GIs were dropped into a crime drama, analogies crept in about a civilized society's hypocrisy, demanding the "ultimate sacrifice" from young men, then forgetting them once the enemy is vanquished. A terse assessment of this was offered by Joe Rolfe (John Payne) in *Kansas City Confidential*, as he's grilled about his role in a robbery. "He won a Bronze Star and a Purple Heart," notes an interrogator. "Try buying a cup of coffee with them," Rolfe snaps back.

When Johnny marched home to Dark City, he wasn't met with a ticker-tape parade or a job offer. He was usually greeted by a grifter with an easy-money scam. Sometimes, he woke up in the psych ward, suffering from a head wound, crucial patches of his memory missing.

The Crooked Way (UA, 1949) was a prime example. Decorated infantrymen Eddie Rice (John Payne) is turned loose from a VA hospital with a few bucks in his pocket and not much in his head. When he hits Union Station, he's braced by the bulls, who know him as Eddie Ricardi, a local hood. Eddie's ex-wife Nina (Ellen Drew) shows up, now the main squeeze of gangster Vince Alexander (Sonny Tufts),

once Eddie's partner. Vince thinks Eddie enlisted to skip out on a job gone sour, for which Vince took the rap.

Director Robert Florey is a bit too empathetic with his protagonist: His pacing is as foggy as the hero's frontal lobes. But *The Crooked Way* is enlivened by John Alton's sinister cinematography, which turns adoring when the camera creeps in for close-ups of Ellen Drew. The most memorable moment occurs in the climactic shoot-out, when Vince uses Eddie as a shield against a battalion of cops. Wizened old Petey (Percy Helton), an ailurophile wounded by Vince, slowly crawls to a discarded gun, drags himself up behind the gangster, and takes aim. Then Petey's allergies kick in. He wheezes up some cat dander. Vince turns and pops Petey point-blank. It's a shocking stroke of originality in an otherwise paint-by-numbers picture.

In *The Clay Pigeon* (RKO, 1949), Seamen First Class Jimmy Fletcher (Bill Williams) wakes up in a VA hospital with amnesia. He's stunned to find himself facing court-martial for treason and murder. In finest noir fashion, the muddy-minded swab doesn't wait to be assigned a judge advocate—he breaks out to track down the missing pieces of his memory. Within hours he's the target of a manhunt involving the police, Naval Intelligence, and a gang of southland chiselers. He heads to the home of his closest Navy pal, Mark Gregory, only to learn from the guy's widow, Martha (Barbara Hale), that Gregory is the guy he's accused of murdering. Fletcher kidnaps Martha and hauls her along on his search for answers.

Before an economical sixty-three minutes have elapsed, Fletcher has broken up a counterfeiting ring operated by corrupt Japanese and US soldiers—and gotten hitched to Martha. The matrimonial bond apparently blossomed through some sadomasochistic ministrations: "Don't make me tie you up again," Fletcher threatens at one point with a big "Aw shucks" grin. "You just try it," Martha vamps back, slyly soliciting more rope burns.

The Clay Pigeon, like most noirs about homecoming vets, exploited a soldier's disability for dramatic effect. Battle-induced infirmities—even the ubiquitous amnesia—proved irresistible to scenarists seeking "plausible" motivations for their improbable plot twists.

The Crooked Way and *The Clay Pigeon* were pallid knockoffs of Joseph L. Mankiewicz's *Somewhere in the Night* (Fox, 1946), the first and best of the amnesiac veteran movies. John Hodiak plays ex-Marine George Taylor, who returns to Los Angeles with only two clues to his identity: a nasty letter from an angry woman, and

JOHN **HODIAK** · NANCY **GUILD** · LLOYD **NOLAN**

SOMEWHERE IN THE NIGHT

with **RICHARD CONTE**

20th CENTURY-FOX
Josephine **HUTCHINSON** · *Fritz* **KORTNER** · *Margo* **WOODE** · *Sheldon* **LEONARD** · *Lou* **NOVA** · *Directed by* **JOSEPH L. MANKIEWICZ** · *Produced by* **ANDERSON LAWLER**

SCREEN PLAY BY HOWARD DIMSDALE & JOSEPH L. MANKIEWICZ · ADAPTED BY LEE STRASBERG · FROM A STORY BY MARVIN BOROWSKY

Decorated war vet Rip Murdock (Humphrey Bogart) faces more guns back home, this one wielded by Coral Chandler (Lizabeth Scott) in *Dead Reckoning*.

another missive signed by "Larry Cravat." The hazy vet pursues Cravat through a demimonde of nightclubs, police stations, and dingy dives, confronting a menagerie of colorful bit players. In the end, he learns that all along he's been chasing himself (a twist exhumed years later with devilish overtones in *Angel Heart* [Tri-Star, 1987]).

As these scenarios suggest, the vexed veteran was the perfect protagonist for films that combined the "Why me?" suspense of Blind Alley thrillers with hard-boiled hegiras indigenous to Shamus Flats. The symbolism of a lost and lonely recruit, searching for his identity, was too tempting for writers to resist, even after the novelty wore off.

A less vulnerable serviceman returned home in *Dead Reckoning* (Columbia, 1947). Flinty paratrooper Rip Murdock (Humphrey Bogart) investigates the disappearance of jump-mate Johnny Drake (William Prince), who rabbits before he's to receive the Congressional Medal of Honor. Rip's search leads to Gulf City, a humid Floridian sister to Dark City, where he encounters local gangster Martinelli (Morris Carnovsky), husky-voiced songbird Coral Chandler (Lizabeth Scott), and the charred body of his war buddy cooling in a morgue drawer. The classic recipe is spiced by the contempt Bogart dishes to crooks who've gotten rich at home while he's risked his life overseas.

Martinelli goes out of his way to insult Murdock, boasting that his casino proffers only the best "prewar" wines and pâtés. No ration stamps for the well-connected. The gangster's private arsenal is assembled from contraband military ordnance. Rip turns the hunt for Johnny's killer into a recon mission, making it clear that even though he's back on US soil, this vet is still behind enemy lines. In a satisfyingly symbolic climax, Rip uses an incendiary grenade to flambé Martinelli and his minions.

Dead Reckoning served up a full ration of hard-boiled noir, assembled from all the requisite ingredients—seasoned hero on a dark quest, oily gangster with pretensions to refinement, flavorful femme fatale, sultry nocturnal environs, vinegary voice-over narration—all coated with the sentimental righteousness of the solitary warrior. But director John Cromwell couldn't quite raise a soufflé from the leaden script, for which no fewer than five writers, including trusty Steve Fisher, earned Purple Hearts.

By '47, Bogart had patented his tough-guy persona. Martinelli and his henchmen were no match for the resourcefulness of this battle-hardened soldier. Liz

Scott jerks his string pretty good; in Dark City women represent a more formidable adversary than puffed-up mobsters. Bogey kisses her off like all the other Vixenville dames who spent the '40s trying to bring him down. It would be a few more years before Bogart tempered his screen image with an edgy humanity, culminating in his portrayal of another military man, paranoid Captain Queeg in *The Caine Mutiny* (Columbia, 1954).

High Wall (MGM, 1947) showed the flip side of the rough-and-ready fighting man Bogart embodied. Steve Kenet (Robert Taylor), an Army pilot, is put in an overcrowded veterans' asylum after he's found unconscious in an overturned car, his dead wife Helen (Dorothy Patrick) beside him. Evidence of strangulation points to Kenet as her killer. A head wound sustained in combat has left him suffering periodic blackouts, and Kenet claims no recollection of the incident. The authorities suspect he's using his brain injury to back up a "temporary insanity" defense. Dr. Ann Lorrison (Audrey Totter) persuades the troubled vet that a second operation, to remove a hematoma from his brain, will free his memory. Kenet's in a quandary. He wants to overcome his disability so he can care for his young son—but he's afraid his restored memory will reveal him as the murderer. *High Wall* was one of numerous noirs that shifted fear and treachery from city streets to the penumbra of the unconscious.

Giving Kenet an injection of sodium pentothal—recommended by ten out of ten Dark City shrinks—Dr. Lorrison dredges up buried details of the fateful night. Kenet had discovered Helen in the apartment of her boss, Willard Whitcombe (Herbert Marshall), a publisher of religious tracts. Spotting her overnight bag on Whitcombe's bed, he lunged for Helen's throat—and blacked out. Convinced Kenet is innocent, Dr. Lorrison helps him reconstruct the fateful night, and the story climaxes with her jabbing the needle of truth into Whitcombe to extract a confession.

Dr. Lorrison is a noir rarity—a compassionate psychiatrist. Typically, doctors in noir were burbling fonts of Freudian psychobabble. Their role model was Dr. Murchison (Leo G. Carroll) in Hitchcock's *Spellbound* (UA, 1945), a condescending European-educated egghead, whose newfangled techniques scrambled old-fashioned common sense—and who won't stop at murder to protect his exalted station in academia. Fear of someone gaining access to—and control of—the deepest parts of one's psyche resulted in many disparaging portrayals of psychiatrists, from Val Lewton horror shows like *Cat People* (RKO, 1942) and *The 7th Victim* (RKO, 1943), to Woolrich-inspired thrillers, to private eye stories in which quack doctors exploit helpless clients. In Dark City, psychiatrists are as corrupt as gangsters, misusing their "power over the mind" to dominate the hapless and disturbed. Such charlatans appear in *Shock* (Fox, 1947), *Nightmare Alley* (Fox, 1947), *Whirlpool* (Fox, 1950), and *Nightmare* (UA, 1955), among others.

High Wall eluded critical evaluation for years, though it contains seminal noir elements. The flashback-within-flashback structure was challenging for an MGM "A" of this period, and may have contributed to the public's lukewarm response. Kenet's anguish was vividly depicted by director Curtis Bernhardt, who excelled at conveying tortured states of mind through sinuous, Expressionistic visuals. When Kenet attacks Helen, and then reenacts the incident with Dr. Lorrison, the camera looms over the women's terrified faces in a startling display of subjective camerawork.

As a specimen of shell-shocked noir, *High Wall* was unique in other ways. Its asylum scenes offered a glimpse of the military generally deemed off-limits. Ample time was devoted to the mental casualties of war; there are references to patients housed in the asylum since World War I. When Kenet demands to see Dr. Lorrison immediately, he's told: "There are 250 patients in this hospital and twelve doctors. We'll get to you when we can." A shard of hard truth woven into the film's baroque design.

Screenwriter Lester Cole, who cowrote *High Wall* with crime specialist Sydney Boehm, would soon be formally accused of slipping subversive messages into his scripts. Only weeks after *High Wall* wrapped, Cole was cited for contempt of Congress as an "unfriendly witness" before HUAC. As one of the Hollywood Ten, he was jailed for refusing to provide the names of suspected Communists.

Cole was an industry stalwart, a screenwriter since the early 1930s. He was a member of the Communist Party of the USA and an early campaigner for unionization of Hollywood scribes. None of these affiliations then had the stigma they'd assume after 1947, when the Cold War plunged discourse into the deep freeze. At the time of his appearance before HUAC, Cole was a favorite of Louis B. Mayer, about to gain lofty writer-producer status at MGM. After the HUAC hysteria, Cole found himself blacklisted, like other artists committed to "progressive" work.

The highest-profile "friendly" witness to testify before HUAC in 1947 was Robert Taylor, who seemed to still be suffering from Steve Kenet's amnesia: "If I were even suspicious of a person being a Communist with whom I was scheduled to work," he declared, "I am afraid it would have to be him or me, because life is a little too short to be around people who annoy me as much as these fellow travelers and Communists do." Cole's work on *High Wall* must've impressed Taylor for the actor to set aside his deeply held ideology.

Taylor had sparked an uproar months earlier, when HUAC's scouting party first went hunting for Hollywood stool pigeons. He claimed President Roosevelt had postponed Taylor's Naval service so he'd be able to film *Song of Russia* (MGM, 1944), a musical that became a touchstone of political debate. Republicans, still smarting from Roosevelt's taxation-based New Deal, sought to discredit Democrats by tarring the late president as a Commie sympathizer. To them, federally sponsored work programs were Socialism by any name. Linking FDR to "pro-Soviet" propaganda, like *Song of Russia*, seemed like a bombshell revelation to political animals in a feeding frenzy. But Taylor soon shrank from the furor and recanted his story.

As anti-Communist fervor gained momentum, treatment of war-related themes became a litmus test for determining an artist's patriotism—or suspicious pacifism. Films that focused on problems of readjustment, or that refused to celebrate victory with the world in disarray, tended to be written by liberals like Dalton Trumbo, Albert Maltz, Carl Foreman, or John Howard Lawson—many of whom had long-standing ties to the film colony's left wing.

Their loyalties were challenged by the Motion Picture Alliance for the Preservation of American Ideals, which, under the leadership of hawks such as Sam Wood, Leo McCarey, Gary Cooper, Robert Montgomery, John Wayne, and Ronald Reagan, sought to root out the "Red Menace" and make movie screens safe for loyal, God-fearing Americans. The reactionary pogrom worked. Hundreds of artists—Communists, progressives, and free thinkers alike—were blacklisted, outright or covertly.

It would be another thirty years, post-Vietnam, before Hollywood used the disabled veteran's plight as grist for drama. In the meantime, crime dramas were the only films willing to suggest that disorientation and mental instability were real problems for combat-scarred soldiers.

Although *High Wall* offered the drama of a wounded vet accused of murder, there was never a doubt that Steve Kenet was innocent—and not only because he

LEFT: Pressbook for *The Blue Dahlia* ABOVE: Demobilized soldiers William Bendix, Hugh Beaumont, and Alan Ladd encounter an active duty GI (Anthony Caruso) in *The Blue Dahlia*.

was played by heartthrob Robert Taylor. While vets were great vulnerable protagonists, it was an unwritten rule they never be guilty of any crime. That was too insensitive—as Raymond Chandler found out when he concocted his own psych ward mystery, *The Blue Dahlia* (Paramount, 1945).

The film's creation is Tinseltown legend, burnished by an application of apocrypha. In '45, Paramount desperately wanted another hit from its biggest star, Alan Ladd, before he reentered the Navy. Ladd had served a hitch in '43, primarily in a morale-boosting capacity. Producer John Houseman, learning that Chandler was halfway through a new novel, convinced studio execs to offer the popular writer a hefty sum to turn his manuscript into an original screenplay. Chandler accepted, and a cast and crew were quickly assembled, topped by Ladd and his mirror-image leading lady, Veronica Lake.

The script turned on the troubles of two demobilized vets, Johnny Morrison (Ladd) and Buzz Wanchek (William Bendix). Johnny has come home to discover his wife Helen (Doris Dowling) is now a squirrelly tramp, canoodling with a local gangster who (yes!) runs a Sunset Strip nightclub, the Blue Dahlia. Helen even

admits to her husband it was her drunk driving that killed their son (she'd written to him it was an illness). Buzz, fresh out of the VA hospital, has a plate in his head that causes tantrums and memory lapses. Things get complicated when Helen is bumped off in her bungalow. Johnny is suspected, and he spends the rest of the film tracking down the real killer, with help from sexy stray Joyce Harwood (Lake) and loyal bulldog Buzz.

Chandler's twist was that Buzz was the killer. His plate started humming when Helen made disparaging cracks about Johnny, but then he blacked out—a twist borrowed from Cornell Woolrich's *Black Angel*. To Chandler's credit, Buzz was at the head of the woozy line of amnesiac vets that trooped through Dark City. The writer envisioned a poignant wrap-up, as Johnny realizes his addled pal is guilty and he has to turn him over to the law.

Helming the production was George Marshall, a journeyman who rarely let an original idea interrupt a shooting schedule. His marching orders were to churn 'em out, so Marshall started shooting before Chandler finished the script. Day by day, Marshall gained on him, cranking scenes into the can before new ones could be written. Halfway in, word came from the Department of the Navy that Chandler's ending didn't pass muster: Buzz could not be the culprit—bad for the Navy's image. Chandler was incensed. He threatened to drop the project. Ladd's reenlistment loomed. A $5,000 completion bonus was dangled before the author. He took umbrage and got crankier. Houseman was at a loss. Finally, Chandler proposed a disingenuous solution: He must work from home, with two secretaries at his disposal, a doctor on call, a pair of Cadillacs to ferry script pages to the set, an open line to Paramount—and the studio's understanding that he could only perform under this pressure mooned to the nuts. Paramount agreed. As Marshall knocked off shot after shot, so did Chandler. Chauffeurs funneled pages to the set, thrashed out by the writer in the midst of a massive bourbon bender.

The film wrapped ahead of schedule and Chandler was fêted like a gallant war hero. His solution to the murder, however, was a clunker: The house detective did it, although the motive didn't seem to extend beyond some convenient lurking at windows and behind curtains—exactly the kind of lame dénouement Chandler detested in other writers.

Ladd's real life was far more intriguing. According to his biographer, Beverly Linet, the actor never did reenlist—he hung around his ranch in Hidden Valley while his wife, agent Sue Carol, negotiated a new deal with Paramount. And Ladd's friendship with Bendix, forged when the pair made a version of Dashiell Hammett's *The Glass Key* (Paramount, 1942), didn't survive the war. The two had been so tight they lived across the street from each other. But when Ladd returned from stateside Naval duty in 1943, grousing about its indignities, Bendix ribbed him: "Quit griping, Laddie. You know you're living the plush life down there in San Diego." Ladd let it pass, but his wife upbraided Bendix: "You're a fine one to talk," she volleyed, "considering you're not rushing off to join up." Bendix, a 4F asthmatic, huffed out. He and Ladd never crossed the street and patched things up. Just another war story, of the Hollywood variety.

NEVER TRUST A GUY YOU MEET IN A BOWLING ALLEY. That's advice vet Howard Tyler (Frank Lovejoy) should have gotten when he did his basic training. Howard never got shipped over, so he didn't even have a war record to parlay into a peacetime paycheck. He'd moved his wife and kids from Boston to Santa Sierra, California,

looking for a fresh start. "How did I know a million other guys would have the same idea?" he snaps at his cloying wife Judy (Kathleen Ryan) before stomping out to look for nonexistent work. When he stops by the lanes for a beer to buzz the edge off his misery, he meets another vet, Jerry Slocum (Lloyd Bridges).

"What outfit were you with?" asks the rakish Slocum, combing his gleaming locks.

"No outfit, really," mumbles Howard. "I never got over. Took my basic at Fort Roberts."

"So did I," beams Slocum. "What a lousy joint—I couldn't wait to get over."

"So you got over. Pretty rugged, huh?"

"That's the rumor I heard in Paris," Slocum smiles. "Ah, *Paree*. You know what I could get for one lousy pack of cigarettes? Boy, the mark-up was terrific."

"I wish a guy could get a buck that easy these days."

"Got a car? Maybe I can put you onto something."

So begins *Try and Get Me!* (UA, 1950), an unheralded picture that's one of the most disturbing of all film noirs. Howard spends the afternoon basking in Slocum's swagger, sizing up the monogrammed silk shirts, expensive cologne, fancy cuff links. "Those are platinum, you know, not silver," Slocum points out. Before Howard drifts, Slocum lays out his cards: He needs a wheelman for some filling station stickups. Howard caves under Slocum's insistence that it's only a few nights' work, in and out, no funny business.

Howard tells himself he's only detouring into petty crime to finally give Judy the middle-class comforts she craves. But the nocturnal knockovers put him on the highway to hell. Jerry ups the ante from robbery to kidnapping. They snatch Donald Miller, scion of a wealthy Santa Sierra family, visions of a big green windfall pushing them on. But as soon as Slocum grabs the rich kid, his hateful envy starts bubbling. "Where'd you get the suit?" he asks, fingering the material. "New York," Miller answers. Slocum sneers: "You guys sure treat yourselves right, don't you?"

In a fit of psychotic rage, Slocum kills their hostage, dumping the body in a desolate quarry. Jerry forces Howard to go through with the plot, dragging him along on a double date to another town, where they mail the ransom note. Howard's shaky mental state is further rattled by his spooky date, Hazel Weatherwax (Katherine Locke, in a strange, unsettling performance). He lurches through a lubricious night on the town, convinced the whole world is watching him, laughing

at him, accusing him. When he passes out on Hazel's couch, the lonesome spinster makes love to him. She finds Donald Miller's tie clasp in the cuff of Howard's trousers. He goes wild and tries to strangle her, before running off. Hazel goes to the police. Howard is trapped like a cowering dog in a shed behind his clapboard house. "What did my daddy do?" his son yelps as the cops close in.

Newspaper columnist Gil Stanton (Richard Carlson), at the urging of his publisher (Art Smith), writes articles playing up the brutality of the killing, fueling public outrage. The sheriff begs him to ease off; the town is too small for the heat of the flames being fanned. Slocum gets nabbed, but Howard's attempt to pin the killing on him is futile. The media, and the vengeful townsfolk, see no distinction between a sociopath and a stupid sap.

In the terrifying climax, a horde of "respectable" citizens, whipped up by Stanton's editorials, storm the jail. Trapped in his cell, Howard Tyler sees death coming in the form of fresh-faced college boys in a frenzy of bloodlust. Slocum greets his seemingly predestined fate with screams of "Try and get me!"

One of the most emotionally charged and bleakest of all noirs, *Try and Get Me!*

was adapted by Jo Pagano from his novel *The Condemned*. Its factual basis was the 1933 lynching in San Jose, California of Jack Holmes and Harold Thurmond, who had kidnapped and killed affluent college student Brooke Hart. *San Jose News* publisher G. Logan Payne fueled citizens' unrest with editorials declaring that "If mob violence could ever be justified it would be in a case like this. . . . There was never a more fiendish crime committed anywhere in the United States . . ." Ten thousand people filled San Jose's town square to cheer the administration of vigilante justice.

Director Cyril Endfield made hardly a false move rendering the shocking story. The insertion of a humanistic Italian professor who lectures Stanton—and the audience—on how society's lack of compassion breeds criminals, is a ham-handed gesture in an otherwise dexterous film. (The preachy doctor is a holdover from the novel, despite Endfield's attempts to remove him.) For most of its ninety

Try and Get Me! adapted a true story from 1933 to reflect the disillusionment of World War II veterans. The ransom scheme of former soldiers Howard Tyler (Frank Lovejoy) and Jerry Slocum (Lloyd Bridges) goes haywire with the murder of their hostage (Carl Kent).

minutes, *Try and Get Me!* (originally titled *The Sound of Fury*) is every bit the equal of Fritz Lang's similarly themed *Fury* (MGM, 1936), also inspired by the San Jose lynchings. The finale, with Bridges pacing his cell like a rabid beast as the crowd seethes below, is shot by DP Guy Roe with an early, highly effective use of handheld camera. The vigilantes' assault is as scary as anything made in Hollywood up to that time. As the prisoners are engulfed by the mob, Endfield cuts to Tyler's son waking up in bed, crying for this father. Gil Stanton sits quietly in his office, wincing at the roars from the crowd as it metes out "justice."

Producer Robert Stillman knew *Try and Get Me!* was special, and he proudly emblazoned his name on the film's haunting final image. But the distributor, United Artists, buried the film after release, another casualty of the anti-Communist crusade. Endfield, a one-time drama teacher and magician, started popping up among The Names, and soon relocated to England.

The fear and confusion rampant in the studios was exemplified by UA's wildly misleading advertising for the film after they tried rereleasing it with a new campaign: "Try and get me! And they tried . . . 6000 people . . . Including the blonde with the ice-cold nerves and the deep, warm curves!!! [That would be Adele Jergens, a character superfluous to the plot] . . . And now you can join . . . Every excitement-packed step of the way . . . From the first angry cry . . . To the roar that explodes the climax!"

A sincere plea against vigilantism, sold as a rip-snorting crowd-pleaser. Those were strange days.

FRANK ENLEY IS NO HARD-LUCK HOWARD TYLER. He's worked his war-hero status into a thriving contractor's business, married a beautiful woman, and has the middle-class program so knocked, he has time to enjoy fishing trips in the mountains. He's left the service with no visible scars, no mental damage. But then Joe Parkson, his one-time bombardier buddy, drops back into his life and the buried horrors emerge into the light.

Act of Violence (MGM, 1949) bristles with anger and guilt, the first postwar noir to take a challenging look at the ethics of men in combat. Enley (Van Heflin) is stalked by the apparently deranged Parkson (Robert Ryan), who seems bent on destroying his former friend's tranquil life. The viewer empathizes with Enley, a solid citizen promoting growth and prosperity. But Parkson's tenacity splinters Enley's psyche, and the truth about his war record leaks out.

In a Nazi prison camp, Enley ratted out his unit, revealing their escape plan. All his comrades—except Parkson—were killed. He told himself he'd squealed to *save* the lives of his mates. Now Parkson wants revenge. "But Frank, they won't listen to Parkson," his wife, Edith (Janet Leigh), assures him. "They'll listen to you." Edith understands her husband's tormentor is the kind of brooding, ill-tempered vet common folk ignore. Her husband, by contrast, is a pillar of the community, a charismatic man with a gift of gab, who has recast the truth to make himself heroic.

"Do I have to spell it out for you?" Enley snaps. "The Nazis even paid me a price. They gave me food and I ate it. I hadn't done it just to *save* their lives. . . . They were dead and I was eating and maybe that's all I did it for—to save one man. Me."

Enley flees from the sanctuary of his suburban home into the underbelly of

Dark City, where he's adrift among gamblers, thugs, procurers, and whores. He finds refuge with a played-out hooker, Pat (Mary Astor, superb) whose pimp, Johnny (Berry Kroeger), offers to kill Parkson for a fee.

Robert Richards's screenplay was adapted from an unpublished story by Collier Young, an ambitious assistant to Harry Cohn. Young would soon embark on a career as an independent producer with his bride-to-be, Ida Lupino. The film was originally to be a small indie production starring Howard Duff (who would, coincidentally, succeed Young as Ida Lupino's third husband). Then Mark Hellinger picked it up, with the notion of pairing Gregory Peck and Humphrey Bogart. Finally filmed at MGM, *Act of Violence* benefited from Robert Surtees's photography, which contrasted the brightness of budding suburbia with the murkiness of the underworld into which Enley sinks.

"That bad, huh? What is it, love trouble or money trouble? I've seen all the troubles in the world and they boil down to just those two. You're broke or you're lonely. Or both." Burned-out prostitute Pat (Mary Astor) hasn't been where Frank has been in *Act in Violence*.

This was Fred Zinnemann's lone excursion into Dark City. A dispassionate but serious-minded director, Zinnemann was clearly influenced by such recent releases as *The Killers* and *Crossfire*, since none of his subsequent films had the moody flourishes displayed here. Zinnemann wasn't a natural on this turf; the pervasiveness of noir pushed him into it.

The casting of Robert Ryan as Joe Parkson was also part of a trend. Ryan had won notice—and an Oscar nomination—for his role in *Crossfire* (RKO, 1947), which, like *Act of Violence*, was conceived as a "message" picture, camouflaged as crime drama. The driving force behind it was Adrian Scott, whose status at RKO was top drawer in the wake of two hits, *Murder, My Sweet* and *Cornered* (1945). Scott was committed to producing movies that "mattered," although his fear of repercussions played hell with a nervous stomach. *Cornered*, for example, was a thriller steeped in antifascist sentiment, although the final cut wisely left most of Communist writer John Wexley's dogma on the cutting-room floor.

With *Crossfire*, Scott fashioned another film reviling fascists. It's a murder mystery, set in an odd liberty limbo, filled with GIs hanging around Washington, DC, awaiting discharge. A civilian (Sam Levene) is beaten to death, and a soldier's ID belonging to Jeff Mitchell (George Cooper) turns up in his room. Captain Finlay (Robert Young), a local homicide detective, hunts Mitchell down with the help of two other soldiers, Keely (Robert Mitchum) and Montgomery (Robert Ryan). Monty's blatant bigotry makes him suspect, as the victim was a Jew. A young grunt, the butt of Monty's cruel jabs, is used to set him up, and Montgomery is revealed as the real killer.

By 1946, Jews in the film industry had been galvanized by facts emerging about Hitler's death camps, and the campaign for a homeland in Palestine. Semitic issues became, for the first time, possible subjects for mainstream movies. Ironically, Jewish studio moguls—Mayer, Goldwyn, Cohn, Warner, Selznick—had spent years cloaking their ethnicity, fearing it would hurt their films in a largely Gentile mass market. Mayer even kept a portrait of Cardinal Spellman on his desk, next to one of J. Edgar Hoover, ensuring he simultaneously mollified the Catholic church and America's most powerful anti-Semite.

When Jack Warner offered Julius Garfinkel a contract, he demanded that he change his name to James Garfield. The actor protested: "You wouldn't name a goddamn actor 'Abraham Lincoln,' would you?" No, came the response: "Abe is a name most people think is Jewish, and we wouldn't want people to get the wrong idea." "But I *am* Jewish," barked the soon-to-be John (not James) Garfield, clinging to a vestige of his heritage. Sam Goldwyn, explaining why Frank Sinatra got the part Sam Levene had played in *Guys and Dolls* on Broadway, said succinctly: "You can't have a Jew play a Jew. It wouldn't work on the screen."

Fox's Darryl Zanuck was determined to be the first studio boss to mainstream the issue of anti-Semitism, adapting the novel *Gentleman's Agreement*. It told the story of a Gentile who learns about bigotry by pretending to be a Jew. Ring Lardner Jr., viewing the finished product, disdainfully assessed its moral: "Never be mean to a Jew, because he might turn out to be a Gentile."

Crossfire's creative team of Adrian Scott, writer John Paxton, and director Edward Dmytryk feared the film might never get made, but Dore Schary, newly installed as head of production at RKO, eagerly gave them the green light—he wanted to get his low-budget thriller into theaters first, stealing Zanuck's thunder. Scott claimed his film wasn't specifically about anti-Semitism. In a memo to Schary, he wrote: "This is a story of personal fascism as opposed to organized fascism. [It] indicates how it is possible for us to have a Gestapo, if the country should go fascist. A character like Monty would qualify brilliantly for the leadership of the Belsen concentration camp. Fascism hates weakness in people; minorities. Monty hates fairies, Negroes, Jews, and foreigners. In the book, Monty murders a fairy. He could have murdered a Negro, a foreigner, or a Jew."

Despite the message being thickly ladled at times, *Crossfire*'s story was deftly told. Robert Young's earnest homilies about brotherhood don't carry half the weight of Robert Mitchum explaining how ugly realities released by the war can't be neatly tucked away. "The snakes are loose," he says, like a man who knows how bad it's going to get.

Crossfire shocked everyone, including Schary and Scott, by being a box-office hit. Whether its success was due to a timely message or taut storytelling, no one was sure (although surveys prior to the film's release suggested little public interest in ethnically themed stories). As the picture reaped humanitarian awards, anti-Communist crusaders moved in on Scott and Dmytryk. Both were branded Red and sent to jail, members of the infamous Hollywood Ten. Scott's dream of making significant movies was over. In the '50s, he'd write TV scripts using a "front."

Dmytryk, along with director Elia Kazan (who'd helmed *Gentleman's Agreement*), became famous examples of blacklistees who bartered their way back into Hollywood by repudiating ties to the Communists and fingering colleagues for federal investigators.

Robert Ryan, Robert Mitchum, and Robert Young in *Crossfire*

A GOOD MAN
IN A BAD TIME

Chalk up the lasting impact of *Crossfire* to Robert Ryan. While Scott and Dmytryk worried themselves sick about its reception, Ryan showed no fear shouldering the film's rancid burden. His sneering ferocity got his career on track—and cast him in an evil mold he'd spend the rest of his professional life trying to break. Ryan was, in truth, the antithesis of the venal characters he excelled at portraying.

Born in Chicago in 1909, to an Irish family in the building trades, Ryan was a shy kid with a precocious fondness for Shakespeare. His father nudged him into the boxing ring to knock the bookishness out of him. The gangly kid surprised: At Dartmouth, he studied theater and held the university's heavyweight boxing crown four years running. Ryan's first love was writing, and he diligently punched out prose in hopes of becoming a playwright or journalist. The Depression encouraged him to be practical.

Ryan's peripatetic pursuit of a living wage was S.O.P. among Depression-era men: engine-room janitor on an Africa-bound freighter, ranch hand in Montana, cemetery plot pitchman, collector for a loan company, miner, prospector—anything with promise of a payday.

In '38, the winds shifted when Ryan risked a $300 buy-in on a friend's oil well, and it came a-gusher. He took his two-grand grubstake and headed west. The nest egg funded a year in Max Reinhardt's acting school. Even though Paramount scouts, after viewing a screen test, said that he was "not the type for pictures," Ryan persevered. He hit the local boards hard, even singing and dancing. He ended up with a $75-per-week contract at Paramount.

Ryan also signed a matrimonial deal with actress Jessica Cadwalader, a fellow student in Reinhardt's class. She was ambitious and talented, but as was often the case back then, she sacrificed her career for her husband's.

(She became a successful author of young adult fiction.) In the early '40s, awaiting the actual draft, Ryan fought the Axis on Paramount soundstages, fattening a growing résumé of B war films, if not his reputation. He returned to the legit stage in the Broadway production of Clifford Odets's *Clash by Night*. It bombed, but an RKO scout caught Ryan's act and signed him once his Paramount pact expired.

For two more years, Ryan sank into studio foxholes, playing soldiers who rarely drew breath at the fade-out. One of these, a homefront weeper called *Tender Comrade* (RKO, 1943), was his first starring role, and it united him for the third time with director Edward Dmytryk. He played the groom of Ginger Rogers, with whom he enjoys a single night of wedded bliss before shipping out. He dies in combat, leaving her to cope as a widowed mother. The actress's mother, Lela, who guarded Ginger's career like a junkyard dog, insisted the studio remove the pinkest lines of Dalton Trumbo's script: "This is a democracy—that means share and share alike," for example. Lela Rogers was a proud Red-sniffing pioneer.

Later that year Ryan hitched up with the real military. First role: Marine Corps drill instructor at Camp Pendleton. Two years of that helped distill the lathered-up fury he'd bring to future films. Mustering out, Ryan met fellow jarhead Richard Brooks, who'd recently published *The Brick Foxhole*. Ryan said he'd kill for the part of Monty, and Brooks said he'd put in the good word if a film version ever materialized. Two years later, renamed *Crossfire*, it launched Ryan's career.

Much later, after he'd breathed life into some of the most miserable bastards ever seen on movie screens, Ryan professed regret at ever making *Crossfire*. He became so identified with tightly wound characters, no casting director could see him as a heroic leading man. Ryan rued losing "A" roles to Gregory Peck. Even as a good-hearted charmer in *About Mrs. Leslie* (Paramount, 1954), a thundercloud of ambiguity hung over Ryan. Was he projecting it? Or was it that viewers couldn't shake the anger they'd seen in Monty Montgomery (*Crossfire*), Joe Parkson (*Act of Violence*), Smith Ohlrig

(*Caught* [MGM, 1949]), Stoker Thompson (*The Set-Up*), Jim Wilson (*On Dangerous Ground*), Nick Scanlon (*The Racket*), and Earl Pfeiffer (*Clash by Night*)? A critic for the *New York Times*, reviewing *Act of Violence*, captured Ryan's persona perfectly: "infernally taut."

In the '50s, studios shied away from contemporary urban dramas in favor of colorful wide-screen spectacles, free of political pitfalls. Ryan was sent west. He loathed making westerns, but found himself saddling up with monotonous regularity. *Inferno* (Fox, 1953), was a 3-D Technicolor inversion of *The Postman Always Rings Twice*, in which Ryan played a cuckolded husband left to die in the desert by his two-timing wife (Rhonda Fleming). As always, Ryan is exceptional, enacting his solitary ordeal twice—once on location and again in a recording booth, in an extraordinary stream-of-consciousness voice-over.

Steve Brodie is menaced by Robert Ryan in *Crossfire*.

Ruminating on his career in 1971 for *Films and Filming*, the actor talked about how he envied urbane Cary Grant and the fabulous locations—Monte Carlo, Paris, the Riviera—in which the debonair star always seemed to work. "I'm fated to work in faraway, desolate places . . . In deserts with a dirty shirt and a two-day growth of beard and bad food. But that's an act of birth. I get all the worst locations because of the way I look. But I am an urban character. I was born in the big city. I have a long, seamy face which adapts itself to Westerns—but I don't for one moment consider myself a Western actor essentially."

In the prime of his career, Ryan, Jessica, and their three children lived with an anti-Hollywood modesty. The parents took intense interest in their children's education, going so far as to fund and construct, in 1953, the Oakwood School, a private center offering an alternative to crowded public schools and rich-kid country clubs. Ryan called it "watered-down progressive," and it was the first time his political and philosophical beliefs brought him grief. Conservative neighbors egged the building and painted crosses on its doors. A committed leftist, Ryan had eluded persecution during the HUAC witch hunt; but by the mid-'50s he was active in the ACLU, a big supporter of the UN, and president of the Southern California branch of the United World Federalists.

Meanwhile, he continued to portray men he despised—amoral racists like Reno Smith in *Bad Day at Black Rock* (MGM, 1954), a contemporary western in which Spencer Tracy played a one-armed vet who rides into a dusty desert town to present a Japanese farmer with his son's posthumous war medal. Surprise: A gang of rabid townsfolk, led by Ryan, has murdered the old man in a fit of racism, masquerading as patriotism.

You'd think Ryan's roles couldn't get more evil, but somehow he upped the ante in the exceptional *Odds Against Tomorrow* (UA, 1959) and Peter Ustinov's salty adaptation of Melville's *Billy Budd* (Allied Artists, 1962). *Films in Review* called Ryan's turn as Master-at-Arms John Claggart the "apotheosis of screen villainy."

Although he built his career with the diligence of a stonemason, Ryan felt trapped by the roles he was offered. During the '50s, he poured his frustrations over ice and drank them down, becoming a functioning alcoholic.

He believed his rejection of the Hollywood lifestyle worked against him. Thinking it might help his career, Ryan moved the family into a tony Holmby Hills spread. Daughter Lisa said it "swallowed us up." She recalls many nights when her father would sit in the dark kitchen, nursing one of many beverages, railing to the acting gods: "Goddamned 'B' pictures! That's all they give me. Goddamned 'B' pictures!"

By the early '60s, Ryan was one of Hollywood's highest-profile liberals, a "militant dove" leading the Southern California Committee on Sane Nuclear Policy and an outspoken fixture at early Vietnam War protests. In '62, he uprooted the Ryan clan and moved to New York, to pursue theater work and dodge death threats from the John Birch Society.

After several years of stage work, Ryan again went west, literally and figuratively. Now in his sixties, his leathery countenance was ideally suited to a new generation of gritty westerns, such as *The Professionals* (Columbia, 1966) and *Hour of the Gun* (UA, 1967). As Deke Thornton in Sam Peckinpah's *The Wild Bunch* (WB, 1969), he and William Holden waged a Mexican standoff over which craggy veteran projected more bone-deep weariness.

Ryan's last act was perhaps his best. In John Frankenheimer's film version of Eugene O'Neill's *The Iceman Cometh* (American Film Theater, 1973), Ryan gave a searing portrayal of derelict political activist Larry Slade. In an all-star cast, Ryan dominated with a performance of life-or-death intensity. He wasn't reaching far for inspiration. His wife Jessica, only fifty-seven, had died the previous year from cancer. Ryan had also developed the disease and he knew his days were numbered.

On July 11, 1973, he succumbed. New York columnist Pete Hamill offered this tribute: "There should be a poem of farewell for Robert Ryan. [It] should express his quiet presence through so many lonely years when few people were struggling to bring decency to the world. . . . Life, death, loneliness, loss: these were some of the things we learned from the quiet art of Robert Ryan, who was a good man in a bad time."

Ryan is an unhinged handyman who terrorizes Ida Lupino in *Beware My Lovely* (RKO, 1952).

KNOCKOVER SQUARE

P IECE OF CAKE. FIVE MINUTES. STAY FOCUSED. FIRE THE DRILL. DEEP BREATH. THE BIT'S GOING IN LIKE BUTTER. LET THE REST OF THIS STINKING TOWN PUNCH A CLOCK AND LIVE ON HAND-TO-MOUTH PAYCHECKS. *SIRENS*. NO. NOT SIRENS, *SCREAMS*. SOMEBODY ELSE'S PROBLEM. *C'MON. DIG!* ALL THOSE LOSERS BUSTING THEIR HUMPS ON EIGHT-HOUR SHIFTS. I'LL BE LAUGHING AT THEM. FOUR MINUTES AND WE'RE OUT WITH A QUARTER MIL. "SPEED IT UP!" *SHUT UP*. DON'T WATCH ME, KEEP AN EYE OUT. *OH, NO!* BIT BROKE. *HAND ME THE SPARE*. WAIT. "DID YOU HEAR THAT?"

After seven years in stir, Doc Reidenschneider (Sam Jaffe) has returned to Dark City. His legend as a criminal mastermind precedes him; Doc knows the law will be on him like white on rice. But the old gent's angling for a last takedown: more than a million bucks' worth of gems from an impregnable jewelry exchange. The little general, who hides his predilections beneath a genteel Old World veneer, sets out to assemble his crew: a stake horse, a fence, a hooligan, a driver, and a box man.

"What boxes have you opened?" he asks Louis Ciavelli (Anthony Caruso), reputed to be the most versatile of safe crackers. "Cannonball, double-door, even a few Fire Chests, all of them," says Ciavelli. Confident but not arrogant—just the yegg the doctor ordered.

This commando unit, operating in the umbrae of *The Asphalt Jungle* (MGM, 1950), gave an injection of realism to the postwar crime picture. Instead of the snarling miscreants seen in hundreds of gangster shoot-'em-ups, *The Asphalt Jungle*

The Asphalt Jungle: Sam Jaffe, Anthony Caruso, and Sterling Hayden clock in for work.

offered an underworld of struggling laborers, alienated loners, even honorable family men—in addition to garden-variety leeches and shysters. These were neorealist thieves, after bigger scores than bicycles.

Director John Huston had an affinity for veteran novelist W. R. Burnett's approach to the crime thriller. He'd scripted Burnett's *High Sierra*, another rugged outlaw caper, in 1940. Burnett had also penned one of the seminal 1930s gangster stories, *Little Caesar* (WB, 1931). Huston leapt at the chance to film Burnett's *Jungle* when *Quo Vadis*, an Eternal City costume drama he was to direct, was postponed. Huston was more comfortable with the dynamics of small groups of men under pressure than he was with hordes of toga-draped extras.

Huston had a flair for capers. In addition to *High Sierra*—which revolved around the robbery of a mountain resort—he'd worked with fledgling screenwriter Richard Brooks to expand Hemingway's story "The Killers" into a feature for producer Mark Hellinger. The film revolved around a factory robbery only hinted at in the original story (Due to contractual conflicts, Anthony Veiller is the sole credited writer on *The Killers*).

Huston's first bold move in adapting *Jungle* was to eighty-six Burnett's structure, which framed the story from the perspective of the police, who cope with ". . . the nightly toll of crime coming in over the commissioner's radio, the voice of the asphalt jungle . . ." Huston stuck with Doc and his cohorts. Co-scribe Ben Maddow credited Huston with writing the scene that delineated the picture's theme: "When I think of all the awful people you come in contact with, downright criminals, I get scared," says May (Dorothy Tree), wife of corrupt attorney Alonzo D. Emmerich (Louis Calhern), fence for the purloined jewels. To which Emmerich replies: "There's nothing so different about them. Crime is only a left-handed form of human endeavor."

Huston's take on such sinister pursuits stressed the motivations of his crooks. They're not hostile hoods looking for a way to wield power; they're disgruntled city dwellers trying to score some breathing room. Louie Ciavelli doesn't crave a penthouse or fancy cars; he just wants enough dough to move his family from a cramped tenement into a decent middle-class home. Doc dreams of retiring to Mexico, where he can while away his twilight years ogling pretty girls on the beach. Dix Handley (Sterling Hayden), the hooligan, is a bluegrass boy bushwhacked by the big city. He needs to pay off gambling debts before he can have any hope of buying back the family ranch in Kentucky. "First thing I'm gonna do is take a bath in the creek and wash this city dirt off me," he tells his girl, Doll Conovan (Jean Hagen).

Gone are the gangland flourishes of previous crime movies, including Huston's own *Key Largo* (WB, 1949), in which Edward G. Robinson played a Lucky Luciano–type mobster with the broadness audiences had come to expect from larger-than-life perpetrators. In *The Asphalt Jungle*, crime is as routine as an eight-hour shift on the packing line. Huston directs with business-as-usual detachment, eschewing sensationalism at every turn.

As a guide, Doc Reidenschneider is a font of sagacity: "Experience has taught me to never trust a policeman—just when you think one's all right, he turns legit." Later, he explains the wisdom of his personal disarmament policy: "I never carry a gun. You carry a gun, you shoot a cop. Bad rap, hard to beat. You don't carry a gun, you give up when they point one at you."

Doc's first visit in town is with Cobby (Marc Lawrence), a bookmaker running a clearinghouse for clandestine activity. Cobby underwrites the venture, allowing Doc to hire his crew for flat fees, rather than a percentage of the spoils. Emmerich, the slippery solicitor, is the fence who'll move the stolen gems. But he's far from the solvent sophisticate he purports to be. He's blown his savings on sexy "niece" Angela

(Marilyn Monroe), who allows "Uncle Lon" to reclaim some of his faded youth. When Emmerich can't call in a single marker to pay for the jewels, he concocts a swindle. "It's my whole way of life," he admits sadly. "Every time I turn around, it costs thousands of dollars. I've got to get out. I've got to get out from under."

Hollywood's Production Code was created to ensure that the public would never empathize with criminals, but it was helpless when it came to caper movies. In caper films, a man's character is determined by his steadiness under pressure, more than his adherence to right over wrong. Audiences identified with the nervy thieves as they tried to pull off a seemingly impossible job. The blurring of moral distinctions was part and parcel of noir. It reached its apex in *The Asphalt Jungle*, and the dozens of heist stories it inspired (including the 1956 French masterpiece *Rififi*, directed by Hollywood ex-pat Jules Dassin, which may even be superior).

ABOVE: "Why are you staring at me like that, Uncle Lon?" Angela Phinlay (Marilyn Monroe) is a catalyst for crime in *The Asphalt Jungle*. OPPOSITE: No honor among thieves: Emmerich (Louis Calhern) has his henchman (Brad Dexter) pull a shakedown at the post-heist square-up in *The Asphalt Jungle*. Dix is about to earn his cut, although he gets a bullet for his trouble.

A RELUCTANT STAR

Sterling Hayden shared Dix Handley's desire to escape. By his own admission not much of an actor, Hayden was trapped in the life by 1950. For him, Hollywood *was* Dark City, a place that drained his soul and stuffed cash into the pockets of the poseur he allowed himself to become.

When John Huston cast Hayden in *The Asphalt Jungle*—opposite such refined craftsmen as Louis Calhern and Sam Jaffe—he was taking a huge inspired gamble. In the 1940s, Hayden did little more than display, in vivid Technicolor, flowing blond locks and a manly physique. By the close of the decade, he was branded with a reputation as a surly malcontent. Paramount fired him when he froze before the camera. He needed therapy to sort out conflicted feelings about being an actor. "Shit!" Hayden railed in his autobiography, *Wanderer*. "I went through the war. I jumped out of bombers. I played kick-the-can with E-boats. . . . Yet whenever I get a close-up in a nice warm studio I curl up and die. Why?" It would be a while before he learned the answer, but when Huston chose him for the role of Dix, Hayden was just happy to find a kindred spirit, a virile man of action. MGM tried to talk Huston out of using the troubled actor, but the director hung tough. He saw in Hayden real-life parallels to Dix's predicament: a simple guy pigeonholed by a résumé that read like a rap sheet, struggling to reclaim his true identity.

Born Sterling Relyea Walter in Montclair, New Jersey, in 1916, the strapping lad chucked a middle-class upbringing in his teens, running away (under the name John Hamilton) to become mate on a schooner. His dream was to operate a merchant shipping company on the coast of Maine. He earned his sea legs dory-trawling for haddock off Newfoundland. At twenty-two, he sailed the brigantine *Florence C. Robinson* to Tahiti. At a muscled six-five, wind burned and sun-bleached, he was a woman's daydream of a potent Poseidon. Film director Edward Griffith saw an article about the young mariner and arranged an interview. Hayden's decision to forgo the sea for a movie career racked his conscience for years to come.

He inked a $150-a-week pact with Paramount, debuted in *Virginia* (1941) opposite Madeleine Carroll, and married the English actress the next year. Before his career could take off, he was summoned to military duty, where his skills as a salt were used in nautical espionage in the Mediterranean, Atlantic, and North Sea. He'd return from the war with his conscience even more conflicted: While most vets struggled to reassimilate, Hayden demob'd into a lucrative life as Paramount's latest beefcake attraction. The Publicity Department billed him as "The Most Beautiful Man in the Movies," and issued bare-torso promo photos. He divorced Carroll and married socialite Betty de Noon. Hayden was perpetually at odds with the easy life, embarrassed by how much money he made for "doing nothing."

"If you don't believe in taking what you don't earn," he inquired rhetorically in *Wanderer*, "then how can you be reconciled to the astronomical figures [an actor is paid]? I never was. Furthermore, I couldn't stand the work." He excoriated himself for cashing the checks and "posing." "Where did the weakness lie?" he asked. "The weakness that forced you to give up ten or twelve of what might have been the most vital years of your life? It lay, did it not, in the fact that you were flawed. You were big and strong on the surface, but something was wrong inside. You were strong enough to rebel—not strong enough to revolt."

This was the angst channeled into *The Asphalt Jungle*; Hayden's tortured introversion finally meshed with a character. He was comfortable as an actor for the first time. After *Jungle*, Hayden would roam Dark City a few more times, playing hard-bitten cops and crooks, sickened by the cheapness of urban life, longing for their day of liberation. Not a big stretch for the one-time "Beautiful Blonde Viking God."

Just as Hayden's career was revitalized, another crisis of conscience struck. HUAC called Hayden's politics into question: He'd served with distinction in World War II, but Hayden had been a member of the Communist Party.

He toyed with the notion of facing down HUAC by running an ad in the trades declaring that he'd been a Communist—*but so what?* When his therapist, Ernest Philip Cohen, asked why he didn't go ahead with the ads, Hayden erupted: "Because I haven't got the guts, that's why. Maybe because I'm a parlor pink. Because I want to remain employable in this town long enough to finish this fucking analysis.

"Because when it comes time for the divorce, I'd like to be able to see my children, and the courts downtown are full of judges who would look askance at a divorced man who was an ex-Communist to boot. That's why. How many reasons do you want, sitting there on your throne?"

Hayden spoke to the FBI privately, stressing he did not want to name names. He'd offer anything about himself, but didn't want to play the implication game. "They know I was a Party member," he fumed to Cohen before leaving for Washington. "They don't want information, they want to put on a show, and I'm the star. They've already agreed to go over the questions with me in advance. It's a rigged show: radio and TV and the papers. I'm damned no matter what I do. Cooperate and I'm a stool pigeon. Shut my mouth and I'm a pariah."

In front of HUAC, Hayden played it contrite. The Dix Handley death-stare wasn't in evidence. But seven other people were: He ultimately named names, including his ex-mistress, and emerged with his career—if not his mental health—intact. He told Cohen, "I'm thinking of quitting analysis. . . . I'll say this, too, that if it hadn't been for you I wouldn't have turned into a stoolie for J. Edgar Hoover. I don't think you have the foggiest notion of the contempt I have had for myself since the day I did that thing. . . . Fuck it! And fuck you, too."

Hayden's kiss-off came too late. In a twist straight from the Dark City rewrite room, a flood of rumors swirled that therapist Phil Cohen—a former Communist Party member with a long, liberal client list—was funneling information from his private sessions straight to the Feds.

"I know he was reporting confidences to the FBI," Abraham Polonsky told Victor Navasky in the latter's 1980 book *Naming Names*. "There's no question about that. And he was turning patients into stool pigeons."

Although Hayden made several more memorable films, the cost of maintaining his career proved too high. "Incredible, really—how I got away with it; parlaying nine years at sea into two decades of posturing. Poor wanderer: trapped in the greenback cradle of Outer Hollywood; laced in the straitjacket of the big time—big houses big salaries big fuss when you walk down a street big fuss as you check into hotels—big big big. . . . What does a man need—really need? A few pounds of food each day, heat and shelter, six feet to lie down in—and some form of working activity that will yield a sense of accomplishment. That's all—in the material sense. And we know it. But we are brainwashed by our economic system until we end up in a tomb beneath a pyramid of time payments, mortgages, preposterous gadgetry, playthings that divert our attention from the sheer idiocy of the charade."

On January 20, 1959, Sterling Hayden executed the escape Dix Handley dreamed of. Defying court custody orders, he loaded his four children onto his schooner *Wanderer* and sailed out of Sausalito, California, headed for the South Seas. He chucked the $160,000 annual salary, the rest of his film career, the mounting debts, the threat of punitive action by the government. He had no money, no job, no prospects. But he had the sea, a small crew—inexperienced but eager—and many journal pages to fill.

The ship runs free, he exults in those scribblings. *Your ears are bathed with wind and the sun comes pouring down. Face south and fill your soul with the far horizon's rapture. Now pivot clockwise slowly and rest for a time, looking west. What do you see? Nothing. Nothing but the sea and sky. Turn quietly north, with the line of the sea and the low-hung spread of cloud, the shimmer of light and shade, and the spell of loneliness mixed with the call of the sea—the beckoning, bursting, smiling call with a wild promise of worlds unknown and dreams undreamed and a life to live.*

Hayden pulled off one of the most incredible capers in Hollywood history: He re-created himself. *Wanderer*, his briny, blood-on-the-page autobiography, written as he sailed for Tahiti, became a best seller. He returned to acting on his own terms, creating memorable mad-bomber General Jack D. Ripper for counterculture compatriot Stanley Kubrick's *Dr. Strangelove* (Columbia, 1964). In Francis Ford Coppola's *The Godfather* (Paramount,

1972), Robert Altman's *The Long Goodbye* (UA, 1973), Bernardo Bertolucci's *1900* (Fox, 1976), Frank Pierson's *King of the Gypsies* (Paramount, 1978), and William Richert's dizzy adaptation of Richard Condon's *Winter Kills* (Avco Embassy, 1979), all remnants of actorly affectation had been scraped from Hayden like barnacles from the hull of a battered but seaworthy brigantine. He only had to float to be majestic. His epic seafaring novel *Voyage* was the product of awesome solitude, the crowning achievement for a man who had left all conventions at dockside to become master of his own leeward life.

Hayden with wife Betty de Noon after testifying before HUAC on March 10, 1951. He declared that joining the Communist Party was "The stupidest, most ignorant thing I have ever done."

HAYDEN DID SPEND SOME TIME ON THE RIGHT SIDE of the law, as in the jaunty seventy-three-minute *Crime Wave* (WB, 1954). Playing Sergeant Eugene Sims, he had a field day as the sort of self-righteous bully with a badge that Hollywood liberals saw coming after them in their sleep.

Sims has it in for Steve Lacey (Gene Nelson), a paroled thief gone straight, who becomes entangled with former cohorts who've broken out of San Quentin. Doc Penny (Ted de Corsia) and Ben Hastings (Charles Bronson), hole up with Lacey, forcing him to act as the driver for a bank job Doc's got planned. They hold Steve's wife Ellen (Phyllis Kirk) hostage to encourage his cooperation.

Sims figures Lacey's still aligned with his old comrades and he persecutes him without mercy, ranting, "Once a crook always a crook," and vowing to send him back to the joint. Could enacting this role have been part of Hayden's post-stoolie therapy?

Director André de Toth, whose only other genuine noir was *Pitfall*, enlivens this programmer with unexpected vigor. Bert Glennon's camera snakes through the streets of Glendale, capturing actual locations with a hybrid of chiaroscuro and crisp natural light. Sims's hostility is mitigated by subtle humor. The script gives him the added frustration of nicotine withdrawal, which prompts the already high-strung cop to gnaw toothpicks in place of his beloved tar-bars. Hayden, who smoked furiously, looks quite annoyed being deprived of the actor's favorite prop. de Toth makes great use of Hayden's massive dimensions: rooms, furniture, and cars are too small for his towering, shambling frame—everything gets in his way.

But Hayden's only the surly ringmaster here. The real show is the supporting cast. Surrounding fresh-faced Nelson and Kirk is a post office wall's worth of creeps. Ted de Corsia, who made his on-screen debut in Orson Welles's *The Lady from Shanghai*, is one of the great noir character actors. Barrel-chested and beady-eyed, hair glistening with a lacquer of Wildroot Cream, de Corsia looks like a guy who'd spent his whole life in boxing gyms and bookie joints. The visage was

ABOVE: Sergeant Sims and his men don't need a search warrant when trying to bust up a *Crime Wave*. **BELOW:** The gang and their hostages in hiding, with (from left) Phyllis Kirk, Gene Nelson, Jim Hayward, Timothy Carey, Ted de Corsia, and Charles Buchinsky (Bronson)

only an accident of birth: The son of a vaudevillian, he was in touring companies as a youth before becoming a radio actor. Credit Welles with spotting de Corsia's nefarious potential, and Jules Dassin for exploiting it. Dassin cast de Corsia in the pivotal role of killer Willie Garza in *The Naked City* (Universal, 1948), and the actor lent a sweaty, feral tone to the film's overwrought urban poetry. De Corsia lurked in westerns, strutted in crime dramas, and skulked in prison pictures, always inducing a shiver of menace when he finally stepped into the light and made his play. In *Slightly Scarlet* (RKO, 1956), de Corsia was immortalized in John Alton's burnished light, which chiseled the actor's hawkish features into a sinister rictus. A just dessert for any great heavy is a memorable death scene, and, in *Slightly Scarlet*, de Corsia goes out grandly: Rhonda Fleming blows a harpoon into his burly chest.

De Corsia's sidekick in *Crime Wave* is the young Charles Bronson, who flexes impressively and growls a few great lines. Leveling his gun at Ellen, he says to her husband, "You want I should clip a curl off the cutie?" de Toth loved the contours of Bronson's face, and his atavistic grace. He used him smartly in several pictures, including the 3-D *House of Wax* (WB, 1954). The gang also included the amusingly unstable Timothy Carey, who is so brain-damaged that midway through sexually intimidating Phyllis Kirk he becomes distracted and forgets what he's doing. *Crime Wave* was one of the first films that prompted viewers to ask of Carey, "What the hell is *wrong* with that guy?"

THE NEXT TIME SUCH A COLORFUL CREW ASSEMBLED for a caper, Hayden was again front and center. In 1955, an upstart twenty-seven-year-old New York film-maker named Stanley Kubrick, who didn't believe Hollywood held the patent on American filmmaking, teamed up with neophyte producer James B. Harris to bust into the big leagues of movie production. Their passport was a paperback thriller they'd bought the rights to, Lionel White's *Clean Break*.

Kubrick was a prodigy, working as a photographer for *LOOK* magazine while still a teenager. The bookish Bronx kid was also wired on noir. His first two features, *Fear and Desire* (Joseph Burstyn, 1953) and *Killer's Kiss* (UA, 1955) were examples of a budding aesthete attempting to distill crude poetry from iconographic terrain. Kubrick had virtually no money, but he was fueled by the belief he had a better way to conjure the dark visions that had inspired him.

Harris and Kubrick danced with United Artists to secure funding for their low-budget picture. The money only came after Sterling Hayden committed to star. Maybe he saw it as a logical addendum to *The Asphalt Jungle*. In that film, Dix tells Doll, "One of these days I'm gonna make a killing." Five years later, reincarnated as Johnny Clay, older and wiser, he'd get one more crack at the Main Chance—in *The Killing* (UA, 1956).

Like Doc Reidenschneider, Johnny is fresh out of prison, where he had plenty of time to plot the perfect heist, a brazen lift of a quarter million from the Lansdowne racetrack, in broad daylight. He has it figured step-by-step, into the counting room and out, five minutes, no gunplay. The trick is installing the right guys—losers all, but stand-up losers—at every stress point in the plan.

The Killing was a tribute to classic noir and caper films, and a fresh gust of filmmaking in one clever package. Kubrick cast his caper with the choicest ensemble of noir actors ever. Marvin Unger (Jay C. Flippen) underwrites the job because he's infatuated with Johnny, who's too preoccupied to catch the drift when Marvin says, "I think of you as if you were my own son." Fay, Johnny's befuddled sweetheart, is played by Coleen ("I may not be pretty and I may not be smart . . .") Gray, the most utilitarian of Dark City dames. Ted de Corsia is bent cop Randy Kennan, who has a pony jones and patrols a narrow barroom and bookie joint beat. Kola Kwarian, a friend of Kubrick's from New York chess clubs, plays Maurice Oboukhoff, a wrestler hired to create a brawling diversion at the racetrack bar (he should have been matched against his bullet-headed twin, Gregorius [Stanislaus Zbyszko], from *Night and the City*.) Most memorably, there's demented sharpshooter Nikki Arano (Timothy Carey, again clenched and inexplicable) and George and Sherry Peatty (Elisha Cook Jr. and luminously wicked Marie Windsor)—voted by a jury of their peers noir's most perfectly matched couple.

George: Been kinda sick today. Keep gettin' pains in my stomach.

Sherry: Maybe you got a hole in it. Suppose you have?

George: How would I get a hole in it?

Sherry: How did you get the one in your head? Fix me a drink, George. I think I'm developing some pains myself.

Unfortunately, Johnny goes soft at the wrong times. When he realizes that George, the crew's weak link, has leaked the plan to Sherry, he passes up the chance to ice her. Instead of "slapping that pretty face into hamburger meat," Johnny sends

Johnny Clay (Hayden) plots the heist with his crew (from left) Ted de Corsia, Joe Sawyer, Elisha Cook Jr. and Jay. C. Flippen.

her home to resume systematic torture of her pitiful husband. Big mistake. She's feeding info she's coaxed out of George to her lover Val (Vince Edwards), who plans to hijack the loot.

Johnny moves through the heist like a firewalker, immune to distraction. Stick to the plan. Play it out, no matter what. Million-to-one shots come in once in a while, you just have to be Johnny-on-the-spot. Mustering all his grace and guile, Johnny Clay—at least for a few moments—is the king of thieves.

Of course, it all falls apart, and the entire gang ends up dead. What glorious delusion, hidden under that stolid façade, made Johnny think he could beat the system? He's so close to that big dream of himself. So close—except for that yapping toy poodle that skitters across the airport tarmac, and the luggage cart swerving, and the cheap latch on the suitcase busting open. Johnny watches silently as his fortune gets scattered like so much confetti. He's too numb to run. Fay guides them through the airport. He's embalmed, can't even hail a cab. "What's the difference?" he mutters, giving up as the net closes.

Kubrick received some notoriety for *The Killing*'s unusual overlapping narrative, which backtracks to show the buildup to the heist from various characters' perspectives. But he was only being faithful to White's novel. A bolder stroke was hiring Jim Thompson to contribute to the screenplay. Celebrated years after his death as the toughest of noir novelists, Thompson at that time was sliding toward Skid Row, struggling under a hefty bar tab. He related to these hard cases and popped wonderful dialogue into the mouths of this mangy menagerie.

"You know, I often thought that the artist and the gangster are the same in the eyes of the masses," Maurice muses for Johnny's benefit. "They are admired and hero-worshipped, but there is always present the underlying wish to see them destroyed at the peak of their glory."

"Like the man said: 'Life is like a glass of tea,' huh?" is Johnny's riposte. "Oh, Johnny, my friend. You were never very bright. But I love you anyway."

TOP: Johnny deftly deals with a potential obstacle to his escape. **MIDDLE:** Johnny's moment of glory: masked up and cleaning out the racetrack's counting room **BOTTOM:** George Peatty (Elisha Cook Jr.) hopes his cut of the loot will impress his two-timing wife, Sherry (Marie Windsor).

When UA execs saw the first cut, they were aghast, claiming it made no sense and that no audience would sit through it. Despondent, Kubrick recut the film conventionally, only to discover what Lionel White knew all along—the nonlinear structure was essential to the story's originality. Kubrick defiantly returned the film to its original state; UA buried it on the bottom of double bills.

But Kubrick's style still drew notice, even if his unorthodox use of the camera irritated the hell out of veteran DP Lucien Ballard, who was at odds with the young director throughout production. Kubrick, showing early indications of his perfectionism, usurped Ballard's camera to photograph the aftermath of the pivotal gun battle himself, in a handheld shot that lingers like gun smoke. Kubrick's aggressive style signaled that a new kind of storytelling was in the air, several years before mainstream critics credited it to France's New Wave directors.

JOHNNY CLAY'S DEMISE WAS FORESHADOWED by the fate of David Purvis (William Talman), who pulls off an *Armored Car Robbery* (RKO, 1950), only to miss his getaway flight at the airport when an incoming plane casts his booty to the wind. This sixty-seven-minute B, directed by the redoubtable Richard Fleischer, was one of the last noirs to present a caper as straight cops-and-robbers stuff. There was no complex moral shading, no sympathy for this crew, because Purvis is as cold and miserable as his fellow masterminds, Doc Reidenschneider and Johnny Clay, were engagingly sympathetic.

Talman played the most reptilian villains in noir (*The Hitch-Hiker*, *Crashout*, *City That Never Sleeps*). With his high forehead and bulging lizard eyes, a forked tongue seemed likely to flash between his lips at any moment. His baleful gaze instantly put any scene on ice. One of the few actors who could withstand the Talman treatment was implacable Charles McGraw, who played Sergeant Cordell, a pit bull out to avenge his partner, killed trying to thwart the robbery. McGraw was built like an armored car and the gruffest voice in movies rumbled out of him; it sounded like a fist was gripping his larynx when he spit out dialogue.

McGraw took taciturn to tight-lipped extremes. Visiting his dead partner's widow in the hospital, he reaches deep for appropriate words of condolence. He fingers the brim of his fedora and finally croaks, "Tough break, Marsha"—then turns and exits, all emotion spent.

In a series of exciting noirs—*The Killers*, *T-Men*, *Border Incident*, *The Story of Molly X*, *The Threat*, *Side Street*, *Roadblock*, *His Kind of Woman*, *The Narrow Margin*, *Loophole*, and *Slaughter on Tenth Avenue*—McGraw's presence lent any scene additional weight. As villains, few players were as physically intimidating. As heroes, few conveyed juggernaut determination so offhandedly, or believably. By the early '60s, his bluntness acquired a weathered quality, used to good advantage by Stanley Kubrick (*Spartacus*), Anthony Mann (*Cimmaron*), and Alfred Hitchcock (*The Birds*). McGraw's career was tragically cut short by a fatal accident. He slipped

John Payne is set up as the fall guy in a daring robbery in *Kansas City Confidential*.

in his shower and crashed through the doors, impaling himself on a huge glass shard—an awful end for one of the great faces and voices of noir.

Talman played many more heavies in the 1950s, second only to Raymond Burr in that regard. Ironically, they'd both end up on the right side of the law on the popular television series *Perry Mason*, where Burr played the titular defense attorney and Talman his nemesis, DA Hamilton Burger. In 1960, Talman lost his job on the show after being busted on a 647—LAPD code for lewd and lascivious behavior. Leaving a "wild party," Talman was cuffed while rambling naked around Beverly Hills. CBS canned him, but a massive write-in campaign reinstated him to the *Perry Mason* cast. It just wasn't the same watching Mason go up against anybody but Hamilton Burger. He continued to lose cases to Perry at a prodigious rate for years to come. How did that guy ever get reelected?

OF ALL THE NEIGHBORHOODS IN DARK CITY, Knockover Square has the most generous ration of unique faces and voices. It's the characters, more than the plots, that make caper films so enjoyable. In *Kansas City Confidential* (UA, 1952), an embittered ex-cop (Preston Foster) engineers an ingenious armored-car robbery, with a motivation emblematic of noir: He's angry about his paltry pension after twenty years of futile crime fighting. He blackmails a trio of petty hoods into executing the job. The simmering hostility within a high-strung crew is compounded because only Foster knows the identity of each man; masks keep them from identifying each other.

Anonymity is key when the robbers reunite later in a Mexican fishing resort to divvy up the loot. Unmasked, no one is sure who's who, or who can be trusted, as the bandits await instructions from the boss—who could be any of the vacationing Marlin fishers.

This gang is in the Knockover Square pantheon: There's skittish Pete Harris, played by Jack Elam, who was manager of the Bel-Air Hotel in Beverly Hills before stepping into the movie business. Elam lost sight in his left eye after a youthful fight, and the resultant wall-eyed stare gave his face a silly-putty oddness that kept him employed for decades.

Chunky, thuggish Kane was a typical role for Neville Brand, whose mug made Charles Bronson look like Cary Grant. He'd reach the height of his popularity playing Al Capone in the hit television series *The Untouchables*, but Brand was as far from a craven crook as you could get: He was the fourth most decorated soldier of World War II.

Playing Mutt (actually Tony) to Brand's Jeff was Lee Van Cleef. The beaked-nosed former accountant would knock around Hollywood as a henchman and saddle tramp for fifteen years before Sergio Leone made him an international star, casting him beside fellow squint-meister Clint Eastwood in spaghetti westerns *A Fistful of Dollars* and *The Good, the Bad, and the Ugly*.

Odd man out in the band of pug-uglies is pretty boy Joe Rolfe (John Payne), set up as fall guy in the robbery. The gang made their getaway in a duplicate of his delivery van, ensuring a diversion. As a result of the suspicion he draws, Rolfe—a vet and paroled jailbird doing straight time—loses his job. He uses his own criminal savvy to hunt down the real robbers and ends up replacing Pete Harris at the south-of-the-border square-up. The goons are none the wiser, since they never saw Harris's face. The clever script, by George Bruce and Harry Essex (from a story by Rowland Brown), makes amusing use of this identity crisis. The question of whether Rolfe will rat out the robbers—or cut himself in on the spoils—generates terrific suspense.

Director Phil Karlson was in stride with *Kansas City Confidential*, having just released the sensational *Scandal Sheet* (Columbia, 1952). Like his two-fisted compatriot Anthony Mann, Karlson spent the '40s grinding out programmers before finding his niche with violent crime pictures. He had a profitable association with actor John Payne and producer Eddie Small, making two other punchy noirs, *99 River Street* (UA, 1953) and *Hell's Island* (Paramount, 1955), in which Payne, a one-time songbird, was transformed into a lonesome nighthawk.

Karlson would later direct *The Phenix City Story* (Allied Artists, 1955), which signaled the end of stylish, artful noir. Replacing it was a slew of crime-busting "exposés"—*New York Confidential* (WB, 1955), *Las Vegas Shakedown* (Allied Artists, 1955), *Miami Exposé* (Columbia, 1956), *The Houston Story* (Columbia, 1956), *Inside Detroit* (Columbia, 1956), *Chicago Confidential* (UA, 1957), *Portland Exposé* (Allied Artists, 1957), *New Orleans After Dark* (Allied Artists, 1958)—films in which noir's moral ambiguity was given the third degree by the Feds, and bureaucrats and G-Men once again held sway.

ABOVE: Producer-actor Harry Belafonte used a heist story to dissect racism in *Odds Against Tomorrow*. Ed Begley is the bitter ex-cop who masterminds the heist. BELOW: Dave Burke (Ed Begley) has to referee the racial tension between cohorts Johnny Ingram (Harry Belafonte) and Earl Slater (Robert Ryan) in *Odds Against Tomorrow*.

ANOTHER RANCOROUS EX-COP PROVIDED THE IMPETUS for the last great caper of the classic noir era. Dave Burke (Ed Begley) was bounced from the force for refusing to rat out his colleagues before a crime commission. In *Odds Against Tomorrow* (UA, 1959), he plots payback with a bank robbery he hopes will free him from the confines of his dingy Dark City apartment.

His plan is to knock over a bank in the upstate town of Melton, easy pickings for a trio of big-city slicks. He enlists the aid of Johnny Ingram (Harry Belafonte), a Harlem jazz musician who needs to pay off his gambling debts, and Earl Slater (Robert Ryan), a callous redneck who comes from the same poisoned family tree as *Crossfire*'s Monty Montgomery.

Just as *Crossfire* used the murder mystery to explore anti-Semitism, *Odds Against Tomorrow* employs the heist formula to offer a hard-edged take on racism. The film was produced by Harry Belafonte's company Harbel, and based on a novel by William (*The Big Heat*) McGivern. Belafonte hired blacklisted Abraham Polonsky to write the script, using John O. Killens, a black novelist, as his front. During excommunication from Hollywood, Polonsky wrote several politically charged scripts on African-American issues, a logical extension of his concern for the struggles of America's underclass. He thought the popularity of Belafonte and Sidney Poitier might open the door for such challenging stories, but neither actor was yet willing to jeopardize his crossover success by jabbing too hard at White America's conscience. For Poitier, films like *The Defiant Ones* and *Lilies of the Field* were a safer bet, sugarcoating anger with sentimentality.

For Belafonte, a crime drama could support the added weight of social significance. The dynamics of men performing under pressure—shelving resentments for the sake of the job—was an acute metaphor for American society. Because it was a crime film, the racial hatred between Johnny and Earl was at a safe remove from the average filmgoer. But its sting is still deeply felt.

Johnny Ingram is a prototypical noir character: a man struggling to hang on to his family and career, with a character flaw—gambling—he hopes won't prove fatal. He bristles at the prospect of committing a crime: "That's the firing squad," he tells Burke. "That's for junkies and joy-boys. We're people." The film underplays the race angle—until Slater pushes Johnny too far.

In one of the film's strongest scenes, the conspirators meet to plan the robbery. Slater dismisses input from Ingram. A veteran and ex-con, he pops off about the firearms they'll need to take the bank by force. Earl reads Johnny's silence as a tip-off that the "boy" is yellow. But then Johnny proposes an ingenious idea for getting into the bank using nothing more than a box of take-out coffees. Burke lights up like a Christmas tree. Earl is humiliated. His resentment of Johnny will doom them all.

Belafonte and his colleagues had their fingers on the pulse of a racial tension few films dared address without requisite Hollywood sanctimony. He presciently suggested that Johnny's innate hipness—his Black badge of cool—was a threat to lower-class Whites afraid of losing their hold on cultural dominance. In his Ray-Bans and turtleneck, and his gravelly jive patter, Belafonte exuded soul, even as his life fell apart. Peckerwood Earl was plenty jealous.

Earl Slater's racism is like gasoline in his veins; it keeps him going when he knows, deep down, he doesn't fit in and has nowhere to go. Scenes of Earl wandering in the wintry city, seething with alienation, are both scary and sad. So are those of his girl Lorry (Shelley Winters) clinging to him in the cramped rooms they call home; she's like a wounded animal huddled with a predatory beast. "It's never easy for you, is it, Earl?" she asks. "Only when I'm angry," he responds. "Then things get *too* easy." Ryan was adept at conveying the tragedy of men like Earl, but pity doesn't make them less terrifying or more tolerable. Ryan cheats on Lorry with neighbor Gloria Grahame in a scene played and shot with a nasty edge that's both sexy and repugnant.

Director Robert Wise created a bone-chilling tone in *Odds Against Tomorrow*, his stripped-down, elliptical direction capturing the lonely lives of desperate men, and desolate environments from wintry Manhattan cityscapes to defoliated upstate New York. Scenes of the trio tensely biding their time in Melton, waiting for the cover of darkness, have a pungent bleakness: Cameraman Joseph Brun shot them on infrared film, conjuring an ominous starkness. Wise also abandoned the orchestral scores of previous noirs for brassy, percussive riffs by John Lewis and the Modern Jazz Quartet. Ingram's life as a jazzman makes the nervy score logical, not an affectation.

After *West Side Story* (UA, 1961) and *The Sound of Music* (Fox, 1965), a generation of film buffs, weaned on the auteur theory, stamped Robert Wise as an A-list hack. It was a bum rap. Wise apprenticed with two geniuses, Orson Welles and Val Lewton, editing *Citizen Kane* and directing Lewton's creepy, touching *The Curse of*

Johnny's clever ruse to get the gang into the bank is wasted when Earl's racial hatred blows up their plans.

the Cat People (RKO, 1944). In films as diverse as *The Body Snatcher* (RKO, 1945), *Born to Kill* (RKO, 1947) *Blood on the Moon* (RKO, 1948), *The Set-Up* (RKO, 1949), *The Day the Earth Stood Still* (Fox, 1951), and *The Captive City* (UA, 1952)—he honed the ability to tell compelling stories concisely, no matter what the genre. Like another sure-handed craftsman of this era, Richard Fleischer, Wise would be entrusted with bigger and bigger budgets—resulting in bloated movies that couldn't help but sag under the weight of studios' expectations. But anyone who dismisses Robert Wise as a stodgy director for hire is only proving they've never seen *Odds Against Tomorrow*, which French noir-meister Jean-Pierre Melville cited as his favorite film.

LOSERS' LANE

THIS LOUSY TOWN THINKS I'M GONNA KNUCKLE UNDER. WELL, THIS TOWN HAS ANOTHER THINK COMING. ALL THOSE PEOPLE UP THERE WILL BE READIN' ABOUT ME SOON ENOUGH. THEY'LL SEE MY PICTURE RIGHT THERE—STARING AT THEM OVER THEIR COFFEE—AND THEN THEY'LL SAY: I SHOULDA DONE RIGHT BY HIM. I SHOULDA KNOWN HE WAS GOING TO BE A BIG MAN. IN THEIR FANCY DIGS, LAUGHING AND THINKING THEY GOT IT MADE. LIKE THEY GOT A LEG UP OR SOMETHING. LIKE THEY'RE BETTER'N ME. THEY'LL JUST HAFTA LEARN. SOMEBODY'S GONNA HAFTA TEACH 'EM.

A guard makes his rounds outside a holding cell. One guy in the tank cranes his neck to watch the bull patrol. "Look at that cheap squirt, passing up and down," he grouses in a high-pitched voice. "For a nickel I'd grab him . . . stick both thumbs right in his eyes . . . hang on until he drops dead." He chortles, like bleats from a raspy sax. The film is *Kiss of Death* (Fox, 1947), the loser in stir is Tommy Udo, and the actor projecting a new strain of dementia is Richard Widmark, in his Dark City debut. "Imagine me in here," he says to sloe-eyed cellmate Victor Mature. "Big man like me getting picked up. Just for shovin' a guy's ears off his head. Traffic ticket stuff."

Once he's sprung and hunting down an informer, Widmark made movie history. He uses a torn-out electrical cord to lash Mildred Dunnock, the squealer's mother, to her wheelchair. Then he pitches her down the stairs of her tenement, cackling all the while. Audiences were brought up short by such berserk mayhem—but also beguiled.

Night and the City: Richard Widmark as Harry Fabian, Dark City's patron saint of last chances and lost cause.

Kiss of Death was an unusual hybrid, between the flamboyantly stylized cinematography of Norbert Brodine and the semi-documentary approach director Henry Hathaway had previously used in *The House on 92nd Street*. Mature played Nick Bianco, a hump trying to shake the crooked life who is enlisted by the cops as a stoolie. Bianco fingers Udo for a job that's been nagging the law, but the prosecution bungles the case and the wacko walks. Nick sends his family away, knowing he'll eventually have to confront the vengeful Udo.

Poor Victor Mature. He gave a swell performance in *Kiss of Death*, but nobody noticed. They were waiting for Widmark to reappear, eager for whatever fresh, twisted tricks he had up his sleeve. Ostensibly a story about Bianco's struggle to go straight, *Kiss of Death* is actually one of the first psycho-stalker movies. All the suspense is generated by wondering when Widmark will pop back into the frame.

Tommy Udo wasn't the type of gangster Jimmy Cagney played to perfection in the 1930s; audiences weren't responding to Udo's angry ambition or relating to the social conditions that made him turn bad. With Widmark, spectators were jazzed merely by his dizzy, dangerous charisma; he played it big and broad, with a spring in his step that could launch him over the top at any moment. He only had about fifteen minutes of screen time, but he funneled bad intentions, annoying habits, grating

obnoxiousness, and total amorality into Tommy Udo—and let it rip. The result was thrilling, and *very* influential. *Double Indemnity* had broached the unthinkable by making murder acceptable screen fare. Widmark went the next step—pathology as squirmy entertainment. He raised the bar for all subsequent nutcases.

It was Darryl Zanuck who recognized the lunacy lurking in Widmark. Henry Hathaway didn't want to cast him, even after seeing the maniacal leer and hearing the freakish titter in a screen test. He thought Widmark was too clean-cut. But Zanuck prevailed, outfitting Widmark with a hairpiece that lowered his forehead, making him look a little stupider and a lot scarier. *Kiss of Death* was in release only a couple of months when college fraternities—ten in all—formed Tommy Udo fan clubs, celebrating this new nastiness, particularly Udo's *I-oughta-smack-you* chauvinism.

Widmark scored an Oscar nomination and Zanuck promptly cast his hot contract player in *The Street with No Name* (1948), an old-fashioned racket-buster out of the 1930s. Director William Keighley sent a battalion of straight-arrow Feds, holdovers from his earlier *G-Men*, after crooked fight promoter Alec Stiles (Widmark)—but it was no contest. Audiences instinctively sided with Widmark, whose nervy malevolence made everyone else on-screen seem tame and tired.

Dark City quickly became home to the man from Sunrise, Minnesota, who'd spent his youth as an honor student growing up in Sioux Falls, South Dakota. Unlike roustabouts Mitchum, Ryan, and Hayden, Widmark enjoyed a secure, stable, all-American upbringing. He was president of the senior class at Illinois's Lake Forest College, a lettered receiver on the gridiron, captain of the debate team, and a movie-crazy member of the Drama Department. In 1942 he went to New York and broke into radio, before landing Broadway roles as a leading man in *Kiss and Tell* and *Kiss Them for Me*. It seemed a sensible, if sinister, progression that *Kiss of Death* be his screen debut.

TOP: Widmark makes movie history, pitching Mildred Dunnock down the stairs in *Kiss of Death*. BOTTOM: *Road House*: Celeste Holm can plead all she wants, but she can't stop the inevitable. Audiences eagerly awaited the scenes where Widmark reached the end of his short tether and flew into a keening, maniacal rage.

After *The Street with No Name*, Widmark was ushered into *Road House* (Fox, 1948). It offered another variation on Tommy Udo, with the psychosis toned down and the hairline reverted to its natural level. It was Ida Lupino's vehicle all the way, and she specifically requested Widmark after being infected with Udo-mania herself. He went toe-to-toe with her, both delivering sensational, drop-dead dialogue.

Road House was a simple story of the eternal triangle. Lily Stevens (Lupino) gets hired by the infatuated Jefty Robbins (Widmark) to work as a chanteuse in his roadhouse. After some initial friction, she falls for Jefty's right-hand man, Pete (Cornel Wilde). When Jefty finds out, he retaliates by framing Pete for theft of the club's receipts. In a queasy twist, Jefty urges the judge to release Pete into his custody. From then on, he tortures the captive lovers while pretending to be a magnanimous benefactor. Widmark brought homicidal petulance to the part.

In *No Way Out* (Fox, 1950), Widmark bunked in Robert Ryan's barracks, playing a fugitive killer who blames a Black doctor (Sidney Poitier) for his brother's death. Although Poitier saves his life, it doesn't stop the bigoted Widmark from race-baiting him at every turn. In a famous scene, Widmark and Poitier grapple and the wound in Widmark's leg reopens. Linda Darnell, who's silently suffered the villain's virulence, snarls: "Tear it some more!" This bit was so loathsome it was clipped from many prints.

By 1950, Widmark, like Ryan, risked being typecast. His defense was to kiss off Tommy Udo with one last blowout. In *Night and the City* (Fox, 1950), he portrayed the quintessential noir loser. Man-child Harry Fabian was the culmination of all Widmark's ranting and raving. Jules Dassin pulled out all the stops, directing in a baroque style that verged perilously close to parody. Widmark matches him every step of the way. Whenever his dervish-like performance threatened to spin out of control, the actor pulled Fabian back to earth with poignant, sympathetic details. Playing a scheming hustler rather than a psycho killer, Widmark found tragedy at the core of a character.

In most crime pictures, Fabian would be a supporting character, a petty climber, the type played by Elisha Cook Jr. The big shots would have patted Harry's cheek and dismissed him offhandedly: "Kid, you've got moxie. I like that." But Harry's naked desire is so wretched it repulses the crooks aspiring to respectability. He's disposed of not because he's a threat, but because he's an *embarrassment* to operators who've cloaked the wannabe inside them with threadbare sophistication. Fabian is

executed for making everybody look bad.

Enough was enough. After Fabian, there were no darker avenues for Widmark to wander. He was cast as the health inspector hero of Elia Kazan's *Panic in the Streets* (Fox, 1950), while Jack Palance essayed the infectious heavy that had been Widmark's stock-in-trade. This time Widmark didn't snicker when he smiled. The audience saw the smirk could also be disarmingly sweet. Probably because it represented a salvation, Widmark called *Panic* the favorite among his many films. Once he'd established heroic leading man credentials, he swung back and forth between the light and dark, bringing shifty charm to noirs such as *Don't Bother to Knock* (Fox, 1952, which featured Marilyn Monroe's best performance) and the previously lauded *Pickup on South Street* (Fox, 1953).

For the next fifteen years Widmark worked steadily in westerns, war dramas, and adventure sagas. In 1968, Don Siegel brought him back to Dark City as *Madigan* (Universal), a veteran cop who embodied the transition between old and new Hollywood. The script, coauthored by Abraham Polonsky, was an Americanized version of Akira Kurosawa's *Stray Dog* (Toho, 1949), in which a cop embarks on a seventy-two-hour odyssey to capture the killer who stole his gun. Widmark was perfect as a tired flatfoot, trying to dodge the myriad miseries of both the underworld and a politicized police department.

During his career, Widmark himself proved to be anything but the crackpot he personified on-screen. He tied the knot with college sweetheart Jean Hazelwood in 1942 and remained happily married to her. His daughter Anne married baseball legend Sandy Koufax. Widmark shunned publicity, living as a gentleman farmer on ranches in California and Connecticut. Though he premiered as a psychopath, Widmark was known as one of the most stand-up guys in the business.

Although Widmark catapulted to stardom as Tommy Udo, he was not the original model for the fair-haired, lanky, laughing loon. That honor belongs to Dan Duryea, who during the 1940s occupied an exclusive enclave in Losers' Lane. He was Dark City's most enchanting villain, the guy audiences loved to hate. For years, Duryea's act was even more popular than Widmark's, although he never entered the upper echelon of leading men the way Widmark did.

The two were remarkably similar, coming to Hollywood from Broadway, where they'd been cast in romantic, blue-blooded parts. Both were slender, with lank, slicked-back blond hair. Both had come-on smiles that exuded cheerful menace.

Lang stages it like a sexual imposition. Bennett stands still, panting slightly, while Duryea insouciantly rummages through her drawers, fondles her clothes, daubs himself with her perfume, and relishes her helplessness. Later, when Joan tries to feed him poisoned scotch, Duryea wises up and turns malevolent. "You drink it," he seethes. When she demurs, he pops her with a backhand and throws her on the bed. "How could you lie like that to Pappy," he sneers. He takes her money and dismisses her with a flick of fingers off his chin. Duryea held the patent on all these rude bits of stage business.

In *Scarlet Street*, the actor upped the ante, having his way with sexy Joan before blithely slapping her around. His reprehensible on-screen behavior proved squirmily popular. Publicists maintained that Duryea got fan mail by the truckload, mostly from infatuated females. Producers developed ever more inventive ways for Duryea to backhand distaff costars. These outbursts always caused his Brillianteened hair to come unglued, spilling long blond strands down his billboard-sized forehead. Duryea was one of the first stars to act with his hair, an affectation that provided tonsorial inspiration for, among others, rock and roller Jerry Lee Lewis.

Beatings administered by Duryea were so telegraphed publicists felt it necessary to offer a disclaimer when promoting *Black Angel* (1946): "Something great has happened in Hollywood, land of great things. Beautiful June Vincent met dangerous Dan Duryea and escaped unscathed. Prolific Dan, beater of such gorgeous femmes as Joan Bennett, touches nary a strand of June's blonde hair in Universal's *Black Angel* . . ."

In *Too Late for Tears* (UA, 1949), Duryea takes a whack at Lizabeth Scott. He plays a private eye who knows Liz is stashing a valise full of cash that was tossed into her convertible. She and Dan hatch a plot to share the loot, with Liz bumping off her husband. Dan thinks several stiff smacks in the kisser will be enough to keep Liz in line, but she proves him wrong. By this time Duryea's facial treatments were so popular the studio used the slapping scene as its poster art.

When Paramount later that year cast Dureya opposite Dorothy Lamour in *Manhandled*, audiences knew what they were getting. First, he slaps Lamour, then hits her with a right cross—twice—and finally tries to throw her off a rooftop. His

Both had high-pitched voices. And, most significantly, considering the milieu they inhabited, both were riveting when they dropped the pretense of civilized behavior and erupted into violence.

During the 1940s, Duryea developed an almost fetishistic forte—slapping women. This was first exploited by Fritz Lang in *The Woman in the Window* (RKO, 1944). He padded the stick-thin actor with a double-breasted suit, bow tie, and straw boater, a getup that was, for a while, his signature ensemble. Suitably decked out, Duryea struck the pose that became his trademark: lounging in a doorframe, worrying a toothpick, a sly smile on his face. "I'm just naturally what they call a cynic, honey," he drawls to costar Joan Bennett. When Duryea paws his way through Joan's apartment, looking for the hidden murder weapon so he can blackmail her, most dastardly act, however, came in a stunning scene where he chases Harold Vermilyea down in a huge Packard and crushes him against an alley wall, gleefully grinding his foot down on the accelerator.

The same year Robert Siodmak cast him as Slim Dundee in *Criss Cross*, providing perhaps the finest visual record of Duryea's dandy duds. And, of course, he tagged Yvonne de Carlo once or twice before giving her a couple of lead ducats to Dreamland. Somehow, he squeezed in another noir that amazing year, *Johnny Stool Pigeon* (Universal), in which he roughed up costar Shelley Winters.

When Duryea made the same crossover as Widmark, playing only slightly crooked heroes in films like *The Underworld Story* and *World for Ransom* (UA, 1954), he sacrificed a bit of his weird allure. He was a serviceable good guy, but a delectable bastard. Duryea's off-screen life paralleled Widmark's as well. While slapping women around made him a millionaire, Duryea lived a simple, modest life by showbiz standards. He was known in Hollywood as a model husband and father. Married in 1931 to Helen Bryan, they remained together until her death in 1967. Duryea followed her the next year.

BEFORE YOU THINK DARK CITY'S INFAMOUS VILLAINS were just clever put-ons, brought to life by talented thespians, let's drop by the station house. Well, wouldn't you know? Look who they've got in the holding cell—Lawrence Tierney. Don't bother asking the desk cop if this is real life or a movie. Makes no difference in this guy's case. If street cred had been a requirement for playing rat bastards, Lawrence Tierney would be the undisputed heavyweight champion of Losers' Lane.

During the heyday of noir crime dramas, Tierney, a Brooklyn-born son of an Irish cop, reeled off a string of rough-hewn B features, made memorable by his authentic mean streak. His breakthrough came at Poverty Row studio Monogram, playing legendary bank robber *Dillinger* (1945). Although he'd had formal acting training, Tierney never lost the "doity poiple boids" in his Brooklyn accent. It made him all the more believable as an on-screen heavy. Pumping more vitriol into his tough-guy persona was the rap sheet he built up with his résumé.

After filming *Step by Step* (RKO) in 1946, Tierney did a five-day stint in the drunk tank. It was only the first of many disagreements with John Law over the course of his checkered career, most stemming from a penchant for barroom brawling. Writers and directors were soon making hay off Tierney's renegade image. Young screenwriter Robert Altman gave him the tongue-in-cheek line "Now you know me better than that—I never get into fights," in *Bodyguard* (RKO, 1948), yet another of Richard Fleischer's sturdy programmers.

Tierney—like his brother, actor Scott Brady—was big, broad-shouldered, and handsome. But his eyes narrowed into slits when he started thinking. And his thin-lipped grin was rapacious. He was the grown-up roughneck from high school who inexplicably had cute girls cozying up to him. Didn't they know he had a nasty nickname for each of them?

In *The Devil Thumbs a Ride* (RKO, 1947), Tierney takes the conniving bully routine around the bend. Only seconds in, he shoots an old man in the back as the guy's making a night deposit at a bank. He fast-talks a soused newlywed (Ted North) into giving him a lift up the coast. At a filling station, he picks up two gals fresh off the bus. He wastes no time schmoozing Carol (Nan Leslie), the dishier of the pair, into a backseat clinch. When he commandeers the wheel, he promptly runs over a motorcycle cop. The group ends up AWOL at a beach house, where Tierney shuts off every avenue of escape and resumes his lupine pursuit of the gullibly innocent Carol. When she realizes he's a fugitive, he drowns her.

Written and directed by Felix Feist, *The Devil Thumbs a Ride* is one of those mesmerizing, dirt-cheap B jobs that steamrolls any logic that might creep into the plot. With Tierney in the driver's seat, it's a fast ride filled with jittery laughs. He indulges in plenty of cruel put-downs, his forte. When a gas jockey proudly displays a picture of his baby, Tierney cracks: "From the look of those ears, she's gonna fly before she walks." After he pitches dreadfully purple woo at beautiful Carol, her shopworn friend Agnes (Betty Lawford) turns up the car radio: "Anything not to have to listen to that." Snaps Tierney: "Quit your gripin', Grandma—you'll never have to listen to it." Chock-full of goofy character actors, *The Devil Thumbs a Ride* is a surreal, live-action cartoon.

Darker and meaner is Robert Wise's *Born to Kill* (RKO, 1947), featuring Tierney as Sam Wild, perhaps the most amoral leading man in movie history. After he kills two people in Reno, his weasely buddy Mart (Elisha Cook Jr.) scolds him: "Honest, Sam—You can't go around killin' people whenever the notion strikes you. It's not feasible." But Sam finds it justifiable: "When I see what I want, I take it. Nobody cuts in on me." The cold-blooded killer insinuates himself into

a clique of affluent San Franciscans. "Marrying into this crowd will make it so I can spit in anybody's eye," he tells Mart. Sam meets his match in Helen Trent (Claire Trevor), a lustful society deviant, engaged to a local scion. Sam marries her half-sister Georgia (Audrey Long) but carries on a torrid affair with Helen. Their heavy-breathing scene in the kitchen pantry was hot stuff for its time:

"All my life I've lived on other people's money," Helen pants. "Now I want some of my own. There is another kind of security Fred can give me—without him I'm afraid of the things I'll do, afraid of what I might become. Fred is goodness and safety."

"And what am I?" Sam sneers. "You're strength and excitement—and depravity," she gasps. "There is a kind of corruptness inside you, Sam." Tierney smiles like he's being pinned with merit badges. They grapple in a wanton embrace. This pair would mug Walter Neff and Phyllis Dietrichson and leave them hog-tied by the side of the road.

Tierney gained more notoriety as he started rehearsing his pugnacious patter in saloons. In '48 he did three months for busting a guy's jaw in a bar. Same year he was charged with kicking a cop while drunk and disorderly—his seemingly perpetual state. In '52 he sparred with a professional welterweight on the corner of Broadway and 53rd. He was the only actor in Hollywood who posed for more mug-shots than publicity photos: belted a cop in '56; simple assault in '57; kicked in a dame's door the same year; another jawbreaker in '58, as well as a dust-up with cops outside a 6th Avenue tavern. The day his mother killed herself in 1960, Tierney was arrested for breaking down a dame's door and beating up her boyfriend.

Another scrapper of note, Norman Mailer, cast him in the author's foray into neo-noir, *Tough Guys Don't Dance* (Cannon, 1987) and Quentin Tarantino resurrected Tierney as belligerent ringleader of the *Reservoir Dogs* (Miramax, 1991). A hulking, chrome-domed, still-menacing version of his once virile self, Tierney often showed up in cameos—none more appropriate than his uncredited stint as a drunken victim of a bloody beating on the television hospital show, *ER*. Alas, Tierney proved not to be immortal. He checked out in 2002, reportedly of natural causes.

Lawrence Tierney, exuding malevolent menace in *The Devil Thumbs a Ride*

Laurie Palmer (Isabel Jewell) about to meet a dismal fate at the hands of Sam Wild (Lawrence Tierney) in *Born to Kill*

SHE WAS NOT ASHAMED

If there was a distaff version of Lawrence Tierney, it was Barbara Payton. The 1949 Eagle-Lion offering *Trapped*, directed by Richard Fleischer, was the first major role for the twenty-two-year-old actress, who was born Barbara Lee Redfield in Cloquet, Minnesota. In 1944, she'd married decorated fighter pilot John Payton and the couple moved to Los Angeles so he could study at USC on the GI Bill. Barbara helped pay their way working as a model. Within a few years, despite a newborn baby, the high life proved too enticing to the young mother. She dumped her husband and became a fixture at Sunset Strip clubs, a '40s equivalent of today's celebrities who are notable for being notable. One guy who took note was Universal exec Bill Goetz, who signed Payton to a contract despite her having no résumé. She'd had only bit parts before being cast in *Trapped*.

Her next picture was a *big* step up—costarring with Jimmy Cagney in *Kiss Tomorrow Goodbye* (WB, 1951). She's terrific in it, playing the Virginia Mayo role in what was Cagney's follow-up to *White Heat*. The star's brother, producer William Cagney, was so entranced with Payton he paid her five grand a week—insane money for someone with only three film credits.

But, then, Payton was a fast worker. Off-screen she cut a swath through Hollywood, claiming affairs with George Raft, Howard Hughes, John Ireland, Bob Hope, Guy Madison, Steve Cochran, Woody Strode—to name only a few, women included. The one that stuck was Franchot Tone, to whom she was

Barbara Payton made a vivid impression in *Trapped* (Eagle-Lion, 1949) with Lloyd Bridges, but her acting career would soon earn less notoriety than her off-screen scandals.

engaged in 1951. That didn't stop her from carrying on a combustible affair with Tom Neal, a B-movie hunk who was Payton's equal in sexual appetite. When Tone caught them together, Neal administered a beating that fractured Tone's skull and put him in a coma for eighteen hours.

Yet Tone forgave his beloved Barbara, and they were married in her hometown. But Payton couldn't lay off the clandestine cavorting with Neal—and Tone filed for divorce. From there, Payton and Neal plunged into a vortex of sex and booze that pretty much finished off their careers. They did road-show theater together—including a stage version of *The Postman Always Rings Twice*—selling tickets based on their salacious notoriety. Payton got a few more film offers, mostly in England. *The Flanagan Boy*, made in 1953, was retitled *Bad Blonde* for American audiences. Treading bourbon, she made *Murder Is My Beat* (Allied Artists, 1955) for Edgar Ulmer, a production even more destitute than his legendary *Detour*.

To pull her life together, Payton dropped out of the business, marrying a furniture store owner and moving to Nogales, Arizona. It didn't take. She was back in LA by the end of the '50s, a full-fledged drug and alcohol abuser, passing forged checks and being busted for solicitation on Sunset Boulevard. In 1963 she accepted a thousand bucks to drunkenly dictate her tell-all autobiography, *I Am Not Ashamed*. After reading it, Barbara Stanwyck said, "Well she damn well should be!"

Offered a try at rehab, Payton said, "I'd rather drink and die." She moved to San Diego to live with her parents—both raging alcoholics. That's where she got her wish on May 8, 1967, dying of heart and liver failure at thirty-nine years of age.

Payton appearing in divorce court with her attorney Milton Golden, seeking alimony from Franchot Tone.

Every year when the carnival rolls into the outskirts of Dark City, you've got a chance to meet Stanton Carlisle, one of the wildest characters this town has ever seen. As Stanton the Great, he once had it all in the palm of his hand. But his fall was even steeper than his rise. The twisting tale of his life is told in *Nightmare Alley* (Fox, 1947).

Stan (Tyrone Power) is a handsome roustabout, learning the ropes of the carny dodge. He's fascinated by the flat joints the rubes fall for, night after night. A student of human nature, Stan is particularly entranced by the chicken-gnawing geek, wondering what could make a man sink so low. The carny hustle fuels his imagination. "It gives you kind of a superior feeling—as if you were on the inside and everybody else is on the outside, looking in," he tells Zeena (Joan Blondell), the veteran "mentalist" with whom he's having an affair. Zeena doesn't need tarot cards to see the avarice in Stan. It's in his eyes.

Stan is after more than a fleshy fling with Zeena. He wants "the code," a "mind-reading" system she and her husband Pete (Ian Keith) devised. It took them to the heights of the business, before booze brought Pete to his knees. One night, Stan accidentally switches Pete's moonshine with a bottle of wood alcohol used in his act. With Pete dead, Zeena needs a new partner. But once Sam's mastered the code himself, he dumps Zeena for Molly (Coleen Gray), a sexy young shill who's the main squeeze of the show's strongman, Bruno (Mike Mazurki). Stan and Molly zoom to the top, leaving the carny life for ritzy clubs where Stanton the Great entertains Dark City's elite with amazing mental feats.

Stan finds a kindred spirit in Dr. Lilith Ritter (Helen Walker), a psychologist intrigued by his shameless hucksterism. She's even more beguiled by Stan's devious plan to bilk her wealthy clients. Using information Lilith feeds him from her sessions, Stan convinces several wealthy socialites of his miraculous powers. He enlists Molly to portray one patron's dead lover: The old kook will give all his earthly riches to see his dead sweetheart one more time. Molly balks, accusing Stan of being a Skygrifter:

"Everything you say and do is so true and wonderful," she blurts, "and you make it sound so sacred and holy—when all the time it's just a gag with you. You're laughing your head off at those chumps! You think God's gonna stand for that? He'll strike you dead!"

But Stan gives Molly his best God-fearing spiel and coaxes her into participating in his ultimate hoax—convincing the delirious mark there's life after death by having the appropriately attired Molly float ethereally around the man's estate. As the chump slumps to his knees in ecstasy, Stan imagines the riches he's about to bilk from this sucker. But Molly's guilty conscience blows the gaff. In the ensuing confusion, Stan knocks the old guy down, accidentally killing him.

He flees to Lilith to get his share of the dough they've scammed, then takes it on the arches. But he frantically returns to her office when he realizes she's pulled the old Gypsy Switch, substituting a single buck for each C-note. Stan has been fleeced by an expert. Lilith has a wax recording of Stan admitting his role in Pete's death. She gives him the bum's rush. Flat broke and a fugitive from the law, Stan rides the rails like a tramp. Like Pete before him, he hits the bottle, hard. Soon he's running routines on his new associates—hobos. When he tries to catch on again with the carnival, there's only one job left for such a broken-down, boozed-up bum.

"You know what a geek is?" asks the carny manager. "Think you can handle it?" Stan downs another proffered shot of rotgut. "Mister," he says, "I was made for it."

Even an ill-advised coda, reuniting Stan and Molly, can't force a ray of light into *Nightmare Alley*. It's one of the most cynical movies Billy Wilder never made. This exceptional film was directed by Edmund Goulding, whose facility with soap operas gave no indication of the depths he'd explore in this venture. It was a departure for everyone involved, especially Tyrone Power. He'd just made the popular and critically praised *The Razor's Edge* (Fox, 1946), playing a character deeper than his norm. Power felt unappreciated as an actor and wanted to unleash a bigger surprise on the public. When he read William Lindsay Gresham's novel *Nightmare Alley*, he had Darryl Zanuck buy the film rights; Stan Carlisle was far more intriguing than the swashbucklers the studio wanted him to play forever.

Power's mesmerizing performance makes Carlisle one of the most compelling characters in all film noir. He's supported by terrific turns from Joan Blondell, Coleen Gray, and, especially, Helen Walker. When she reveals the frosty psychologist to be a calculating bitch, it's enough to make anyone swear off therapists.

Nightmare Alley is unique for noir. There's no gunplay, no gangsters, and the lone "crime"—the death of Pete—is handled with ambiguity. In spirit it resembles *Force of Evil*, which also delineated the predatory elements of the American "success story." Just as Polonsky's film presciently envisioned a future filled with mob-infested lotteries and a criminal pox on Wall Street, so *Nightmare Alley* presaged

Zeena (Joan Blondell) wonders what devious musings run through the mind of Stanton Carlisle (Tyrone Power) in *Nightmare Alley*.

"Two people dead! Just so we can live without working! Why? Why do you do it? Why do you have to kill people? Why can't you let them live?"

—Bart (John Dall) to Laurie (Peggy Cummins) in *Gun Crazy*

a world of televangelists, home shopping hucksterism, and New Age charlatans.

Stan, you were born too soon.

A COUPLE OF YEARS AFTER Stan Carlisle returned to the carnival, the geek was no longer the midway's star attraction. Acing him out as the hottest act was a comely sharpshooter from the British Isles named Annie Laurie Starr (Peggy Cummins). In her Annie Oakley outfit, twirling her six-guns, eyes sparkling in the spotlights, she was everything young Bart Tare (John Dall) wanted in a woman. She was, like him, *Gun Crazy* (UA, 1950).

Laurie immediately recognizes the gunpowder glaze in Bart's eyes as he gazes up at her from the front row. When he accepts the house's challenge of a shooting contest, movies reached the zenith of outrageous sexual symbolism: flirtation by firearms. These two are turned on by firing bullets at each other. Sidearms are a more powerful thrill than sex itself.

The film is ostensibly about Bart's fixation with guns. It sketches his youthful yearning for weapons, but stresses that he doesn't want to kill anything. "It's just that when I shoot, I feel like I'm good at something," he explains to a judge after being caught swiping a majestic Colt revolver from the local hardware store. He's sent to reform school and joins the military, finding his niche as a shooting range instructor. But he returns to his hometown aimless—until he outshoots the sexy Miss Starr. From then on, he's got only one direction—following her.

It's clear who runs this show. "I want action," Laurie declares. Literally in the blink of an eye, film noir's answer to Bonnie and Clyde career across the countryside, pulling stickups with a frenzy. Laurie pretends the robberies are about money, but they're really about the thrill. In the heat of the heists, her face turns feral, like a cat shredding raw meat. Bart is tortured by their outlaw life, but not Laurie: "I told you I was no good, and I didn't kid you," she purrs.

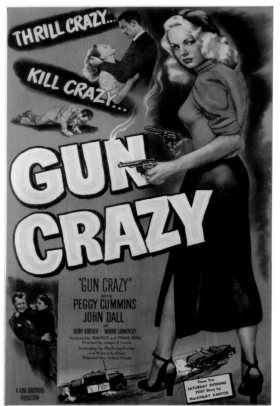

Sick of living like nomads, they decide to pull one last job—knocking over the payroll office of a meatpacking plant. As they're fleeing, Laurie pumps a slug into the office manager who dared sound the alarm. Bart still can't shake his attraction to Laurie. They run like wild dogs, back to Bart's hometown, where he's shunned by his family and hunted by his childhood buddies, now a reporter and a sheriff. The fugitives hide out in a foggy marsh. As his old friends close in, begging Bart to give up, Laurie shrieks: "Come any closer and I'll kill you! I'll kill you all!" Distraught, Bart *finally* kills another living thing—his beloved Laurie. Hearing the gunshots, his pursuers open fire, killing Bart.

The script by blacklisted Dalton Trumbo (under the front provided by Millard Kaufman), couldn't have been honed any closer to the bone. Even though John Dall is saddled with chunks of speechifying that were a Trumbo trademark, for the most part the movie is paced at a breakneck speed not conducive to philosophizing.

Joseph H. Lewis's propulsive direction has a vigor that the frantic editing and visual pyrotechnics of his filmmaking progeny never quite surpassed. *Bonnie and Clyde* (WB, 1967) may be a more significant and sophisticated movie, but nothing in it matches the breathtaking single take in which Cummins and Dall rob a small-town bank. This uninterrupted take, in which the audience is a virtual accomplice in the crime, is moviemaking at its exhilarating best.

Another rush is the scene in which the lovers flee in separate cars after the payroll heist. Unable to abandon each other, they wheel their land yachts into screeching U-turns and fall back into each other's arms. It should be laughable. Instead, it's the most ecstatic moment in noir. Lewis fires off one sharp scene after another, like Bart fanning the hammer on his favorite Colt. Even today, there's a freshness to *Gun Crazy*. The storytelling is so visually adept it could have been a silent movie, complemented solely by Victor Young's score. With due respect to Dalton Trumbo's dialogue, it would have worked just as well.

ABOVE: Eddie Miller (Arthur Franz) stalks the streets of San Francisco with a high-powered rifle, exacting his "revenge" on women in *The Sniper*. BELOW: Marie Windsor was usually a little more savvy about men, but in *The Sniper* she plays a tavern singer who enflames Eddie's tortured psyche.

EDDIE MILLER (ARTHUR FRANZ) IS ANOTHER HABITUÉ of Losers' Lane whose obsession with firearms is inspired by libidinous urges. His fear of, and desire for, women—instilled in him by a loveless mother—drives him to murder. Intimacy only comes through a telescopic sight, his only release from pulling the trigger. *The Sniper* (Columbia, 1952) was the first film to explore what would become a shameful national pastime—serial killing.

Harry Brown's screenplay was based on research by associate producers Edna and Edward Anhalt, who disdained the romanticism of films like *Gun Crazy* in favor of a straightforward account of violent sex offenses. The story is a manhunt thriller, familiar to film viewers of the past eight decades. But in '52, the murder scenes were so shocking the movie was pulled from release prematurely. For the first time, a contemporary film addressed the homicidal rage of a lonely, disturbed man lashing out at women. There are provocative innuendos throughout, suggesting women are predestined victims of male instincts, and that Miller's killing spree is the culmination of a chromosomal predilection. Eddie Miller is the original Incel.

For decades *The Sniper* was seldom seen, but it was central to a shift that took place in noir in the early 1950s. It was emblematic of what Paul Schrader, in his 1972 "Notes on Film Noir," called the genre's "third and final phase"—the descent into psychopathology:

"After ten years of steadily shedding romantic conventions, the later noir films finally got down to the root causes of the period: the loss of public honor, heroic conventions, personal integrity and, finally, psychic stability." The themes of alienation, sexual confusion, and violent revenge in *The Sniper* extended through the 1960s, to Don Siegel's *Dirty Harry* (WB, 1972), in which modern marshal Clint Eastwood patrols the same San Francisco streets Arthur Franz terrorized in *The Sniper*. It reached its apex in Schrader's screenplay for the über-noir *Taxi Driver* (Columbia, 1976)—which seemed a culmination of his 1972 essay on noir.

The Sniper neither sympathizes with its killer nor treats him like a rabid animal. It's one of the first films to take seriously the threat of brain-damaged individuals loose in a modern city. Miller *wants* to be put away—he *knows* he's dangerous—but the system is too overloaded to deal with him. The overcrowding of the VA Psych Ward had, by 1952, spilled over to the General Hospital (the police focus their manhunt on "section eights"—military mental cases). The film is full of scenes that capture the transition between an era when sexual deviance was considered a marginal problem—fodder for cavalier humor—and a new generation of armed sexual predators.

After the guilt-racked sniper intentionally burns his firing hand on a hot plate, he gets old-school counseling from a male nurse bandaging him: "A man's got no business fooling around with a stove. They're strictly women's business. You're not married, huh? You're missing a big deal, friend. So you get married, your wife does all the cooking—so she's the one that gets burned. So what happens? She comes crying on your shoulder. You pat her head, give her a kiss or two—yeah, that's living."

A few years earlier that would've passed for homespun wisdom in a Hollywood movie. Here, the camera tracks in on Miller's eyes as the nurse spouts off, his words stoking the killer's fury.

The idea that society was in the crosshairs of a new urban menace—and unprepared to defend itself—is reflected in a police show-up in which sexual deviants are paraded before a room filled with cops. The inquisitor (Ralph Peters, brilliant) can't help himself: He treats it like vaudeville shtick, offering quips about each man's perversion. The film clearly suggests that the joke is on the cops, who can't distinguish between garden-variety Peeping Toms and murderous psychos.

In an extraordinary scene, Miller goes to an amusement park and enjoys pitching baseballs at a bull's-eye, which dunks a swimsuit-clad woman in a tank of water. His faultless aim attracts a crowd as she's soaked over and over. Miller's misogynist rage finally erupts; he hurls balls directly at the woman, sending her screaming in terror. Despite the anxiety it builds as the manhunt closes in on Miller, the film climaxes with brilliant restraint: With the street cordoned off and residents warned of a gun battle, cops break into Miller's apartment to find him huddled on the bed, clutching his rifle. The camera dollies in to show a single tear dripping from his eye.

With *Murder, My Sweet*, *Cornered*, and *Crossfire* already on his résumé, Edward Dmytryk's reputation was secure as a director of exceptional noir. But his personal life overshadowed his artistic achievements. After serving a one-year sentence as one of the Hollywood Ten, the blacklisted Dmytryk lived in exile in England, until he turned informer against his formerly Communist comrades. The rancor his decision inspired always affected his reputation. The two films he made in England, *Give Us This Day* (Eagle-Lion, 1948) and *The Hidden Room* (Eagle-Lion, 1949) remain obscurities. The former is a solemn adaptation of Pietro di Donato's 1939

novel *Christ in Concrete*, about the ordeals of the American working class. Dmytryk uses the same visual flourish he'd employed at RKO, but seemed overwhelmed by the seriousness of the subject. He's on surer footing with the genre hijinks of *The Hidden Room*, a tale clearly inspired by Cain's novels, in which Robert Newton, in a fabulous performance, devises a diabolical scheme to dispatch his wife's lover. Simplicity is its greatest virtue; it's among the director's best films.

Back in Hollywood, Dmytryk picked up the pieces of his career by embracing the fast and resourceful style he'd mastered at RKO. Dmytryk insisted to his nine brethren that he was not selling out, that he would never knuckle under to "the enemy." What must they have thought when, for the role of Lieutenant Kafka (!) in *The Sniper*, Dmytryk cast Adolphe Menjou—who before the original House Un-American Activities Committee, in 1947, smugly offered himself as an expert on the Red Menace and indicted half of Hollywood?

Although it's too obscure to be considered influential, *The Sniper* predated stalker movies as a subset of the crime genre. Like those odd entertainments, its structure anticipates the predatory "catch and release" progression of pornographic films. Instead of sexual hookup and consummation, you get rejection and retaliation—the basic structure of all "slasher" films to come—reflecting a social problem that, as *The Sniper* warned, has become an epidemic.

OF ALL THE GUN-TOTING CRAZIES that passed through Losers' Lane, none achieved greater infamy than Cody Jarrett (James Cagney)—a mama's boy who turned homicidal whenever the *White Heat* (WB, 1949) cut through his brain like a buzz saw.

In the 1930s, Cagney juked his way to fame in a series of Warners gangster pictures: *The Public Enemy* (1931), *The Lady Killer* (1933), *Jimmy the Gent* (1934), *Angels with Dirty Faces* (1938), and *The Roaring Twenties (*1939), bedrock of the studio's golden era. Those films were notable for a "progressive" take on crime: It was the result of rugged conditions endemic to the modern city; the gangster was creating an organizational alternative to the legit enterprises a poor boy couldn't crack. Jarrett's lawlessness, on the other hand, stems from a mental disorder. Don't delve any deeper than his mother to find the root of his problem. Ma Jarrett (Margaret Wycherly) is a hard case who'll alibi her boy for anything, including murder.

White Heat typifies the conservative subversion of the crime thriller. In the wake of the studios' Communist purge, social criticism was out. Films could no longer suggest that people did bad things due to economic pressure. Criminal instincts weren't the by-product of a social system; they were inherited from your mother. Eric Johnston, head of the Motion Picture Association of America, who once defied HUAC's attempt to influence film content—only to later spearhead the studios' surrender to it—told the Screen Writers Guild in 1948: "We'll have no more *Grapes of Wrath*. We'll have no more *Tobacco Roads*. We'll have no more films that show the seamy side of American life. We'll have no more pictures that deal with labor strikes. We'll have no more pictures that show a banker as a villain." *Grapes of Wrath* author John Steinback certainly saw this day coming. "A communist is anybody who wants thirty-five cents an hour when we are paying twenty-five," he sarcastically explained in that novel.

Ben Roberts's and Ivan Goff's script for *White Heat* came along as Cagney reached a professional crossroads. After playing George M. Cohan in *Yankee Doodle Dandy*, Cagney protected his fame by rejecting the association he'd had with left-wingers during his days at Warners. But by '48, his misjudgments as an independent producer dimmed his luster and he was angling for a comeback. *White Heat* was just the ticket—a fresh take on the old crook.

An Oedipus complex, not poverty, is what drives Cody Jarrett to pull dangerous heists. The script charts his renegade career: daring robberies to prove his worth to Ma; his capture and imprisonment; the betrayal by his wife Verna (Virginia Mayo) with Cody's underling, Big Ed (Steve Cochran); Ma's death, and the transference of Cody's affections to Hank Fallon (Edmond O'Brien), an undercover agent planted in stir with Cody. After he escapes from prison, Cody plots revenge against Verna and Big Ed, but doesn't realize it's Hank who's the real "traitor."

Cagney's flamboyant "toppers"—bits of show business that kick a scene over the top—are in ample evidence: falling into his Ma's lap when he's struck by a headache, gnawing a chicken leg as he shoots a cohort, kicking a chair out from beneath Virginia Mayo—all hundred-proof Cagney, with a psychotic twist. Most famous are the mess-hall breakdown, when he goes wild after learning of Ma's death, and the climax, in which he's trapped atop a refinery tank. Realizing it's curtains, Cody kisses tomorrow goodbye by pumping bullets into the tank and bellowing the most famous exit line in movie history: "Made it, Ma—Top o' the world!" Credit Roberts and Goff for concocting the first cataclysmic climax to a crime thriller, but credit Cagney for the crazy smile, the wounded dance steps, and the giddy laughter—this was his ultimate "topper."

Despite the growing hue and cry against crime pictures in 1949, *White Heat* was a smash. Maybe people wanted nothing more than a riotously entertaining melodrama; thanks to Raoul Walsh's rambunctious direction, *White Heat* delivered in spades. But critics were largely unkind. The film was deemed brutal and mean-spirited. One week after he'd written a laudatory review in the *New York Times*, critic Bosley Crowther recanted under pressure from social guardians and branded the film potentially harmful. In the intervening years, more viewers—and critics—have come to see *White Heat* as a savage black comedy, a send-up of Cagney's former persona. (Cagney came to loathe the film, angry this snarling loser was the role with which he'd be most identified.)

An intriguing take came from John Howard Lawson, of the Hollywood Ten, who viewed *White Heat* with other inmates while serving his prison sentence. In a 1953 essay, titled "Film in the Battle of Ideas," Lawson said the film made a deep impression on the incarcerated audience, many of whom he described as "decent, well-intentioned people . . . who recognize the forces which drove them to vice or crime are inherent in our present social system. Related to this partial understanding is a deep bitterness, a feeling that the individual has no chance in a jungle society unless he adopts the way of the jungle. . . . . *White Heat* idealizes this code of the jungle and advertises it as a way of life. The prison audience—and this is probably true of any audience—associated the fictitious character with Cagney's reputation. The spectators saw him as an attractive symbol of toughness, defending himself against a cruel and irrational society; at least [inmates] said, 'He has the guts to stand up and fight back!'

"This emphasis on the individual's total depravity in a depraved society rejects the possibility of rational social cooperation," Lawson concluded. "Man is doomed to prowl alone, a beast in the jungle."

"Made it, Ma! Top o' the world!"
—Cody Jarrett (James Cagney) goes out in a blaze of glory in *White Heat*.

A scene from *Canon City* (1948), shot inside the Colorado State Penitentiary

THE BIG HOUSE

A T NIGHT I PLAY A GAME WHERE I DRIFT AWAY, BACK TO THE PLACE WHERE I USED TO LIVE. BACK BEFORE ALL THE MISTAKES, WHEN I STILL HAD SOMETHING TO GIVE. BACK WHEN IT WAS JUST YOU AND ME AND ENDLESS DAYS AHEAD. NO LIARS, NO CHEATERS, NO NEVER-ENDING DREAD. I COUNT THE DAYS 'TIL I CAN TELL THE ROTTEN BULLS GOODBYE. BUT YOU KNOW ME, I'M AN IMPATIENT GUY. DON'T KNOW HOW MUCH LONGER I CAN HACK IT IN THE CLINK. SO I'LL JUST SIGN OFF BY SAYING CLOSE YOUR EYES AND YOU'LL SEE ME AGAIN—SOONER THAN YOU THINK.

To the moviegoing public, prison movies are like penitentiaries: They're everywhere, always have been, yet they're shunted to the outskirts and rarely discussed. The genre has been around as long as any other, for obvious reasons: Every character comes with a gripping backstory—true or false—and when they're crammed into hostile confinement, something's got to explode. The Big House, looming just outside the Dark City limits, is government-funded purgatory for miscreants whose detours to the dark side haven't ended in death. Yet.

In *Scoundrels & Spitballers: Writers and Hollywood in the 1930s*, journalist Philippe Garnier relates the remarkable story of two convicts who used their criminal histories to brilliant advantage—writing Depression-era screenplays for studios eager to cash in on the public's fascination with crime. Robert Tasker and Ernest G. Booth were crooked from the get-go, surviving off burglaries and armed robberies until the state of California provided them free room and board in a series of Greybar Hotels. During their time in San Quentin, Tasker and Booth wrote for *The Bulletin*, Q's in-house literary magazine (which Tasker edited). Screen stories followed. During the late 1920s, Booth alone earned $28,000 writing from stir.

The work caught the attention of H. L. Mencken, editor and publisher of the influential *American Mercury*. Mencken was fond of discovering writers in low places, like gypsy-king Jim Tully, whom he helped turn into a literary sensation. Mencken pulled strings in 1929 to get Tasker, the less hardened of the pair, released early—straight into the waiting arms of Hollywood producers, eager to put an authentic imprimatur on their jailhouse potboilers.

Tasker worked uncredited with Frances Marion on MGM's *The Big House* (1931), and by some accounts shared more with her than just tips on the criminal life. Marion did not, however, share with him the Oscar their script won for Best Adapted Screenplay. The ex-con wrote many more films in the '30s, including *Doctor X* (WB, 1932); *Hell's Highway* (RKO, 1932); *The Notorious Gentleman* (Universal, 1935); and *The Accusing Finger* (Paramount, 1937), which starred another paroled ex-con, Paul Kelly, who'd served a manslaughter jolt at Q for killing his lover's husband in a drunken brawl. Tasker cavorted with the likes of Rowland Brown, eccentric writer-director of *Hell's Highway*, *Blood Money* (Fox, 1933), and *Quick Millions* (Fox, 1933), even appearing in the latter as a hired killer.

Other writers jumped on the hoosegow bandwagon: Seton I. Miller cowrote *The Criminal Code* (Columbia, 1931, Oscar-nominated) and *The Last Mile* (KBS Productions, 1932), while Brown Holmes scored with three penal colony classics: *I Am a Fugitive from a Chain Gang* (WB, 1932), *20,000 Years in Sing Sing* (WB,

1933), and *Ladies They Talk About* (WB, 1933). The latter was based on a play by jailbird Dorothy Mackaye, imprisoned as an accessory in the death of her husband—killed by her lover, actor Paul Kelly! Jim Tully's chain gang novel *Laughter in Hell* (Universal, 1933) was made into a jaw-dropping seventy-minute feature, filled with adultery, murder, executions, and plague.

Robert Tasker had his biggest credit cowriting *San Quentin* (1937) with John Bright; the picture, starring Pat O'Brien and Humphrey Bogart, was a hit for Warner Bros. Ex-con Tasker was living the Hollywood high life, already having married and divorced an heiress, by the time fellow felon Ernest Booth was paroled in 1937.

Booth immediately alighted in Tinseltown, ready to get his share of the pie. But by the end of the decade the flood of prison pictures had dried up. Booth managed only a few credits, including *Women Without Names* (Paramount, 1940, based on his 1931 play *Ladies of the Mob*) and *Men of San Quentin* (PRC, 1942). So, Booth augmented studio earnings by returning to the life he knew best, knocking over banks and robbing houses. He was arrested by the LAPD while dining at Musso & Frank's and was summarily shipped back to the slammer, where he stayed until his death in 1959. At least he outlived partner-in-crime Tasker, who died under mysterious circumstances in Mexico in 1942, at forty-three years of age.

ON ONE OF HIS FIRST HOLLYWOOD SCRIPTS, a comedy called *Penrod's Double Trouble* (WB, 1938), Ernest Booth collaborated with Crane Wilbur, a man whose entire career revolved around prisons, although, unlike Booth, he'd never been a guest of the state. No one wrote, produced, and directed as many prison pictures as Crane Wilbur. He

ABOVE: **Robert Tasker, convict turned screenwriter** BELOW: **Crane Wilbur in his *Perils of Pauline* matinee idol days**

worked this grim outpost of the movie business for more than twenty-five years, yet he's virtually unknown today. He made a dozen movies set entirely or partially in the Big House (five of which he directed): *Alcatraz Island* (1937); *Over the Wall* (1938); *Crime School* (1938); *Blackwell's Island* (1939); *Hell's Kitchen* (1939); *Roger Touhy, Gangster* (1944); *Canon City* (1948); *The Story of Molly X* (1949); *Outside the Wall* (1950); *Inside the Walls of Folsom Prison* (1951); *Women's Prison* (1955); and *House of Women* (1962). That's not counting films that dealt with characters on parole and probation.

Although he hailed from an upstate New York farming community, theater was in Wilbur's blood. His mother, Carrie Crane, had been a stage actress and his aunt Edith was married to Tyrone Power Sr. His father, Henry Wilber, hung himself when his son was six years old, the first of several untimely deaths that haunted the stagestruck kid. (He'd lose a young wife to sudden illness, and their child, as well.) Only in his teens, Wilbur (he changed the spelling), produced and acted in self-penned shows that displayed avidity for crime and the macabre.

The handsome young man made his acting debut in 1911 for New Jersey's American Pathé studio, which teamed him with actress Pearl White in a slew of silent shorts before their breakthrough with the series *The Perils of Pauline*, in which Wilbur and White routinely engaged in death-defying escapes that thrilled audiences nationwide.

Despite success as an actor, Wilbur preferred writing and producing. His first Broadway show, *The Ouiji Board* (1920) was a murder mystery about bunko spiritualists. Its follow-up, *The Monster*, mixed humor, mystery, and horror and was optioned by producer-director Roland West for a 1925 picture starring Lon Chaney.

In 1930 Wilbur starred on Broadway in Edgar Wallace's *On the Spot*, in which he played Tony Perrelli, a thinly veiled caricature of Al Capone, with Anna May Wong as his Chinese mistress. When the play traveled to Capone's home turf, Scarface demanded a command performance at his Chicago headquarters. "There must have been forty or fifty gangsters there," Wilbur recalled in an interview. "I did the whole play for them. I played all of the parts. I told them scene by scene what was happening. I never had such an audience." (Paramount adapted *On the Spot* in 1938, retitled *Dangerous to Know*, with Anna May Wong reprising her role but Akim Tamiroff replacing Wilbur.)

From 1932 to '34, Wilbur produced his own shows on Broadway, *Border-Land*, *Halfway to Hell,* and *Are You Decent?* Then his agent, Ivan Kohn, set up a meeting in Hollywood with Bryan Foy, who'd change the course of Wilbur's professional life.

Foy, like Crane Wilbur, had a theatrical upbringing. He was the oldest of the seven kids in their father's vaudeville act—Eddie Foy and the Seven Little Foys. "Brynie" entered pictures in the 1920s as a writer for Warner Bros. In the studio's first all-talking picture, *The Lights of New York* (1928), he wrote a line that became synonymous with gangsterism: "Take him for a ride."

When Foy left Warners in 1934 to establish Bryan Foy Productions, he hired Crane Wilbur to direct a pair of films by provocative African-American novelist Wallace Thurman—though the casts were exclusively White. First was *Tomorrow's Children* (1934), about forced sterilization. Teenage pregnancy was the hot button pushed in *High School Girl* (1934). Wilbur acted in both and coscripted *Tomorrow's Children*. For the next few years he worked on Poverty Row as a director-writer-actor, making everything from dramas about human trafficking (*Yellow Cargo* [Grand National, 1936]) to musicals (*The Devil on Horseback* [Grand National, 1936]).

When Foy returned to Warners in '37 to run its B unit, he brought Wilbur on as a staff writer. *Alcatraz Island* was the first of Wilbur's Big House scripts. It featured a gangster (John Litel), based on Capone, sentenced to The Rock on a tax rap. "It was what we call a 'sleeper,'" Foy said, "and it made a lot of money, so I was always looking for another one." In short order, Foy turned out four more prison pictures, Wilbur writing on them all: *Over the Wall* and *Crime School* in 1939, *Blackwell's Island* and *Hell's Kitchen* the year after.

After a detour into radio—writing and producing episodes of CBS's *Big Town*, starring Edward G. Robinson as a crime-fighting newspaperman (Daniel Mainwaring and Maxwell Shane also wrote for the show)—Wilbur followed Foy to 20th Century-Fox to work on a biopic about gangster Roger Touhy. Framed

Crime School **(WB, 1938) was one of the first of dozens of Wilbur scripts set at least partially behind prison walls.**

by Capone for a kidnapping he didn't commit, Touhy served time at Statesville Prison in Joliet, Illinois. On October 9, 1942, he and several other inmates staged a breakout. Foy jumped all over the story, gaining the cooperation of the governor to restage the escape where it happened, with prison guards playing the convicts. *Roger Touhy, Gangster* was released in 1944 with Preston Foster in the title role. Touhy, who was apprehended and returned to the slammer, later sued Fox for defamation, winning a five-figure judgment after Capone's frame-up was verified.

When Foy ditched Fox to take over production at upstart Eagle-Lion Pictures (where he green-lighted *T-Men* and *Raw Deal*), Wilbur followed his peripatetic pal. Could a prison picture be far behind?

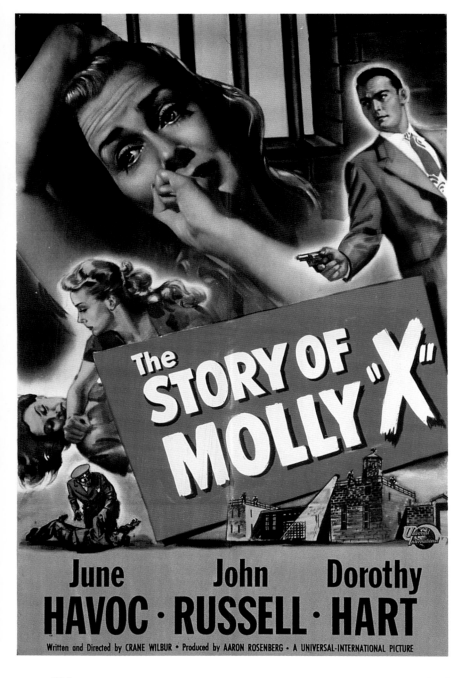

The STORY OF MOLLY "X"

June **HAVOC** · John **RUSSELL** · Dorothy **HART**

Written and Directed by CRANE WILBUR · Produced by AARON ROSENBERG · A UNIVERSAL-INTERNATIONAL PICTURE

On December 30, 1947, a dozen cons busted out of the Colorado State Prison, sparking a statewide manhunt. Only six months later, *Canon City* (Eagle-Lion, 1948) was in theaters—written and directed by Crane Wilbur and photographed by the great John Alton. Bryan Foy had called in a favor from warden Roy Best (whom he'd met making *Roger Touhy, Gangster*), gaining permission to shoot inside the prison even before the escapees were recaptured. "I spent a lot of time there," Wilbur said. "I knew practically every one of those inmates, even the warden's dogs." Following the success of *Canon City*, Wilbur and Foy scored again with *He Walked by Night* (1948), an influential police procedural (see page 31).

Wilbur parted ways (briefly) with Foy to direct and write a pair of pictures at Universal-International. *The Story of Molly X* (1949), set largely at the California Institute for Women in Tehachapi, was about the rehabilitation of the titular criminal (June Havoc). As was his modus operandi, Wilbur spent time interviewing inmates, including one doing life for killing a man who'd kicked her cat.

Unlike dames in most WIPs (industry lingo for women-in-prison films), Molly X is no naïf, jailed by mistake. She's a professional thief who takes over her husband's robbery ring when he's murdered. When she learns that his killer is in their gang, she guns him down. Convicted, she's sent to the state's new all-female prison (Tehachapi was the first of its kind in California). Her rehab is detoured when her victim's moll (Dorothy Hart) winds up in the same cellblock. Their reunion leads to the film's highlight: a knock-down, drag-out brawl between Havoc and Hart, the greatest catfight in Hollywood history.

Wilbur followed *Molly X* with *Outside the Wall* (1950), again writing and directing, from a story by Henry Edward Helseth (*Cry of the City*). Parolee Larry Nelson (Richard Basehart), determined to go straight, gets hired at a sanitarium. A shifty blond nurse (Marilyn Maxwell) and a former prison mate (John Hoyt) threaten to push Nelson off the straight and narrow. Like a moth to the flame, Wilbur shot the prison scenes in Philadelphia's Eastern State Penitentiary.

When Bryan Foy reupped at Warner Bros. in 1951, he brought his old pal in to write on an anti-Communist propaganda piece (every studio was making one). *I Was a Communist for the FBI* (1951) was based on a *Saturday Evening Post* serial by Matt Cvetic, who had posed as a Red to infiltrate a spy ring supposedly operating inside the Pittsburgh steelworkers' union. Directed by Gordon Douglas and starring Frank Lovejoy as Cvetic, the movie was presented as fact, but was really trumped-up melodrama—making it particularly ironic when the film, fabricated entirely on studio sets, was nominated for the 1951 Academy Award as Best Documentary.

Wilbur was back in the director's chair for *Inside the Walls of Folsom Prison* (WB, 1951). Not as artful as *Canon City*, nor as entertaining as *The Story of Molly X*, it's still a signature Crane Wilbur work, notable for being narrated by the prison itself (an idea Steve Fisher cribbed for 1953's *City That Never Sleeps*, Chicago itself providing the voice-over):

> I am Folsom Prison. At one time they called me Bloody Folsom—Ha! And I earned the name. I've been standing here in California since 1878. My own prisoners built me, shutting themselves off from the free world. Every block of my granite is cemented by their tears, their pain—and the blood of many men.

The story pits Folsom's ruthless warden (Ted de Corsia) against his college-educated captain of the guards (David Brian), with Steve Cochran leading the inevitable prisoner revolt. Per usual, Wilbur ingratiated himself with Folsom's staff and inmates. "I went there a couple of weeks in advance . . . to round out what I had written. I wanted to see that it was true. I didn't want it all to be a lot of crap." Bits of real-life business he'd incorporate include an aging con who refuses parole because of his attachment to a dog that won't leave the prison. Wilbur stayed at Folsom long enough for some cons to hatch a plan to take him hostage in a prison break. Several inmates—including a murderer, a robber-kidnapper, and a racketeer—later bragged to Wilbur, individually, that *his* influence is what spared Wilbur from the kidnapping plot.

Some of Wilbur's best work followed, none of it behind bars: He scripted the 1954 Warners release *Crime Wave*, a small-scale classic brilliantly directed by André de Toth. Wilbur then called on his early stage horrors to create, again with Foy and de Toth, the 1953 smash *House of Wax*, which reenvisioned 1933's *The Mystery of the Wax Museum* in the new 3-D process that was Hollywood's latest fad.

In 1955, Wilbur reunited with his *Big Town* radio show compatriot Daniel Mainwaring to script *The Phenix City Story*, one of the best of the industry's wave of crime "exposés." Pugnaciously directed by Phil Karlson, it recounts the campaign by Alabama attorney Albert Patterson to run organized crime out of Phenix City,

This publicity photo of inmate Steve Cochran may have been shot on a set, but the film it promotes, *Inside the Walls of Folsom Prison* (WB, 1951), was shot largely within the California prison.

Alabama, a bastion of gambling and prostitution that catered to soldiers stationed across the river in Fort Benning, Georgia. It was the last great movie Wilbur worked on. His final script, fittingly, was 1962's *House of Women* (WB)—yes, for Bryan Foy Productions—a throwback to '30s prison yarns with little of the sexploitation that started sensationalizing the genre in the 1960s.

When Crane Wilbur died in 1973, at age eighty-six, his *Los Angeles Times* obit was headlined **SCREEN ACTOR CRANE WILBUR DIES,** with the first four paragraphs focusing on *The Perils of Pauline*. Not much respect for a guy integral to the development of both the "police procedural" and the "semi-documentary"—not to mention his being the undisputed Potentate of Prison Pictures.

CRANE WILBUR DID NOT HAVE A HAND in the most powerful prison picture of the noir era. *Brute Force* (Universal, 1947) was produced by Mark Hellinger as his follow-up to *The Killers* and it was—and remains—the most explosive prison movie ever made.

The film at first appears to be a vilification of fascism in all its forms. The message-mongering by screenwriter Richard Brooks is broad enough for the picture to be read as a polemic against Hitler, Franco, or any totalitarian regime. (At the time, resilient Nazism was still a greater public fear then nascent Marxism.) But within a few short years, the film's director, Jules Dassin, would have his Hollywood career snuffed out by the House Un-American Activities Committee. Dassin and company were, in fact, predicting the parallels between demagogic politicians like Senator McCarthy and Captain Munsey, *Brute Force*'s terrifying captain of the guards.

The prisoners of Westgate Penitentiary are recipients of inhumane cruelty, dispensed, Gestapo-style, by Munsey (Hume Cronyn), a small, miserable man who finds fulfillment in a uniform and the license it gives him to abuse power.

Brooks's script paints Munsey as the archetypal crypto-Nazi, just doing his job to maintain order: "I really want to help the warden. It's just that he's confused. He doesn't know that kindness is actually weakness. And weakness is an infection that makes a man a follower instead of a leader." Munsey even listens to Wagner records as he wields the truncheon in his interrogation room: "There is no reward for bringing them back alive," he reminds the guards.

Joe Collins (Burt Lancaster) is determined to lead his cellmates in a breakout,

even though he knows it could ignite a full-scale riot. Hours tick down to the big bust-out. Flashbacks reveal how each man in Cell R-17 came to be trapped in his personal hell. In the type of by-the-numbers writing that characterizes the worst of film noir, each man's transgression revolves around a woman (at Hellinger's insistence). The petty schemes that led to their arrests wither beside the full-throttled hatred that consumes all the men, on both sides of the bars.

The only ones opting out of the rush to destruction are the warden, a feeble, useless administrator, and the prison sawbones, Dr. Walker (Art Smith), a pie-eyed pinko who has the chore of regularly underlining the film's themes. "That's it, Muncie, that's it," he says, after provoking the top bull into hitting him. "Not cleverness, not imagination, just force. Brute force. Congratulations. Force does make leaders. But you forget one thing. It also destroys them."

The jailbreak runs off the rails when Collins uncovers an informer in his crew. "What's the plan now?" he's asked. "The plan's a flop. You're on your own. It's a million to one."

The climax displayed the most harrowing violence ever seen on movie screens. After discovering that Freshman (Jeff Corey) is the informer, Collins straps him to the front of a railcar and sends him out of the prison's drainpipe to be ripped apart by the guards' machine gun fire. A pair of cons with whom we've empathized, Soldier (Howard Duff) and Kid Coy (Jack Overman), die instantly. Regardless, the prisoners surge forward with a fatal determinism unmatched until *The Wild Bunch* (1969), but minus any blaze of glory. Collins kills his way into the tower, where he grapples with Captain Munsey hand to hand, finally throwing him to his death amid the rioting inmates. As he watches the prison go up in flames, Dr. Walker says: "No one escapes. No one ever escapes."

Brute Force is the bleakest of film noirs. By the time it ends, all its political posturing has been burned beyond recognition by its searing nihilism.

The climactic prison break in *Brute Force* featured some of the most harrowing violence yet seen in movie theaters. Convicts Jeff Corey, Howard Duff, Jack Overman, and Burt Lancaster will not escape. "No one ever escapes."

Caged: Eleanor Parker enters the joint a naive innocent, but she'll leave it a bitter, hardened criminal.

THE NEXT GREAT PRISON PICTURE would barely have a man in it. Since its release in 1950, *Caged* (WB) has come to be known, unfortunately, as a camp classic. That's largely because the tropes of prison films, when enacted by a female cast, would soon be fodder for titillating sexploitation. By the 1970s, R-rated pictures like *The Big Bird Cage* (New World, 1972) and *Caged Heat* (New World, 1974) existed solely to show Pam Grier or Erica Gavin battling through the Big House in various states of undress. Tom Eyen's 1975 stage parody *Women Behind Bars* featured a warden played by drag superstar Divine. After that, all WIPs were instantly and retroactively reclassified as "camp."

Women had been brutalized behind bars in movies since the silent era, when Cecil B. DeMille made a couple of groundbreaking WIPs, *Manslaughter* (Paramount, 1922) and *The Godless Girl* (Pathé, 1929). Such films typically had two things in common—they were written by women, and they all featured a saintly priest or social reformer, always male, to steer the star to redemption.

Virginia Kellogg, the woman behind *Caged*, had a hand in two of the most testosterone-fueled films of the era—*T-Men* and *White Heat*—both based on her original stories. A former reporter, Kellogg's strong suit was firsthand research—and for *Caged* she surpassed even Crane Wilbur. She'd brought the idea to Warner Bros.'s producer Jerry Wald in 1948, under the title *Women Without Men*, and Wald enthusiastically had the studio send Kellogg around the country, investigating women's prisons. In one case she was incarcerated for two weeks and treated like any other prisoner. There was nothing "campy" about the experience—it scared the hell out of Kellogg. She telegrammed Wald that she was learning "shocking facts that far surpass *The Snake Pit*," the 1948 Fox film that revealed the horrors inside mental institutions.

Kellogg's investigative essay, "Inside Women's Prison," was published in *Collier's* to coincide with the release of *Caged*. Her descriptions of institutional corruption and the ritual humiliation of prisoners hit especially hard because *the inmates were women*. Kellogg voiced contempt for prison matrons, whom she revealed as often being on the payrolls of crime syndicates or "related to politicians . . . and just hanging on long enough to get a pension." Kellogg was so unnerved by her experience, and fearful of reprisal, she never left home without a gun in her handbag.

Wald hired Bernie Schoenfeld, who'd already scripted two noir gems, *Phantom Lady* and *The Dark Corner*, to turn Kellogg's research into a polished screenplay, which Jack Warner wanted to call *Locked In*, a title Wald hated. There'd be many name changes before Wald came up with the perfect title.

Wald's initial inspiration was to cast—take a deep breath—Bette Davis as Warden Benton and Joan Crawford as naïve first-timer Marie Allen. *Whatever Happened to Convict #93850*? Both actresses, of course, coveted the Marie Allen role, so their epic pairing would have to wait a few more years. Patricia Neal turned down the role of the warden, telling Wald she had no interest in supporting "whoever played the plum role." For that part, Wald considered Doe Avedon, Betsy Drake, and Ruth Roman—before settling on studio contract player Eleanor Parker, who'd spent several years as a second lead, but never had anywhere near this juicy a part. Venerable character actress Agnes Moorehead signed on as the warden, enjoying, for her, a rare sympathetic turn.

For the role of prison matron Evelyn Harper, the villain of the piece, there was only one choice: six-foot two-inch, 230-pound Hope Emerson, who'd made a huge impression in Fox's *Cry of the City*, intimidating tough guy Richard Conte. Emerson became one of the most memorable villains of all-time, terrorizing a cast that included Betty Garde, Jan Sterling, Ellen Corby, Lee Patrick, Olive Deering, Jane Darwell, and Gertrude Michael. The cellblock is literally packed with great actresses—none of whom wear a speck of makeup in this decidedly unglamorous film.

The male do-gooder who routinely redeemed the hard-luck female con—that guy never shows up in *Caged*. Far from rehabilitating her, prison destroys Marie Allen, turning an innocent woman into a hardened criminal. This was not easily snuck past the Production Code office. Reviewing the script, chief censor Joseph Breen noted that, at the end, Marie is ". . . presumably leaving prison to join a house of prostitution." Somehow Bernie Schoenfeld convinced Breen his script was "simply emphasizing the fact that she had some talent as a booster"—meaning, in underworld slang, a pickpocket.

Other things, however, didn't get past the PCA. Like drug use. On her research tour, Virginia Kellogg was amazed at the prevalence of narcotics in prisons, so she created a character called "Twitch," an addict. Breen demanded "Twitch" be cut. It'd be five more years before *The Man with the Golden Arm*—released *without* the PCA's approval—showed drug addiction on American movie screens (although if you read between the lines, Veronica Lake is addicted to heroin in 1949's *Slattery's Hurricane* [Fox], directed by her then-husband, André de Toth).

"Smoochie," played by Jan Sterling, is the rare woman in a film of the era actually ID'd as a CP—common prostitute. There were dozens of films in which prostitution was implied, but only a handful where it's stated openly. Jerry Wald

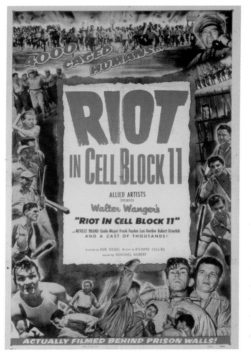

had to be persuasive to get that past Breen and his minions. Although the PCA gave ground, the film still suffered cuts in parts of the country with their own censor boards; Pennsylvania and Kansas banned it outright. *Caged* stirred up protests like no Warner Bros. picture since 1932's *I Am a Fugitive from a Chain Gang*. The American Prison Association sent Jack Warner a letter complaining that *Caged* was causing "considerable resentment among wardens and superintendents . . . with its sweeping condemnation of correctional policy and administration."

Jerry Wald wanted Michael Curtiz or Vincent Sherman to direct *Caged*, but he ended up with veteran John Cromwell, who turned in his best film in years. Cromwell followed with two more crime pictures in 1951, both for RKO—*The Company She Keeps*, coincidentally about a female parolee, and *The Racket*, a remake of the silent 1928 cops-and-robbers yarn. After making those, Cromwell was rewarded by being named a Communist by RKO boss Howard Hughes—a false charge, but it didn't stop Cromwell from being blacklisted for the next seven years.

Caged earned three Oscar nominations—Best Actress (Eleanor Parker), Best Original Story and Screenplay (Virginia Kellogg and Bernard Schoenfeld), and Best Supporting Actress (Hope Emerson). In real life, Emerson was nothing like the monster she portrayed. She had performed in vaudeville as a kid and became a nightclub performer, singing bawdy ballads and playing a mean boogie-woogie piano. In the late '50s, she portrayed "Mother" on the TV series *Peter Gunn*, earning an Emmy nomination. Sadly, she died shortly afterward of liver disease at only sixty-two years of age.

PRISON PICTURES HAD A SURGE of popularity in the mid-1950s. *Riot in Cell Block 11* (Allied Artists, 1954) led the wave, inspired by producer Walter Wanger's own prison stint, served in the relative luxury of the Castaic Honor Farm. Wanger had caught his wife, Joan Bennett, having an affair with agent Jennings Lang. "Wanger

did what any crazed cuckold would do," explained Billy Wilder. "He shot Lang in the balls."

Wanger hired Richard Collins to write compassionately about the inmates, who riot to gain better living conditions and to expose the prison's institutionalized brutality. Collins, a former Communist who kept his career by naming names to HUAC, essentially revised *Brute Force*, trading its fabulist symbolism for starker realities. The prisoners extract concessions from the Prison Board following a tense hostage standoff, but the governor refuses to sign them into law. Don Siegel directed with typical vigor and Neville Brand had his best role ever as leader of the inmates' uprising.

Crane Wilbur and Bryan Foy were back at it in *Women's Prison* (Columbia, 1955), in which Wilbur's rewrite tipped Jack DeWitt's original story toward campiness, and a cellblock of overheated actresses—including stalwarts Ida Lupino, Agnes Moorehead, Jan Sterling, Audrey Totter, and Phyllis Thaxter—ripped the scenery and each other to shreds. The hook was male and female prisons existing side by side—with no earthly force capable of keeping wanton wenches and horny hoodlums from fulfilling their carnal desires—albeit in chaste '50s style.

Released the same year was *Betrayed Women* (Allied Artists), in which scribe Steve Fisher found no reason to tamper with the formula. Its sole claim to originality is that women were busting out of the Big House. The spectacle of Amazonian boss con Beverly Michaels (*Wicked Woman*) leading the break is worth every one of the seventy minutes it takes veteran director Edward L. Cahn to reel out Fisher's refried plot.

Big House, U.S.A. (Allied Artists, 1955), an independently produced film shot in the same Colorado prison and environs featured in *Canon City*, is a flat-looking '50s film, directed only serviceably by Howard Koch, but throbbing with meanness and cruelty. The script, by noir veteran John C. Higgins, was enacted by one of the heaviest casts ever: Broderick Crawford, Ralph Meeker, William Talman, Charles

Bronson, and Lon Chaney Jr. Meeker plays a kidnapper whose ransom plot goes haywire when the rich kid he's nabbed falls off a cliff. He secures the ransom and buries it, but is caught and imprisoned (for kidnapping, not murder, since the boy's body is never found). Crawford's gang of cons then ropes Meeker into their breakout, forcing him to take them to his buried loot. Things do not end well.

The hard cases of *Big House, U.S.A.* had nothing on the mugs in *Crashout* (The Filmakers)—yet another 1955 release. It's the best of the jailbreak yarns, thanks to a well-wrought script by Cy Endfield, written prior to his exile in England (he has no credit).

Former newspaperman Lewis R. Foster directs with a startling amount of brutality (bordering on sadism), especially a tense scene where the escapees hold roadhouse patrons hostage. William Talman, who'd broken out of *Big House, U.S.A.* the

The escaped cons in *Crashout* flee on a train in stolen civvies: William Talman, William Bendix, Gene Evans, and Arthur Kennedy.

seizes his chance. He disembarks with the girl. The gang senses a betrayal. As she waits for Billy outside the station, Talman hurls his knife into the lovestruck kid's back. He dies not even knowing the girl's name.

Beverly Michaels is also on hand (playing a decent woman for a change), giving Arthur Kennedy a whiff of what could have been. She's a kindred spirit, a wounded soul who barely bats an eye when the cons take over her house. It's the rare prison-break movie in which the best scenes are quiet conversations about the pain of missed chances.

All these similar 1955 releases exhausted the public's interest in prison yarns. The challenge of putting a new spin on the formula fell to director Russell Rouse, who in 1957 adapted a Jack Finney story into *House of Numbers* (MGM), scripted not by Rouse and his usual writing partner, Clarence Greene, but by Herman Mankiewicz's son, Don. The plot stretches credulity to the breaking point—Jack Palance plays a San Quentin inmate who convinces his twin brother (also Palance) to break *into* the joint and trade places with him. The far-fetched premise is helped by being shot inside the actual prison, and by supporting players Barbara Lang and Timothy Carey, who reprises his spacey nutcase routine as Palance's cellmate. It's a fascinating fumble—just not *quite* inspired enough to overcome its absurdity.

same year, plays a Bible-quoting psycho adept at knife-throwing. William Bendix, tougher than ever, leads a crew that includes Talman, Arthur Kennedy, Luther Adler, Gene Evans, and Marshall Thompson. A sense of doom permeates the film, made all the more palpable by the tiny rays of hope that appear—only to be quickly snuffed out.

A scene in the middle of the action is, by itself, a mini-masterpiece: The cons, in stolen civvies, board a train and blend with the passengers. Billy (Marshall Thompson), the youngest of the gang, sits with a pretty girl (Gloria Talbot) returning to her small town after failing to crack the big city. The kids are instantly drawn to each other. After a heartfelt conversation with this vulnerable stranger, Billy

THE LAST GREAT PRISON MOVIE of the 1950s only ends in the Big House. Most of *I Want to Live!* (UA, 1958) recounts the true story of party-girl/prostitute Barbara Graham. Producer Walter Wanger marshalled an A-team to bring this "ripped from the headlines" story to the screen. The script by Nelson Gidding and Don Mankiewicz (apparently a prison specialist after *House of Numbers*) was adapted from newspaper articles by Pulitzer Prize–winner Ed Montgomery of the *San Francisco Examiner*. In interviews with the reporter, Graham presented herself as a hard-luck dame roped into a robbery scheme that ended in the death of widow Mabel Monohan. Graham felt she'd never get a fair shake because of her reputation as a "loose" woman. She was proven right on June 3, 1955 when, after many torturous stays of execution, she was put to death in San Quentin's gas chamber.

"I probably got more emotionally invested in that film than any other," admitted director Robert Wise. Yet his genius was to tell the tale without melodrama or mawkishness. He contributed mightily to Susan Hayward's Oscar-winning performance by stripping the actress of her notorious vanity and bringing her innate hardness to the surface, photographed by Lionel Lindon minus any glamorous affect. Wise uses a jazz score by Johnny Mandel (featuring great work from Gerry Mulligan and Art Farmer) to propel the story, the first time he'd collaborated with a composer from the start of production; together they devised musical transitions that distilled long expository stretches to mere moments.

The depiction of the execution was groundbreaking. It had always been standard Hollywood practice to "look away," in films ranging from *Angels with Dirty Faces* to *The Postman Always Rings Twice* to *Beyond a Reasonable Doubt*. Wise would have none of that: "I didn't want reviewers to say, 'Well, that's a Hollywood version of what goes on in the death cell and the gas chamber.'"

His handling of the death house scene was inspired by a conversation Wise had with the priest who consoled Graham in her final hours: "He said, 'I don't suppose you have any idea of the terrible atmosphere that permeates a prison the day before, the night, the morning of an execution. The whole prison knows an execution is coming up, they know all the steps that are being made to take a human life.' . . . I went right back to the prison and said, 'Show me everything that goes on from the moment you start to prepare for an execution until it's over—all the details, every routine you go through.' That gave me the spine around which to hook the third act."

That last act, in which Graham bides time in her cell, hoping for the governor's commutation, is excruciating; the preparations for her death, harrowing. "When you hear the pellets drop, count to ten and take a deep breath," suggests a guard. "It's easier that way."

"How would you know?" snarls Graham, a hard-ass to the end.

Susan Hayward enters the death chamber in her Oscar-winning performance as Barbara Graham in *I Want to Live!*

THIEVES' HIGHWAY

Escape was the only option. Follow the blacktop out of Dark City, into a fresh start. Two hours ago the city lights vanished from the rearview, like stars blinking out a million miles away. Out here there'll be room to live, to make a move without knocking against somebody. Listen—a train whistle. Not car horns, or an ambulance, or a siren. I'll find a town where people look you in the eye and call you by your first name and know you're good for an IOU. Ah, look at this poor guy—his car must've conked out, in the middle of nowhere. "Hey, Buddy, you need a lift?"

In the 1950s, America reached its greatest prosperity since the mid-1920s. The Cold War was terrific for business; consuming became a patriotic duty. And there was no greater badge of affluence than the automobile. President Dwight D. Eisenhower had a vision that hooked up the Cold War to the nation's burgeoning car culture: the Interstate Highway Act, a massive federal program that linked rural and urban America in what proponents called "farm to market" unity. The sinister aspect of the plan was that the new four-lanes were also designed as escape routes, should Soviet missiles rain on major US cities.

The Highway Act had an unexpected dark side. It ensured that troubles once limited to the big city were free to travel, in a big roadster, wherever they wanted to go. In terms of crime—and noir—"Check the bus and train terminals! Put a roadblock at the bridge!" would rarely be heard again.

A highly publicized example of a new type of criminal in the nation's

bloodstream was William Edward Cook Jr., a twenty-two-year-old ex-con who in 1951 went on a murder rampage in the Southwest, cadging rides from his victims. Among the unfortunate Samaritans were a vacationing family from Illinois and a traveling salesman from Seattle. America thought it had buried the terrors of the Old West under a veneer of gray flannel civility, but here was a clear indication that murder was just as likely to happen in the sticks as on city streets.

When Cook was apprehended, all the major magazines ran profiles. Journalists recounted the story of his brutal childhood—absent father, taunting from other kids because of a facial deformity, Dickensian boarding schools—searching for clues to his motives. Cook offered a succinct explanation for his homicidal behavior: "I hate everybody's guts and everybody hates mine."

Billy Cook represented an unrepentant viciousness that all but obliterated any notion in the media—especially the movies—of the criminal as social rebel. Rebelliousness was kid stuff, left to the slew of juvenile delinquent movies spawned by rock 'n' roll and the rise of leather-clad motorcycle cults. Hardened criminals got more murderous than ever, in reality and in the movies. Their motives were still trotted out, but in Ike's America mitigating circumstances didn't count for much. A

Films such as *Moonrise* (Republic, 1948), starring Dane Clark and Gail Russell, showed that noir also thrived beyond the Dark City limits.

Red was a Red and a crook was a crook. Both were threats to peace and prosperity. In films such as *The Night Holds Terror* (Columbia, 1955), *The Killer Is Loose* (UA, 1956), *A Cry in the Night* (WB, 1956), *Cry Terror* (MGM, 1957), and even the A-list *The Desperate Hours* (Paramount, 1955), the focus is on murderous outcasts invading lives of middle-class tranquility.

In 1953, *The Hitch-Hiker* (RKO) recounted the terrifying eight-day ordeal two vacationing men suffered at the hands of Billy Cook. The story follows the outline of Cook's killing spree, changing the character's name to Emmett Myers (William Talman). When Ray Collins (Edmond O'Brien) and Gil Bowen (Frank Lovejoy) give Myers a lift, he commandeers their '52 Plymouth, and their lives. He revels in his animal instincts, which make him superior to the bourgeois vacationers. Because Myers's deformed right eye cannot close, his captives are never sure if he's asleep as he holds them at gunpoint every night.

Myers represents the worst part of each man's ego, turned loose. When he asks what they do for a living, he learns that Gil is an architect, Roy a mechanic. "That makes you smarter," he sneers, jabbing the pistol at Gil. Even Myers's idle sniping wounds.

In a beautiful touch, Gil covertly slips off his inscribed wedding band and leaves it on the pump of a desolate Mexican filling station. It will either be the clue that rescues them or the last trace he leaves behind when he's gone. Roy, meanwhile, is mired in a masculinity crisis: Because he won't confront Myers—or run away— he's afraid Myers's tagging him as "soft" is all too true. Roy is suckered into seeing life through Myers's eyes—the eyes of a predator. In that narrow view, failure to best his antagonist brands him as prey. The breakdown of his psyche follows. Gil doesn't get baited as easily. He's able to plot escapes more feasible than the mano-a-mano brawl Roy fantasizes. After riding the pair endlessly about how differences in class and education mean nothing now, Myers relishes one last joke—forcing Roy to trade clothes with him and walk into a trap the police have set. Symbolically, Roy yells into the darkness: "I'm not Myers! I'm not Myers!" Gil, who'd seemed resigned to his fate, strikes quickly: He overpowers the distracted Myers and wrestles the gun away from him. Without a weapon, the killer surrenders meekly.

Frank Lovejoy, William Talman, and Edmond O'Brien in *The Hitch-Hiker*

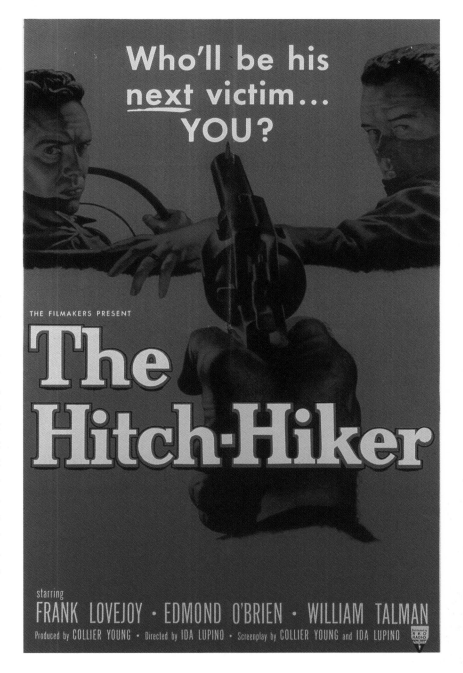

Who'll be his
next victim...
YOU?

THE FILMAKERS PRESENT

The Hitch-Hiker

starring
FRANK LOVEJOY · EDMOND O'BRIEN · WILLIAM TALMAN
Produced by COLLIER YOUNG · Directed by IDA LUPINO · Screenplay by COLLIER YOUNG and IDA LUPINO

THE MOST TALENTED WOMAN IN TOWN

The Hitch-Hiker has the distinction of being the only film noir directed by a woman, Ida Lupino. If anything proved she was one of the boys, this did: There isn't a woman in the film, yet the dynamics of machismo swirl at every turn. Although [ea]rlier films had traces of noir, *The Hitch-Hiker* was her only drive into [(or out of?)] Dark City. She had further excursions planned. An investor's [prosp]ectus for The Filmakers, the production company she operated with [husband] Collier Young, mapped several noir projects: *I Bought a Gun*, about [how a] handgun in the house affects a family; *Something for Nothing*, a tril[ogy of] gambling stories; and *The Story of a Murder*, described as "The first [serious] scientific approach . . . to tell audiences why people kill and why [murder] can be prevented." Finally there was *Fire Bug*, featuring an arsonist [who at]tempts to burn down the whole damn city. None of these were ever [produc]ed, however.

[Lu]pino turned to crime dramas only after attempts at socially conscious [films] foundered. Inspired by the neorealists, her independent productions [were] heartfelt tales of ordinary people. *Not Wanted* (Film Classics, 1949), [Lupino]'s first film, was a look at unwed mothers. Elmer Clifton is credited as [directo]r, but the old veteran took ill before shooting and Lupino helmed it, [uncre]dited. She didn't have a Guild card, so she kept a low profile. [*Never*]*Fear* (Eagle-Lion, 1950) was a romance about polio victims, featur[ing an] inspired wheelchair dance. Collier Young proudly declared to Hedda [Hopp]er: "We're working on the theory that the ticket-buying public is more [intere]sted in *what's* in a picture then *who's* in it."

Ida Lupino in her element, sans glamour, directing *The Hitch-Hiker*

The Filmakers was broke in no time.

To salvage their investment, Lupino and Young signed a deal with RKO head Howard Hughes. Lupino didn't trust Hughes and once the pact was inked she didn't trust her husband, either. Young basically gave Hughes control of their creative lives. Rejected by Hughes was *The Atom Project*, on development of the A-bomb. Approved was *Outrage* (1950), concerning a rape victim. "Hughes liked things dealing with sex," said Malvin Wald, *Outrage*'s writer.

In addition to *Outrage* and *The Hitch-Hiker*, Lupino directed *Hard, Fast and Beautiful* (1951) for RKO, a sports melodrama. More intriguing was *The Bigamist* (1953) in which Edmond O'Brien kept two families and became equally bored with each. Lupino played against conventions, making both women regular sorts instead of the typical virgin/whore dichotomy. The film couldn't top Lupino's own story, however. After the Hughes debacle, she'd split from Collier Young, falling into the arms of Howard Duff, who became her third husband. Young consoled himself with Joan Fontaine, whom he'd marry. Young and Lupino would, however, remain business partners. In *The Bigamist*, Lupino plays one of O'Brien's wives—and Joan Fontaine plays the other. The following year, in *Private Hell 36* (written and produced by Young and Lupino), Ida would make love on-camera to Steve Cochran, under the eye of costar and current husband Howard Duff, while her *ex*-husband observed from out of the frame. Director Don Siegel recalled the principals as being intense, and intoxicated, throughout production.

Lupino went on to a long career acting and directing in television. In the 1980s, her films were rediscovered but disappointing to revisionists seeking to proclaim her a maverick feminist who strained at her Hollywood bonds. Her films didn't have a gender-specific perspective. That's probably because Lupino saw herself as the equal of anybody in the industry, and because her taste in material encompassed all of society, not just the distaff side. Although her ambition exceeded her achievements, she left a body of work that proved her to be a capable director, a good writer, an excellent producer, and a superior actress. Most important, she was a total pro, and the most multitalented woman in the history of Hollywood.

Lupino is visited by producer Joan Harrision while directing "Sybilla," a 1960 episode of *The Alfred Hitchcock Hour*.

ROY AND GIL CAME OFF THE ROAD in better shape than Al Roberts did in *Detour* (PRC, 1945). In this tawdry masterwork of bargain-basement filmmaking, an innocent man picks up a psychopath only slightly less lethal than Billy Cook.

Roberts (Tom Neal) is a New York piano player whose girl, Sue (Claudia Drake), leaves him to seek a career in Hollywood. He pines for Sue, and decides to follow her, hitching west. Somewhere in the Southwest, he gets a lift from Charlie Haskell (Edmund MacDonald), a high roller in a half-track-sized convertible. Al scopes fresh scratches on Haskell's face and hands: "Whatever it was, it must've been big and vicious."

"It was a woman," Haskell admits—an ingrate hitcher who went wild when he made a pass. Nice guy Charlie flashes a suspicious cash-roll and treats Al to a hash-house dinner, which the hitcher inhales like a starving animal. Belly-full and drowsy, Haskell lets Al take the wheel. As Al ponders a reunion with Sue, Haskell drops into the big sleep. It begins to rain, and when Al stops to put up the ragtop, Haskell pitches out of the car and cracks his skull. Convinced he'll be accused of murder, Roberts hides the body, switches wallets, and continues toward LA in Haskell's car. Bum move.

At a filling station, he makes a worse one: He picks up a woman hitching a ride. After several miles of small talk, she blurts: "Okay, what'd you do with his body?" The woman, Vera (Ann Savage), turns out to be the feisty gal who raked Haskell miles back.

Vera is, hands down, the meanest, bitchiest shrew to ever escape from Dark City. She's got Al knuckling under in no time. If he doesn't follow her orders, she'll finger him as Haskell's killer. Her plan is to sell off the dead guy's wheels once they hit LA. But in a

Take this **DETOUR** *for a New type of Screen Thrill!*

with TOM **NEAL**
ANN CLAUDIA
SAVAGE · DRAKE
Edmund MacDonald
Tim RYAN · Esther HOWARD
Roger CLARK

A P.R.C. Production

Associate Producer
Martin MOONEY
·
Directed by
Edgar G. ULMER
·
Screen Play and Story
Martin GOLDSMITH

fluke not uncommon in the impoverished areas of Dark City, she learns Haskell was heir to a dying millionaire. She demands Al pose as Haskell so they can collect the inheritance. In a cheap hotel room, Al and Vera battle it out like tethered cat and dog. Al calls her bluff, daring Vera to dial up the cops. She does, and he backs down before she drops the dime, becoming, in essence, her slave. Vera celebrates by getting tight and locking herself in the bedroom, taking the telephone with her. Afraid she'll call the cops, Al tries to snap the phone cord, tugging with all his might. Something is wrong. Breaking down the door, he finds Vera dead, the cord wrapped around her throat.

Fearing he'll be blamed for two murders, Al returns to the road. He waits for the day when the law will finally swoop down. Hitching yet another ride, imagining his inevitable arrest, he utters one of the most famous lines in noir: "Fate, or some mysterious force, can put the finger on you or me for no good reason at all."

Detour was based on a 1939 novel by Martin Goldsmith, a young writer who, to finance his avocation, ran a coast-to-coast car service, hauling half a dozen passengers at a time in a Buick station wagon for $25 a head. The novel grew out of this experience. It smacks more of the Depression than the postwar period in which the film is set. Goldsmith rued that he'd sold the rights to producer Leon Fromkess in 1944—before learning that John Garfield had read the book and wanted Warners to buy it. Garfield envisioned Ann Sheridan or Ida Lupino as his costar. Fromkess relished telling a major studio to pound salt. He turned down $25,000 for the property.

Fromkess's outfit, Producers Releasing Corporation (PRC), was the epitome of Poverty Row. The entire budget for *Detour*, including money paid for the rights and Goldsmith's own screenplay adaptation, was $30,000. The

TOM NEAL
A CURSED LIFE

arallels between the lives of Al Roberts and Tom Neal are the stuff of B-movie legend. Some *Detour* fans suggest its strange power haunted Neal, causing the film's fatalism to infect the actor's real life. In truth, Neal was a sight more aggressive than Al Roberts. He'd have smacked a woman senseless if she popped off at him as Vera does. Neal was a "poor man's Clark Gable," who worked steadily during the '40s. He developed a reputation as a solid pro—and quite the ladies' man. "He had a chemical buzz for me that sent red peppers down my thighs," said Barbara Payton. Their tempestuous on-again-off-again affair had ugly overtones that coldcocked their careers. Neal quit the business, moved to Palm Springs, and married Patricia Fenton. He started a landscaping business, and had a son, Tom Jr. But Patricia died of cancer when the boy was only a year old and Neal sent him to live with his sister in Illinois. He met Gail Kloke at the Palm Springs Tennis Club and married her in 1961. Four years later, Kloke was shot to death and Neal was charged with murder. Despite evidence indicating first-degree murder—Neal claimed it was an accident, but the gun was never found—Neal was sentenced to prison for involuntary manslaughter. He was freed after six years, but died of heart failure in a Hollywood apartment several months later. His son, who'd come to California to live with him, found the body. In 1990, Neal Jr., starred in a remake of *Detour*, in the role of Al Roberts.

Neal's manslaughter of antagonist Ann Savage in *Detour* would come back to haunt him later in life.

shooting schedule was reputed to be only six days (a legend; it was actually nineteen). But only fifteen thousand feet of film was allotted for a sixty-three-minute movie. With that kind of budget and schedule, production could only be entrusted to one man—Edgar G. Ulmer. Born in Vienna, Ulmer had studied philosophy at the University of Vienna, and was a contemporary of future cinema giants F. W. Murnau (Ulmer worked on his 1927 silent masterpiece, *Sunrise*), Ernst Lubitsch, Robert Siodmak, and Billy Wilder. Once he came to the states, Ulmer earned a reputation as a director who could deliver despite almost inconceivable limitations. Any hopes he had for an A-list career were dashed when he and Shirley Castle, continuity girl on his first major film, Universal's *The Black Cat* (1934), fell in love. She divorced husband Max Alexander, cousin of Universal chief Carl Laemmle, and married Ulmer. Laemmle got even by blackballing Ulmer at every major studio. Poverty Row became Ulmer's home, but Castle was a devoted wife for the rest of his life.

In *Detour*, he used every trick in his quiver to make an engrossing movie out of virtually nothing. His first bit of magic was making more than half of Goldsmith's 144-page script disappear—and improving it in the process. The Arizona desert in which much of the action takes place was all filmed within fifteen miles of the PRC lot. Ulmer's vision was to transform the cross-country journey into a head trip: The action is literally confined to Al Roberts's mind. The bulk of the running time is consumed with tortured close-ups of Tom Neal, pondering his miserable luck, under the ultimate "Why me?" voice-over.

Ulmer crafted a haunting blend of claustrophobia and paranoia. Roberts may believe there's a cruel force working against him, but in truth he's his own worst enemy. *Detour* is a nightmare, one in which the unconscious overwhelms rational thought and takes off on mesmerizing and implausible leaps of logic. That's why it works best viewed at 2:30 a.m., through half-closed eyes, with Neal's self-pitying soliloquies snaking around your defenseless mind.

Watching movies that late, there's always a chance of nodding off. Ann Savage obliterates any possibility of that. The twenty-four-year-old former bowling instructor was like Susan Hayward on a coke jag—a harpy from hell, with a singularly irritating nails-on-slate voice. Her spewed taunts—"I'm not through with you by a long shot," and "Not only don't you have any scruples, you don't have any brains," and "Shut up! You're making noises like a husband!"—are scarier than

anything Widmark slung in *Kiss of Death*. Savage's career was short, but her *Detour* performance ensured her a suite in the Pantheon Hotel, home of characters you will never forget. Try as you might.

HITCHHIKING IS NOT THE IDEAL TRANSIT OPTION. Safer to ride the rails—unless you were a passenger on a particular Union Pacific train from Chicago to LA in 1952, when all manner of intrigue squeezed through the corridors and into the cloistered sleepers. In *The Narrow Margin* (RKO, 1952), a ration of cops, dames, and hit men were all aboard for the ultimate "can" movie—slang for a picture set in the confines of a moving vehicle.

Writer Martin Goldsmith has the honor of writing the source material for what may be the two best B movies ever, *Detour* and *The Narrow Margin*. The latter is based on his unpublished story, adapted by Earl Felton. As in *Detour*, logic is locked in the baggage car while momentum rides up front.

Cops Walter Brown (Charles McGraw) and Gus Forbes (Don Beddoe) are assigned to escort a gangster's widow from Chicago to LA. "I hear she's a dish," says Forbes as they alight in the Windy City. "She's the sixty-cent special," growls Brown. "Cheap, flashy, strictly poison under the gravy." McGraw is at his surliest and it doesn't get better than that. At least until we meet their baggage, Mrs. Neil (Marie Windsor). From the first shot of her, sucking on a tar-bar, flipping back a jet-black wave, and giving the cops the once-over with her huge, sexy eyes, we know McGraw has met his match.

Before they get Mrs. Neil into a waiting taxi, Forbes takes a fatal bullet. The syndicate is out to ensure she won't rat them out to the grand jury in LA. The death of his partner ignites Brown's contempt for Mrs. Neil. "You make me sick to my stomach," he snaps. "Well, use your own sink," Windsor fires back. Nobody could throw brass-knuckled palaver like these two.

Aboard the train, Brown meets Ann Sinclair (Jacqueline White), traveling with her wiseacre kid, Tommy (Gordon Gebert). He pulls a clever ruse, redirecting heat by letting the hoods think Sinclair is Mrs. Neil. Meanwhile, Windsor and McGraw shovel verbal coal. "The food stinks and so does your company, but I'll hand you one thing, Brown—you're beginning to show real genius," Mrs. Neil cracks. "Making this other dame the target shows you're using your head."

"For your information, I didn't plan it that way," Brown counters. "Well, if you didn't, the DA's entitled to a refund," she sneers.

Richard Fleischer's inventive direction reached its peak in *The Narrow Margin*. Some scenes couldn't be done any better: the killing of Forbes and McGraw's back alley pursuit of the shooter; a brutal fistfight between McGraw and David Clarke in a cramped train compartment; multiple planes of action layered on the train windows; inspired visual transitions (dissolving from Windsor scraping her nails with an emery board to the wheels chugging inside the train's journal box to the chattering crawl of a Western Union ticker, all in about four seconds). Despite all that, it's the omission of a single image that keeps *The Narrow Margin* from being easily heralded as a masterwork: Where is the shot of McGraw watching Marie Windsor's dead body being taken off the train? It's unpardonable neglect of a character who is, frankly, the most memorable part of the movie.

Sadly, this rude dismissal was typical of a career that included *Cat Women on the Moon*. Although indelible in every part she played, Windsor never broke into the top rank of female stars. She was too physically intimidating—a statuesque five-foot-nine, with a balcony that could support a double run of pinochle. Sexy, evil femmes were her lot. She handled the role effortlessly in such noirs as *Force of Evil*, *Double Deal* (RKO, 1950), *Two Dollar Bettor* (Realart, 1951), *City That Never Sleeps*, *Hell's Half Acre* (Republic, 1954), *No Man's Woman* (Republic, 1955), and, most effectively, *The Killing*.

Windsor was a one-time Miss Utah whose ambition was to follow in the footsteps of her screen idol, Clara Bow. Legendary pinup artist Alberto Vargas certainly felt Windsor had "It" when he hired her as a model. She put herself through Maria Ouspenskaya's famous acting school by working as a cigarette girl at the Mocambo nightclub, where she caught the eye of producer Arthur Hornblow Jr. She started her career in the early '40s and was once Gloria Grahame's understudy onstage. Windsor married realtor Jack Hupp in 1943 (he remained a devoted fan, seeing one of her later plays, *The Bar Off Melrose*, twenty-nine times). They remained happily married.

Windsor stayed active in television right up to the '90s. She was a dedicated and staunchly conservative member of the Screen Actors Guild, and spearheaded charities aimed at helping orphans and mentally disturbed children. Though never given the meaty roles she deserved, she was the undisputed Queen of B noir. Who wouldn't have forgiven Charles McGraw for making the obvious play: locking himself in Marie's compartment and enjoying the rhythm of that long ride to the coast.

The pairing of Marie Windsor and Charles McGraw in *The Narrow Margin* provided sufficient combustion to fuel a cross-country train trip.

Out in the painted desert is the town of Chuckawalla, setting for a very strange crime "drama." Hal Wallis's *Desert Fury* (Paramount, 1947), scripted by Robert Rossen and A. I. Bezzerides, is the gayest movie ever produced in Hollywood's golden era. Recitation of the plot is hopeless: the action swirls around a band of sexually ambiguous miscreants hiding out in the middle of nowhere. Fritzie Haller (Mary Astor) runs the Purple Sage casino while dominating her gorgeous and spoiled daughter Paula (Lizabeth Scott). The two women play it like sapphic temptresses. When Scott appears, an ogling Astor says, "You look good, baby—gimme a kiss." Liz, in her full Technicolor glory, looks like fifty million bucks. Determined to break away from "mother," she romances on-the-lam gangster Eddie Bendix (John Hodiak), another character of indeterminate sexuality. Their dalliance doesn't sit too well with Bendix's longtime companion, Johnny Ryan (Wendell Corey, in a memorable debut as the gangster's housewife-moll)—nor Paula's other suitor, the town's stud sheriff, Tom Hanson (Burt Lancaster, in what was truly his first movie role).

In this air-conditioned desert everyone saunters around in fabulous Edith Head fashions, pondering all kinds of offbeat sexual desires. The script was expanded, deliriously, from a short story ("Bitter Harvest") by twenty-five-year-old Ramona Stewart, who then turned it into her first novel, *Desert Town*, in which the swirling homoerotic undertones were more explicit. The film, directed by Lewis Allen, is *saturated*—with incredibly lush color, fast and furious dialogue dripping with innuendo, double entendres, dark secrets, outraged face-slappings, overwrought Miklos Rozsa violins. How has this film escaped revival or cult status? It's borderline noir, but mid-century Hollywood at its most gloriously berserk.

Johnny isn't too pleased to find Paula bending Eddie's bisexual tendencies in a more distaff direction in the outrageously suggestive *Desert Fury*.

Nick Garcos (Richard Conte) wants revenge on crooked produce broker Mike Figlia (Lee J. Cobb), who cheated and crippled his old man while Nick was off at war. Hope Emerson is a savvy produce buyer who sees the battle brewing: "I'll take odds on the kid."

COMBINE THE FERTILE SOIL of California's Central Valley with year-round sunshine and a steady supply of water from the Sierra Nevada Mountains, and you've got food for practically all of America. Mix in the treachery of how that bounty gets to market and you've got *Thieves' Highway* (Fox, 1949), an unjustly overlooked film Jules Dassin made between his more famous *Naked City* (1948) and *Night and the City* (1950). It didn't have a high-powered producer like *Naked City*'s Mark Hellinger, nor as much style as *Night and the City*. What it did have was a terrific screenplay by A. I. Bezzerides (based on his novel), a fantastic cast, and Dassin's most graceful direction.

Bezzerides grew up in Fresno—raisin capital of the world—during the Depression and he learned firsthand about making a living off the land and surviving the betrayals that crop up in the grower-to-consumer food chain. His novel *Thieves' Market*, on which the film is based, was about the greed and chicanery infecting the agribusiness system.

Nick Garcos (Richard Conte) returns from the war to find his old man crippled by a trucking accident. The culprit is Bay Area produce broker Mike Figlia (Lee J. Cobb), who has a rep for cheating small operators and "fixing" them if they protest. Nick, an immigrant child, has picked up an American brand of piss and vinegar in combat. He reclaims the truck his father sold and looks for a load that will get him to Figlia. Another driver, crafty Ed (Millard Mitchell) knows of a hidden orchard of early apples, and the two strike a deal. Tailing them to the Bay Area are two other truckers, Pete (Joe Pevney) and Slob (Jack Oakie), who don't think Ed's dilapidated truck will survive the run. They're poised to scavenge the load.

Dassin handles the trucking montages with panache, including a suspenseful scene in which Conte is pinned by his rig while trying to fix a flat on the highway's sandy shoulder. Ed, a conniver up until then, shows his true colors by rescuing Nick, and Bezzerides's off-the-cuff dialogue sketches a masculine bond between them, now pals for life.

Arriving at the bustling produce market in the dead of night, Nick and Figlia engage in some nasty negotiations. Knowing he can make a killing on the first apples of the season, Figlia tries all his grifts to cheat Nick. He cuts his tires to force him to unload; he complains about the fruit's "pulpy" quality; he lies about the going price. When all else fails, Figlia pays sexy Italian refugee Rica (Valentina Cortese) to lure Nick to her room.

In her garret, Rica's stranger-in-a-strange-land pathos has an erotic charge. The Production Code forced Bezzerides and Dassin to be creative, and they conjure the kind of exquisite sexual byplay that would disappear from screens once the Code was obsolete: Nick and Rica shower in the cramped room with only a curtain separating them; in an embrace, Cortese rubs her dark curls on Conte's face; she uses her fingernails to play tic-tac-toe on his bare chest. In her American film debut, Cortese uses her exotic accent, sharp features, and cunning eyes to create one of the most full-blooded women in Dark City.

While Rica flirts with Nick, Figlia sells his load right off the truck. Bezzerides depicts the marketplace as an arena and business as a cutthroat American sport. When Nick demands full price from Figlia for his fruit, they square off like heavyweights. Early morning buyers watch from ringside. "Figlia is going to eat that kid

alive," chimes one. "I'll take odds on the kid," says a savvy broad (Hope Emerson) who's gone toe-to-toe with Figlia herself.

Meanwhile, Ed struggles to bring in his load, vexed by a weak driveshaft. On the winding roads of the Altamont Pass, it blows. Ed cracks up. Apples avalanche down the hillside. Ed burns to death in the truck's cab. Pete and Slob, stunned, head on to Frisco to give Nick the news.

Nick has forced top dollar—six bucks a box—out of Figlia. He celebrates by calling his Waspy girlfriend Polly (Barbara Lawrence), telling her to come to the city so they can be married. But Rica's sweet on Nick, and on a stroll through the railyards, she tries to convince him to forget Polly. They're jumped by Figlia's boys, and Nick's money is stolen. When he wakes up in Rica's room, he's convinced she set him up. But Rica has picked up Polly at the train depot and escorted her back to the crib. When Polly sees her fiancé in another woman's bed—and learns he's lost all his money—she dumps him flat. Exactly as Rica expected. "Polly and I have one thing in common," she tells Nick, slyly smiling. "She loves money, too."

Figlia finds out that Ed's haul of Golden Delicious was spilled but undamaged. He offers Pete fifty cents a box to bring in the dead man's load. Pete takes the money, but Slob spurns him. When Nick emerges in the cold morning light, he learns from Slob what's happened. Nick goes wild. "Four bits a box!" he screams, kicking over crates. "Four bits a box!"

Slob drives Nick to the spot where Ed died. He finds Figlia celebrating in a roadside tavern. Smashing his hand with an ax handle, Nick forces Figlia to confess that he's shorted Pete on the apples. As Pete and Slob keep Figlia's thugs at bay, Nick beats Figlia senseless—"For Dad." In one of the few uplifting fade-outs in noir, Nick returns for Rica and takes her away from Dark City in his rumbling rig.

Your tour guide confesses a soft spot for *Thieves' Highway*. It was the first noir he'd ever seen, although, at the time, there wasn't a handy label for this kind of dark, crime-tinged melodrama. All he knew was the mix of crime, business, sex, loyalty, and politics was intoxicating. From then on, he was always looking for the 90-proof kick only a ninety-minute thriller, laden with meaning but light on its feet, can provide.

Ruth Roman and Steve Cochran on the run in *Tomorrow Is Another Day*

ON THE WAY TO FRISCO with his load of Golden Delicious apples, Nick Garcos surely passed some Central Valley lettuce fields, worked by itinerant laborers living in clapboard shanty towns. Two of those field hands, newlyweds Bill (Steve Cochran) and Cay (Ruth Roman), are keeping a low profile after a cross-country trek from Manhattan. See, Bill was a simpleton ex-con who served time for killing his abusive old man. Cay was a part-time prostitute he met in a dance hall only days out of the joint. She was too jaded to fall for this dopey virgin, even if he is handsome as all get-out. But when Cay was accosted in her crib by a dirty cop (who moonlights as her pimp), Bill waded in swinging. He got conked and blacked out. Cay grabbed the gun they'd been fighting over and plugged her pimp. When Bill woke up, Cay told him *he'd* pulled the trigger. A return to the Big House loomed. Bill and Cay took the noir route—run like hell.

Tomorrow Is Another Day (WB, 1951) is such a crummy title it's no wonder the film escaped critical reappraisal for decades. Too bad, since it's brimming with simple and stylish pleasures, like a jazz standard played hundreds of times—but then you're amazed to hear it played in a fresh and soulful way.

The lovers-on-the-lam premise is familiar to anyone who's seen *You Only Live Once* (UA, 1937) or *They Live by Night* (RKO, 1948) or *Gun Crazy* (UA, 1950) or *Shockproof* (Columbia, 1949). In fact, Sam Fuller, writer of *Shockproof*, could have sued for plagiarism, since the last half of *Tomorrow Is Another Day* seems lifted directly from his script. I'll give *Tomorrow*'s story writer Guy Endore (it's based on his unpublished novel *Spring Kill*) and screenwriter Art Cohn the benefit of the doubt; after all, there was definitely something in the Hollywood air at the time. The movie plays like *Gun Crazy*—if *Gun Crazy* had been written by John Steinbeck.

But it's not the story that makes the film special. Director Felix Feist had a flair for volatile characters in confined spaces, as he'd shown in *The Devil Thumbs a Ride* and *The Threat*, both of which showcased his creative manipulation of a minuscule budget. Warner Bros. once had bigger plans for the picture, tailoring it for John Garfield and Susan Hayward. Prior to this, Steve Cochran was a sinister supporting hunk, swaggering through *White Heat*, *The Damned Don't Cry*, and *Storm Warning* (WB, 1951), where he's a KKK goon who rapes Ginger Rogers. Not a move that would typically get you promoted to leading man. But as boss of the "Tri-State Gang" in 1950's *Highway 301*, Cochran showed what Elvis might have been if, instead of singing and playing the guitar, he robbed banks for a living. As man-child

Bill Clark, Cochran gives a more vulnerable performance than was asked of him in tough-guy roles.

His costar, Ruth Roman, was cut out for noir—one of her first professional jobs was modeling for covers of *True Detective*. By 1950, she'd appeared in major movies without ever having a memorable role. Cay Higgins may be her best, a hard-as-nails dame who gradually opens up to the possibility of kindness and affection.

Unfortunately, a studio-enforced ending forces this bluesy film to finish as a sunny pop tune. The ending was changed after negative reaction from a preview audience, probably the usual pack of Pasadena teens whose immature taste altered the endings of so many films intended to have downbeat finales. With a noir ending—Cay mortally wounds Bill, trying to stop him from shooting it out with the cops . . . only to learn they *weren't* being chased after all—it's a classic.

FARMWORKERS ALSO FIGURED PROMINENTLY in *Border Incident* (MGM, 1949), released two months after the left-leaning *Thieves' Highway*, but showing the corruption of America's agribusiness from a more Republican perspective. The film aimed to coattail on the success of *T-Men*, made the previous year. Again, undercover agents infiltrate a crime ring—not counterfeiters, but labor racketeers. Director Anthony Mann and DP John Alton transposed their vision to the Southwest, mesas and fertile fields assuming the same ominous shadows found in the big city.

Mann, who'd displayed his flair for brutality in *Desperate*, *T-Men*, and *Raw Deal*, offered greater shocks in the wide-open spaces. When agent Jack Barnes (George Murphy) has his cover blown, he's set up for a farming "accident": He's shredded by the swirling blades of a reaper as his colleague, Pablo Rodriguez (Ricardo Montalban), looks on helplessly. Truly, one of the most harrowing scenes ever.

Border Incident, like *T-Men*, is undermined by its association with the federal government. In exchange for the imprimatur of the Justice Department and the Immigration and Naturalization Service, the film was obligated to show criminal labor practices as the work of a few renegades. In 1949, unlike today, the trail of crime could never lead to corporate America. *Border Incident* ends with the voice of authority assuring us that we can rest easy; the crisis of illegal farmworkers has been eradicated through the work of dedicated federal agents.

LAST ACT FOR THE LADIES' MAN

Cochran with costar Mamie Van Doren in *The Beat Generation* (MGM, 1959)

Steve Cochran may have been underrated as an actor, but certainly not as a lover. Take it from Mamie Van Doren. I asked her, point-blank: *Who were the duds and who were the studs?* For her, Cochran was alone atop the stud list: "He'd do me in the morning and Mae West in the afternoon."

Professionally, the actor followed in the footsteps of actors-turned-producers John Garfield, Dick Powell, and Burt Lancaster, forming Robert Alexander Productions—his real first and middle names. He produced one terrific film, *Come Next Spring*, costarring Ann Sheridan. After that, Cochran powered through middle age in a blaze of booze, sex, and moviemaking—leaving him frayed around the edges while only in his forties.

In 1965, after wrapping what would be his last film, *Tell Me in the Sunlight* (Films International, 1967)—which he wrote, produced, directed, and starred in—Cochran placed an ad for an all-female crew to help him scout locations for his next film, *Captain O'Flynn*. This was on his private yacht, *The Rogue*, traveling between Acapulco and Costa Rica. Eleven days out, the boat was found adrift, its mast broken. Cochran had suffered exposure trying to guide the ship through a squall. An autopsy listed the cause of death as an infection caused by water in his lungs. Since none of the three "crew members" were competent mariners—Cochran's ad specified "No Experience Necessary"—they couldn't pilot the ship and Cochran died at the helm. And there's a bizarre epilogue: After the actor's burial, Merle Oberon—who starred with him in *Of Love and Desire* (Fox, 1963)—demanded his body be exhumed because she suspected the women had killed him. No foul play was discovered—but Oberon's husband, Italian industrialist Bruno Pagliai, couldn't have been too pleased by her concern. Mamie, Mae, and *Merle*—all in one day?

"SOMEDAY I'D LIKE TO SEE SOME OF THIS COUNTRY we've been traveling through," the young man tells his sweetheart. "By daylight, you mean? That'd be nice." Some hope. It's not going to happen for Bowie (Farley Granger) and Keechie (Cathy O'Donnell) because *They Live by Night* (RKO, 1949). These starry-eyed kids—"never properly introduced to the world we live in . . ."—are fugitives, skulking through the back roads and motor courts of an angry every-man-for-himself country.

Based on Edward Anderson's Depression-era novel *Thieves Like Us*, *They Live by Night* was the directorial debut of Nicholas Ray, a man of considerable heart and talent. Producer John Houseman, who prospected many creative talents, had known Ray since their days at New York's Federal Theater. He sensed a future for Ray as a movie man. Houseman gave him Anderson's novel and Ray produced a treatment that displayed a firm grasp of the filmmaker's art. (Philippe Garnier uncovered an earlier adaptation of the novel by Rowland Brown, which Brown hoped to direct. There are many similarities between Brown's work and the final shooting script by Charles Schnee—but enough differences to make the notion of plagiarism moot.)

The story line is simple: Bowie, a youngster sent up on a specious murder rap, escapes prison with a pair of seasoned criminals, T-Dub (Jay C. Flippen) and Chickamaw (Howard da Silva). Hiding out, he finds his soul mate, Chickamaw's niece, Keechie. They gradually drop their defenses and imagine living normal lives. But the crooks won't let Bowie loose. He assists in another bank job, deluding himself that his share will buy a lawyer to clear him of the murder charge. Fleeing, Chickamaw shoots a cop—and Bowie's gun, covered with fingerprints, is left at the scene. His innocence is gone forever. Bowie and Keechie get married, but it's honeymoon interruptus when the gang puts the touch on him for another knockover. T-Dub is killed this go-round, and Bowie and Chickamaw angrily split.

With Keechie pregnant, the lovers hit the road. Every time they feel like "real people," reality kicks them in the teeth. They return to Hawkins (Ian Wolfe), the crooked judge who married them, hoping he might rig passage to Mexico. "I believe in helping people get what they want as long as they can pay for it," Hawkins tells them. "I marry people cause there's a little hope they'll be happy. But I can't take this money of yours. No, sir. In a way I'm a thief just the same as you are—but I won't sell you hope when there ain't any." T-Dub's sister-in-law Mattie (Helen Craig) sells out Bowie, in a deal to win release of her own convict husband. Realizing that Keechie can never get straight while attached to him, Bowie returns

to their motel to bid her farewell. He never makes it. The law is lying in wait, and he's shot to death. Keechie finds a goodbye note on his body, professing love for her and their unborn child.

During the '30s, Nicholas Ray journeyed through rural America with the legendary Alan Lomax, helping him record indigenous folk music for the Library of Congress. The experience was influential. At his best, Ray worked like a jazzman (in fact, a treatment called "Jazz Man" was one of his earliest proposed projects), his eyes and ears open to nuance, colorations, unexpected ways of riffing a familiar refrain. Where some directors saved wind for flashy solos, biding time in the bridges, Ray committed to the whole piece. He constructed a brilliant soundtrack, giving as much attention to aural aspects as did Welles. George Diskant offered camerawork that captured the swings between fitful repose and frantic flight. The cast was perfect, with the hardened mugs of the veterans looming over the wet-behind-the-ears newcomers. There's hardly a note in *They Live by Night* that doesn't resound with freshness and conviction.

Made in 1947, the film wasn't released in the United States until late '49, due to confusion wrought by Howard Hughes's takeover of RKO. More noirs were issued that year than any other, and Ray's was lost in the shuffle. Had it been distributed earlier, perhaps Ray would've garnered more enthusiastic reviews, leading Hughes to offer him better material than tired soapers like *A Woman's Secret* (1949) and *Born to Be Bad* (1950). On loan to Columbia, Ray directed the Humphrey Bogart–sponsored *Knock on Any Door* (1949), in which the script's message-mongering overwhelmed Ray's finesse. The association would, however, lead to the creation of *In a Lonely Place*, a genuine masterpiece.

Ray was a great artist, but a mediocre craftsman. When inspired—as in *They Live by Night*, *In a Lonely Place*, *On Dangerous Ground*, *The Lusty Men*, *Johnny Guitar*, and *Rebel Without a Cause*—his work was emotional, evocative, and inventive. When less than fully engaged, torpor could creep in. After *Rebel*, Ray's identification with lonely outsiders became too strong, and too self-destructive, for him to survive in Hollywood. He battled chronic illness and depression with drink and drugs. Eventually, that struggle did him in. He finished his cinematic career as a teacher, appropriate considering his thematic obsession with the (often-doomed) promise of youth. He reached mythic stature among his charges, but he probably would've traded it for the relentless health and stamina of his comrade Samuel Fuller.

Farley Granger and Cathy O'Donnell are star-crossed young lovers "never properly introduced to this world" in *They Live by Night*.

As Ray was making his debut, aging director Frank Borzage was spiraling downward. A two-time Oscar-winner, Borzage started in films with Thomas Ince in 1913. Although he'd helmed popular '30s titles such as *A Farewell to Arms* (Paramount, 1932), *Desire* (Paramount, 1936), and the fabulous *History Is Made at Night* (UA, 1939), Borzage's ninety-eight-film legacy is fat with fodder. By 1946, Borzage, who once stalked the plush carpets of Paramount's executive offices, was reduced to a three-picture deal at Republic—the magenta-colored lots on Hollywood's Monopoly board.

If ever there were proof that noir "infected" Hollywood—like a virus of resurgent creativity—it was Borzage's *Moonrise* (Republic, 1948). The film, based on Theodore Strauss's novel, was originally proposed as an "A" picture, to be directed by William Wellman and starring either James Stewart or John Garfield. When talks with the majors didn't pan out, independent producer Marshall Grant took the project to Republic, where Borzage was handed the reins. The story resembles *They Live by Night*, as both concern young men branded as outcasts, living on the fringes of the rural South. They are also the two most romanticized, poetic works in noir.

Danny Hawkins (Dane Clark) is haunted by the legacy of his father, hanged for murder. Taunted throughout his life in the town of Woodville, Danny fears his "bad blood" will doom him to an unhappy life. When boyhood rival Jerry Sykes (Lloyd Bridges) competes with Danny for the attention of schoolteacher Gilly (Gail Russell), Jerry sneers that she'll never go for a guy with "killer's blood." The two brawl out back of a summer dance. In a blind rage, Danny crushes Jerry's skull with a rock. He hides the body in the swamps.

Sykes's disappearance throws the town into an uproar. As the manhunt closes in, Danny comes to believe his fate is predestined. He takes to the swamps, convinced he's no better than a wild animal, unfit to live among humans. When Sykes's body turns up, the philosophical sheriff (Allan Joslyn) muses: "If you went into all the reasons why that rock struck Jerry Sykes's head, you'd end up writin' the history of the world."

Borzage directs with a simplicity that is earnest and deep. His most vital work was done in the silent era (7th *Heaven* [Fox, 1927], *Street Angel* [Fox, 1928]) and *Moonrise* is an example of an artist returning to his roots for a call shot of adrenaline. The opening montage is stunning: In several heartbeats, we see the senior Hawkins's execution, Danny's birth, his torment at the hands of other children, and his emergence as a sullen adult. The images flow darkly, like the "tainted" blood in Danny's veins. Borzage's style is a kind of magical unrealism. John L. Russell's camera prowls swamps with reeds of the deepest black and highlights shimmering like jewels, presaging Charles Laughton's similar visions in *Night of the Hunter* (UA, 1955). The young lovers meeting in a deserted antebellum mansion were precursors of James Dean and Natalie Wood in Ray's *Rebel Without a Cause* (WB, 1955).

As in *They Live by Night*, analogies are drawn between animals and hunted humans. Borzage's symbolism is brazen—dissolving from a close-up of Dane Clark to the face of a terrified raccoon. But in the finest tradition of silent storytelling, Borzage transcends the obvious. Accompanying a band of hunters near the spot where he buried Sykes, Danny climbs a tree to shake out the trapped 'coon. Man and animal stare at each other. We shiver as Danny recognizes his kinship with the helpless critter. But Danny must sacrifice it, to divert attention from Jerry's grave. The 'coon is shaken loose, falling into a circle of predators. As we hear the hounds and hunters pounce, Danny breaks down in tears.

Danny's disintegration comes on a Ferris wheel at the county fair. He explains to Gilly that his father murdered a doctor in a rage after his negligence resulted in the death of Danny's mother. His soul-searching is interrupted by the appearance of the sheriff, who also boards the ride. Disoriented and panic-stricken, Danny leaps from the top of the Ferris wheel. In a vertiginous shot, we assume his point of view for a terrifying fall into the carnival crowd.

These scenes exemplify the visual poetry Borzage created in the silent days, a craft that evaporated from movies around the time the last of these pioneers faded away. Because crime dramas relied on hypercharged emotions, an old warhorse like Borzage was able to indulge his flair for pictorial storytelling, not restrain it. Like the best of his silents, *Moonrise* drew emotion directly from its juxtaposition of images. With title cards instead of dialogue, it would have been the greatest silent picture Borzage ever made.

Gail Russell is one of the true angels of film noir. When she finds Danny hiding amid the cobwebs of the vacant plantation house, she offers a lovely benediction: "You should have sent me away when I might have gone. It's too late now." True to his reputation as a romantic, Borzage would never allow Gilly to betray Danny. She is a savior, not a femme fatale.

Unfortunately, Russell had no savior. She chased stage fright with booze and

spent the '50s shuttling between soundstages and sanitariums. In '57 she drove her convertible through the front of Jan's Coffee Shop in LA, nearly killing an employee. In August 1961, she was found dead in her Hollywood apartment, amid dozens of empty vodka bottles.

There is no such grim demise for Borzage's characters. *Moonrise* is unique for being one of the few noirs in which the redemptive power of love keeps nihilism at bay. The ending—in which Danny reclaims his place in society by turning himself in for Jerry's murder at first seems false, like any other Code-mandated square-up. But in the thin air of Borzage's ethereal realm, the ending works. It may have been written as a typically pat wind-up, but Borzage's commitment to the idea of redemption convinces you that peace of mind counts all the more in a world where injustice and hatred rule.

FOR MANY YEARS THE AUTHORITIES TRIED to nail down the facts surrounding the death of "classic film noir." Some reports indicated it died in 1958, on the edge of a polluted creek in the border town of Los Robles. Others claimed that in 1959 it was blown to kingdom come in a refinery explosion outside the upstate New York town of Melton. Our sources indicate that Noir—the original, the one bred from the craft and politics of the Hollywood studio system—actually perished in a lonely

motel room in California's Central Valley.

Noir had registered under an assumed name—Marie Samuels—after stealing forty grand from the real estate office in Phoenix where she worked. Typical of Noir—an impetuous crime, committed in the throes of passion. We'd been down this road before—the volatile sexuality leading to criminal behavior, the moral ambivalence, the desperate flight. All the tropes and imagery were firmly in place.

Then Noir had a long talk with lonely young Norman, the motel's proprietor, and she decided crime didn't pay after all. Like Danny Hawkins in *Moonrise*, she decided to turn herself in and face the music. A nice hot shower would cleanse her of her sins.

That was the night Noir died.

When he stepped into that bathroom, brandishing a butcher's knife and clad in his dead mother's housecoat and wig, it was one small step for Norman Bates, one giant leap for the movies. When Norman—reverting to his normal schizophrenic self—cleaned up the gory mess, he washed the last vestiges of "classic noir" down the drain with his victim's blood.

Alfred Hitchcock was the real culprit. If he tried to profess innocence, he'd be lying. He knew exactly what he was doing. Can't you see that schoolboy smirk right now? This was a case of murder, open and shut: Hitchcock slaughtered our expectations.

Psycho (Paramount, 1960) was an astonishing landmark in the history of cinema. A generation of movie-watchers who came of age in the '70s and '80s, when the bloodletting of slasher movies became standard adolescent fare and MTV provided a daily visual and aural assault, simply cannot comprehend the impact *Psycho* had when first released. Before audiences had recovered from the unsettling image of a toilet, actually shown functioning on-screen (a Hollywood first)—Hitchcock murdered his star (Janet Leigh), a third of the way into the film, in a scene that has never been surpassed for filmmaking artistry and pure shock.

It's not a stretch to contend that *Psycho* did for movies what the assassination of JFK would soon do for politics. It loosened all the bearings, shattered all preconceived notions of how things worked, and ushered us into a new American fear-scape, where suspicion replaced complacency as the pervasive national backdrop.

Psycho didn't manage this all by itself. But its influence over a subsequent generation of filmmakers had a lot to do with it. For all its cinematic brilliance, *Psycho* is also a tent show, a freak carny attraction. "No One Seated After the Show Has Begun!" screamed the ads. "Don't Dare Reveal the Shocking Ending!" Hitchcock liked to say he perceived *Psycho*—and the surrounding hoopla—as a "black comedy." No doubt it was, for him.

When it was released, no one was laughing, rest assured. It was only later, when the cultural elite adopted its post-everything attitude, disregarding the main thrust of any popular art in favor of the deconstructive irony beneath, that critics detected humor—and began to appreciate how Hitchcock had hustled audiences with mesmerizing technique.

Hitchcock had a lot of Stanton the Great in him. He set up his audience with cold disdain, confident he could fleece them with dazzling sleight of hand, and audacious powers of misdirection. Like Stanton Carlisle, Hitchcock knew we were suckers for a story, and like the ill-fated huckster, he knew the euphoria that came with "getting over" on a crowd. "It gives you a kind of superior feeling," Stan had said. "As if you were on the inside and everybody else was on the outside, looking in."

It was a sensation sought by many of America's next wave of filmmakers, for whom Hitchcock was the master, and *Psycho* the medium's touchstone. They were responding not just to the film, but to its facility for manipulating viewers.

That shiver of cruel power would become a goal to which many filmmakers aspired. There was scant reward for those who embraced subtlety, or restraint, or even seamless, coherent storytelling. Sensation would compensate for any shortcomings. *Psycho*'s sensational power spawned a legion of imitators—copycat killers, if you will. They've taken many of the dark themes once emblematic of classic noir and steadily pushed them toward vulgar excess, in hope of garnering attention in a market saturated with noise and violence.

If the film noirs of the late '40s were warning flares, as suggested at the start of this excursion, their radiance would be barely noticed in the bomb blasts of today's cinematic offerings. As far as "classic film noir" is concerned, *Psycho* was the movie that brought down the curtain on that now-lost world.

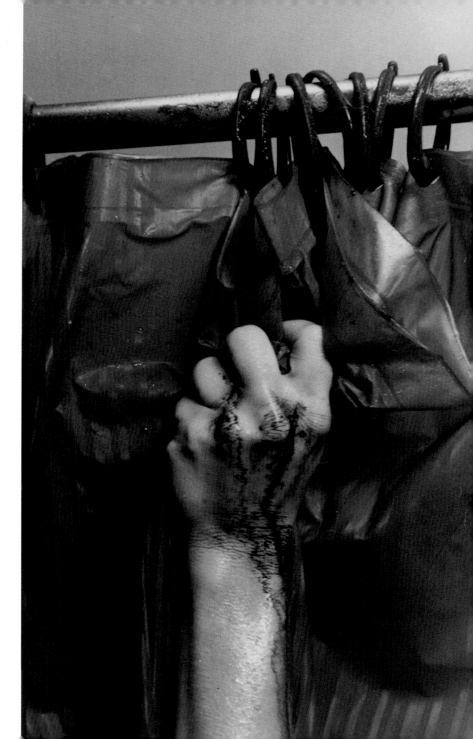

548-42

THE STAGE DOOR

DARK CITY, IT SHOULD BE EVIDENT BY NOW, IS HOLLYWOOD.

New York, Chicago, San Francisco, and other actual cities provided necessary backgrounds to our stories. But the sense of desire and despair, the greed and alienation, and the unflinching take on the venal depths of human nature are the product of a specific place and time—the final days of the once-powerful studio system, a volatile period when politics and paranoia, economics and ego, and avarice and alcohol conspired to bust up one of the great rackets of the twentieth century. But while scandal had always been entwined in Hollywood's history, studio bosses had a gentleman's agreement never to show their business in a negative light.

Consider one of the earliest examples of noir to emerge from a major studio, 1941's *I Wake Up Screaming*, from the novel of the same name by Steve Fisher. His book was a roman à clef about sexual shenanigans within a Hollywood studio—something Fox chief Darryl Zanuck and other studio heads declared off-limits after re-enforcement of the Production Code in 1934. So the film's setting was switched to New York's theatrical milieu. Hollywood didn't want more rumors about its sordid underbelly.

Anthony John and his wife Brita (Ronald Colman and Signe Hasso) rehearse the roles of Othello and Desdemona in *A Double Life*.

I Wake Up Screaming has been neglected as a progenitor of the noir movement largely because of the casting of Betty Grable, Fox's biggest musical-comedy star. The studio blundered by releasing the film as *The Hot Spot*, misleading the public into thinking it was a nightclub-based musical. In this early stage of the noir movement, studios weren't sure what they were creating. America had joined the war, and the industry was trying to determine if the public wanted serious movies reflecting that turmoil—or escape from it. As a result, early examples of noir, like *I Wake Up Screaming* and *This Gun for Hire* (1942), leavened the grimness of their source novels with comedy and romance, even if the plots revolved around sexual obsession (*Screaming*) and assassination (*Gun*).

Par for the course, a pair of promising players in this proto-noir suffered dire fates in real life. Carole Landis, who played murdered actress Vicki Lynn in *I Wake Up Screaming*, had become a star opposite Victor Mature in *One Million BC* (Fox, 1940), thanks to how fetchingly she filled a cave-girl outfit. Zanuck was impressed enough to give her a contract . . . and more. Landis became a popular comedienne and a pinup favorite of GIs. Her tireless touring to entertain the troops resulted in a book, *Four Jills in a Jeep*. She'd star in Fox's 1944 film version. After her affair with Zanuck ended, she went to England to make pictures (including the fine 1948 noir *The Silk Noose*). She fell in love with British actor Rex Harrison, their

ABOVE: Disturbed cop Ed Cornell (Laird Cregar) stalks the object of his obsession, Vicky Lynn (Carole Landis, center) and her sister Jill (Betty Grable) in *I Wake Up Screaming*, an early and often overlooked landmark in the film noir movement. BELOW: Ronald Colman won the Best Actor Oscar for his portrayal of a schizophrenic Broadway actor in *A Double Life.*

affair becoming an open secret in Hollywood—which didn't please Harrison's wife, actress Lilli Palmer. When Harrison ended the affair, Landis committed suicide with a handful of Seconal. She was twenty-nine.

The actor who murders Landis's character in *I Wake Up Screaming* had his own tragic demise. Laird Cregar burst on the scene in the early '40s, playing heavies with a streak of perversion (*This Gun for Hire*, *The Lodger* [1944]). But Cregar saw himself as a leading man, like Fox stablemate Tyrone Power. Merle Oberon told him he needed to lose weight to play romantic roles, so the actor went on a regimen of fasting and amphetamines. He dropped more than a hundred pounds, as evidenced in 1945's *Hangover Square*, where he was the lead opposite Linda Darnell. He was still a disturbed misfit, but a slim one, clutching the studio's sexiest starlet. Cregar never read the good reviews he earned. He died two months before the film opened, from complications of drug use and drastic weight loss.

A DISTURBED ACTOR is the central character in one of the most prestigious noir films of the 1940s, *A Double Life* (Universal, 1947). Although the role was intended for Laurence Olivier, Ronald Colman won a Best Actor Oscar for his portrayal of Broadway star Anthony John, whose identification with the characters he plays leads to schizophrenia. After costarring with his wife Brita (Signe Hasso) in more than a hundred performances of Shakespeare's *Othello*, the character's jealousy of Desdemona becomes the actor's reality. He kills a Greenwich Village waitress (Shelley Winters) while rehearsing Othello's kiss of death, and after being suspected of the crime by a wily cop (Edmond O'Brien), the actor switches to a real dagger for the play's climactic scene. It's Anthony John's final performance.

The clever script by playwrights Ruth Gordon and Garson Kanin was directed by George Cukor, who encouraged cameraman Milton Krasner to heavily apply the noir atmospherics de rigueur at the time. Reviews were gushing, even from *New York Times* curmudgeon Bosley Crowther ("rich, exciting . . . plushy"), who typically dismissed genre pictures. Back then, film critics were duty-bound to rate theater and literature (and movies made from them, or about them) above original works of cinema. Even decades later, reviewer Jerry Renshaw would say "*A Double Life* is an unusually intelligent, literate noir that is a classy departure from the pulpy 'B' atmospherics often associated with the genre."

Rosalind Russell followed Ronald Colman to the dark side, playing a Broadway actress who kills her producer in *The Velvet Touch*. Sydney Greenstreet is the inspector investigating the crime.

As soon as Colman clutched his Oscar for *A Double Life*, Rosalind Russell had her husband, producer Frederick Brisson, develop a distaff version. *The Velvet Touch* (RKO, 1948) is emblematic of noir's influence. Russell was a charming and gifted comedienne, but like many of her male counterparts she was eager to delve into darker material. The same motivation applied to Russell's character, Valerie Stanton, a Broadway actress eager to perform *Hedda Gabler*, not another frothy farce. During an argument with her producer (and former lover), she kills him and covers up the crime. In a twist dear to any noir fan, her archrival is accused of the murder—Claire Trevor! *The Velvet Touch* was a one-and-done venture into noir for Russell—and for its director, Jack Gage, dialogue director on several of Russell's previous films. He acquits himself well, thanks to the witty Leo Rosten script and the support of Trevor, Leon Ames, and Sydney Greenstreet, playing the sly inspector who puts the pieces together.

Whether it was a trim sixty-four-minute B, like *Smooth as Silk* (Universal, 1946), or a top-of-the-line masterpiece, such as *All About Eve* (Fox, 1950), any show business skullduggery depicted by Hollywood was limited to legitimate theater. Such aberrant, and abhorrent, behavior could never happen in Hollywood . . . right?

Nobody saw through that sham as mordantly as Billy Wilder. He didn't invent film noir, but with *Double Indemnity* he came as close as anyone to defining it and perfecting it. Six years later, his film having spawned countless imitations, Wilder laid the noir template over his own industry, producing a singular example of Hollywood Guignol, *Sunset Boulevard* (Paramount, 1950). It left no doubt that Wilder was the most talented writer-director ever to work in Hollywood.

Sunset Boulevard takes off from the traditional detective story. A cynical writer, down on his luck, is retained by a bizarre client. He treads warily through sepulchral secrets and the flames of narcissism, dealing with an array of grotesque and possibly dangerous eccentrics. Wilder parodied the first-person narration that by 1950 had become common in crime dramas. The writer, Joe Gillis (William Holden), recaps the story while floating, dead, in the swimming pool he'd always wanted. Gillis recounts how he was kept by faded silent screen queen Norma Desmond, writing the script she imagines will return her to the big time. He fatally underestimates the mix of neediness, desperation, and vanity he's unleashed. Norma is Hollywood incarnate, the ultimate femme fatale, too much for Joe to handle. Like many chumps before him, and more to follow, he thought he could take what he wanted, toss it aside when he was done, and walk away unscathed. Norma nudges him along with a few parting shots. Joe was a hack anyway, only a couple of lousy Bs to his credit. Dime a dozen in this town.

Wilder offered Hollywood as America under a distorted magnifying glass: bustling with activity, surging with fresh ideas, its residents relentless in their quest for success. They barrel-ass through a pretense of community, zooming past side streets where isolation, misery, and rejection fester into madness. Wilder surveyed it with a baleful gaze and a cynical laugh—perhaps the only appropriate attitude in this terrain.

AT THE SAME TIME WILDER WAS CONCOCTING *Sunset Boulevard* at Paramount, an equally dark assessment of Hollywood life was being created nearby at Columbia. *In a Lonely Place* (1950) used its crime drama spine to support a jumble of raw nerve

Even the poster for Billy Wilder's film thumbed its nose at the industry's habit of sanitizing its image, blatantly declaring his tale of neuroses, madness and murder "A Hollywood Story."

endings. It laid open the lives of its principal creators and transcendently charted sad corners of the human heart.

After making *Knock on Any Door* together in 1948, Humphrey Bogart and Nicholas Ray wanted another project they could make through Bogart's company, Santana Productions. They chose Dorothy B. Hughes's 1947 novel *In a Lonely Place*, a startling novel about a misanthropic and misogynistic serial killer. They retained the premise and evocative title, but made significant changes that brought the project closer to home. Los Angeles remained the setting, but the protagonist changed from a psychotic veteran masquerading as a writer to a veteran screen-writer, possibly psychotic, mired in a fallow funk. Instead of the killer of Hughes's novel, Ray and Bogart made the character slippery and ambiguous—the artist as suspect. Not an uncommon notion in 1949 Hollywood, but for Bogart and Ray the character had personal dimensions.

Dixon Steele (Bogart) is a once major talent whose deft touch with a script has been undermined by attachment to the bottle and an uncontrollable temper. His loyal agent Mel Lippman (Art Smith) sets Dix up with one last shot, adapting a turgid best seller for a major studio. Dix and Joe Gillis are cut from the same cloth: intelligent, witty men filled with self-loathing because they can't wean themselves from Hollywood's glamorous, sugary teat. To achieve the kind of status Joe craved, Dix has encased himself in a carapace of cynicism. He must have laughed like hell when he opened the morning paper to the headline: **FADED MOVIE QUEEN KILLS WRITER**.

Dix is so disdainful of his assignment he brings home a coat-check girl familiar with the odious best seller. She describes the plot while he nurses a drink, amused at the sound of the wind between her ears. Eventually, he sends her home. The next day she turns up murdered. Dix is the prime suspect. The only witness to his actions on the night in question is Laurel Gray (Gloria Grahame), an aspiring actress who's moved in across the courtyard. She gives Dix an alibi and their mutual attraction sparks into romance. As so often happens, the attention of a woman inspires the dissolute artist. Fresh ideas and smart dialogue stream from Dix's typewriter.

But Laurel soon realizes that jealousy and violence are part of Dix's character. Seething because the cops still consider him a suspect, Dix throws a tantrum and attacks a motorist on a beach road. Laurel fears Dix may be a killer after all. She holds little hope for a life together. The stronger bond is between Dix and Mel, who

The artist as suspect: Frank Lovejoy, Carl Benton Reid, and Gloria Grahame are all suspicious of what makes screenwriter Dixon Steele (Humphrey Bogart) tick in *In a Lonely Place*.

understands that for the chance to tap Dix's genius, he must absorb his anger and contempt. Laurel, however, doesn't work on commission. When Dix realizes she intends to leave, he tries to strangle her. The police call to say they've caught the actual killer, but the news comes too late. Looking in Laurel's horrified face, Dix understands—he may as well be a murderer.

It's not a tragedy, nobody dies at the fade-out, the world keeps on spinning . . . but it's crushingly sad. And it almost didn't end that way. In the original script (by Andrew Solt, extensively reworked by Ray) Dix actually chokes Laurel to death, just before the cops arrive to tell him he's been cleared as a suspect. That ending was shot: The cops find Laurel's corpse in the bedroom and Dix at his typewriter, reading the romantic lines he'd written for Laurel, the love of his life.

Ray shot it, but couldn't live with it. Too horribly melodramatic. He wanted something truer to life. So, he rewrote the scene, letting Laurel live and having *her* take the call from the cops. Dix isn't guilty of murder, only of destroying the best chance for love he'd ever have.

Bogart and Ray didn't need guns, gangsters, or byzantine schemes to get to the heart of darkness. They'd been there. Ray had fallen in love with Gloria Grahame when they made *A Woman's Secret* together in 1948. She'd inspired in him the same excitement Laurel provided Dix Steele. Then she got pregnant and Ray, adhering to his Midwestern principles, saw marriage as the only course. By the time they tied the knot, however, the bloom was off the rose. Gloria spent their Vegas wedding night alone in a hotel room, while Nick—in a real Dix Steele move—drunkenly gambled away forty grand in an all-night stand at the casino tables.

Ray's commitment to his craft—characterized by some as obsessive—made him an outcast. "He always felt people were out to get him," said Rodney Amateau, a do-everything guy at RKO who worked on several Ray films, including *In a Lonely Place*. "And nobody was out to get him, you know? But if you feel somebody's out to get you long enough. . . . They play the part."

For Bogart, the role of Dix Steele could have been rote. Instead, it was revelatory. Bogart's nasty streak was legend. A notorious needler, he'd get several sheets to the wind at Romanoff's and insult anybody he felt deserved it. That part of Dix came naturally. The revelatory part was the sadness he exposed at the character's core. This too was familiar to Bogart, although unlike Dix, he found a way past it. When *In a Lonely Place* was released, America was still enthralled with the romance between Bogart and Lauren Bacall, a match-up milked for all it was worth by Warner Bros. and the starstruck public.

Less well known was the tricky feat Bogart pulled off extricating himself from wife Mayo Methot. She, too, had come to Hollywood seeking stardom, a big beautiful blonde, primed to take the place by storm. But her marriage to Bogart, and their boozing and brawling, took its toll. Her looks went first, then the film offers. As Bogart's star rose, so did Methot's jealousy. She begged him not to leave her for Bacall, promising she'd stop drinking. Bogart was loyal; he steered clear of Bacall and gave it another go with his wife. But when Warner Bros. reunited Bogart and Bacall for *The Big Sleep*, the Bogarts' booze and bouts were uncorked again.

Methot spiraled into depression. She humiliated herself by pleading with Bogart—in the press—to return to her. After Bogart divorced her and married Bacall, Methot fled Dark City, crushed and alone. In an 80-proof haze, she drifted down Thieves' Highway, back to her home state of Oregon.

Not long after the release of *In a Lonely Place*, Mayo Methot was found dead in a roadside motel.

No lights, no cameras, no retakes.

Norma Desmond, having dispatched her ungrateful screenwriter, is ready for her close-up at the climax of *Sunset Boulevard*.

When I created *Dark City: The Lost World of Film Noir* in the waning days of the twentieth century, I had no idea of the impact it would have. The book changed my life. Not because it was a best seller, but because of the doors it opened.

The American Cinematheque in Hollywood invited me to program a festival based on the book, at its newly refurbished Egyptian Theatre. Opening night, March 15, 1999 was the first step in a still unfolding adventure. Producer Stanley Rubin, director Richard Fleischer, and actress Marie Windsor appeared to discuss *The Narrow Margin*, the first of many relationships the festival fostered with writers, directors, and performers from the original noir era. Another book followed, *Dark City Dames: The Wicked Women of Film Noir* (HarperCollins, 2002) which explored the lives of noir stalwarts I had the privilege of befriending—Windsor, Audrey Totter, Coleen Gray, Jane Greer, Ann Savage, and Evelyn Keyes.

San Francisco's Castro Theatre then asked me to curate and host an even grander festival, which I dubbed Noir City. It was embarrassingly successful, with sell-out crowds and box-office receipts some of these films had never before enjoyed. Noir City, from its opening night, was a lightning rod for fans who craved the style, wit, sexiness, and cynicism of noir. People arrived every January from around the globe, dressed to kill and primed to wallow in glorious darkness. A woman from Scotland earned an MBA for her thesis on the festival's grassroots success.

From that nexus grew a circuit of annual Noir City festivals around the country: Seattle; Chicago; Austin; Washington, DC; Detroit; Boston. In 2005, I founded the Film Noir Foundation (FNF), a nonprofit dedicated to rescuing and restoring "orphaned" noir films. I was now a veritable Sam Spade, tracking down wayward movies. I went from knowing literally nothing about film restoration and preservation to becoming an internationally known advocate.

To date, the Film Noir Foundation has restored and preserved more than thirty films, including significant titles missing from *Dark City*'s original blueprint: *Woman on the Run*, *Too Late for Tears*, *Cry Danger*, *The Guilty*, *High Tide*, *Trapped*, *The Man Who Cheated Himself*, and dozens more—once again available thanks to the efforts of the Film Noir Foundation and its partners, particularly the UCLA Film & Television Archive, the Hollywood Foreign Press Association's Charitable Trust, and digital media publisher Flicker Alley.

My advocacy for noir has taken me around the world, to festivals and archives and cinema societies, including Paris's legendary Cinémathèque Française, which in 2011 invited me to curate and host a forty-film program called "Black Pearls." An expanding network of colleagues has enlightened me to noir being a global phenomenon, not limited to Hollywood. The FNF's rescue of *Apenas une delicuente* (1949), *No abras nunca esa puerta* (1952), *La bestia debe morir* (1952), *El vampiro negro* (1953), and *Los tallos amargos* (1956), achieved in collaboration with my Buenos Aires colleague Fernando Martín Peña, led to an acclaimed series at New York's Museum of Modern Art, a catalyst for reappraisal of Perón-era Argentine cinema.

And then Turner Classic Movies called. I always was an avid TCM viewer but it never occurred to me I'd play a leading role on the network. I'm grateful to my boosters at TCM who designed a special place for me—*Noir Alley*—and let me run the show, and my mouth, as I see fit. I'm honored to play a part in the stewardship of American film history, providing content and context for a new generation of cinephiles.

Above all, I'm grateful for the noir fans I've met on this unexpected and exciting journey. When I started building *Dark City* more than twenty-five years ago, it was a shot in the dark. Imagine my surprise, discovering that films about desperation, deceit, betrayal, and paranoia can unite people around the world in a shared passion.

"It's a bitter little world," all right, but noir also makes it just a little better.

BIBLIOGRAPHY

Barson, Michael. *The Illustrated Who's Who of Hollywood Directors, Vol. 1: The Sound Era.* New York: The Noonday Press, 1995.

Bernhardt, Curtis (Interviewed by Mary Kiersch). *Curtis Bernhardt: A Director's Guild of America Oral History.* Metuchen, NJ and London: The Scarecrow Press, 1986.

Bessie, Alvah. *Inquisition in Eden.* New York: Macmillan Co., 1965.

Bishop, Jim. *The Mark Hellinger Story: A Biography of Broadway and Hollywood.* New York: Appleton-Century-Crofts, 1952.

Bloom, Howard. *The Lucifer Principle.* New York: Atlantic Monthly Press, 1995.

Bogdanovich, Peter. *Who the Devil Made It.* New York: Alfred A. Knopf, 1997.

Cameron, Ian and Elizabeth. *The Heavies.* New York: Praeger, 1969.

Caute, David. *Joseph Losey: A Revenge on Life.* New York: Oxford University Press, 1994.

Ceplair, Larry, and Steven Englund. *The Inquisition in Hollywood: Politics in the Film Community, 1930–1960.* Garden City, NY: Anchor Press, 1980.

Christopher, Nicholas. *Somewhere in the Night: Film Noir and the American City.* New York: The Free Press, 1997.

Clarens, Carlos. *Crime Movies: An Illustrated History.* New York: W. W. Norton & Co., 1980.

Clark, Al. *Raymond Chandler in Hollywood.* New York: Proteus Publishing, 1982.

Cole, Lester. *Hollywood Red.* Palo Alto, CA: Ramparts Press, 1981.

Conant, Michael. *Antitrust in the Motion Picture Industry: Economic and Legal Analysis.* Berkeley and Los Angeles: University of California Press, 1960.

Cook, Bruce. *Dalton Trumbo.* New York: Charles Scribner's Sons, 1979.

Crawford, Christina. *Mommie Dearest.* New York: William Morrow & Co., 1978.

Curcio, Vincent. *Suicide Blonde: The Life of Gloria Grahame.* New York: William Morrow & Co., 1989.

Daniel, Douglass K. *Tough as Nails: The Life and Films of Richard Brooks.* Madison: University of Wisconsin Press, 2011.

Davies, Nigel. *The Rampant God: Eros Throughout the World.* New York: William Morrow & Co., 1984.

Davis, Mike. *City of Quartz: Excavating the Future of Los Angeles.* London and New York: Verso, 1990.

De Toth, André. *Fragments: Portraits from the Inside.* London and Boston: Faber & Faber, 1994.

Donati, William. *Ida Lupino: A Biography.* Lexington: University Press of Kentucky, 1996.

Eisenschitz, Bernard. (Translated by Tom Milne). *Nicholas Ray: An American Journey.* London: Faber & Faber Ltd., 1993.

Eisner, Lotte. *Fritz Lang.* London: Martin Secker & Warburg Ltd., 1976. (Reprinted by Da Capo Press, New York, 1986.)

Fleischer, Richard. *Just Tell Me When to Cry: A Memoir.* New York: Carroll & Graf, 1993.

Friedman, Lester D. *The Jewish Image in American Film.* Secaucus, NJ: Citadel Press, 1987.

Friedrich, Otto. *City of Nets: A Portrait of Hollywood in the 1940s.* Berkeley and Los Angeles: University of California Press, 1986.

Fuller, Samuel. *A Third Face: My Tale of Writing, Fighting and Filmmaking.* New York: Alfred A. Knopf, 2002.

Gabler, Neal. *An Empire of Their Own: How the Jews Invented Hollywood.* New York: Crown Publishers, 1988.

Garnham, Nicholas. *Samuel Fuller.* New York: The Viking Press (in association with the British Film Institute), 1971.

Garnier, Philippe. *Goodis: A Life in Black and White.* Alameda, CA: Black Pool Productions, 2014.

————. *Scoundrels & Spitballers: Writers and Hollywood in the 1930s.* Alameda, CA: Black Pool Productions, 2020.

Gelman, Howard. *The Films of John Garfield.* Secaucus, NJ: Citadel Press, 1975.

Gifford, Barry. *The Devil Thumbs a Ride & Other Unforgettable Films.* New York: Grove Press, 1988.

Grobel, Lawrence. *The Hustons.* New York: Charles Scribner's Sons, 1989.

Hayden, Sterling. *Wanderer.* New York: Alfred A. Knopf, 1963.

Hecht, Ben. *A Child of the Century.* New York: Simon & Schuster, 1954.

Higham, Charles. *The Films of Orson Welles.* Berkeley: University of California Press, 1970.

————. *Howard Hughes: The Secret Life.* New York: G. P. Putnam's Sons, 1993.

Hill, James. *Rita Hayworth, A Memoir.* New York: Simon & Schuster, 1983.

Hirsch, Foster. *Film Noir: The Dark Side of the Screen.* San Diego: A. S. Barnes & Co., 1981. (Reprinted by Da Capo Press, New York, 1983.)

Hoopes, Roy. *Cain: The Biography of James M. Cain.* New York: Holt, Rinehart and Winston, 1982.

Houston, David. "The Two Tom Neals: A Legacy." Evanston, IL: *Filmfax #11* (July 1988).

Huston, John. *An Open Book: The Autobiography.* London: Virgin Books, 1981.

Johnson, Diane. *Dashiell Hammett: A Life.* New York: Random House, 1983.

Kahn, Gordon. *Hollywood on Trial: The Story of the Ten Who Were Indicted.* New York: Boni & Gaer, 1948.

Kaplan, E. Ann, ed. *Woman in Film Noir.* London: The British Film Institute, 1978.

Klein, Robert. *Wounded Men, Broken Promises: How the Veteran's Administration Betrays Yesterday's Heroes.* New York: Macmillan Publishing Co., 1981.

Kuhn, Annette, ed. *Queen of the B's: Ida Lupino Behind the Camera*. Westport, CT: Praeger, 1995.

Lasky, Betty. *RKO, The Biggest Little Major of Them All*. Englewood Cliffs, NJ: Prentice-Hall, Inc., 1984.

Leemann, Sergio. *Robert Wise on His Films: From Editing Room to Director's Chair*. Los Angeles: Silman-James Press (in cooperation with the Directors Guild of America), 1995.

Linet, Beverly. *Ladd: The Life, The Legend, The Legacy of Alan Ladd*. New York: Arbor House, 1979.

LoBrutto, Vincent. *Stanley Kubrick: A Biography*. New York: Da Capo Press, 1997.

MacShane, Frank. *The Life of Raymond Chandler*. New York: E. P. Dutton & Co., 1976.

McArthur, Colin. *Underworld USA*. New York: The Viking Press (in association with the British Film Institute), 1972.

McGilligan, Patrick. *Cagney: Actor as Auteur*. San Diego: A. S. Barnes & Co., 1975.

———. *Fritz Lang: The Nature of the Beast*. New York: St. Martin's Press, 1997.

Madsen, Axel. *Stanwyck*. New York: HarperCollins, 1994.

Miller, Mark A. "Marie Windsor Interview." Evanston, IL: *Filmfax #30* (December/January 1992).

Mumford, Lewis. *The Culture of Cities*. New York: Harcourt, Brace & Co., 1938.

Murphy, Michael and Cheryl. "The Devil Thumbs His Nose: To Hell and Back with Lawrence Tierney." New York: *Psychotronic #8* (Winter 1990).

Navasky, Victor S. *Naming Names*. New York: The Viking Press, 1980.

Nevins, Francis M., Jr. *Cornell Woolrich: First You Dream, Then You Die*. New York: The Mysterious Press, 1988.

Nielsen, Mike, and Gene Mailes. *Hollywood's Other Blacklist: Union Struggles in the Studio System*. London: British Film Institute, 1995.

Nott, Robert. *He Ran All the Way: The Life of John Garfield*. New York: Limelight Editions, 2003.

O'Brien, Geoffrey. *Hardboiled America: The Lurid Years of Paperbacks*. New York: Van Nostrand Reinhold Co., 1981.

Ott, Frederick, W. *The Films of Fritz Lang*. Secaucus, NJ: Citadel Press, 1979.

Parrish, James Robert. *The Tough Guys*. New Rochelle, NY: Arlington House Publishers, 1976.

Polonsky, Abraham. (John Schultheiss and Mark Schaubert, eds.) *Force of Evil: The Critical Edition*. Northridge, CA: The Center for Telecommunications Studies, Film as Literature Series, 1996.

———. *Odds Against Tomorrow: The Critical Edition*. Northridge, CA: The Center for Telecommunications Studies, Film as Literature Series, 1999.

Pratley, Gerald. *The Cinema of Otto Preminger*. New York: Castle Books, 1971.

Ragan, David. *Movie Stars of the '40s: A Complete Reference Guide of the Film Historian or Trivia Buff*. Englewood Cliffs, NJ: Prentice-Hall, 1985.

Rode, Alan K. "Caged: Classic, Not Camp." Alameda, CA: *Noir City Sentinel #31* (published by the Film Noir Foundation) (Second Quarter, 2010).

Sarris, Andrew. *Interviews with Film Directors*. New York: Avon Books, 1969.

Selby, Spencer. *Dark City: The Film Noir*. Jefferson, NC: McFarland & Co., 1984.

Server, Lee. *Sam Fuller: Film Is a Battleground: A Critical Study*. Jefferson, NC: McFarland & Co., 1994.

Schatz, Thomas. *Boom and Bust: American Cinema in the 1940s. (History of the American Cinema, Volume 6: 1940–1949)*. Berkeley, Los Angeles, and London: University of California Press, 1997.

Skenazy, Paul. *James M. Cain*. New York: Continuum Publishing Co., 1989.

Silver, Alain, and Elizabeth Ward, eds (with Carl Macek and Robert Porfirio). *Film Noir: An Encyclopedic Reference to the American Style*. Woodstock, NY: The Overlook Press, 1979.

Silver, Alain, and James Ursini, eds. *The Film Noir Reader*. New York: Limelight Editions, 1996.

Sperber, A. M., and Eric Lax. *Bogart*. New York: William Morrow and Company, 1997.

Spoto, Donald. *The Dark Side of Genius: The Life of Alfred Hitchcock*. Boston: Little, Brown & Co., 1983.

Taylor, John Russell. *Hollywood 1940s*. London: Multimedia Publications (UK) Ltd., 1985. (Published in the United States by Gallery Books, New York, 1985.)

Thomas, Bob. *Joan Crawford*. New York: Simon & Schuster, 1978.

Thomas, Tony. *Howard Hughes in Hollywood*. Secaucus, NJ: Citadel Press, 1985.

Thomson, David. *America in the Dark: The Impact of American Films on American Culture*. New York: William Morrow & Co., Inc., 1977.

———. *A Biographical Dictionary of Film*, 3rd ed. New York: Alfred A. Knopf, 1994.

———. *Rosebud: The Story of Orson Welles*. New York: Alfred A. Knopf, 1996.

Tierney, Gene (with Mickey Herskowitz). *Self-Portrait*. New York: Wyden Books, 1979.

Turner, Peter. *Film Stars Don't Die in Liverpool*. New York: Grove Press, 1986.

Twomey, Alfred E., and Arthur F. McClure. *The Versatiles: A Study of Supporting Character Actors and Actresses in the American Motion Picture, 1930–1955*. Cranbury, NJ: A. S. Barnes & Co., 1969.

Walker, Brent. "Crane Wilbur: Pondering the Potentate of Prison Pictures, from *The Perils of Pauline* to Police Procedurals." Alameda, CA: *NOIR CITY, Vol. 6 No. 1* (Published by the Film Noir Foundation) (Spring 2011).

INDEX

Page numbers in **bold** refer to illustrations or their captions. Book titles that are the same as movie titles are followed by the author's name in parentheses.

ACKNOWLEDGMENTS

Crafting a book is a caper. It requires a dedicated and resourceful crew. In the case of this volume, returning to the scene of the original crime required fresh cohorts. Foremost among them was Cindy Sipala, my editor at Running Press. She's pulled off more than a few jobs like this one, so there was no question she had the mettle. But her advocacy on my behalf—not only maintaining but enhancing my vision of the book—was stellar. Kudos to Josh McDonnell for taking my original design notions and giving them the deluxe treatment. Many thanks as well to Heather Margolis and John Malahly at TCM for helping shepherd this new edition to fruition. Fondest regards to all my colleagues at Turner Classic Movies—they didn't have anything to do with this book, but I'll take any opportunity to express my respect and appreciation to them all.

The saddest part of creating a new version of this book is that my most valued colleague, Erik S. McMahon, isn't here to celebrate this second score. First time around, he was a mastermind, boxman, and hooligan all in one; he had my back through the whole run. I couldn't have asked for a tougher, sharper, more literate lieutenant . . . or friend. RIP, pal.

Before the arrival of digital media, Lawrence Chadbourne supplied an arsenal of films, feeding me hard-to-find titles with unsurpassed generosity and kindness. I never even met his henchmen, Dave Martin, Bob Yamada and Arthur McMillan, but they all came through in a pinch. As did the staff at the bygone Movie Image video rental store (remember those?) in Berkeley, California. Many thanks to owner Roland De La Rosa and staffers Randy Beucus, Jeremy Gross, and Will "Vic Valentine" Viharo, who also became a lifelong friend.

Eternal gratitude to a pair of this book's original stake horses, Cal Morgan and Gordon Van Gelder, who oversaw its initial incarnation at St. Martin's Press. I am extremely grateful for the time and insights offered by Abraham Polonsky, who provided essential grounding for the book's unique approach to the subject. Likewise, Geoffrey O'Brien provided a spark of inspiration through his superb book, *The Phantom Empire*. Lisa Ryan was wonderfully open about her father, Robert, and I'm grateful this book initiated our friendship. Like virtually everyone who researches a book on the movies, I owe a debt to the staff and patrons of the Margaret Herrick Library at the Academy of Motion Picture Arts and Sciences.

Other important contributors on the first go-round: Lester Glassner, Michael Abbott, Paul Toner, Ted Bonnitt, Jerry Ohlinger, Ron and Maria Blum, Andrew Taylor, Pierce Rafferty, Tracey Janzen, and Dennis Parlato, who furnished invaluable camaraderie, and a hideout, when I was on the lam. Special thanks this go-round to two invaluable colleagues and friends, Daryl Sparks and Michael Kronenberg.

As for the dozens of other authors to whom I am indebted—you can pick up your cut in the bibliography.

Lastly, I thank my wife Kathleen, to whom this edition is dedicated. I owe her everything.

CHECK OUT OTHER TITLES IN THE  LIBRARY

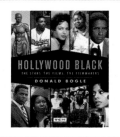

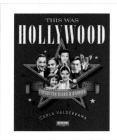

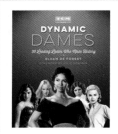
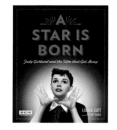

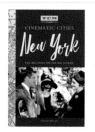

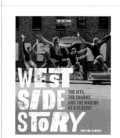

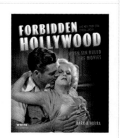

RUNNING
PRESS

Witness...
by Fake Co...
Fight to
Vice Sy...

JOHN
HODIAK
NANCY
GUILD
LLOYD
NOLAN

...MEWHERE
...E NIGHT

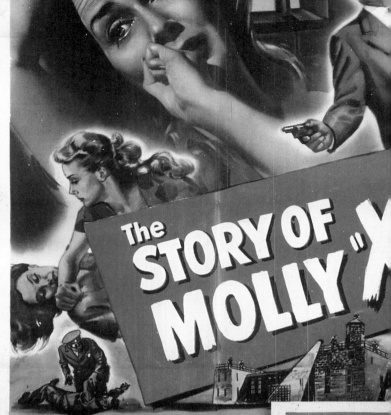

The
STORY OF
MOLLY "X"

June
HAVOC · John
RUSSEL

Written and Directed by CRANE WILBUR · Produced by AARON ROSENBERG

Copyright 1949 by Universal Pictures Co., Inc. Country of Origin U.S.A. PRINTED IN U.S.A.

Take this
DETOUR
for a
New
type of
Screen
Thrill!

DETOUR

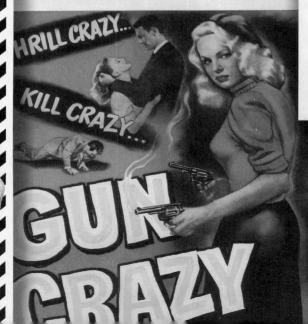

...HRILL CRAZY...
KILL CRAZY...

GUN
CRAZY

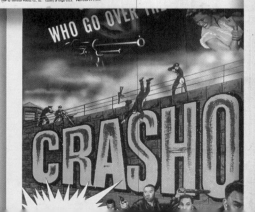

WHO GO OVER T...

CRASHO...

THE FILMAKERS PRESENT

Th...